Harriet Wood Wheeler, J. N. (John Nelson) Davidson

In unnamed Wisconsin

Studies in the History of the Region between Lake Michigan and the Mississippi

Harriet Wood Wheeler, J. N. (John Nelson) Davidson

In unnamed Wisconsin
Studies in the History of the Region between Lake Michigan and the Mississippi

ISBN/EAN: 9783337140250

Printed in Europe, USA, Canada, Australia, Japan

Cover: Foto ©ninafisch / pixelio.de

More available books at **www.hansebooks.com**

IN

UNNAMED WISCONSIN

STUDIES IN THE HISTORY OF THE REGION BETWEEN LAKE

MICHIGAN AND THE MISSISSIPPI

BY

J. N. DAVIDSON, A. M.

TO WHICH IS APPENDED

MEMOIR OF

MRS. HARRIET WOOD WHEELER

MILWAUKEE, WISCONSIN
PUBLISHED BY SILAS CHAPMAN
1895

PREFATORY NOTE.

If, in the pages that follow, sons and daughters of Wisconsin find reason for deeper interest in the history of their own state, and for increase of honorable civic pride, I shall be glad. But if any reader look for the indifference, real or affected, that treats of men and causes, good and bad, as if all were alike merely curious, he will surely count what I have written as most unphilosophical, if indeed he take the trouble to think about it.

Most of my story is of a time when there was no Wisconsin; when this region was only an undefined portion, first of New France and in part, perhaps, of Louisiana; then of the province of Quebec; next of Virginia, when she was passing from the condition of a colony to that of a state; then of the old Northwest Territory and, afterward, successively of Indiana, Illinois and Michigan. In the course of my study one thing has been made clear to me: The who first settled on this soil were not the founders of Wisconsin. There was a wide difference between those who would have had this region remain a part of Canada,—whether under France or under Britain,—and those who established here the institutions of an American state.

One thing I hope,—that good done by humble and unpretending men and women may, by these pages, become a little more widely known and that they who did it may receive somewhat more of honor. Their cheeks will not flush now, if we speak their praise. For one of them filial love has prepared a memorial that is fittingly appended to the record herein given of her own and of others' faithful service.

The knowledge that this work was in progress brought to the writer, even after the first few chapters had been sent to the press, certain material which, had it been found earlier, might have been better used. Hence, notwithstanding the awkwardness of so doing, there was reason to add some closing paragraphs containing statements that properly belong in the narrative itself.

Among those who, in Wisconsin's early days, came hither from a land that we can scarcely call foreign, was one who, by precept and by life, gave me a faith from which I have found no reason to depart; who taught me that "man's chief end is to glorify God and to enjoy him forever;" who, without effort and almost unconsciously, showed me that the eternal things are as real as those that perish with the using; who, through all my life, has upheld me with a strong tenderness. They who read thus far will say "his mother," and to her, without permission, this book is dedicated with a son's reverent love.

TWO RIVERS, WISCONSIN,
July, 1895.

ILLUSTRATIONS AND FAC-SIMILES.

REV. CUTTING MARSH

facing page 116.

REV. LEONARD HEMENWAY WHEELER

facing page 165.

MRS. HARRIET WOOD WHEELER

facing page 229.

FAC-SIMILE pages of Muh-ḥe-ka-ne-ew booklets.   See end of

volume.

CONTENTS.

CHAPTER I.— DISCOVERY AND EXPLORATION.

Settlement of the Northwest Territory — Discovery of the Wisconsin region — Death of Jean Nicolet — Radisson and Groseillers — Their Discovery of the Upper Mississippi — Voyage on Lake Superior — Their "Fort" on Chequamegon Bay — Their Explorations in what is now Minnesota — Return to the French Settlements and Escape thence to Boston — They enter English Service - - - - - 1–6

CHAPTER II.— EARLY MISSIONS.

Renahis Menard — His labors with the Ottawas — His death — Claude Allouez — Jacques Marquette — Mission at Depere — *Proces-verbal* at Sault Ste. Marie — Nicholas Perrot — Accusations against the Jesuits — Louis Hennepin — *Coureurs de Bois* — The Outagamies - - 7–16

CHAPTER III.— THE OUTAGAMIE WAR.

Plundering the Traders — "Siege of Detroit" — Attempted Destruction of the Outagamies — Building of Forts St. Francis and Beauharnois — A Summer of Horrors — Effect of the Outagamie War - - 17–23

CHAPTER IV.— END OF FRENCH DOMINION.

Perriere Marin — Massacre of Outagamies — Treaty of Paris — The British take Possession of Green Bay — French Kings who ruled in the Wisconsin Region - - - - - - 24–27

CHAPTER V.— BRITISH DOMINION.

Keeping the Western Posts — The "Quebec Act" — Carver's Travels — Langlade — Events of the Time of the Revolution — Dr. Manasseh Cutler — Ordinance of 1787 — Settlement at Marrietta — Witchcraft — Slavery — Events of the War of 1812 — Americans take Possession of the Wisconsin Region - - - - - 28–44

CHAPTER VI.— THE IONA OF OUR INLAND SEAS.

Michilimackinac — David Bacon and his Mission Work — The American Fur Company — Expedition to the Pacific — Dr. Morse at Mackinaw — Mission Re-established there — Appeal for a Mission among the Ojibways — Robert Stuart - - - - - 45–51

CHAPTER VII.— DR. MORSE AND HIS ERRAND IN THE WEST.

First Protestant Service in what is now Wisconsin — Projected Indian Territory — The "New York Indians"— John Metoxen - - 52-61

CHAPTER VIII.— ONEIDAS AND THE BROTHERTOWNS.

Samuel Kirkland — Eleazar Williams — John Clark — First Methodist Church-Building in Wisconsin — Samson Occom - - - 62-72

CHAPTER IX.— THE MUH-HE-KA-NE-OK.

Their Legendary History — Their Language — Settlement at Stockbridge, Massachusetts — John Sergeant — A Total Abstinence Movement — David Brainerd — Specimens of the Mohegan Language — British Gifts to the Stockbridge Mission — Wars with the French — Jonathan Edwards — Dr. Stephen West — John Sergeant, the Younger — Muh-he-ka-ne-ew Service in the Revolution — Removal to New York — Council in Indiana — Tatepahqseet — Removal to Indiana - - - 73-108

CHAPTER X.— STATESBURG AND STOCKBRIDGE.

Removal from Indiana and New York to Fox river — The first Congregational Church in Wisconsin — Rev. Jesse Miner — First Protestant Church-Building in Wisconsin — First School-Mistress here — Rev. Cutting Marsh — Commissioner McCall — The "Orchard party" of Oneidas — A Booklet and a Psalm in the Mohegan Language — Letter to Jefferson Davis — Mission Work Begun among the Sioux — An Indian Temperance Convention — Letter by Chauncey Hall — Mission Trip beyond the Mississippi — Stockbridge (Wisconsin) Built — Capital Punishment by Indian Tribal Authority — The Muh-he-ka-ne-ok are made Citizens — Divisive Religious Movements — Removal to Shawano County — Present Condition of the Tribe - - - - - - - 109-145

CHAPTER XI.— AMONG THE OJIBWAYS.

Legendary History — Trading-Station at La Pointe — Alexander Henry — The Cadottes and the Warrens — Alvin Coe and J. D. Stevens — "Manner of Traveling on the Upper Waters of the Great Lakes" — Mission begun at La Pointe — Jeremiah Porter and W. T. Boutwell — Naming of Lake Itasca — First Book written here — First Organization of a Congregational Church in Wisconsin — Meeting-Houses at La Pointe, Congregational and Roman Catholic — Missions in Minnesota — Fight at Pokeguma — Murder of Benjamin Terry and Mrs. Spencer — Ojibway New Testament — Rev. L. H. Wheeler — Odanah founded — Mission Work by the Methodists — Rev. Alfred Brunson — Attempt to remove the Ojibways — Effect of the War — Rev. Frederic Baraga — Death of Mr. Wheeler — Covenant of the Ojibway Churches - - - 146-174

CHAPTER XII.— BY THE MIZI SIBI.

Louisiana — Religious Intolerance — Prairie du Chien — Fort Crawford — Mr. Lockwood's Narrative — First Sunday-School in Wisconsin — Rev. Aratus

CONTENTS. vii

Kent — David Lowrey — Abolitionists from the South - 175–186

CHAPTER XIII.— AMONG THE MINES.

An "Island in a Sea of Drift"— Discovery of Lead — The Winnebago War — Surrender of Red Bird — Dr. Newhall's Letter — Father Kent comes to Galena — Black Hawk and his "British Band" — War — Henry Dodge becomes Governor - - - - - 187–200

CHAPTER XIV.— WISCONSIN'S OPEN DOOR.

Permanent Settlement at Green Bay — British leave the place — Fort Howard — A. G. Ellis and other Early Teachers — First Methodist Services in the Green Bay Region — Rev. R. F. Cadle - Episcopal Mission — Organization of the First Presbyterian Church of Green Bay - 201–206

CHAPTER XV.— FORT WINNEBAGO.

Topography - "Wau-bun" — Rev. A. L. Barber — "Portage of the Siskoinsin" — Transportation there - - - - 207–210

CHAPTER XVI.— BY THE LAKE AND ON THE PRAIRIE.

A Sloop of War at "Millwakey" — Threat by Robert Dickson — Joliet and Marquette — The Brothers La Framboise — Jacques Vieau — Juneau — Samuel Brown — Reports from the "Home Missionary" — Protestant Episcopal Service at Milwaukee — J. F. Ostrander — Organization of the First Presbyterian Church — First Protestant House of Worship for Whites in Wisconsin — Rev. Gilbert Crawford — Settlement of Racine — Scarcity of Food — Jesse Walker and Cyrus Nichols — Settlements formed at Kenosha and Beloit — Madison — Rev. S. A. Dwinnell — His Account of Chicago and Wisconsin in 1836 - - - - - 211–226

APPENDIX.

Memoir of Mrs. Harriet Wood Wheeler — Ancestry — Education — Marriage — Arrival at La Pointe — Work there — Guests — Covenant — Visit to Fond du Lac — Education of Children — Mr. Wheeler Founds Odanah — Mrs. Wheeler as Teacher — Anniversary Days — Winter at the Lowell Home — Small-pox at La Pointe and Odanah — Medical Service — Odanah Training School — Reservations Saved for the Indians — Removal to Beloit — Invention of Wind-Mill — Death of Mr. Wheeler and a Daughter — Mrs. Wheeler's Last Years — Her Injury and Death - 227–261

TRIBUTES.

Memories of Home — Tribute of Mrs. Kennedy - Letter and Poem of Rev. H. C. McArthur - Letter of Mrs. Mary Warren English - Of Mrs. M. E. Vaughn - Of Professor Whitney - Of Mrs. Anna S. Rogers — Of Dr. Roy — Of Mrs. Mary H. Hull — A Neighbor's Message — From a Friend of Mrs. Wheeler's Last Years - - - 262–274

Biographical Sketches of Rev. Frederic Ayer and Rev. Cutting Marsh — Chauncey Hall - Additional Paragraphs - Corrections - 275–280

CHAPTER I.

DISCOVERY AND EXPLORATION.

Not Ohio alone but the entire Northwest Territory received Christian civilization when, 1788, April 7th,[1] the historic company of the second Mayflower landed at the mouth of the Muskingum. Marietta is a second Plymouth as, in some respects, Ohio is a second Massachusetts. For the possession of the great empire, part of which was thus entered upon, a series of wars lasting almost a century had been fought. We may call this the second War of a Hundred Years. Its beginning properly dates from the time when a great-grandson of William the Silent, representing the principles of his murdered ancestor, was crowned king in Westminster in 1689. The first Hundred Years' War, notwithstanding the brilliant victories of Edward the Black Prince, saw the Briton driven from the mainland of Europe; in the second, the armies of the French were driven from North America. The descendants of the men who conquered at Crecy and Poitiers were themselves victorious at Louisburg and Quebec. Then the struggle took a new aspect, and it was settled that those living in America should rule it. Britons and Protestants had founded a new nation of which Wisconsin is a part. Hence it comes to pass that we who dwell in Wisconsin are American, not Canadian; Saxon, not French; a fact that seems to be lost sight of in some academic discussions on the early history of our state.

But the first whites who saw the western shores of Lake Michigan and the southern shores of Lake Superior, the first to row up the Fox and to float down the Wisconsin, were Frenchmen from Canada, then New France. To their settlements on the St. Lawrence rumors came of the "Men of the Sea." For the purpose of making a treaty with these people, whom imagination pictured as Orientals rather than Indians, Jean Nicolet, "interpreter and clerk of the gentlemen of the company of New France," left Quebec 1634, July 1st,[2] and came to the Green Bay region, having made, it is said, a voyage of one thousand one hundred miles in a birch-bark canoe. To meet with suitable ceremony the people whom he had come so far to see on such important business, he clothed himself "in a large garment of China damask strewn with flowers and birds of various colors," and went forward carrying a pistol in each hand.

[1] The day of the week was Monday as was that of the landing at Plymouth. Of course both parties were led by men who honored the Sabbath.

[2] A date more easily remembered is the 4th of July, the time when he left Three Rivers, then almost the outward post of civilization. Nicolet probably went up the Ottawa.

The "Men of the Sea" were the Ouinipigou, or, as they are commonly called, the Winnebagoes. The sight of these naked savages must have been a rude shock to Nicolet's fancies. However, he made a treaty with them, and went farther up the Fox to a village of the Mascoutins probably in what is now Green Lake county. Here he heard of the "Great Water," by which he understood the sea, but which is probably the Mississippi. There is reason to think that from the Mascoutin country he went southward to the region inhabited by the Illinois. In the autumn of 1635 he returned to Quebec. In December of that same year, occurred the death of the governor of New France, the illustrious Samuel de Champlain, the founder, in 1608, of the French colony that has since grown into the Dominion of Canada. His death seems to have put an end for the time to further explorations. Nicolet, still in the company's service, was stationed at Three Rivers. Seven years after his return from the West, while at Quebec, he was sent for to come to his home to save, if possible, the life of a New England Indian whom captors that lived near Three Rivers were threatening with death by torture. Nicolet started promptly, but on his way up the St. Lawrence was accidentally drowned, 1642, November 1st. The Indian was afterward sent home in safety.

Nicolet's discovery, which he does not seem to have regarded as of any special importance, seems to have been soon forgotten. Only the patient labor of historians of our own time has rescued from oblivion the name of the first civilized man who saw any part of what is now Wisconsin. We honor him as a man who came hither on an errand of peace and died on one of mercy. He was deeply religious.

For many years the French were kept from further exploration. Champlain, dying, left to the colony the heritage of war with the Iroquois, often called the Five Nations, to whom the Dutch and, later, the English supplied fire-arms while the French furnished their allies with "kettles and missionaries."

Among those hostile to the Iroquois was a kindred tribe, the Hurons,[1] who were utterly defeated and driven from their former homes. These were within the present limits of New York. Leaving their domain to enlarge the possessions of their conquerors, the Hurons fled into the interior of the continent. After the fiercest of the struggle was over, an expedition of thirty-one Frenchmen, accompanied by a number of Hurons, started about the middle of June, 1658, to go up the Ottawa river, and thence to Lake Huron and beyond. An attack by Iroquois turned back all the whites except two, Pierre d'Esprit and his brother-in-law, Medart Chouart, better known by their titles as Sieur Radisson and Sieur des Groseilliers (pronounced Gro-zay-yay). These two had made a compact "to travel and see countreys." Radisson, the first named, though the younger, seems to have been the leader. At any rate he has the advantage of telling the story, which he did, in perplexing English and very bad

---

[1] "*Quelles hures.*'" [word used of a boar etc.: "What heads of-hair!"] said the French when they first saw them; hence the word "Hurons."—CHARLEVOIX.

They called themselves Wyandots (Y-en-dats).

spelling, in a narrative probably intended for the use of Charles II. of England. He and his companion made almost the entire circuit of Lake Huron. On one of the Manitoulin islands they aided the Hurons in a fight with the Iroquois. What followed Radisson thus describes : "The dead weare eaten and the living weare burned with a small fire to the rigour of cruelties." Invited by Pottawattomies who were then living on the islands at the mouth of Green Bay and the peninsula between the bay and the lake, our travelers spent the winter with that tribe. "I can assure you I liked noe country as I have that wherein we wintered," says Radisson, "ffor whatever a man desired was to be had in great plenty ; viz., staggs, fishes in abundance, & all sorts of meat, corn enough." The aboriginal population of the Green Bay country was very large.

In the spring of the following year, 1659, they visited "an other nation called Escotecke [Mascoutins], which signified fire."[1] These people were living where Nicolet found them twenty-five years before. Here the Frenchmen heard of "a nation called Nadoneceronon[2] [Sioux] which is very strong." They were told also of the Christinos [Crees, now of British America]. "Their dwelling was on the side of the salt watter [Hudson's Bay] in summer time & in the land in the winter time, for it's cold in their country." The account of a great discovery is thus given ;

"We weare 4 moneths without doing anything but goe from river to river. We mett several sorts of people. We conversed with them, being long time in alliance with them By persuasion of som of them we went into the great river that divides itself in 2." Radisson calls it the "forked river" and adds : "It is so called because it has 2 branches, the one toward the west, the other toward the South, which we believe runs toward Mexico by the tokens they gave us." How far south they went we do not know, but speaking of the barbarous punishment[3] of a captive by some Indians whom they visited they remark : "So they doe with them that they take, and kill them with clubbs, & doe often eat them. They doe not burn their prisoners as those of the northern parts."

The "forked river" is doubtless the Mississippi. "A beautiful river, grand, wide, deep and comparable to our own great river, the St. Lawrence," says a description made at the time from Radisson's reports. To measure the greatness of this discovery we must remember that, with the possible exception of some wandering fur-traders like themselves, there were at that time,—summer of 1659,—probably, no other white men west of the Alleghany mountains.

[1] Charlevoix, a Jesuit traveler and historian, states that the true name is "Mascoutenec," signifying "an open country." The Pottawattomies' word for fire was like their corruption of this name "Mascouten." From them, it is said, the French obtained the incorrect form and the untrue meaning.
Francis S. Drake, in his great work "The North American Indians," says : "*Mushkoosi* is grass or herbage in general. *Ishkado* means fire. The only difference in the root-form is that between *nahko* and *ishko.*"
[2] NADOWSIE, an Algonquin expression signifying enemy. It is derived from *Nadowa*, an Iroquois or a Dakota; the word was originally applied to a serpent The termination in *sie* is from *awasie*, an animal or creature. This term is the root, it is apprehended, of the French soubriquet Sioux.—H. R. SCHOOLCRAFT.
[3] "His arms & leggs weare turned outside."

For the missions,—even those as far east as the Mohawk valley,—that the Jesuits had established among the Hurons, were utterly broken up in the destruction of the homes of that people.

Before our adventurers returned to the French settlements, they coasted along the eastward part of the southern shore of Lake Superior.[1] Thus they were the discoverers not only of the upper Mississippi but probably also of our greatest North American lake. About the 1st of June, 1660, they came by way of the Ottawa to Three Rivers on the St. Lawrence. Thus ended what Radisson calls his third "voyage."[2]

In August, 1661, Radisson began his next and fourth "voyage." His brother-in-law again accompanied him. They intended to go by way of Lake Superior to the "salt watter" of which they had heard two years before. They coasted along the southern shore of Lake Superior, entered Chequamegon[3] bay by a portage across Oak Point, which is on the east side of the bay, and in the autumn or early winter, built what they call "a fort of stakes"[4] This was doubtless the first structure put up by civilized men in what is now Wisconsin. "There we stayed still full 12 days without any news. The 12 day we perceived afarr off some 50 yong men coming toward us, with some of our former compagnions. They stayed there three days." These "compagnions" were probably Hurons. Some of this tribe, driven westward by their relentless enemies the Iroquois, had first sought refuge on an island in the Mississippi above Lake Pepin. Driven thence by the Sioux, they came into the country about the head waters of the Chippewa. To one of their villages on "a little lake some 8 leagues in circuit,"—probably Namekagon in the southern part of

---

[1] In the spring of 1660.

[2] Radisson's first "voyage," in 1652, an individual experience, was in the character of prisoner, a party of Mohawks having captured him in the neighborhood of Three Rivers and carried him with them to their village, where he was adopted; but he ran away. October 29, 1653, went to the Dutch at Albany and from Manhattan sailed for Holland. In May, 1654, he was back again at Three Rivers. In July, 1657, he accompanied the Jesuit Fathers, Paul Raguenean and Joseph Inbert Duperon, to their mission among the Onondagas, which was clandestinely abandoned on the night of March 20, 1658. This constituted Radisson's second "voyage."—REUBEN GOLD THWAITES.

Radisson's narrative was republished in this country by the Prince Society of Boston, an organization named in honor of Rev. Thomas Prince, so long pastor of the old South church of that city.

[3] I use this conventional orthography, though I do not like it. In the opinion of Rev. Edward Payson Wheeler, of Ashland, a native of Madelaine island, it is peculiarly unfortunate that we get names used by the Indians under a Gallicized disguise. What seems to me evidence of the correctness of this opinion is found in the changing of "Ojibway" to "Chippeway," and also in the spelling of the name of the bay mentioned above. This, by William Whipple Warren in whose veins flowed honorably Ojibway blood, is written "Chagouamigon" ("History of the Ojibways" *Minnesota Historical Collections, vol. V.*). The meaning, "place of shallow water," is given by Mr. Wheeler (*Sheh* "the," *gu* "of," *wah* "shallow [water]," *mi* a particle denoting specific place, *kung* "place"). The italicized syllables suggest also his pronunciation (*a* like *oo* in *cool*; other vowels short). "Shah-kah-wah-mee-kunk," seems to represent the name as I heard it spoken by Rev. John Clark, the native pastor lately at Odanah. The last syllable receives the primary accent. Mr. Wheeler, whose boyhood was spent among the Ojibways, in the mission that Mr. Warren's father helped to found, thinks that the younger Warren's pronunciation of the name was like his own as given above.

[4] This may have been at the mouth of Whittlesey creek, about three miles from Ashland and between that city and Washburn. See note on the place of Allouez's mission, page 11

what is now Bayfield county,—came the Frenchmen accompanied by friends who had visited the "fort." "The winter comes on, that warns us; the snow begins to fall, soe we must retire from the place to seeke our living in the woods. Soe away we goe, but not all to the same place. Butt let where we will, we can not escape the myghty hand of God, that disposes us as he pleases, and who chastes us a good & a common loving ffather, and not as our sins doe deserve." Among the Hurons with whom they were spending the winter there was distress for want of food. "To augment our misery we receive news of the Octanaks [Ottawas] "who weare about a hundred and fifty with their families. They had [had] a quarrell with the hurrons in the Isle where we had come from some years before in the lake of the stairing hairs[1] [Huron]. "But lett us see if they have brought anything to subsist withall. But they were worse provided than we; having no huntsmen they are reduced to famine."

Our travelers wandered westward and were the first white men to enter what is now Minnesota. Before winter was over they were in the country of the Dakotas, otherwise called Sioux, a little south-of-west from Lake Superior, in the Mille Lacs region, whose streams are tributary to the Mississippi. As to food, they were then in better condition than they had been. Yet there was still such a degree of famine that some of the company saved the snow upon which fell the blood of a half-starved dog which Radisson killed one night for food, having previously stolen the wretched creature from two Sioux as they lay asleep. More than five hundred Hurons and Ottawas died that winter of starvation.

In the late winter or early spring, they visited "the nation of the beefe" [Bœuf, or Buffalo, Sioux]. Thence they went seven days' journey, apparently northward, and visited the Christinos. The ice was still in the lakes. "Coming back we passed a lake hardly frozen" [frozen hard]. They came again to Oak Point which they had crossed the autumn before. "Here we built a fort." In August of the next year, 1662, they returned to Three Rivers, bringing with them furs to the value of 200,000 livres ($37,000). New France was burdened with a monopoly which sought to control the fur trade. Radisson and Groselliers, finding the governor intent upon plundering them, escaped to Boston. Thus the explorers of our Wisconsin streams and forests found refuge in the city of the Puritans. It would be interesting to know what they thought of the home of John Endecott[2] and Increase Mather. From Boston they sailed to England. There Radisson married the daughter of a Sir John Kirk.[3] Here, after the fashion of a romance, we might leave our adventurers.

---

[1] Probably, hair brushed or pushed up. Compare the speech of Brutus in Shakespeare's "Julius Cæsar:"
   Art thou some god, some angel, or some devil,
   That mak'st my blood cold and my hair to stare?

[2] Commonly spelled Endicott.

[3] Sir John Kirk (or Kertk) was a zealous Huguenot. The daughter probably shared her father's faith. It is not unlikely that Radisson himself, with the change in his political allegiance, made a corresponding change in his religious connection. But I do not know that he did. Like many another he probably held, in a general way, the Christian faith without car-

But they were yet to do some of their greatest achievements. They entered English service and, in 1667, led an expedition to the "salt watter" mentioned above. There they established trading-posts and thus became active agents in founding the Hudson's Bay company which virtually controlled for two hundred years the northern half of our continent, and more than once has vitally affected the history of the United States.[1] Thinking themselves wronged by some officials of the company, they again entered French service, sailed in 1682 to Hudson's Bay, captured Port Nelson, which they themselves had founded, raised over it the lilies of France and changed its name to Port Bourbon. This action was of course made the subject of diplomatic correspondence. Lord Preston, the English ambassador at Paris, thus wrote home, under date of 1684, January 19: "Sent to know if the king had ordered any answer concerning the attack upon Nelson's post. I find the great support of Mons de la Barre, the present governor of Canada, is from the Jesuits of this court, which order hath always had a great number of missionaries in that region. who, besides the conversion of infidels, have had the address to engross the whole castor [beaver] trade from which they draw considerable advantage."

Presumably his lordship had no objection to "the conversion of infidels." But that "the Jesuits of this court," whose "address" he probably somewhat exaggerated, or any other Frenchmen, should have a monopoly of the fur trade, was intolerable. To put an end to such a state of things, there were no better agents than Radisson and Groseilliers. By the persuasions of Lord Preston and their friend Sir James Hayes of the Hudson's Bay company, aided perhaps by the entreaties of Radisson's English wife, they again exchanged, this time for good, the land of their nativity for that of their adoption. A second time they aided in establishing English authority over the Hudson's Bay region. Thus these men who have so large a part in the history of the exploration of North America widened therein the domain of Saxon Protestantism.

---

ing much for differences in doctrine or ritual.

[1] Thus it is probable that but for its influence British Columbia would now be one of the states of our Union.

CHAPTER II.

EARLY MISSIONS.

In order of time, the brief, touching story of one who is often called Wisconsin's first missionary belongs between Radisson's third "voyage" and his fourth. On the 28th of August, 1660, Renahis (commonly written Rene) Menard, who had labored among the Hurons before their utter defeat by the Iroquois in 1649 and the blotting out of the missions in the same year, started from Three Rivers in search of the vanquished tribe, who were so broken in spirit that they hid even from their former teachers. He came on the 15th of October, St. Theresa's[1] day, to the most prominent cape on the southern shore of Lake Superior, Keweenaw Point, in what is now Michigan. No Hurons there; only Ottawas, who seem, like most other Algonquians,[2] to have been friendly to the whites, with perhaps a partiality for the French. But these Ottawas treated Menard with a cruelty that might be expected from a tribe

---

[1] Though not the discoverer of the adjacent bay, Menard gave it St. Theresa's name. We have here a suggestion, first recognized by the late eminent Roman Catholic historian J. G. Shea, that dates of discovery can, in some cases, be determined by the names that were given by the early explorers. This principle must, of course, be applied with caution. Thus of the Arched Rock, Lake Superior, Radisson writes: "I gave it the name of the portal of St. Peter, because my name is so called, and that I was the first Christian who ever saw it."

St. Theresa is known to some by the fact that an account of her vision of hell has been published under the sanction of Roman Catholic dignitaries. Many "visions" of some of the saints suggest that the subjects thereof would, with a slightly different religious training, have made first-class "spirit mediums." We shall not understand men like Menard and his compeers unless we remember that narratives of the sort indicated formed no small part of their reading and were regarded by them as almost on a parity with divine revelation. The "lesser devotion" paid to the saints was not only a matter of religious observance, it was a dictate of prudence as well. For their aid was almost indispensable in contests with Satan, whose dominion the missionaries were invading, whose subjects they were endeavoring to wrest from him, and who might be expected to appear in tangible presence under almost any guise, in almost any place and at almost any time.

[2] The spelling given above is that used by the Bureau of Ethnology (Smithsonian Institution). For the entire Algonquian (Algonquin, Algonkin) family Schoolcraft suggested the term "Algics." Using this name, thus wrote W. W. Warren, of whom we have already heard, a descendant of a Mayflower pilgrim, as well as of Ojibways:

"The red men who first greeted our pilgrim fathers, and who are so vitally connected with their early history, were Algics. The people who treated with good William Penn [with whom good William Penn treated] for the site of the present city of Philadelphia, and who named him 'me guon,' meaning, in the Ojibway language, 'a pen' or 'a feather,' were of the Algic stock. The tribe over whom Pow-hat-tan (signifying 'a dream') ruled as chief belonged to this wide-spread family."

But J. Hammond Trumbull says that Powhat-hanne, or Powhau't-hanne, denotes "falls in a stream." Also that the famous chief and his people derived their name from the falls in the James river, near Richmond, Virginia.

some[1] of whose number as known the next winter by Radisson called forth from him this fierce invective: "They are the coursedest, unablest, the most unfamous & cowardliest people that I have seene amongst fower score nations that I have frequented." Of Menard's success or, rather, want of success, among such a people let the "Jesuit Relations" speak:

"During the winter that he spent with the Outaouak, he started a church among these savages, a very small one indeed but very precious, for it cost him much sweat and many tears. Hence it seemed to be composed only of predestined souls, the greatest part of whom were dying infants whom he was obliged to baptize stealthily, for their parents used to conceal them when he would enter their wigwams, having the old erroneous notion of the Hurons that baptism caused their deaths.[2] Among the adults he found two old men whom grace had prepared for Christianity." Here follows an account of them and of some good women who also became Christians. "Excepting these elect, the Father, amongst the rest of these barbarians, found nothing but opposition to the faith, on account of their great brutality and infamous polygamy. The little hope he had of converting these people, plunged in all sorts of vices, made him resolve to undertake a new journey of a hundred leagues in order to instruct a tribe of poor Hurons, whom the Iroquois had caused to fly to that end of the world. Among these Hurons there were a great many old Christians who asked most urgently for the Father. They promised that at his arrival at their place all the rest of their countrymen would embrace the faith. But before starting to this distant country, the Father begged three young Frenchmen of his flock to go ahead to reconnoiter." These young men, "after undergoing many hardships, finally arrived at the village of this poor, agonizing tribe. Entering the wigwams they found but living skeletons, so feeble that they could scarcely stir and stand on their feet." Having returned, Menard's messengers sought to persuade the old missionary not to attempt the difficult and dangerous journey. He answered: "This is the most beautiful occasion to show to angels and men that I love my Creator more than the life which

---

[1] The "hundred and fifty with their families."

[2] We have the following with its delicious bit of absurdity from Rev. Chryostom Verwyst, historian of these early missions in the Lake Superior region, himself a Romanist:

"As the early Jesuit Fathers realized the absolute necessity of Baptism for salvation, they most eagerly sought to confer that Sacrament upon the dying children of Pagan parents. Seeing that their children generally died after Baptism, the natives in their ignorance and superstition attributed their death to Baptism, which they regarded as an evil charm for the destruction of their offspring."

Mr. Verwyst is surely right in assuming that such a belief as that he indicates on the part of the Indians is evidence of both ignorance and superstition. The kindlier belief of the Jesuits, shared evidently by himself, that children dying unbaptized will be eternally lost must be regarded, of course, as evidence of wisdom and piety. But as the Indians were not to be blamed for their belief so, perhaps, the Jesuits are not to be praised for theirs.

"I have been most amply rewarded for all my trials and sufferings," says one of the early Jesuits who labored in some part of the interior of our continent, though not, so far as I know, in the Wisconsin region, " I have this day rescued from the burning an infant who died from hunger, its mother's resources in the general famine having failed her; I administered to the dying infant the sacred rites of baptism; and, thank God, it is now safe from the dreadful destiny which befalls those who die without the pale of our most holy church." He himself had been compelled by hunger to eat part of an Indian moccasin. This group of starv-

I have from him, and would you wish me to let it escape?") "Some Hurons," continues the "Relation," "who had come to traffic with the Outaouak offered themselves to the Father to act as guides. He gave them some luggage to carry, and chose one of the Frenchmen (Jean Guerin, a blacksmith) to accompany him. So he set out on his journey the 13th of July, 1661, nine months after his arrival in the Outaouak country. But the poor Hurons, though they had little to carry, soon lost courage; their strength failed through want of nourishment. They abandoned the Father, telling him they were going in haste to inform the head men that he was on the way coming, and thus induce some strong young men to get him. About fifteen days the Father stopped near a lake," perhaps Lac Vieux Desert on the boundary between Michigan and Wisconsin, "expecting help." But, as the Hurons did not come, he continued the journey. "About the 10th of August," says the "Relation," "the poor Father, whilst following a companion [around a portage] went astray." It is almost certain that he was murdered. "His camp-kettle was found in a Sauk's hand, and some years after his disappearance his robe and prayer-book were found in a Dakota lodge, and were looked upon as 'wawkawn,' or supernatural."[1]

There seems no sufficient reason for the supposition that Menard went by way of Green Bay and the Fox-Wisconsin route to the Mississippi and thence up the Black. The so-called evidence supporting this notion is late, and comes from what is almost conclusively shown by Mr. Verwyst to be a mistake of Perrot's. The "Jesuit Relations" seldom indulge in the rhetoric of understatement in speaking of the hardships, dangers and achievements of any of their order. They call Menard's proposed journey one "of a hundred leagues." But twice that distance would not equal such a journey as that described by Perrot. Nor does the narrative speak of any such discovery as that of the Mississippi. Its language accords with the probability that Menard went to Lac Vieux Desert and thence followed the Wisconsin. This route was probably also that of his three messengers whom, it is reasonable to suppose, he would endeavor to follow. "It took them fifteen days to return to the place whence they had started." The village which they visited and to which Menard was going was near the headwaters of the Black river, perhaps in what is now Taylor county. If they went by the upper Wisconsin we can understand the statement that "they set out on their way to return, which was a great deal harder, being obliged to go up the river in returning, whereas they had gone down stream when going to the Huron village." But this account does not harmonize at all with the theory that, on their return, they went down the Black, down the Mississippi, up the lower Wisconsin, and down the Fox. Mr. Verwyst thinks that Menard perished near the confluence of the Copper river with the Wisconsin, not far from the present village of Merrill.

Though the writer of the "Relation" thinks it probable that Menard was

---

ing figures, in a wretched wigwam or, perhaps, shelterless, would form a fitting subject for the pencil of a Dore, and the entire narrative a theme for a Dante.

[1] Rev. Edward Duffield Neill, historian of Minnesota and one of the first, if not the first, to labor therein under commission from the American Home Missionary society.

murdered, yet he indulges the following supposition, which we copy as illustrating a source of great suffering in the Wisconsin woods:

"Behold the priest left, abandoned; but in the hands of Divine Providence. God, no doubt, gave him the courage to suffer with constancy, in that extremity, the deprivation of all human succor when tormented by the stings of mosquitoes, which are exceedingly numerous in these parts, and so intolerable that the three Frenchmen who had made the voyage [journey to the Huron village] declare that there was no other way of protecting themselves from their bites than to run incessantly, that it was even necessary that two of them should chase away those little beasts whilst the third was taking a drink. Thus the poor Father, stretched out on the ground or on some rock, remained exposed to their stings and endured their cruel torment as long as life held out. Hunger and other miseries completed his sufferings and caused this happy soul to leave its body, in order to go and enjoy the fruit of so many hardships endured for the conversion of savages."

Four years passed before the work in which Menard had lost his life was undertaken by another. Meanwhile Chequamegon bay became the gathering place of a large Indian population of whom the first to come were the Hurons and the Ottawas. The successor to Menard in missionary labor among them or, rather, for them was another French Jesuit, Claude Allouez. French traders who had been at Chequamegon bay invited him to return with them. He thus writes:

"The eighth day of August of the year 1665, I embarked at Three Rivers, with six Frenchmen, in company with more than four hundred savages of divers nations. The devil formed all opposition imaginable to our voyage, making use of the false prejudice these Indians have, namely, that baptism causes death to their children. On the second of September, we entered into the upper lake (Superior), which will hereafter bear the name of Monsieur Tracy.[1] After having gone a hundred and eighty leagues along that coast of Lake Tracy that looks toward the south, we arrived on the 1st of October, 1665, at Chequamegon. It is a beautiful bay at the head of which is situated the large village of Indians, who there cultivate fields of Indian corn and do not lead a wandering life. There are at this place men bearing arms who number about eight hundred; but these are gathered together from seven different tribes, and live in a peaceable community." The particular place where he made his home he thus describes: "The section of the lake shore where we have settled down is between two large villages, and is, as it were, the center of all the tribes of the countries, because the fishing here is very good, which forms the principal source of support to these people. We have erected there a small chapel of bark, where my sole occupation is to receive the Algonquin and Huron Christians, instruct them, baptize, and catechise the children," etc. The name of the Holy Spirit was given by Allouez to mission, chapel and place.

---

[1] Jean Baptiste Tracy, then intendant of New France, an office which was designed to be a check upon that of governor.

EARLY MISSIONS.

This was probably where Radisson and Groseilliers built their first "fort," or but little distance therefrom.[1] What Allouez calls "La Pointe d'Esprit" is the wide cape on the west side of the bay, not the part of Madelaine island now known by that name, where the first mission established was that of the American Board.

One reason, apparently, that so many Indians chose the shores of Chequamegon bay as a home was that there they were at a safe distance from the Iroquois on the east and supposed themselves to be out of danger from the Sioux on the west or had not yet had reason to fear them. Says one of the writers in the "Jesuit Relations" for 1668 and 1669: "God has found some elect in every tribe during the time in which the fear of the Iroquois has kept them assembled there. But finally the danger having passed, each tribe returned to its own country." However, the Hurons, Ottawas and perhaps some of other tribes remained.

In 1667, the year in which Marquette was sent to found a mission at Sault Ste. Marie, Allouez went back to Quebec, arriving there on the 3rd of August. He returned to the mission of the Holy Spirit where he stayed two years longer. In 1669 he went again to Quebec whence he once more came west to establish a mission in the Green Bay region.

James Marquette succeeded Allouez in the mission on Chequamegon bay. This worthy man, whose bad fortune it has been to receive more honor for the deeds of others mistakenly attributed to him than for what he did himself, arrived at his new station on the 13th of September, 1669. "I went," he says, "to visit the Indians, who were living in clearings divided, as it were, into five villages. The Hurons, to the number of four or five hundred souls, are nearly all baptized, and still preserve a little Christianity.[2] Those of the Keinou-

---

[1] The late Secretary L. C. Draper, of the Wisconsin Historical society, believed that Radisson's "fort" and the mission of Allouez were on or about the same site. Where was this? One suggestion has been given. Mr. Wheeler believes that it was in the southwestern part of Washburn itself. These are his reasons:

1. There were two Indian villages on the Chequamegon; one at the head (sometimes called the "bottom") of the bay; the other probably at the mouth of Onion river, and so a short distance south-west of Bayfield. (A reason for supposing that this second village was at the mouth of the river is that there is second-growth timber there and not at Bayfield.) Allouez says that he set up his establishment "between two large villages."

2. The Ojibway name of Washburn, handed down from the earliest times, is Gah-nu-kwash-koh-dah-ding: "that which was the place of meeting" (u like oo; a in kwash long; other vowels short).

3. Convenience of landing.

4. Policy of traders to have their posts outside of Indian villages to prevent collision of hostile bands.

[2] This remark of Marquette's is suggestive. He and John Eliot, the Puritan apostle to the Indians, were contemporaries. After contrasting the wanderings of the Jesuits with the much shorter journeys of the Protestant missionaries, the historian Parkman adds: "Yet in judging the relative merits of the Romish and Protestant missionaries, it must not be forgotten, that while the former contented themselves with sprinkling a few drops of water on the forehead of the proselyte, the latter sought to wean him from his barbarism and penetrate his savage heart with the truth of Christianity."

In speaking of this early work among the Massachusetts Indians, Bancroft says that no pains were spared to teach them to read and to write and that in a short time the proportion of them who could do so was larger than the corresponding number among the inhabitants of Russia at the present day. And on the same subject Edward Fiske Kimball ("New England

che tribe[1] (an Ottawa clan) declare loudly that the time is not yet come [to embrace the Christian religion]. The Outaouacs (Ottawas) seem to harden themselves against the instructions imparted to them. The Kiskakonk nation, which for three years has refused to receive the gospel announced to them by Father Allouez, finally resolved, in the autumn of the year 1668, to obey God. This resolution was taken in a council and declared to the Father who was to winter with them for the fourth time in order to instruct and baptize them. The Father having gone to another mission, the charge of this one was given to me."[2]

At this time the Illinois were living west of the Mississippi. Some of them came to the mission. Marquette gives an account of them and adds: "When the Illinois come to La Pointe, they pass a great river about a league in width. It runs from north to south and so far that the Illinois, who know not what a canoe is,[3] have not heard of its mouth. It is hardly credible that this large river empties [into the sea] at Virginia; and we rather believe that it has its mouth in California. If the Indians who have promised to make me a canoe do not fail in their word, we shall travel on this river as far as possible." As is well known, this purpose was carried out in 1673 when Joliet and Marquette entered the upper Mississippi by the Fox-Wisconsin route as Radisson had done fourteen years before.

Marquette's stay at Chequamegon bay was a short one. The last account of the mission of the Holy Spirit is in the "Relations" for 1671 and 1672: "The quarters of the north have their Iroquois, as well as those of the south: there are certain called Nadouessi [Sioux] who make themselves dreaded by all their neighbors.[4] Our Outaouacs and Hurons had, up to the present time, kept up a kind of peace with them; but affairs having become embroiled, and some murders having been committed on both sides, our savages had reason to appre-

---

Magazine," September, 1892) writes: "It was the missionaries as well as the soldiers who saved New England."

It is evident from accounts given by the Jesuits themselves, that many of their "converts" looked upon the rites of the church as a new kind of magic which it might be worth while at least to try. Says Rev. S. S. Hebberd, author of "French Dominion in Wisconsin:" "All revered the black-robed stranger as at least a mighty magician armed with a mysterious power and possessed of more potent spells than had ever before been witnessed in the wilderness. One day a war party (among the Fox Indians) were so wrought upon by the harangues of Allouez that they daubed the figure of a cross upon their shields of bull-hide before going to battle; they returned victorious, extolling the sacred symbol as the greatest of 'war-medicines.' This test convinced multitudes. It is the first recorded attempt to apply the scientific method to the verifying of religious truth."

[1] Keinouche, the kind of fish known as pike. Of this name, a modified form is Kenosha.

[2] Marquette made a fatal mistake as a minister of Christ. He allowed the Indians to retain such sacrifices to imaginary spirits as he thought were harmless.—REV. E. D. NEILL.

[3] "How did they cross the river?" is a natural inquiry. But Marquette had in mind, probably, the larger boats made by Indians who dwelt on the shores of the Great Lakes.

[4] These Nadouessi having been irritated by the Hurons and the Outaouacs, war was kindled among them, and they pursued it with so much fury that some prisoners which were made on both sides were put to death by burning them."—*Relation of the Mission of St. Ignatius at Missilimackinac.*

We wish that the record added that Marquette tried to prevent the burning of living men by the Indians of his own party. But I find no such statement.

hend that the storm would burst upon them, and judged that it was safer for them to leave the place. They retired to the Lake of the Hurons. Father Marquette was obliged to follow his flock, submitting the same fatigues and encountering the same dangers with them." The Hurons went to "Missilimackinac," the mainland north of the island now called Mackinaw though the name was applied to both. The "Outaouacs" found a home on the island of Ekaentouton, now called Manitoulin. Not until our own Mr. Ayer came in 1830 was the gospel of Christ again proclaimed on the shores of Chequamegon bay. Then another Indian nation, the Ojibways, held the land.

But before the mission of the Holy Spirit came to an end, another had been established. Reference has already been made to the large aboriginal population about Green bay. To the mouth of the Fox river or thereabout, came Allouez on the 2nd of December, 1669. French traders were there ahead of him,[1] and on the following day, dedicated in the calendar of the church of Rome to St. Francis Xavier, eight of them attended mass. This mission, named from the day on which its first service was held, was maintained for almost sixty years. It may be that Allouez built its first chapel somewhere between the mouth of Fox river and Sturgeon bay. In 1671 the headquarters of the mission were established where is now the village of De Pere (originally Des Peres; that is, "of the father").

Following the establishment of the mission of St. Francis Xavier came the formal act of taking possession of this continent by the deputy of the French king. This took place 1671, June 14th, at a great gathering of the Indian tribes held at Sault Ste. Marie. Nicholas Perrot gathered the Indians together. Allouez was there, and made an address to the Indians concerning the king in terms that lead us to wonder what more he could have said had he been speaking of the Lord of earth and heaven. The ceremony is spoken of in the "Jesuit Relations" as one "worthy of the eldest son of the church and of a most Christian sovereign." These expressions are not meant for irony, though the king spoken of is no other than the infamous Louis XIV. who was so soon (1685), with the support and almost certainly at the instigation of Jesuits, to drive into exile thousands of his best subjects because they were Protestants. It is a curious fact that one time the only forms of religion that would have been tolerated in what is now Wisconsin were Romanism and the various forms of heathenism that prevailed among the Indians.

It is evident from the terms of the *proces-verbal*, set forth at Sault Ste. Marie by "Simon Francois Daumont, Esquire, Sieur de St. Lusson, commissioner subdelegate of my Lord the Intendant of New France" (Jean Baptiste Talon), that he did not intend that anything should be lost because it had not been claimed. "We take possession of the said place of Ste. Mary of the Falls

---

[1] Despite Bancroft's statement, in regard to the exploration of the interior of North America, that "not a cape was turned, nor a river entered, but a Jesuit led the way," the trader, almost without exception, preceded the missionary. Professor Frederick Jackson Turner of our state university stated, to the writer hereof, in regard to this entire region, that he knew of no case in which a Jesuit led in the work of exploration.

as well as of lakes Huron and Superieur, the island of Caientonton [Manitoulin] and of all other countries, rivers, lakes and tributaries, contiguous and adjacent thereunto, as well discovered as to be discovered, which are bounded on the one side by the Northern and Western Seas and on the other side by the South Sea (Pacific ocean) including all its length or breadth."

Nicholas Perrot, commanding for the king at the post of the Nadouesioux (Sioux) took formal possession of the country about the Bay des Puants[1] and the upper Mississippi at Post St. Anthony, 8th of May, 1689. He called attention to our Wisconsin lead mines, discovered, it is believed, by a previous explorer Le Sueur who came to the Upper Mississippi from Green Bay, in 1683.

To human sight it would have seemed, in 1671, that the St. Lawrence and Mississippi valleys were to be closed forever to other than French and Roman Catholic influence.[2] We honor the early missionaries though they erred both in method and teaching and were the active supporters of an abominable political despotism, and the agents of an ecclesiastical tyranny which has justly brought upon itself the suspicion of the world. "The individual Jesuit might be, and often was, a hero, saint, and martyr, but the system of which he was a part; and which he was obliged to administer, is fundamentally unsound, and in contravention of inevitable laws of nature, so that his noblest toils were forever doomed to failure, save in so far as they tended to ennoble and perfect himself, and offered a model for others to imitate."[3] The courage and devotion of men like Menard, Allouez and Marquette are the clean pages upon the blood-stained history of French rule in the region of the Great Lakes and the Upper Mississippi. But the Jesuit missions there were failures. To be sure there were many baptisms. Marquette who returned to the mission of St. Francis Xavier late in September, 1673, and spent there possibly the following winter and certainly the next summer puts the number at two thousand. In 1676, a chapel was built at De Pere. This with the mission house was burned eleven years later, by hostile Foxes, Kickapoos and Mascoutins. There was no school house to burn. "No evidence can be found that the Jesuits ever opened a missionary school in Wisconsin before the American troops took possession of Fort Howard."[4] No doubt there was oral religious instruction. It is said, how-

---

[1] "Bay des Puants,"—Bay of the Bad Smell,—was the unpleasant name given to Green bay by the French who first came thither. They sometimes, also, applied the name to Lake Michigan. The reference, however, is to the Winnebago Indians, and to them not on account of their habits as might well be the case, but because of the tradition that they originally came from the "ill-smelling," that is the salt, water. "The Bay," says Marquette, "bears a name that has not so bad a meaning in the Indian language, as they call it Salt Bay rather than Fetid Bay, although among them it is about the same."

[2] On the western side of the Mississippi the profession of any form of Christian faith save Romanism was illegal until (1800, October 1st) Spain receded the province of Louisiana to France. In practice, however, there was tolerance to the American settlers who even at that early day had found homes beyond the Mississippi. An inquisitor who came to New Orleans to exercise the functions of his "Holy Office,"—which a son of General Sherman thinks so beneficient in its practical working,—was shipped back to Spain by (acting) Governor Estavan Mi...

[3] ...v. R. F. Littledale, LL. D., D. D., D. C. L.

[4] ...W. C. Whitford, ex superintendent of public instruction.

ever, that there was a school at Michilimackinac (Point Ste. Ignace).

But the pagan Indians were not the worst foes whom the early missionaries had to encounter. Nor was the fact that most of their "converts" continued in practical heathenism, the only charge brought against them. "With the Jesuits the conversion of souls is but a pious phrase for trading in beaver skins." These bitter words of Frontenac, governor of New France from 1672 to 1682, and again from 1688 until his death in November, 1698, show a feeling which he did not possess alone. La Salle accuses the Jesuits of plotting against his life. Yet it dulls the edge of these charges to know that they were made by those who were virtually business rivals, and that one of the points of controversy between Frontenac and the ecclesiastical authorities was in regard to the sale of liquor to Indians, which the missionaries wished to forbid. And I believe the frightful accusation made by La Salle to be wholly false. Yet we must grant that the Jesuits should not have gone into the fur trade. As it was their missions here came to an end under suspicion and reproach. The civil authorities and rival orders[1] within the church of Rome itself were alike hostile to them. Thus Louis Hennepin,—a Franciscan of the stricter sort known as Recollects,—who, in his wanderings with La Salle in 1679, came into Green Bay[2] ignores the existence of the mission of St. Francis Xavier. This is the more remarkable because in the following year, 1680, he enjoyed the hospitality of those laboring there.

Besides this strife within New France there was a contest between the authorities of that province and those of Louisiana. A bad government at home naturally produced its like in the colonies. Corruption in administration seems to have been expected as a matter of course. Burdensome monopolies were made legal. Unchristian intolerance and exclusion were expressly commanded. "Precise orders were given by Louis XIII. that no Protestant should settle in Canada, and that no other religion than the Catholic should be tolerated."[3] There was not even the thought of popular education.

That the government of New France was less oppressive than that of the mother country was merely because men in Canada could easily find the freedom of lake, forest, and prairie, a freedom, however, that was purely natural and not legal. Thus the fur trade monopolies could not prevent the existence of a large class of unlicensed traders, or *coureurs de bois*. Among these were found some of the most venturesome explorers, men like Radisson and Groseilliers. The trader rather than the priest was the first who found a path in the

---

[1] No true judgment of the church of Rome can be formed which ignores the denominational divisions within her ranks. These are known as "orders," and the history of their mutual contests forms some of the worst chapters of sectarian controversy.

[2] This was soon after his discovery (1680) of the falls at the present city of Minneapolis. These, called Rara by the Dakotas from *irara* to laugh, he named after St. Anthony of Padua (Italy). Five hundred feet was the hight he gave them in his narrative as first published. Later he put it at six hundred feet.

[3] John Law, a eulogist of the Jesuits, addressing the Young Men's Catholic Literary Institute of Cincinnati.

wilderness, and it was commonly in canoes laden with goods for the Indians that the missionary found conveyance to his Western home.

The French, willing to step down almost to the plane of barbarism, were for the most part successful in winning allies among the Indians of the interior. But the cargoes of goods which the traders brought were of course tempting objects of plunder. Soon the Indians, especially the Outagamies, or Foxes,[1] learned enough of the ways of civilization to make themselves toll-gatherers. Their service was to help bring the laden canoes up the Fox river rapids,—since developed into some of the best water-powers in the United States,—and over the portage to the Wisconsin. Their charges were quite as just as those of the French colonial authorities and far more reasonable. Thus the governor demanded of Radisson and Groseilliers, as the price of a license, one-half of all they might get. Refusal to pay forced them to go without legal permission and so exposed them to the exactions from which, as already narrated, they fled to Boston. In the general game of grab, the Outagamies,—crude reasoners of the wilderness!—may have thought themselves entitled to all that they could compel others to pay.

Of the many evils with which New France was afflicted, none was more hurtful to the Indians than the fur-trade monopoly. It lowered the price of what they had to sell and increased the cost of what they wished to buy. They soon learned that the English would give sometimes from four to six times as much for beaver skins as the French did. But these commanded the lakes and were at hand; the English were far away. The sturdiest young men of the Puritan commonwealths and of New York did not go into the wilderness to become semi-savages. The British colonists sought to turn forests into farms and thus found enough to do at home. Moreover, the great water-courses were not open to them, and the frequent wars made their settlements compact and put them much of the time on the defensive.

---

[1] The Foxes were of two stocks: one calling themselves Outagamies, or Foxes, whence our English name; the other, Musquakink, or men of red clay, the name now used by the tribe. They lived in early times with their kindred the Sacs east of Detroit, and some say near the St. Lawrence. They were driven west and settled at Saginaw, a name derived from the Sacs. Thence they were forced by the Iroquois to Green Bay; but were compelled to leave that place and settle on Fox River."—C. W. BUTTERFIELD.

CHAPTER III.

THE OUTAGAMIE WAR.

With the accession of William and Mary to the thrones of England and Scotland began the struggle between the French and the British, elsewhere called the second War of a Hundred Years. During its first distinct phase, known in American history as King William's war, the Outagamies, or Fox Indians, became bold enough to plunder,[1] as early as 1693, some of the French traders who, they alleged, were furnishing arms to the Sioux, the Outagamies' traditional enemies. The war that followed in the Mississippi valley and the Upper Lake region was virtually the beginning of the struggle by which the French were dispossessed of their North American dominions.

The history of much of this war is obscure as to both time and circumstance. But it is known that few wars of modern time have surpassed it in ferocity or in the number of those slain as compared with the number taking part. There is reason to think that by 1712 the French and their Indian allies had formed the purpose to destroy the Outagamies. In the spring of that year a large force of that tribe, with whom were Mascoutins and some Sauks, encamped near Detroit where a post had been built by the French to keep the British from the upper lakes. Here the Outagamies and their allies made themselves troublesome. But though the fort was virtually at their mercy they made no assault and took no lives. On the 12th of May, Indian allies of the French arrived. The united force immediately beset the camp of the Outagamies, whom the fire of the enemy, hunger and the want of water brought to the humiliation of offering surrender. "My father," said their great war chief Permoussa to Du Buisson, the French commander, "I come to you to demand life. It is no longer ours. You are masters of it. All the nations have abandoned us." (He speaks for the Outagamies and Mascoutins; the Sauks had deserted.) "But do not believe I am afraid to die. It is the life of our women and children that I ask of you." "I confess," says Du Buisson, "that I was touched with compassion at their misfortunes; but as war and pity do not agree together, and particularly as I understood they were paid by the English for our destruction, I abandoned them to their unfortunate fate; indeed I has-

---

[1] The charge made by the French that the Outagamies were incited to hostility by the British is not supported by evidence. However, it would be probable enough save for the lack of communication between the English colonies and the distant interior.

tened to have this tragedy finished, in order that the example might strike terror to the English and to themselves."

In their first encampment the Outagamies withstood a siege of nineteen days. Then, under cover of storm and night, they sought a second place of defence where they held out against overwhelming odds four days more, "fighting with much courage," says Du Buisson, who adds: "Finally, not being able to do any thing more they surrendered at discretion to our people who gave them no quarter. All were killed except the women and children, whose lives were spared, and one hundred men who had been tied but escaped.

"All our allies returned to our fort with their slaves" [the captive women and children, it would seem]. "Their amusement was to shoot four or five of them every day. The Hurons did not spare a single one of theirs.

"In this manner came to an end these two wicked nations who so badly afflicted and troubled all the country. Our Rev. Father chanted a grand mass to render thanks to God for having preserved us from the enemy. The enemy lost a thousand souls, men, women and children."

Thus ended the so-called siege of Detroit.

At the end of his report which is dated "au Fort du Detroit, Pontchartrain, June 15, 1712," Du Buisson expresses to Marquis de Vaudreuil, governor-general of Canada, the hope that "you will not suffer a devil to be reduced to beggary." He means himself, using the term devil after the manner of those who mistake coarseness for humor. Most of us, however, will be inclined to give his expression a very literal interpretation.

Notwithstanding the fond hopes of Du Buisson, the Outagamies were not exterminated. According to the estimate of the missionary Gabriel Marest,[1] who lays the blame of the war on his own countrymen, there were four hundred warriors of that nation at Green Bay. With diplomatic skill the Outagamies sought alliances. They almost annihilated French trade in what is now Wisconsin and Minnesota. They blocked the Fox-Wisconsin route[2] and threatened that of the Chicago and the Illinois. It was evident that something must be done. It was even proposed to bring about reforms in law and ad-

[1] We turn for a moment from graver matters to note that in connection with the name of Marest, there may be offered a humble contribution to the history of a bad joke. Writing 1712, November 9th, from "Cascaskias" (old Kaskaskia, Illinois), which he describes as midway between the Ohio and the "Pekitanoui" (the Missouri), Marest states that "omne genus muscarum" (every kind of fly) abounds in the valley of the Mississippi, and that since Frenchmen came thither the mosquitoes have caused an unmeasured amount of profanity. We could wish that the statement of the age of this bit of supposed humor might prevent its use hereafter; a use that, in regard to a senseless and wicked habit, is too often both suggestion and apology.

Marest for a time was at Plymouth, Massachusetts, as a captive, having been taken with other prisoners when, in 1695, the English seized the forts on Hudson's bay.

[2] These were the principal routes from the Great Lakes to the Ohio and the Mississippi:
1. From Lake Erie, by way of the Miami and the Wabash.
2. From Lake Michigan, by way of the St. Joseph river and the Wabash.
3. From the St. Joseph, by way of the Kankakee river, to the Illinois.
4. By the Chicago river to the Illinois.
5. The Fox-Wisconsin route.
6. From Lake Superior, by way of the Bois Brule and the St. Croix.

ministration. But this was too revolutionary, of course, and instead of doing justice to the Indians, as was advised by Perrot and others, the French authorities resolved to try a second time to exterminate their hated enemies.

Accordingly there set out from Quebec 1716, March 14th, the first hostile expedition of white men that ever trod Wisconsin soil. "Every one believed," said Charlevoix, "that the Fox nation was about to be destroyed, and so they themselves judged. They, therefore, determined to sell their lives as dearly as possible."

It was, according to tradition, at the little Butte des Morts, near the present city of Menasha, at the outlet of Lake Winnebago, that the Outagamies prepared for what they supposed to be their final defence. But their bravery won from De Louvigny, the French commander, honorable terms, which we are sorry to say they did not faithfully keep. So the war went on. In these years of strife and bloodshed the mission of St. Francis Xavier found shelter in a fort, to which it gave name, built some time between 1718 and 1721 a mile and a half from the mouth of Fox river and on the site of the present city of Green Bay. Hither, in the summer of 1721, came Peter Francis Xavier Charlevoix, and found there his fellow Jesuit, Jean Baptiste Chardon, one of the last of the early missionaries in the region west of Lake Michigan. Chardon was present at a great council held at Green Bay, 7th of June, 1726, for the real or pretended purpose of making peace between the French and Indians. Of these, Outagamies, Sauks and Winnebagoes took part in the council. The truce rather than peace then agreed upon lasted less than two years. But it gave Beauharnois, then viceroy of New France, the opportunity of sending an expedition to establish among the Sioux a fort on the west side of Lake Pepin. To command this force he chose Rene Boucher, the Sieur de la Perriere, who in 1708 left behind him in New England[1] a trail of blood. The Foxes permitted this Boucher to pass unmolested from Fort St. Francis to the site chosen for the new fort to which the viceroy's name was given. Nor did they interfere with his return.

Strengthened by their new military post Fort Beauharnois, the French became bolder. Rev. Emanuel Crespel, of the order of Recollects, gives an account of an expedition which he accompanied as chaplain. His story needs no comment and little explanation. He writes very unconcernedly about the proposed destruction of a people. "Four hundred French, to be joined by eight or nine hundred Indians of several nations, the whole under command of M. de Lignerie, were dispatched with orders to destroy a nation of Indians, called

---

[1] On the 29th of August, 1708, a force of two hundred fifty men, consisting of French and Indians, reached Haverhill. The house of Rev. Benjamin Rolfe was the first attacked. It was garrisoned by three soldiers, who when the enemy appeared became terrified and fled. The enemy broke through the door and soon captured Mr. Rolfe whom they tomahawked. Mrs. Rolfe and one child were also killed.—REV. G. L. GLEASON, Haverhill, Massachusetts.

A more vivid narrative says that Rene Boucher, the Sieur de la Perriere was "the officer in command of the Indians who," with a party of French, 1708, August 29th, "surprised Haverhill, Massachusetts, killed," among forty others, "the minister of the town, scalped his wife and broke the skull of his child against a rock."

by the French the Fox Indians; but in their own language the Outagamies.

"We halted on the 17th [of August, 1728], to avoid arriving at the post of La Baye before night, wishing to surprise our enemies, whom we knew to be in company with the Saguis [Sauks], whose village lay near Fort St. Francis. The enemies had information and all the inhabitants escaped except four, who were delivered to our Indians; and they, after having long amused themselves with tormenting them, shot them with arrows, making them suffer the pain of twenty deaths before they deprived them of life. I was a painful witness to this cruel transaction, and wished to point out what I thought reprehensible in their proceeding; but all our interpreters were on the other side of the river."

"After this affair we ascended the Fox river. The 24th of August, we arrived at the village of the Puans Indians. Our men were well disposed to destroy such men as they found there, but the flight of the inhabitants saved them, and we could only burn their huts, and destroy the harvest of corn on which they subsist."

"The next day, being St. Lawrence's, we had mass, and entered a small river which led us to a marshy ground, on the borders of which was situated the chief settlement of those Indians of whom we were in search. We found in their village some women only, whom our Indians made slaves, and an old man whom they burned by a slow fire, without manifesting the least repugnance for committing so barbarous an action."

These murders of five helpless victims moved the chaplain to give the offending Indians a moral lecture. It does not appear that he gave De Lignery who permitted these atrocities the benefit of any part of his excellent sermon. He goes on with something like unconscious satire to say, "I was proceeding to give further reasons, when orders were given to advance against the last post of the enemy which was situated on a little river which runs into another river, that communicates with the Mississippi. We did not find any Indians, and as we had no orders to advance farther, we employed some days in laying waste the country to deprive the enemy of the means of subsistence.

"After this expedition, if such a useless march deserves the name, we prepared to return to Montreal, from which we were now four hundred and fifty leagues distant. In our passage we destroyed the fort at La Baye, because being so near so near the enemy, it would not afford a secure retreat to the French who must be left as a garrison."

Beauharnois did not regard the march as useless. "It is certain," he wrote 1728, September 1st, to the French minister of war, "that one-half these nations, who number four thousand souls, will die of hunger, and that the rest will come in and sue for mercy."

"The Foxes would have found refuge with the Sioux, if the French fort had not been established there," said an official dispatch from New France to the home government. But the Sioux, whom the Outagamies had won to a brief alliance, proved faithless to them in their hour of greatest need. Yet so much dreaded were the Outagamies, even in defeat, that Fort Beauharnois was abandoned at their approach. Fugitives themselves, they did not pursue the garrison but sought refuge among the Iowas. Soon they returned to the Wisconsin region. Not the Sioux alone, but all their allies, the Mascoutins and the Kickapoos, the Sauks and the Winnebagoes, had deserted them. And of these the Mascoutins and at least some of the Winnebagoes became open enemies.

Almost fifty-nine years elapsed from the coming of Allouez to Green Bay in 1669 until the departure of the last missionary with the garrison of Fort St. Francis in September, 1728. Yet the Indian allies of the French seem to have received very little practical Christianity. They continued to act like savages. Thus, probably in the autumn of 1729, an expedition of Ottawas, Ojibways, Menomonees and Winnebagoes surprised a hunting party of Outagamies. Of this event the cheerful Beauharnois made report under date of 1730, May 6th:

"I have the honor to communicate to you the favorable news I have received this winter, through different letters of officers who command in the upper country.

"A party of over two hundred Indians, Outaouacs, Sauteux, Folles-Avoines and Puants, fell on the Foxes, surprised and destroyed twenty flat-boats of this nation who were returning from a buffalo hunt, containing eighty men, who were all killed or burned, except three,—the allied Indians having burned the boats, three hundred women and children shared the same fate.

"I have the honor, my lord, to communicate the news with so much the more pleasure, as there is no doubt existing on the subject, circumstances and letters, received by me from all parts, which do not contradict themselves concerning this affair, corroborate the fact."

Then the Outagamies did sue for peace. Their chief, in the depth of winter, sought the distant fort that the French had built on the river St. Joseph, near the southern end of Lake Michigan. But though he asked "for nothing, except the lives of the women and children,"[1] and "promised that his people would send deputies the next spring to Montreal to sue for mercy,"[1] he appealed in vain to a people of whom one of their own number, La Mothe Cadillac, said: "Among the wolves we have learned to howl." In March, 1730, some of their number were attacked by a French force under command of Marin, of whom we shall hear again, and an action ensued " of the warmest kind." More of this fight, unless it is identical with one yet to be described, we do not know.

On the opposite side of the river from the site of Fort St. Francis, near the place where, eighty-six years later, American troops built Fort Howard, the French, in 1730, established a military and trading post. But the mission was not revived. The general name La Baye, already in use, was given not only to the station but to what may be called in modern phrase the "sphere of influence" which it commanded. That summer was given to a campaign against the persecuted Outagamies. Its scenes suggest the words of the prophet Joel:

---

[1] Hebberd's "History of Wisconsin, under the Dominion of France," page 130.

"Blood, and fire, and pillars of smoke." The war became, if possible, even more cruel. The slaughter of warriors in battle is to be expected, but not when the fight is over the burning alive of captives and the destruction of women and children. To the eternal disgrace of the French commanders these things were done.

The worst events of the war occurred near Rock St. Louis[1] on the Illinois river. They are thus described in a letter addressed 1730, November 3rd, by Beauharnois and Hocquart to the French government:

"An affair took place in September under the command of the Sieur de Villiers, commanding at the river St. Joseph's, to whom were united the Sieur de Noyelle commanding the Miamis, and the Sieurs de St. Ange, father and son, with the French of that distant colony, together with those of our posts, and all the neighboring Indians our allies (we numbered from twelve to thirteen hundred men) which resulted in the almost total defeat of the Foxes. Two hundred of their warriors have been killed on the spot, or burned after being taken as slaves, and six hundred women and children were absolutely destroyed.

"This is a brilliant action which sheds great honor on Sieur de Villiers."

The battle began on the 19th of August, 1730; the massacre began on the 9th of September. The whole affair lasted twenty-two days. Nor was this the end of slaughter. At Starved Rock nine hundred of the Outagamies, men and women, were destroyed either in battle or in murder by knife and fire. Two years later, 1732, October 17th (it may be), their village on the Wisconsin and near the mouth of the Kickapoo was surprised by Indian allies of the French, — Iroquois[2] from the St. Lawrence, who had become Christians (of a peculiar sort, certainly), and some Hurons. These fell upon the peaceful village and soon massacred three hundred men, women and children.

A party of seventy or eighty of the survivors went to Green Bay to sue for mercy. Among them was the chief Kiala, who was sent as a slave to Martinique, one of the West Indies. His wife chose to share his living death.

Some of the unhappy remnant of the Outagamie nation found refuge for almost a year among the Sauks (Sacs) near Green Bay. When these refused to surrender the fugitives they became themselves the objects of French hatred. A fight occurred in which De Villiers, the French commander, was killed.[3] Then the Sauks and Outagamies fled. According to Augustus Grignon the former, at least, found refuge on the Wisconsin river where they built a village. Another account states that the united party found a home beyond the Mississippi on the Wapsipinnicon river.[4] In August, 1734, the French with some of their "Christian" Indians set out to attack them there. They fled to the Des

---

[1] Sometimes called Starved Rock. It is in the town of Deer Park, La Salle county, Illinois, on the south side of the river, between the cities of La Salle and Ottawa.

[2] Very few of that people were friendly to the French.

[3] Different versions are given of this story, all agreeing that the French commander was slain.

[4] As the Sauk village may have been built after this time both stories may be true. It

Moines where the French, failing of success, made a kind of peace at least with the Sauks. Under date of 1737, October 16th, Beauharnois announced that peace had at length been established with the Sauks and the Foxes. We do not know how long it lasted. But we do know that in 1742 the French distributed presents among those whom they had sought, so long and fiercely, to destroy.

If we reckon from the destruction, in 1687, of the mission establishment at De Pere we have half a century of conflict. The deed mentioned shows matured rather than incipient hostility. It occurred before British influence had penetrated this region, before England herself had "flung the burden of the second James." Her government was then in a state almost of vassalage to Louis XIV. and her colonies were but a fringe on the Atlantic sea-board. It could not, then, have been in hope of alliance with the people of these distant settlements, that the Outagamies first braved the enmity of the French. For this action of theirs the simplest explanations seem most likely to be true. The Outagamies desired to rule rather than to be ruled, and they coveted a share of the traders' profits. If they were incited to hostility, or encouraged in warfare, by the Iroquois the support does not seem to have been of the kind that shares danger or helps fight a battle.

Events yet to be narrated may belong to the history of this long struggle; if not, they mark a renewal of it. But in 1737 the attempted destruction of a people was at an end. Twenty-five years of such fighting as the world has seldom seen had weakened the power of the French and not exterminated the Outagamies.

Taking, for a moment, a forward look, we see that almost a century later these same people with their kindred Sauks (the Sacs and Foxes) were again in arms, this time against a nation the greatness of which, if not its very existence, they had helped to make possible. For theirs was effective aid in the overthrow of French power in North America. By this overthrow the American Revolution was, if not occasioned, at least brought more quickly to pass, and the United States had opportunity to become a great as well as an independent nation.

will be noticed also that a general name as "Foxes" is sometimes used now of one party and again of another, and that what is said of one of these two closely related tribes may be true also of the other or of both.

CHAPTER IV.

END OF FRENCH DOMINION.

Perriere Marin is one of the notable men of what we may call the Green Bay district of New France. Himself a trader, having posts nine miles west of Mackinaw (probably the old fort) and on the eastern bank of Mississippi [1] eight or nine miles below the mouth of the Wisconsin, he was deeply interested in putting a stop to the exactions of the Outagamies. He planned a massacre. With armed men hidden in boats, under oil-cloth or tarpaulin as goods were covered from the rain, Marin approached Winnebago rapids which are near the outlet of the lake. The unsuspecting Outagamies had come to the river side to levy their customary tribute. Marin's men sprang from their concealment and poured a murderous fire upon the hated toll-gatherers. Unprepared for fight, the Outagamies fled to their village to find that it was in flames, and that an enemy, the Menominees, whom the crafty Marin had sent thither, awaited them. No quarter was asked and none was given. If the stories are to be believed, there perished of fifteen hundred Outagamies not fewer than a thousand.

This assault, with that of De Louvigny, have made the country about the outlet of Lake Winnebago a veritable Aceldama, a field of blood.

Stories are told of two other expeditions against the Outagamies, and Marin's name is connected with both. One, if it occurred at all,[2] was a following-

---

[1] Each of these is called Fort Morand by Grignon, who writes thus the trader's name also.

[2] Hon. Moses M. Strong ("Wisconsin Historical Collections," volume VIII., page 247) says: "The only account of this expedition is a traditionary one." This remark follows his statement that in May, 1730, "Du Buisson, who commanded at Mackinaw, left that post with six hundred men, among whom were fifty Frenchmen, to complete the extermination of the Foxes, so effectually commenced two months before. Marin went with him." Mr. Strong's reference in "effectually commenced" is to the massacre by Marin,—the one described above. It took place, Mr. Strong believes, in 1730. The "winter expedition," against the Outagamies near the mouth of the Kickapoo, he credits to Marin, and follows, substantially, Augustus Grignon in saying that the victor, "having fully conquered the Foxes, and having the last remnant of them in his power, gave them their freedom; but required them to retire beyond the Mississippi, which they did." He adds: "It seems probable that the Foxes and Sauks, having become confederates, wrested from the Illinois their possessions, and, incorporating the remnant which they spared of that numerous tribe with their own, occupied the territory which had been the home of the Illinois. The principal seat of their power was the country about the mouth of Rock river, whence in 1831, and more formidably and effectively in 1832, they made those forays upon the pioneer settlers of Illinois and Wisconsin which resulted in what is generally known as the Black Hawk war."

up of the horrible "victory" at Winnebago rapids. The attack was a surprise to the fugitives,— who had made a stand or, at least, an encampment near the Great Butte des Morts,[1] — and, for them, another hopeless defeat.

"The surviving Foxes," says Augustus Grignon,[2] "located themselves on the northern bank of the Wisconsin, twenty-one miles above its mouth, and some little distance below the creek next below the mouth of Kickapoo river; when I first passed there, in 1795, I saw some crude remains of this village. As soon as the enterprising Morand [Marin] heard of the new locality of his determined enemies, who still seemed bent on obstructing his great trading thoroughfare, he concluded it would be unsafe for him to suffer them to remain there, and consequently lost no time, even though winter had commenced, to collect his tried and trusty band of French and Indians, and make a distant winter expedition against the Foxes. Perhaps he thought, as he had once defeated them by stratagem and then by the usual mode of Indian warfare, that it would now be policy to push his fortunes by a winter campaign, fall upon his inveterate foes and strike a fatal blow when they would least expect it. Captain Morand pursued on foot with troops up Fox river and down the Wisconsin, taking with them snow-shoes to meet the exigencies of the season and pursue their tedious march over the snow for a distance of fully two hundred miles. The Foxes were taken completely by surprise, for Morand's men found them engaged in the amusement of *jeu de paille*, or game of straw; and surrounding the place and falling suddenly upon them, killed some and captured the others. So well planned was Morand's attack and so complete the surprise, that not one of the Foxes escaped. Only twenty warriors were taken, with a large number of women and children."

As we read this story of Grignon's we wonder if it is not merely an incorrect version of the narrative, in chapter III., that it so much resembles.

The time of Marin's bloody deeds is uncertain. Grignon seems to think that they resulted in driving the Outagamies beyond the Mississippi. This removal took place, he thinks, in 1746. Some writers change the order of these battles; and the approximate dates given vary, in the case of the massacre at Winnebago rapids, not less than forty years. There is reason for adopting Grignon's view of a later date. The events in question may have occurred even as late as Marin's administration at Green Bay, which began in 1750 and ended two years later.

Savage as was Marin's treatment of the Outagamies, he seems to have had more humanity than most of those who preceded him in warfare against them. He was brave and efficient. He won to the support of the French all or nearly all the tribes in the region of the Upper Lakes and the Upper Mississippi. It may be that even the remnant of the Outagamies agreed to do service against the British. The treaty bringing all these tribes into alliance with the French, during (at least part of) the "French and Indian war,"

---

[1] On the Fox river above Oshkosh, and in what is now Winnebago county.
[2] "Wisconsin Historical Collections," volume III., pages 208, 209.

was made in 1754. "I conquered more than twenty nations," wrote Marin, "who have since made war on our behalf." Transferred by Du Quesne to command on the Ohio, Marin was succeeded here by his son, who in 1749 had been stationed on the Chequamegon. The feeble hold of the French was soon lost.

La Baye is a name foreign to mission annals. It would seem that from the day when priestly lips last sang "Introibo ad altare Dei,"[1]— "I will go to the altar of God,"— at Fort St. Francis until John Metoxen, of whom we are yet to learn, here led in the worship of God according to the simple rites of the ancient churches, as followed by our Puritan fathers, there was within the limits (of the then future) Wisconsin no regularly maintained public Christian service. In the first part of this long interval of ninety-five years, there seem to have been no pastoral or missionary visitors, and in the later time so little shepherding did the nominal Romanists of Green Bay receive that even marriage was entered into by many of them without any religious or civil rite.

Thus for almost a century there was resident within the present limits of our state neither minister nor so-called priest. Meanwhile the authority of the French in North America came to an end. The greatest failure in colonization that the world has ever known became an acknowledged fact. The treaty of Paris, 1763, February 10th, gave to Britain "a vast, compact and flourishing empire, reaching from the Arctic zone to the Gulf of Mexico."

But earlier than this (1761, October 12th), when British troops occupied La Baye,— to which their commander, Captain Henry Belfour gave the name Fort Edward Augustus,— French dominion in what is now Wisconsin had come to an end. It left here imperfect explorations, abandoned missions, two or three miserable trading-posts, and a non-Indian population few in number and so poor in quality that it required the authority of the first American court established among them to compel proper honor to the rites of marriage. The story of French rule in the country between Lake Michigan and the Mississippi has been written,[2] and we feel as we read it that, save for the places mentioned, it is utterly foreign. It is part of the annals of New France. The cruelties that disgraced it bring reproach chiefly upon men of another race and language than our own. We may not in pharasaic manner blame the French people.[3] But we may say with truth that the Bourbons had fitting agents in these forests and plains of the interior. It is retributive justice that sovereignty like theirs should be overthrown.

When Nicolet came to Green Bay in 1634, Louis XIII. was king. He was the eldest son of the famous Henry of Navarre who succeeded to the

---

[1] The first words of the communion service of the church of Rome, commonly called the mass.

[2] "History of Wisconsin under the Dominion of the French," by Rev. S. S. Hebberd, of Viroqua.

[3] On the contrary, we are to remember that the vast majority of them were hopelessly oppressed by their ecclesiastical and political masters. Had the Huguenots received from France such privileges and help in colonization as England extended to her Puritans, her Roman Catholics and her Quakers, a New France might have disputed with New England for the intellectual and moral leadership of North America.

crown of France when, 1589, August 2nd, his distant cousin Henry III. died from the effects of a wound inflicted the day before by a Dominican priest. As Henry IV. had been the leader of the Huguenots, the party of the Romanists opposed by force of arms his accession to the royal dignity until (1593) he "allowed himself to be converted to Catholicism." This action of Henry's has been much commended as master stroke of politics. Those who agree with Gibbon that "to the statesman all religions are equally useful and to the philosopher equally false" will of course agree with the king's alleged statement that "Paris is well worth a mass." Worth a mass, perhaps, but not the integrity of an immortal soul. And it is worthy of note that the infamous sovereigns who, by their tyranny and vice, helped to bring upon France the storm of the Revolution were descendants of the man who denied his faith for the sake of the kingdom which they brought almost to ruin. Those who held what is now Wisconsin as part of their vast domain in North America were Louis XIII.[1] named above, who reigned from the assassination of his father (whose acceptance of Romanism did not prevent his murder by a fanatic of that faith) 1610, May 14th, until his own death, thirty-three years later to a day. Then came his son, Louis XIV., infamous but called Le Grande, whose reign is the longest on record in the history of the world. Dying 1715, September 1st, he left the throne to his great-grandson, Louis XV. who parted with New France (Canada, including all the country of the upper Lakes) by the treaty of Paris, 1763. On the ratification of this treaty Voltaire congratulated the king on having got rid of fifteen hundred leagues of snow! By a secret treaty Louisiana (as afterward bought by the United States) had been ceded to Spain, 1762, November 3rd, as a set-off for Florida which Great Britain demanded as part of the price of peace and which she secured by the same treaty of 1763, thus humiliating his Catholic Majesty of Spain as well as his Christian Majesty of France.

So completely has French influence ceased to exist in Wisconsin that even the church of the early explorers has among us not a Gallican but a German, Irish or Slavic aspect. Its "bishops" in this state trace their ecclesiastical lineage not through the see of Quebec but through that of Baltimore. A few troublesome measurements of land by "arpents" in the neighborhood of Green Bay, and some melodious names,—most of these corrupted forms of Indian words,—are all that is left of a dominion that has utterly passed away and left the world better for its going.[2] The sons of the French are Americans.

---

[1] The French colonies were the special solicitude of the home country. Louis XIII. was proud of Canada, the new France. They had a governor, and an Intendant who had an eye on the governor to report him at home, to see that all the wants of the people were provided for. This in Canada was quite proper, but in New England it would have been hooted at. The French government even selected wives for the colonists; each had a dowry paid by the king, and all bachelors must get married at two weeks' notice or not hunt, catch fish or trade with the Indians. But the experiment failed. The English planted self-supporting colonies. The fittest has survived and the world is the better for it.—PROFESSOR JOHN FISKE.

[2] A careful student of the early history of this region, Rev. A. O. Wright, secretary of the National Board of Charities and Correction, calls attention to the fact that there was an improvement in the condition of the Indians among whom the French had any considerable in-

CHAPTER V.

BRITISH DOMINION.

The period of British dominion in the region bounded on the north and east by the Great Lakes, on the south by the Ohio and on the west by the upper Mississippi lasted from the end of the French and Indian war, in 1763, until the definitive treaty of peace, 1783, September 3rd, between the American states and the mother country. Indeed the northern and northwestern parts of this domain, now comprised within the states of Michigan and Wisconsin, were kept in possession by the British until the 1st of June, 1796. Then the western posts, which had been held without regard to the treaty of 1783, were given up to the Americans. This was in accordance with the treaty signed by John Jay, 1794, November 19th and ratified the following August.[1]

---

fluence. Moreover, among these tribes, the practice of cannibalism almost entirely ceased. The very few instances of it in the war of 1812 were acts of bravado rather than custom.

"Ought you not," asks Mr. Consul Willshire Butterfield, so favorably known as a writer on the history of Wisconsin, "to modify what you say about the entire Northwest territory's receiving Christian civilization, April 7th 1788 ? There was a good deal of it at Detroit, Michilimackinac, Green Bay ("the Baye"), Prairie du Chien, in the Illinois, and on the Wabash before that date, but of course nearly all Roman Catholic."

In reply it may be said that the civilization and the Christianity were both of a questionable kind, and further that these places did not become centers of religious, intellectual or moral life, or even of any kind of business that does not flourish in barbarous communities, until they were changed by American emigration, bringing with it a purer faith and a more vital civilization. These came with the emigrants that crossed the Alleghanies to make homes, not with the wanderers who went up the St. Lawrence and the Great Lakes to gather furs.

[1] "The unexpected reverse in Europe induced Ministers to compromise with the Americans. Jay's treaty was concluded, a cessation of the Indian war promised, the Indians themselves, now unsupported and dispirited by the defeat at the Miamis, concluded a treaty with Waine (Wayne). The cession of one of the finest Countrys on Earth, with Public Works estimated at 300,000 Sterling was the immediate result, the loss of the fur trade and of the Canadas will be the ultimate consequence, if strong measures be not adopted and in due time."

The foregoing is from "a statement of the Province of Upper Canada sent with the approbation of Lieutenant-General Hunter to Field Marshal his royal highness the Duke of Kent (father of Queen Victoria), commander-in-chief of British North America in the year 1800." By the "reverse in Europe" the writer probably means the conquest of the Netherlands (Holland) by the French, 1794-5, and the other successes of that people by which they were able to conclude with Prussia, 1795, April 5th the treaty of Basle.

The "statement" makes admissions that show reason for the strong feeling in the minds of Western pioneers against the British: "The Indians resolved to defend their country extending from the Ohio Northward to the Great Lakes and westward to the Mississippi. They employed the Tomahawk and the Scalping Knife against such deluded Settlers who on

By proclamation "given at our court at St. James's, the 7th day of October, 1763, in the third year of our reign," King George III. established the provinces of Quebec, East Florida, West Florida and Grenada,[1] and enlarged Georgia by the gift of the territory lying between the Altamaha river and the St. Mary's.

This proclamation made Quebec a "royal province" after the models then existing among the original English colonies. By this action two classes were greatly irritated, the Roman Catholic priests, because theirs was no longer the established church of the province, and the proprietors of large estates who had been striving to establish in America the feudal institutions of France. In 1774 when troubles in the English colonies began to threaten war, the British parliament passed the celebrated "Quebec act." By this act the boundaries of the province of Quebec were enlarged so as to include a great part of the present province of Ontario as well as what is now Ohio, Indiana, Illinois, Michigan, Wisconsin and the part of Minnesota east of the Mississippi. The measure was entitled "An act for making more effectual provision for the government of the province of Quebec in North America."[2] It should have been called "An act to please priests and claimants of land and seigneurial titles." This so-called "Quebec act" secured to the Roman Catholic clergy the "dues and rights" as related to members of that church which French law had given. Innocent-looking phrases sometimes cover evil things, and these "dues and rights" practically gave the priests the power to support themselves and build churches by public taxation of their people. The result has been the virtual establishment of Romanism as a state religion in the province of Quebec. It was enacted that "in all matters of controversy relative to Property and Civil Rights, Resort shall be had to the Laws of Canada" (as they were under French rule). Thus those claiming rank and property under the old laws were satisfied. For its immediate purpose the measure was successful. The popular feeling was stifled, the feeling that would have led Canada to join the colonies about to revolt. The invitation held out in the American Articles of Confederation was given in vain to a people ruled by priests and a Bourbon-made gentry. Fortunately for our state it was delivered by the American Revolution from the effects of this mischievous act, as well as from the consequences of other mistakes and wrongs in British legislation of the last century.

---

the faith of the treaty to which they (the Indians) did not consent, ventured to cross the Ohio. Secretly encouraged by the Agents of Government, supplied with Arms, Ammunition and provisions they maintained an obstinate and destructive War against the States."

[1] The latter embraced some islands in the West Indies.

[2] The passage of this act was one of the grievances that led to the Declaration of Independence. Our fathers feared Roman Catholicism both as false religion and political tyranny. They were also jealous of the Church of England and its daughter in this country. This from Carnegie's "Triumphant Democracy" is of interest: "The fear that England would establish the Episcopal Church in America, if the colonies should be subdued, drew together all other sects and all favorable to religious equality, and therefore opposed to the claims of the English Church. 'This,' says John Adams, 'contributed as much as any other cause to arouse the attention not only of the inquiring mind, but of the common people, and urge them to close thinking on the constitutional authority of Parliament over the colonies.' And the intensity of colonial opposition to the State Church is shown by the special instruc-

In settlement, nothing was done in the upper lake region during the time of British occupancy; in exploration, we note the travels of Captain Jonathan Carver, a native of Canterbury, Connecticut. He started from Boston on his long journey in June, 1766, went by way of Albany and Niagara Falls to Mackinaw, and on the 20th of September of the same year left Green Bay for the Mississippi. He returned to Boston in October, 1768, having traversed nearly seven thousand miles. About ten years afterward his "Travels through the Interior Parts of North America" was published in London with a dedication to the eminent Sir Joseph Banks, dated July 20th, 1778. He gives a favorable account of the countries through which he passed, and tells his readers that even before beginning his journey he was convinced that the French had been trying to keep from all other nations, and especially from the English, accurate knowledge of the interior of the great North American continent. Carver was a good observer, and gives an interesting account of his trip up the Fox and down the Wisconsin. He died in London 31st (or the 29th) of January, 1780.[1]

During the storm of the Revolution the Wisconsin region was to the colonists foreign territory. The few civilized or semi-civilized men here were their enemies. One of them, Charles de Langlade, held a commission as captain in the British army. He had commanded a force of Indians against the British and Americans at Braddock's defeat 1755, July 9th, in the French and Indian war, and was with the Indians — perhaps he could not command them or did not wish to, — when they massacred British and colonial troops at Fort William Henry, on Lake George in one of the early days of August, 1757. He was present, — as were also, according to Parkman, "Sac Indians from the river Wisconsin," — when the massacre at Mackinaw occurred, June 4th, 1763, and did nothing to prevent it. Cannibalism was one of the horrors of that frightful time.

British interests in this region were cared for by Colonel Henry Hamilton, at Detroit, and his subordinate, Major A. S. De Peyster, at Mackinaw. Hamil-

---

tions of the Assembly of Massachusetts to its agent in London, in 1768 'The establishment of a Protestant episcopate in America is very zealously contended for (by a party in the British Parliament); and it is very alarming to a people whose fathers, from the hardships they suffered under such an establishment, were obliged to fly their native country into a wilderness in order to peaceably enjoy their privileges — civil and religious. We hope in God that such an establishment will never take place in America; and we desire you would strenuously oppose it!' In addition, therefore, to the dissatisfaction which the State Church produces at home, it is justly to be charged with being one of the chief causes which led to the loss of the colonies abroad."

[1] He was attended in his last illness by the mendacious Tory clergyman, Samuel Peters, LL. D., whose "Blue Laws of Connecticut" still deceive some ill-informed people. Dr. Peters came to this country to prosecute a claim to the so-called "Carver's grant" an account of which does not belong here. He spent some time in Prairie du Chien, and it is in a letter addressed to him that we have an account of the first school there, — one of the first in Wisconsin. To this school reference will be made later. Dr. Peters says that Carver was "by profession an Anabaptist" (Baptist) in religion, and that he was a great-grandson of John Carver, first governor of Plymouth colony. As is well known, Peters was singularly inaccurate, if not habitually untruthful. Thus while the first of the above statements is very likely true, the second in all reasonable probability is not. For Governor Carver left only one child and that a daughter.

ton was taken prisoner 25th February, 1779, by Colonel George Rogers Clark, at Fort Sackville (Vincennes), Indiana. Hearing of this, Langlade who, with a party of Indians was hastening to his relief, turned back at "Milwakie."[1]

Captain (afterward Lieutenant-Colonel) Patrick Sinclair[2] who succeeded De Peyster in command at Mackinaw when the latter took Hamilton's place at Detroit, rejoices in a letter dated 29th of May, 1780, over an exploit of some of his forces. He thus addresses Sir Frederick Haldimand, governor of Canada from 1778 until 1784:

"Your Excellency was informed by my letter of February last, that a Party was to leave this place on the 10th of March to engage the Indians to the Westward in an attack on the Spanish and Illinois country. Seven Hundred & fifty men including the Traders, servants and Indians, proceeded with them down the Mississippi for that purpose on the 2nd day of May.

"During the time necessary for assembling the Indians at La Prairie du Chien, detachments were made to watch the River to intercept craft coming up with provisions and to seize upon the people working in the lead mines. Both one and the other were effected without an accident.

"Thirty-six Minomies (at first intended as an escort) have brought to this place a large armed boat,[3] loaded at Pencour, in which were twelve men & a Rebel Commissary.

"From the mines they have brought seventeen Spanish & Rebel Prisoners, & stopped Fifty Tonns of Lead ore and from both they obtained a good supply of Provisions.

"Captain Langlade with a chosen Band of Indians and Canadians will join a party assembled at Chicago to make his attack by the Illinois River, and another party are sent to watch the plains between the Wabash and the Mississippi."

The expedition which went to Prairie du Chien was fitted out with the design of capturing St. Louis then of course in possession of Spain. The inhabitants sent Charles Gratiot to ask aid of Colonel George Rogers Clark, then at Fort Jefferson on the Kentucky side of the Mississippi a few miles below the

[1] It may be that he met there no friendly reception. After a council of the Indians that year at old Fort Mackinaw on the 4th of July, Major De Peyster addressed some of his Indian allies in verses very poor in quality but unmistakable in meaning:
    Those renegates of Milwakie,
        Must now perforce with you agree;
    Sly Siggenauk and Naakewoin,
        Must with Langlade their forces join.

[2] In his journal (yet in manuscript), written at Michilimackinac in the summer of 1820, ex-Governor Doty describes Sinclair as "a wild, thoughtless, crazy Irishman."

[3] The boat spoken of belonged to Charles Gratiot, a son of an exiled Huguenot. He had been a Mackinaw trader, but at this date was living at Cahokia, in the Illinois country. Unlike Langlade he aided the American cause. "Gratiot's Grove," well known to the early settlers in the mining region, and the town and post-office of Gratiot in La Fayette county, were named in honor of his son Henry. A daughter of Henry Gratiot became 1845, July 31, the wife of Hon. E. B. Washburne, long a citizen of Galena, Illinois, a city whose early history is closely linked with that of southwestern Wisconsin. For many years Mrs. Washburne was a member of the South Presbyterian church of that city. Her son Hempstead Washburne was lately mayor of Chicago.

month of the Ohio. Clark came promptly and the enemies were driven back.

But, though it is not likely that the American flag was displayed in the Wisconsin region more than once, if at all, during the whole Revolutionary war, the schemes of Hamilton, whose fifteen expeditions against the frontier settlements of Pennsylvania and Virginia were probably scalping parties rather than anything else; of De Peyster, who afterward was addressed by Robert Burns in his "Poem on Life" as "my honored colonel" and of Langlade for whom a sapient legislature of Wisconsin named a county, were more than offset by the successes of Colonel George Rogers Clark.[1] His expedition more than any other military movement determined that this region should become in time states of the American Union and not provinces of Canada. However the acquisition on the part of the United States of the entire country lying between the Great Lakes and the Ohio and the Mississippi was a triumph of diplomacy rather than of arms. Thus the old Northwest Territory became a part of the new nation "conceived in liberty and dedicated to the proposition that all men are created equal."

There was significance in the fact that Haldimand, British governor of Canada, in an address dated Quebec, 2nd of July, 1779, and delivered by proxy to the Indians who were wont to assemble at Mackinaw always speaks of the Americans as "Bostonians." Since the landing of the first Mayflower Puritans had taught the world that nations did not need kings nor churches lord-bishops. The Saxon "folk-moot" had become the New England town. The men of these New Testament churches and self-governed towns had established free schools for all the children of their commonwealths. Out of their love for learning had grown the American college. They had given their fellow-colonists as early as 1643, the first lessons in practical union, and thus laid the foundation of our present system of government. They made the American Revolution a necessity and a success. From them more than from any others came the men who won the victory. Next were the sturdy Presbyterians. Among these were the Irish who won so just a fame in the contest with the British king, and who had an honorable place in what Theodore Roosevelt has happily called "the winning of the West." The Episcopal clergy were nearly all Tories. Even Jacob Duche, whose extemporaneous prayer before Congress has been the subject of so much admiration, remained a loyalist, and tried to persuade Washington to renounce the cause of the new nation then struggling to be free. John Wesley, good man as he was, condemned the colonists for their rebellion. We cannot blame him, for we remember that he was an Englishman.

Of all classes in that trying time none were more generally patriotic than

---

[1] On January 2nd 1778, Patrick Henry, then governor of Virginia, issued instructions to Lieutenant-Colonel George Rogers Clark to raise seven companies, to consist of fifty men each, properly officered, with which to attack the British force in the Illinois country, and thus put a stop to their inciting Indian forays against the frontier settlements of Kentucky, Virginia and Pennsylvania. In that year Clark wrested from the British government Kaskaskia and Cohokia in Illinois; and, early in the ensuing year, Vincennes in Indiana.

Congregational clergy of New England. Many, with the younger men of their congregations, engaged in army service. Among these was one who is entitled to rank among the founders of states.[1] William Bradford of Plymouth colony, John Winthrop of Massachusetts Bay, and Thomas Hooker of Connecticut, had a worthy successor of their own faith in Rev. Manasseh Cutler, pastor for fifty-two years of the Congregational church in Ipswich Hamlet, later Hamilton, Massachusetts. He belongs to Wisconsin though he never set foot upon our soil.

While the convention that framed the constitution of the United States was in session in Philadelphia the continental congress was sitting in New York. Hither came 1787, July 6th, Dr. Cutler, "bearing," says Senator G. F. Hoar, "the fate of the Northwest." He was agent of the Ohio company, the object of which was to found a settlement in what was then called the West. For this purpose land was needed and Dr. Cutler came to buy it. That he should have been chosen for this delicate and responsible duty does not surprise us when we learn the varied abilities of this extraordinary man. After graduating from Yale college in 1765 he went into business. Then he studied law and was admitted to the bar. Preferring the ministry, he entered that calling. In the exercise of it he studied medicine to such good purpose that he became a member of the Massachusetts medical society. While serving as chaplain in the army he had at one time under his care forty-two patients ill with varioloid. He was one of the first party of white men that explored the White mountains. He was the second American writer on botany, and made astronomical calculations which at that time had not been surpassed in this country.[2]

There were many reasons why Congress desired to sell land on the Ohio. The proceeds would aid in lessening the enormous public debt. Such a settlement as that proposed would bind the Western country to the rest of the Union. The possibility of separation was then felt to be a real danger. "The West-

---

[1] Manasseh Cutler is entitled to rank with Bradford, Winthrop, Penn, Calvert and Oglethorpe, as the founder of a state."—*The Nation*, 30th August, 1888.

[2] Since writing the above I have found the following in Carnegie's "Triumphant Democracy:"

"Here are the words of Rev. Manasseh Cutler, D. D., LL. D., of Ipswich, Massachusetts, who was at once minister, scientist, statesman and the agent of the New England and Ohio Company, which started [the settlement] at Marietta, Ohio. Blessed man, he it was who succeeded in getting passed the famous ordinance of 1787, which prohibited slavery in the old Northwest Territory, and secured that fair domain forever to freedom. Here is the prediction he made in a pamphlet published in 1787:

"'The current down the Mississippi and Ohio, for heavy articles that suit the Florida (Mississippi) and West Indian markets, such as Indian corn, flour, beef, timber, etc., will be more loaded than any [other] stream on earth! It was found by late experiments that sails are used to great advantage against the current of the Ohio; and it is worthy of observation that, in all possibility, steamboats will be found to be of infinite service in all our river navigation.'

"That was written twenty years before Fulton's practically successful application of steam to navigation, and a quarter of a century before the first s eamboat that ever plowed the Western rivers was built at Pittsburg."

It appears also that while Dr. Cutler was at Marietta he was one of a party that made experiments with a screw-propellor of such sort as those now used by our lake and ocean steamers. Dr. Cutler anticipated the usefulness of the invention though there was no available power to apply to it. See McMaster's account of the Marietta colony.

ern states," Washington wrote, "stand, as it were, upon a pivot. The touch of a feather would turn them either way." The English had not yet given up the Western posts.[1] Against them as well as against the Indians and the Spaniards the new colony would be a defence. Nearly all the men who purposed to go had served in the Revolutionary army. To such an extent was this the case that when a few years later, 1796, the Congregational church of Marietta, the first in the town, was organized nine out of the twenty-five men who entered into covenant had been officers in military service.

Not only in his own character but as the representative of men like these and as the possible purchaser of a million and a half acres of land was the Ipswich pastor a power. Massachusetts as well as Congress had land to sell and this fact doubtless had weight with the latter body. A measure for the government of the Northwest Territory was then pending. But it was not satisfactory to Dr. Cutler and he would make no purchase until an ordinance was passed which pleased him. With consummate tact he addressed himself to the Southern members especially those from Virginia. Some men of the South gave the proposed measure hearty support. Without their aid it could not have been enacted. It was well known that Washington favored keeping slavery out of the West. On the 13th of July, 1787, was passed that "immortal ordinance" as the late President I. W. Andrews of Marietta calls it. For it, he adds, "we are largely perhaps chiefly indebted to Dr. Cutler." Before it was passed his keen eyes read it and his pen amended it in some of its most important articles. Doubtless he insisted on the anti-slavery clause which Nathan Dane who favored it had given up in despair. Without the reservation of land for the purpose of establishing a university he would not buy. He drew up a scheme for the establishment and government of the university system. His, probably, is the noble declaration: "Religion, morality and knowledge, being necessary to the good government and happiness of mankind, schools and the means of education shall forever be encouraged."

Not to speak of the constitution, three state papers have been produced in America which will command always and everywhere the attention of thoughtful men. These are the Declaration of Independence, the ordinance of 1787 and the Emancipation Proclamation. The first, notwithstanding what Rufus Choate called its "glittering generalities," and the strained character of some of its charges against the king, is worthy of its place in history. The second impressed the Puritanism of the free state, the free church and the free school first upon the Northwest Territory and the states formed from it, and then upon a majority of the newer American commonwealths. "Copied in succeeding acts for the organization of Territories" says Alexander Johnson, "and

---

[1] "The government of the United States not having fulfilled some Articles of the treaty of peace, which established their independence, it was thought proper by the British government to retain the Military Posts of Oswego, Niagara, Detroit and Michilimackinac, which had been injudiciously ceded by Oswald the British Commissioner, a man of little political, and less local knowledge, if Men's talents may be estimated by their Measures." See note on page 28.

still controlling the spirit of such acts, the ordinance of 1787 is the foundation of almost everything which makes the American system peculiar." It abolished primogeniture and entail. It secured equal rights of inheritance. It made possible the Emancipation Proclamation, and, in 1865, what is substantially its sixth article, appears as the thirteenth amendment to the constitution of the United States. In it was in embryo the constitution of Wisconsin, and the anti-slavery clause thereof is a transcript of that found in the ordinance. "God is manifest in history."

Under the sanction of the solemn compact thus entered into by Congress the Ohio company made its settlement. The story does not need to be told here. It is not foreign history; it is a part of our own. The Marietta of Manasseh Cutler, the Congregational minister, and of Rufus Putnam who fought for his country and ours in the Revolution, is much nearer to us than the Green Bay of Allouez, the French Jesuit, and Charles Langlade whose ninety-nine real and mythical battles were always fought against the people whose ensign is now the stars and stripes. This Puritan settlement on the Ohio has the same kind of primacy over the old French settlements in all this region that Plymouth has over St. Augustine or Santa Fe.

Wisconsin, as well as her sister commonwealths, received evangelical religion, popular education, English law and language, with attendant civilization, through settlements begun at Marietta. Speaking in that historic place at the centennial celebration 1888, April 7th, Senator George Frisbie Hoar used these words:

"Here was the first human government under which absolute civil and religious liberty has always prevailed. Here no witch was ever hanged or burned. When older states or nations, where the chains of human bondage have been broken, shall utter the proud boast, 'With a great price I obtained this freedom,' each sister of this imperial group, Ohio, Indiana, Illinois, Michigan and Wisconsin, may lift up her queenly head with the yet prouder answer, 'But I was free-born.'"

We could wish that these statements were entirely accurate. It is true that the witchcraft delusion that has slain its hundreds of thousands of victims in Germany, France and Britain, and its twenty or more even in New England, found none in the region between the Great Lakes and the Mississippi after American government was firmly established here. But this statement, even as thus qualified, must not be understood as applying to the Indians. Among them were many cases, doubtless, of the death penalty for supposed witchcraft. One such is mentioned in a late history of Indiana as having taken place within what are now the limits of that state in one of the early years of this century. In or about 1840 a squaw was put to death in Iowa by the famous chief Keokuk, on the charge of having bewitched one of his children.[1] But this supposed witch, more fortunate than the Indiana victim, was not burned. It mr

---

[1] J. B. Newhall, in "Sketches of Iowa."

be remarked, in passing, that death for witchcraft was one of the potent factors in reducing the number of the Indian population both before and after the advent of white men to this country. Major J. W. Powell makes this statement: "It may safely be said that while famine, pestilence, disease and war may have killed many, superstition killed more."

All this many would be ready to believe who yet would be inclined to doubt that an American officer ever gave an order for the execution of the sentence of a court that had commanded death by burning as the penalty of witchcraft. But we have documentary evidence that such an order was given, and that by the uncle or grand-uncle of Mary Todd, the woman who became the wife of Abraham Lincoln. By appointment (dated at Williamsburg, 1778, December 12th) of Governor Patrick Henry of Virginia, John Todd was made "commandant of the country of Illinois" after its conquest by Colonel George Rogers Clark. The subjoined order was found in Colonel Todd's notebook:

"ILLINOIS, to-wit: To Richard Winston, Esq., Sheriff in chief of the District of Kaskaskia:

"Negro Manuel, a Slave in your custody, is condemned by the Court of Kaskaskia, after having made honorable Fine at the Door of the Church[1] to be chained to a post at the Water Side and there to be burnt alive and his ashes scattered, as appears to me by the Record. This sentence you are hereby required to put in execution on tuesday next at 9 o'clock in the morning, and this shall be your warrant. Given under my hand and seal at Kaskaskia, the 13th day of June, in the third year of the commonwealth."

An unknown pen has drawn black lines in Colonel Todd's note-book across the record as found above. From this circumstance some have hoped that the sentence was never carried out. But in the opinion of Edward G. Mason of Chicago, who has carefully studied this subject, "it is probable that the sentence was actually executed."

"The third year of the Commonwealth" was of course 1779. On June 15th of that year another order was given by Todd in regard to the execution of a sentence of death for alleged witchcraft, this time in the case of "Moreau, a slave condemned to execution," doubtless for the same offense; voudouism, or witchcraft. To this unhappy victim was given the more merciful death

---

[1] "To make honorable Fine at the Door of the Church" is a puzzling expression to most of us. In a personal interview with Archbishop F. X. Katzer of Milwaukee that gentleman expressed the opinion that it meant to do some prescribed form of penance. More definitely Bishop S. J. Messmer of Green Bay wrote me under date of 1894, February 12th: "I have asked different gentlemen about it. They all agree that it is only a bad literal translation of the French 'faire une amende honorable,' which means to make proper amends for an injustice or wrong. As to the custom mentioned in your reference, you will get an idea of it by referring to Webster's Dictionary under the word *amende*. Why Webster should call it an 'infamous' punishment, I can not understand except it be in the same sense as the legal phrase *pœna infamis*, a punishment for a crime which renders the culprit legally infamous; *i. e.*, deprives him of his civil rights."

However, the punishment as described by Webster would seem to be infamous enough. And thus, very possibly, it was that the poor victim at Kaskaskia paid part of the penalty of his imaginary offense little more than a hundred years ago.

of hanging. Is he not the last legally to suffer death for his imagined offense?

These condemnations for witchcraft took place under French law. How far the "Quebec act" was responsible for the revival of the statute, or ordinance, under which these convictions were had I can not say. "The law against sorcery held its place in French legal works till at least the middle of the last century."[1] That, as we have seen, was about the time of the enforced separation between New France and the mother country. There the penalty for witchcraft was death by burning. What was law in the Illinois region was, of course, law in what is now Wisconsin.

Accordingly, if the Kaskaskia court was right, witchcraft scarcely more than a century ago, was a legal offense in all this region and the penalty was death by being burned alive. That in a time of panic, such as almost undoubtedly there was at Kaskaskia in the summer of 1779, and in a distant colony, the old law should have been held to be in force is not surprising. For the American officers there is this measure of excuse, that they sought to interfere as little as possible with existing laws and customs. The Revolutionary war was not at an end.

As the stain of death for witchcraft is upon the history of this western part of the old province of Quebec, so the foul mark of negro slavery blots the early record of the same region after the old Northwest Territory was succeeded by those organized from it. With the western movement of emigration from Virginia and other Southern states came a reaction from the lofty sentiment and good sense which found expression in the great ordinance. "No person shall be held in slavery, if a male, after he is thirty-five years of age; or a female, after twenty-five years of age." There was danger that this clause would be incorporated into the first constitution of Ohio. It had the approval, as was known, of President Jefferson who was sentimentally an enemy of slavery, practically a supporter of it.[2] But at Rufus Putnam's call Ephraim Cutler rose from a bed of illness and, by an earnest appeal, prevented the marring of his father's work. "It cost me every effort I was capable of making," and his own proposition utterly forbidding slavery "passed by a majority of one vote only." And that vote was secured by Mr. Cutler's appeal. He adds: "I prepared and introduced all that part of the constitution" which relates to slavery, religion and schools or education."[3] Thus Puritanism secured to Ohio the freedom it had established there.

Negro slaves were held in Indiana and Illinois. In four years as many as five petitions were sent from (the Territory of) Indiana asking for the suspen-

---

[1] Legislation against witchcraft is certainly as old as, and perhaps older than, the "Twelve Tables" of Roman law. Until 1821 there was a statute in force in Ireland enacting "that if a person bewitched in one country died in another the person guilty of causing his death might be tried in the country where the death happened, so that Ireland appears to be distinguished as the last country in which penalties against witchcraft were retained in statute law."

[2] The handwriting (of the proposed clause) "I had no doubt was Mr. Jefferson's."— EPHRAIM CUTLER.

[3] Outside of New England none of the states, except Pennsylvania, had at that time a system of common schools.

sion or repeal of the anti-slavery clause of the ordinance. What wonder that years later she denied to men, simply because they were black, a right to have a home within her borders, and that, during the struggle for the life of the nation, the most malignant copperheadism stained her honor? And in all these respects her shame was shared by her great neighbor on the west. Only by heroic efforts was slavery prevented from getting legal foothold in these states. Illinois furnished a martyr to the anti-slavery cause in the person of Elijah Parish Lovejoy, a Congregational minister who was killed by a mob at Upper Alton, 7th of November, 1837. Even in Wisconsin several negro slaves were held. Of these two at least were returned to slave soil and to legal bondage.[1]

Forty-one men landed at Plymouth; forty-eight at Marietta. Religious belief was strong in both companies. It was fitting that the faith of the men who landed on Plymouth Rock should be the first preached to white men in Ohio. The first sermon to the settlers at Marietta was by Rev. Daniel Breck on the 20th of July, 1788. The text was significant: "Now, therefore, if ye will obey my voice indeed and keep my covenant, then shall ye be a peculiar treasure unto me above all people: for all the earth is mine. And ye shall be unto me a kingdom of priests and an holy nation. These are the words which thou shalt speak unto the children of Israel."—Exodus XIX. 5, 6. In the congregation was Colonel John May of Boston. The following is from his journal of the date given above:

"At eleven o'clock to-day a religious service. Mr. Daniel Breck began the observance by singing, praying and preaching. The place of worship was our bowery, on the bank directly over my ship. A large number of people were assembled from the garrison [of Fort Harmar], Virginia, and our own settlement, in all about three hundred; some women and children, which was a pleasing, though somewhat unusual sight for us to see. Mr. Breck made out pretty well. The singing was excellent. We had 'Billings' to perfection. Governor St. Clair was much pleased with the whole exercise."

The bowery was an arbor prepared for the Fourth of July celebration. The "ship" was the boat in which Colonel May had come from Pittsburg, and in which he lived until he could build a house. "At that time there was not a Protestant church for white people in the Northwest Territory, and not another clergyman there to preach the gospel in the English language."[2] Only one family had then arrived at Marietta. The women and children of whom Colonel May speaks were from the Virginia side of the river.

The second who preached in the new colony was Dr. Cutler himself. His sermon, delivered on the 20th of August 1788, from Malachi I. 11, was worthy of a man who, to use the words of the Westminster catechism, believed that

---

[1] These were girls from the home of Rev. James Mitchell. When it became unsafe to hold them longer as slaves in Wisconsin they were sent to Missouri. This James Mitchell must not be confounded with John T. Mitchell, his father, nor with Samuel Mitchell, familiarly called "Father" Mitchell, his grandfather. While living in Virginia Samuel Mitchell, on becoming a Christian, set his slaves free. See "Negro Slavery in Wisconsin" by J. N. Davidson, "Proceedings of the Wisconsin State Historical Society for 1892."

[2] From an historical sermon by Rev. C. E. Dickinson, Marietta, Ohio.

"man's chief end is to glorify God and to enjoy him forever." It recognizes the excellencies and speaks frankly of the faults of the older Puritan character. It argues against the union of church and state. In it we have evidence that a man might be a Calvinist of the eighteenth century and yet a broad, liberal-minded man. Dr. Cutler never became a resident of the Northwest Territory though Washington offered him a judge's commission therein. Later he was for two terms a member of Congress from Massachusetts. But he kept his pastorate, an example to those upon whom ministerial vows seem to rest with little weight.

Settlements rapidly extended in the Northwest Territory. Twenty thousand came in 1788. By the purchase of Louisiana in 1803 it ceased to be on the west the political frontier of the United States. The army of emigration which swept westward from the Atlantic states was reinforced by those whom the sinister influences of slavery drove from the South. But years elapsed before it took possession of what is now Wisconsin, which thus remained unorganized and without distinctive name or defined area until 1836. In 1800 it was made part of Indiana Territory, in 1809 part of Illinois and in 1818 part of Michigan. When, by act of Congress approved 1836, April 20th, the Territory of Wisconsin was organized, it included not only the present state of that name but also what is now Iowa and Minnesota as well as all that part of South Dakota lying east of the Missouri, and of North Dakota lying east of the Missouri and the White Earth. All this had previously belonged to Michigan. This act made Wisconsin an organized Territory, 1836, July 4th. By act of 12th June, 1838 the Territory of Iowa was organized, taking all of Wisconsin west of the Mississippi. The act of 1846, August 6th, enabling the people of Wisconsin to form a state government separated from the prospective state all that part of what is now Minnesota lying east of the boundary formed by the Mississippi to its source (Lake Itasca) and thence by a line drawn due north to the "northwest corner of the Lake of the Woods," that is to the British possessions. Thus to Wisconsin were given her present limits.

The Americans were slower in taking actual possession of this region between Lake Michigan and the Mississippi than in acquiring title to it. The French hated and dreaded the Yankees. "Great danger both to individuals and to the government is to be apprehended from the Canadian traders." Thus in 1811 wrote Nicholas Boilvin, Indian agent at Prairie du Chien, — the only one in the Wisconsin region, — to the war department.

During the second war with Britain the military posts in Michigan and what was then northern Illinois[1] fell again into the hands of the British. That

---

[1] When, 1809, February 3, the Territory of Illinois was created by act of Congress, her eastern boundary extended to Lake Superior; her western "to the most northwestern point" of the Lake of the Woods. That is northward from the confluence of the Ohio and the Mississippi, her western boundary was that of the United States until the Louisiana purchase. "The most northwestern point," — we use the words of the treaty of 1783, — was then undetermined. It is now known to be in longitude 95 8 56.7 west of Greenwich, and latitude 49 23 50.28 north. Thus even the little point of land projecting into the Lake of the Woods from the west, and now forming part of Minnesota though separated from it, was once a part

at Mackinaw was surrendered without resistance, 1812, July 17th, to a superior force of the enemy. This event turned back Brigadier-General William Hull from his proposed invasion of Canada, perhaps decided the fate of Detroit (surrendered 1812, August 6th) and made the British masters of the region between Lake Michigan and the Mississippi. All that Boilvin, unsupported by military force, could do was more than offset by the influence among the Indians of Robert Dickson, a British trader, whose home had been at Prairie du Chien since about 1790 or 1795.[1]

About the first of May (or perhaps a little later), 1814, William Clark,[2] governor of Missouri Territory and commander of the United States troops of the upper Mississippi, started from St. Louis for Prairie du Chien. There he held a council with the Indians, and left a force under command of Lieutenant Joseph Perkins, of the twenty-fourth United States infantry, to build and garrison a fort. After Governor Clark's return we hear of the expedition in a letter dated at St. Louis, 1814, July 2nd: "On Sunday last [June 26th], an armed boat arrived from Prairie du Chien under command of Captain John Sullivan, with his company of militia and thirty-two men from the gunboat 'Governor Clark,' their terms of service (sixty days) having expired. Captain Zeizer [or Yeizer], who commands on board the 'Governor Clark' off Prairie du Chien, reports that his vessel is completely manned, that the fort is finished, christened 'Fort Shelby' and occupied by his regulars, and that all are anxious for a visit from Dickson and his red troops."

Probably Dickson did not come for he was at Mackinaw when, 1814, August 4th, the Americans made an unsuccessful attack on that stronghold. But an enemy came who put to silence all boastful words. Part of the story is told in an official record from Lieutenant-Colonel Robert McDouall to Lieutenant-General Sir George Gordon Drummond dated at "Michilimackinac," 16th July, 1814:

"I beg leave to acquaint you that on the 21st ulto. I received information

---

of Illinois. But on her admission into the Union all of the former Territory lying north of latitude 42 30,—that is the whole of Wisconsin, except most of the peninsula between Green Bay and the lake, more than half of the Upper Peninsula of Michigan and almost a third of Minnesota,—was added to Michigan "for temporary purposes only."

[1] Perhaps even longer. The following is from the reminiscences of "Colonel" John Shaw, a well known pioneer:
"Colonel Robert Dickson obtained an unbounded influence over the Indians of the Northwest. He established a law that no Indians should engage in war with each other within twenty-five leagues of Prairie du Chien; that wide belt of country should be strictly neutral ground. I think he must have made Prairie du Chien his summer home for some thirty years prior to the final pacification in 1815."
Dickson was faithful in his allegiance to "the best of Kings and Our Glorious Constitution." I use his own words. Shaw continues: "When peace was proclaimed, he spoke to a large assembly of his red children, and informed them that the treaty rendered it necessary for him to retire to the Red River of the North and Hudson's Bay; that it caused the deepest gloom in his mind to be compelled to leave his much loved children, and that he could never recover from this sorrow. The Indians by their tears and grief for many days evinced their strong attachment for their father and friend."

[2] A brother of George Rogers Clark, and the associate of Captain Meriwether Lewis in the famous expedition known by their names; the first sent by the United States government across the Rocky Mountains.

of the capture of Prairie des Chiens on the Mississippi by the American Genl. Clarke who had advanced from St. Louis with six or eight very large Boats with about three hundred men for the purpose of establishing himself at that post by building a Fort the situation being very eligible for that purpose. * *

"I saw at once the imperious necessity which existed of endeavoring by every means to dislodge the American Genl from his new conquest, & make him relinquish the immense tract of country he had seized upon in consequence & which brought him into the very heart of that occupied by our friendly Indians. There was no alternative it must either be done or there would be an end to our connexion with the Indians for, if allowed to settle themselves, by dint of threats, bribes, & sowing divisions among them, tribe after tribe would be gained over or subdued & thus would be destroyed the only barrier which protects the great trading establishment of the Northwest and the Hudson's Bay Companys. Nothing could then prevent the enemy from gaining the source of the Mississippi, gradually extending themselves by the Red River to Lake Winnipic, from whence the descent of Nelson's River to York Fort would in time be easy. The subjugation of the Indians on the Mississippi would either lead to their extermination by the enemy or they would be spared on the express condition of assisting them to expel us from upper Canada. Viewing the subject in this light I determined to part with the Sioux and Winnebago Indians to give them every encouragement and assistance, & even to weaken ourselves here, rather than the enterprise should not succeed. I appointed Mr. Rolette and Mr. Anderson, & Mr. Grignion of Green Bay to be captains of volunteers, the two former raised 63 men in two days, whom I completed, armed and cloathed, the latter takes with him all the settlers of Green Bay. I held several councils with the Indians on this important business. * * *

"Everything being prepared, Lt. Col. McKay sailed under a salute from the garrison on the 28th ultimo, taking 75 of the Michigan Fencibles and Canadian Volunteers & about 136 Indians. He arrived at Green Bay about six days after, at which place such was the great zeal displayed, that his force was immediately doubled, but as every arrangement had been made previous to his departure for the junction of the Winnebago & Follsovine [Folles Avoine [1] or Menomonee] Indians at the portage of the Ouisconsing River, I have scarcely a doubt but that his force at that place will be at least 1500 men, besides being afterward joined by the Sioux from River St. Peters & other tribes.

"If *successful and the thing is practicable*, I have directed him to descend the Mississippi and also to attack the Piorias [2] Fort on the Illinois River."

The "arrangement for the junction of Indians at the portage of the Ouisconsing" was doubtless made with Dickson who had spent the preceding winter in service at Lake Winnebago. [3]

---

[1] Wild oats; a name given by the French to the wild rice, —*zizania aquatica*,—of our marshes. The Indians made much use of this as food.

[2] Fort Clark, at Peoria, built by American troops under General Benjamin Howard, in the autumn of 1813.

[3] Thence, under date of 4th February, 1814, he had written as follows to John Lawe of

When McKay and his men landed at Green Bay on the 4th or 5th of July, they found no American force to oppose them. The United States government had never really taken possession of the place. Here, to use a statement more precise than that of Colonel McDouall, the British received an accession of "thirty militia almost all old men unfit for service," and about one hundred Indians. We do not hear of any increase in number at the "portage of the Ouisconsing." Twenty-one miles from Prairie du Chien the party halted at the old deserted village of the Outagamies. From this place scouts were sent out who found that the Americans were totally unaware of the coming of their enemies. The next day, says one of the scouts (Augustus Grignon), "We reached the town about ten o'clock unperceived. As this was Sunday [July 17th], and a very pleasant day, the officers of the garrison were getting ready to take a pleasure ride into the country, and had McKay been an hour or two later the garrison would have been caught without an officer."

McKay's force of Indians, — four or five hundred Sioux, Winnebagoes, Menomonees, and Ojibways, — was "perfectly useless," he tells us, and he had only one hundred fifty whites of whom twenty were regulars and officers. However he was successful in his attack on Fort Shelby, though Perkins made a vigorous defence. Part of the American force of one hundred fifty was on the "Governor Clark, Gunboat No. 1." "She goes remarkably fast," wrote McKay descriptively not sarcastically, "particularly down the current, being rowed by 32 oars."[1] Driven by the fire of the enemy she was obliged to leave the fort to its fate. It was surrendered on the evening of July 19th, and received the name of its captor. This was the only actual warfare between whites on Wisconsin soil in the war of 1812. No lives were lost at the taking of Fort Shelby.

It required McKay's utmost exertions to save his prisoners from massacre by the Indians, most of whom, as in the Revolution, were hostile to the "Big Knives," as they called the Americans. And the whites of Prairie du Chien, like those of Green Bay, preferred British rule.

To McDouall's more ambitious scheme McKay thus refers: "As to going down the Mississippi and returning" (to Mackinaw) "by way of Chicago, [it] is now rendered impracticable for the present, — no dependence whatever to be placed in the Indians except the Sioux."

Green Bay, then lieutenant in the British service:

"Fort Madison was evacuated & burnt late in the season. * St. Louis might be taken this spring with 5 or 600 men. * From all appearances, even from the Democratic papers, the Americans tremble for the consequences of the war in Europe. They already figure the Russians and Cossacks at their doors. The Emperor of Austria has joined the Russians and Prussians & Swedes & their Combined forces amount to 540,000 men. * Lord Wellington had taken the two important Fortresses of Pampeluna & St. Sebastian, and was advancing into France. I think that Bony must be knocked up as all Europe are now in arms.

"The crisis is not far off when I trust in God that the Tyrant will be humbled, & the Scoundrel American Democrats be obliged to go on their knees to Britain."

[1] But four steamboats had at that time been built on the rivers of the Mississippi valley. Of these the first built, called the New Orleans, had sunk a few days before (July 15th). The other three were the Comet, a diminutive vessel of twenty-five tons' burden, the Vesuvius and the Enterprise.

Though somewhat damaged, the Governor Clark, with Agent Boilvin on board, made her way to Rock Island pursued "till within a league of the rapids" by a force of British. These turned back on meeting another American gunboat which, it is probable, was part of an expedition dispatched under command of Lieutenant John Campbell from St. Louis for the reinforcement of Fort Shelby. Here Campbell at the hands of Indians under command of the famous Black Hawk[1] suffered a defeat deserved apparently by his own carelessness and disobedience (22 July, 1814). Twelve of his men were killed; between twenty and thirty wounded. Soon a British force went down the Mississippi as far as Rock Island and there on the Illinois side erected a battery. Major Zachary Taylor, afterwards President of the United States, started from St. Louis, August 12th, with four hundred fifty men to take this, but, for want of artillery, was repulsed, 1814, September 6th. Again Black Hawk commanded the Indians, thus defeating the future President.

Though the Americans were unsuccessful in their attempt, already mentioned, to recover Mackinaw they put the British in the Upper Lake region to serious inconvenience, and delayed the furnishing of supplies to Fort McKay. Nor was there an abundance when they came. "Here we are," wrote one of the garrison, 14th March, 1815, "posted since last fall without news from any quarter, and destitute of provisions, sociability, harmony or good understanding. Not even a glass of grog nor a pipe of tobacco, to pass away the time, and if a brief period don't bring a change for the better, I much dread the United Irishmen's wish will befall the place,—a bad Winter, a worse Spring, a bloody Summer and no king. Owing to a scarcity of Provisions here a gloom appears on every countenance; and if ever I take an idea to resign, I mean to recommend Mr. Hurtibis to supply my place as I think him the properest person in the time of famine as he has no teeth.

"I must conclude this long and useless letter after having endeavored in vain to give you an idea of the wretchedness of this country—a task for which nature has not qualified me. To give it in its true light would require the pen of an able historian."

The war was then over. Though the British commissioners at Ghent sought to acquire the region on the American side of the upper Great Lakes, or more strictly speaking to have made it into a neutral Indian country under the protection of their government, the treaty of Ghent to the rage and almost the despair of nearly all the whites living there, confirmed it to the United States.

The official announcement of peace did not reach Captain Andrew A. Bulger, then in command at Prairie du Chien until the 22nd of May, 1815. The next day he wrote to Governor Clark of St. Louis, "I propose evacuating this post to-morrow." He did not wish to have British and American troops at Prairie du Chien at the same time. It may be that his departure was earlier by one day than he had proposed to make it. For Lieutenant-Colonel McDou-

---

[1] McDouall states that Black Hawk was in command of the Indians. See "Michigan Historical Collections," volume XIV, page 285.

all states that Bulger evacuated Prairie du Chien May 23rd and arrived at Mackinaw on the 17th of June. Doubtless he went by way of Green Bay. The unknown date of his departure thence marks the end of British dominion in what is now Wisconsin.[1]

It cost McDouall a bitter struggle to give up Mackinaw. His Indian allies shared his feeling. "We hate those Big Knives!" said a Winnebago chief at a council held at Mackinaw 1815, June 3rd. "Our Great Father beyond the Great Lake is a tender parent; but when he agreed to give up this place to the Big Knives, he did not reflect that he was putting us in the power of our great enemy." McDouall had reflected upon it. His reiterated argument is that the region between Lake Michigan and the Mississippi had never really been in the possession of the Americans, but belonged to Indian tribes that were allies of the British.

His protests were in vain. Not only had the British flag for the last time floated in mastery on the banks of the upper Mississippi and at Green Bay; it was now to be taken from the heights of Mackinaw. Accordingly at noon, 1815, July 19th, the British evacuated the Malta of our fresh-water Mediterranean. McDouall withdrew to Drummond's Island. As he went royal authority on the southern and western shores of the upper Great Lakes passed away.

---

[1] Thus British influence was in ascendency at Green Bay during almost all the reign of George III. and he was the only English king who held sway on what is now the American side of the upper Great Lakes. It is a curious fact that (the future) Wisconsin was under royal government during three of the longest reigns known to history, those of Louis XIV. and Louis XV. of France, and that of George III. of Great Britain.

CHAPTER VI.

THE IONA OF OUR INLAND SEAS.

The eastern part of the Upper Peninsula of what is now Michigan was known to early French explorers at Michilimackinac. It gave name (now usually shortened to Mackinac or, spelled phonetically, Mackinaw) to the neighboring strait through which the waters of Lake Michigan pass on their way to the sea. On the north side of this strait, Marquette and the fugitive Hurons found refuge in 1671, when they fled from Chequamegon bay to escape the fury of the Dakotas. The mission of St. Ignatius, thus established, was strengthened by a French military post. But after Cardillac founded Detroit in 1701, he withdrew the garrison from the older settlement, despite the entreaties of the Jesuits, and prevailed upon many of the Indians to leave.[1] To prevent the desecration of their church by pagan Indians, the priests set fire to it with their own hands and abandoned the mission. When, in 1712, De Louvigny came by command of Governor-General De Vaudreuil to re-establish a fort in the Michilimackinac region, he placed it on the south side of the strait. This is what is often called "Old Fort Mackinaw." During the French and Indian war the English flag was raised over Detroit 1760, November 29th, by Major Robert Rogers, a native of New Hampshire. Fort Mackinaw was occupied 1761, September 28th, by British troops under command of Captain Henry Balfour[2] who, with the greater part of his force, sailed on the 1st of the following October to take possession of Green Bay. A part of the war that followed Pontiac's conspiracy was the massacre of the the British garrison at Old Fort Mackinaw.[3] This event the story of which does not need to be told here.

---

[1] There was no love lost between Cardillac and the Jesuits. He thus wrote of them to the home government:
"You wish me to be a friend of the Jesuits and to have no trouble with them. After much reflection I have found only three ways in which this can be accomplished; the first is, to let them do as they please; the second, to do whatever they desire; and the third, to say nothing of what they do." The letter was dated at "Fort Ponchartrain, August 31, 1703." Said fort occupied a site in what is now the business portion of D troit.
According to E. M. Sheldon's "Early History of Michigan," Cardillac was a "zealous [Roman] Catholic." He favored the Franciscans. These, in a sense, are the Methodists of Roman Catholicism, as the Jesuits are its "high church" Episcopalians.

[2] Following the Wisconsin "Blue Book" and "Historical Collections" this name is spelled "Belfour" on page 26. But the British "Army List" gives it as "Balfour."

[3] Pontiac's conspiracy was so far successful that by August 13th of that year (1763), with

took place on the 4th of June, 1763. Remembering, it may be, this occurence, Major De Peyster, who commanded there during the Revolutionary war, made preparations, as a measure of safety from the Americans, to remove the British garrison to Michilimackinac island. On the 4th of November, 1780, his successor, Captain (and Lieutenant-Governor) Sinclair made the formal removal. Thus the beautiful island, now the delight of summer tourists, the supposed birthplace of the legendary Hiawatha, became the center of trade and political influence for all the region of the upper Great Lakes.

It was destined also to be the center of religious, educational and missionary influence. Thither the Roman Catholic congregation hauled over the ice from Old Mackinaw, in 1780, the timbers of their house of worship and there re-erected it. But for half a century they enjoyed the services of only non-resident priests.

In 1800 a young man, David Bacon, was sent West by the Missionary society of Connecticut. "Afoot and alone he was to make his way towards the wilderness, with no baggage more than he could carry on his person, thankfully accepting any offer of a seat for a few miles in some passing vehicle. Such was the equipment with which the good people of Connecticut, seventy-four years ago, sent forth their first missionary to the heathen."[1]

His first tour was one of exploration. He arrived at Detroit on the 11th of September, 1800. Thence he went northward as far as Harson's Island, River St. Clair. Having returned to New England he was married and ordained. Again he came to Michigan and settled at Detroit. Here was born 19th February, 1802, his son Leonard, afterwards the famous New Haven pastor and member of the Yale corporation. In June, 1802, Mr. Bacon removed to Mackinaw and thus became the first Protestant missionary in the region of the upper Great Lakes. Great were the obstacles to his work, among the whites as well as the Indians, both there and Detroit. Those whom he speaks of as "bigoted, persecuting papists" of course opposed his work. British influence, still strong in these regions, was against him because he was a Yankee, by which was meant an American. The fur traders did not wish to have the Indians become civilized. It would seem that Mr. Bacon's best and almost only friends were the officers of the United States army.

This first Protestant mission at Mackinaw ended with the removal of the missionary about the 1st of August, 1804. A canoe voyage from Detroit to Cleveland took him with wife and two infants to what was then known as "New Connecticut" (Western Reserve). Mr. Bacon was one of those who impressed Puritanism upon Northern Ohio, the land of Giddings and Garfield, of Oberlin college and Western Reserve university.

Before the clash of arms in 1812, there was in the fur trade a commercial war of which Mackinaw was in a sense the center and in which John Jacob

---

the exception of the garrison at Detroit, there was not a British soldier in the region of the upper Great Lakes.

[1] Congregational Quarterly, January, 1876.

Astor, his partner, Wilson Price Hunt, and others, represented the American cause. A sturdy Scotchman, Ramsey Crooks, was among Astor's trusted lieutenants. Starting from Mackinaw about the 12th of August, 1809, Hunt and Crooks made their way by the Fox-Wisconsin route,[1] the Mississippi and the Missouri to the Rocky mountains and thence to the Pacific. They are sure of abiding renown for Irving has written of them in his "Astoria."

The importance of Mackinaw both in the Revolution and in the second war with Britain has been shown. With the return of peace came better subjects for the historian than strife and bloodshed. Again Mackinaw became the center of an extensive fur trade. By favoring legislation the American Fur company, in which Astor had a controlling interest, was able to command a great part of the commerce of the Northwest. At no time, perhaps, was it more prosperous than in 1820.

In this year, June 16th, Jedidiah Morse, D. D., father of S. F. B. Morse, the inventor of the telegraph, landed at Mackinaw.[2] He was accompanied by his son Richard Cary Morse, long one of the proprietors of the "New York Observer," who wrote thus of their stay:

"There had not been a Protestant sermon preached in the place for ten years or more. During our fortnight's stay the gospel was preached by us in the court house to full and attentive audiences. At his [Dr. Morse's] suggestion and by his personal aid a Sabbath school and a day school were formed for the children; a Bible and Tract society." From Mackinaw, as already stated, our travelers went to Green Bay.

A letter written by Dr. Morse soon after his return to New Haven shows his interest in supplying the people at Mackinaw with a pastor. He had come west not only under commission from the United States government,—of which service we shall soon hear,—but also as agent of the Northern Missionary society of New York.[3] This organization was soon absorbed by another,

---

[1] They had much difficulty in securing a crew. Irving thus describes the only kind of men to be had: "Like sailors, the Canadian voyagers generally preface a long cruise with a carouse. They have their cronies, their brothers, their cousins, their wives, their sweethearts, all to be entertained at their expense. They feast, they fiddle, they drink, they sing, they dance, they frolic and fight, until they are mad so many drunken Indians. * * * It was with the utmost difficulty they could be extricated from the clutches of the publicans [liquor sellers], and the embraces of their pot companions, who followed them to the water's edge with many a hug, a kiss on each cheek and a maudlin benediction in Canadian French."

[2] Dr. Morse, born 1761, August 23rd, died 1826, June 9th, was one of the corporate members of the American Board, and was once a member of the Board of Overseers of Harvard college. When, 1805, February 5th, the corporation elected Henry Ware, Jr., a Unitarian, to the Hollis professorship of divinity, Dr. Morse, as one of the overseers, strongly opposed the confirmation of their action which he regarded as a breach of trust. For one of the conditions of the gift establishing the professorship was that the incumbent should be, in religion, of orthodox belief. Following the election of Ware, Dr. Morse resigned his office as overseer.

[3] "Organized in 1797. Albany, New York, seems to have been its headquarters. It was 'absorbed,' in your fitting term, about 1821. Its missions, if I am not mistaken, were chiefly among Indians in the state of New York. Dr. Chester, a noble man of great influence, was the pastor of one of the principal churches in that city, and was connected with the Northern Missionary society perhaps as chairman or president. His grandson is in Milwaukee,— Rev. William Chester, pastor of Immanuel Presbyterian church."— Rev. John C. Lowrie, of the Presbyterian Board of Foreign Missions, 1893, March 31st.

and this United Foreign Missionary society, as it was called, representing the Presbyterian, the (then Dutch) Reformed and the Associate Reformed churches, re-established the mission at Mackinaw which, for various reasons, finds place in our Wisconsin history. Here were the headquarters of our missionary work for this part of the world. As we have seen the story of Wisconsin can not be told without reference to that of Mackinaw. And at one time, February, 1828, the committee on Territories in the House of Representatives was committed to the project of making the Upper Peninsula (now) of Michigan with the adjacent islands, Mackinaw among them, a part of the proposed Territory of "Wiskonsin," a name then recently substituted in congressional proceedings for "Chippewau."

In 1822 Rev. William Montague Ferry visited Mackinaw and organized a church there.[1] The following statement of special need for Christian work is from the missionary report of a later year:

"It had long been a common, though not a universal practice, among the many traders, clerks and other whites in this whole region to live with Indian women, either as wives or concubines, and to desert them and their children on returning to civilized life. This practice was introduced while the French held possession of Canada, and the greater part of the half-breeds were still of French descent. They and many of the Indians were nominally Roman Catholics, but were almost entirely ignorant of Christianity."

Mr. Ferry returned next year with his wife, arriving 19th October, 1823. The mission and boarding school which formed part of his plan was opened Monday, 3rd of the following November, with twelve Indian children. The school increased and at one time had an attendance of one hundred eighty. The children from the village attended as day pupils, and those from the several tribes as boarders. These were collected from the whole region extending from the white settlements south of the Great Lakes to Red River and Lake Athabasca. The children were trained in habits of industry, taught trades and how to cultivate the soil, besides receiving a common-school education. Most of the Ojibway traders sent their half-breed children to this school. "Great good was desseminated from it, which spread over the whole Northwest territory. Many of our most promising half-breeds, now engaged as missionaries or in mercantile pursuits, received their education at the Mackinaw mission. After its dissolution such of the traders as were financially able sent their children to receive an education in some of the Eastern states."[2]

The school was first held in the old court house. In 1825, the building now known as the "Mission House," was erected for missionary and school purposes.[3]

---

[1] Previous to the location of this mission, Mr. Ferry spent a year in Mackinaw, in which time he organized a church; persuaded the inhabitants, generally, to abandon secular employments on the Sabbath, and attend public worship."—Missionary Gazetteer by Rev. Walter Chapin, of Woodstock, Vermont.

[2] "History of the Ojibways," by William Whipple Warren.

[3] During the late war this old mission house was used for a time as the home of certain

THE IONA OF OUR INLAND SEAS.

In this same year the United Foreign Missionary society,[1] which, as already stated, had previously absorbed the Northern Missionary society, gave up its own distinctive name and work by union with the American Board. This action was ratified the following year and, in in the proceedings of the Board for 1827, we find—quoted from above—its first report, of the Mackinaw mission. In August of that year, there were one hundred twelve pupils in the boarding school, and there had been several interesting cases of conversion.[2] French priests occasionally visited this region and opposed this mission to the extent of their power.

Thus the mission grappled at once with heathenism and a corrupted form of Christianity. It has a history written in the lives of men and women who have left their imprint upon all this region. It made Mackinaw a St. Columba's island of the West.

Among those who became earnest Christians in a revival there, as early as 1826, was Lyman Marcus Warren, a trader in the employ of the American Fur company. He at once desired that a mission be established at his trading post, La Pointe, on the largest of the many islands in Chequamegon Bay, not far from the scene of the labors of Allouez and Marquette more than one hundred fifty years before. Then, among others, Hurons dwelt there, but Mr. Warren's Indian neighbors were Ojibways. His earnest entreaty reached some students at Hamilton college, and in response to it came, in 1827, Rev. Jedidiah Dwight Stevens who fills so large a place in the early history of our Wisconsin churches. He and his wife arrived July 21st. He came with the purpose of establishing a mission among the Ojibways. But Mr. Ferry thought that this project was premature. Accordingly Mr. Stevens remained at Mackinaw to strengthen the mission there and, to use his own words, "was at once installed principal of the male department of the school. There was gathered a motley mass of boys from five to twenty years of age, of various colors, tongues and bloods, pure and mixed, French and English, Irish, Scotch, American and Indian; nearly all born of heathen mothers. These boys were to be educated and

---

state prisoners from Tennessee.

[1] Formed in New York City in 1817 by a joint committee of the General Assembly of the Presbyterian church, the General Synod of the Reformed Dutch church, and the General Synod of the Associate Reformed church.

[2] Yet the school failed to accomplish the object for which it was founded. "In 1826-7," says the late A. G. Ellis, then a missionary teacher at Green Bay, "I was requested [by the Episcopal church committee] to acquire all the information possible of the best manner of organizing and conducting a large boarding school for Indian children." He visited Mackinaw, "Mr. Ferry received me courteously. I acquainted him with the object of my inquiries; that they were made in behalf of the committee of the Episcopal church, who designed establishing such a school at Green Bay. He candidly advised against it and gave his reasons; informing me that this school, which had been put in operation at great expense, had failed of the object sought, and that he had already received instructions to reduce it in numbers as fast as could be done, and eventually discontinue it entirely; that with all their endeavors they had been able to secure the entrance into it of comparatively very few Indian children; that the great proportion of their nearly two hundred attendants were children of Indian traders, who were reaping all the benefits of education from which the Indian children were being almost wholly excluded." Accordingly, Mr. Ellis reported against attempting to establish a like school at Green Bay.

But was it not as good a thing to educate a half-breed as an Indian?

molded into a Christian civilization and religion, and made to be educators of the tribes now perishing in heathenism."

As we soon leave Mackinaw to follow Mr. Stevens on more adventurous service, we may give an epitome of the remaining history of the mission there. The building known as the "mission church" was erected in 1830. It was dedicated 1831, March 4th. As it was thought that the Indian children could be more advantageously educated near their homes, the school which according to the "Missionary Herald" for June, 1829, had numbered one hundred sixty or one hundred seventy, including thirty or forty from the village of Mackinaw, was, as we have learned, purposely made smaller. Mr. Ferry's health failed and 6th August, 1834, he was released from missionary service.[1] During his stay at Mackinaw there was born to him a son, Thomas White Ferry, who, on the death of the late Hon. Henry Wilson became acting Vice-President of the United States. In 1836 the mission was discontinued. Mackinaw had ceased to be a place of rendezvous for the Indians and of trade for the whites. The island was almost deserted until it became a place of resort for summer visitors. The old church gave to other communities,— Green Bay and La Pointe among them,— its membership and its very life. The work of the mission passed to other stations in some of which it is still continued.

As a picture of what it accomplished, the following from "Wau-bun, the 'Early Day,' in the North-West," is suggestive, though colored no doubt by the warmth of friendship and brightened by the gladness of a young wife's journey to a new home in a land which she had always regarded as a region of romance. At Fort Winnebago, whither at this time, September, 1830, she and her husband were going, we shall again meet the writer, Mrs. John H. Kinzie, well known in the early history of Chicago:

"We were received with the most affectionate cordiality by Mr. and Mrs. Stuart, at whose hospitable mansion we had been for some days expected. After a season of pleasant conversation, the servants were assembled, the chapter of God's word was solemnly read, the hymn chanted, the prayer of praise and thanksgiving offered, and we were conducted to our place of repose.

"It is not my purpose here to attempt a portrait of those noble friends whom I thus met for the first time. To an abler pen than mine should be assigned the honor of writing the biography of Robert Stuart. All who have enjoyed the happiness of his acquaintance, or still more, a sojourn under his hospitable roof, will carry with them, to their latest hour, the impress of his noble bearing, his genial humor, his untiring benevolence, his upright, uncompromising adherence to principle, his ardent philanthropy, his noble disinterest-

---

[1] Mr. Ferry was one of five ministers who, in 1827, established the presbytery of Detroit. From Mackinaw he removed to what is now Grand Haven, Michigan. His was the first white family that settled there. They landed Sabbath, 2nd November, 1834. Directly the father called them into a log house,— he had been at the place previously himself,— and preached from the text: "For who hath despised the day of small things?" He died 1867, December 30th, honored and beloved. By will, he left to various objects of Christian benevolence one hundred forty-seven thousand dollars. Ferry Hall, Lake Forest university, Illinois, bears his name.

edness. Irving in his 'Astoria,' and Franchere in his 'Narrative,' give many striking traits of his early character, together with events of his history of thrilling and romantic interest, but both have left the most valuable portion unsaid, namely, his after-life as a Christian gentleman.

"Michilimackinac! that gem of the lakes! How bright and beautiful it looked as we walked abroad on the following morning! The object of our early walk was to visit the mission house and school. This was an object of especial interest to Mr. and Mrs. Stuart. They had lived many years on the island, and had witnessed its transformation, through God's blessing on Christian efforts, from a worldly, dissipated community to one of which it might almost be said, 'Religion was every man's business.'"

The commercial ruin of Mackinaw was brought about by the use of larger vessels in the Indian trade, especially that on Lake Superior. This, in the way of navigation, was cut off from the other lakes by the falls in the St. Mary's river. As the first canal around the "Sault" was not completed until 1855, May 19th, vessels needed on Lake Superior in the early years had to be built or put together there. That done, La Pointe became, in a sense, the successor to Mackinaw.

CHAPTER VII.

DR. MORSE AND HIS ERRAND IN THE WEST.

Within little more than five years of the time when the British flag was floating at Green Bay, Dr. Jedidiah Morse held public religious service in Fort Howard. He was the first Congregational minister, and, so far as is known, the first Protestant minister, who ever preached in the part of Michigan Territory that is now Wisconsin. He came as did Jean Nicolet, the first explorer of this region, by the broad way of the Great Lakes. Leaving Mackinaw on the 3rd of July, 1820, he attended, at L'Arbre Croche, a council held with the Ottawa Indians, and arrived at Fort Howard July 7th. Having come under a commission issued by the Secretary of War, he was made the guest of Colonel Joseph Lee Smith,[1] commandant at the post. Dr. Morse's mission was one of investigation into the condition and needs of the Indians of the West and South. He made it part of his duty to aid a movement which, after vexatious delays, provided a home for those who are known in the history of our state as the "New York Indians." These aborigines were the first emigrants from any of the older states who came with the purpose of making here their permanent homes. With Dr. Morse and his service, which was especially in behalf of the little tribe of Indians commonly called Stockbridges, begins properly not only the history of Congregationalism in Wisconsin but almost of Christian civilization therein. He was the herald of a great company of the universal church.

As Dr. Morse did not leave Green Bay until the 23rd of July, it is probable that he or his son held service in the fort on both the Sabbaths of their stay, the 9th and the 16th.

A letter written at "Mackinaw, July 25th. 1820," and addressed to "Mr. John Law,[2] Green Bay," shows on what errands Dr. Morse went thither, and implies certain sadly defective social condiitons that then prevailed there:

"I was sorry to leave Green Bay without having another interview with you & your friends on subjects on which we had conversed relating to the Indians, & to the establishment of a school for the children of your village. This was the principal business left unfinished. A few hours employed together

---

[1] Colonel Smith was a native of New Britain, Connecticut, and the father of Brigadier-General Edmond Kirby Smith of the Confederate army.

[2] Mr. John Lawe. The letter itself I copy by permission of Herbert Battles Tanner, M. D.

would have completed it. I have left it with Dr. Comstock to complete it with you, & to forward to me the result at this place before I shall quit it—whh will be in the course of 10 days or probably a fortnight.—Having been expected by this opp'y to write you, I improve it to drop you a line in order to aid the accomplishment of this business, that I may have the result by the return of this vessel—whh will furnish you a good opp'y for you to write me.—I wish particularly to know definitely what funds can be raised & calculated on for the support of a School for the children of mixed blood in your village.—Or if you prefer it, a *subscription* School, to embrace the children of white parents in the village, and of the Officers of the Garrison.—Dr. Comstock suggested this last idea. I had supposed your intention was to have a school for children of mixed blood only & that your subscription was intended to let me know what support you were willing to give to such a school. If this was your idea, as I suppose, you have only to head a subscription to suit yourselves, & to put your names, & annex the sum you are willing to give yearly for one or more years—with liberty to send as many children as you please—or so much for every child you may send—adding what you will do as to furnishing a School room, house & provisions for the Instructor in addition. I shall then know what will be necessary to supply in addition, if any, & thus matters would be prepared for me to act. Without something like this I have no basis to proceed upon.

"If you prefer a *subscription* School to embrace white children—according to Dr. Comstock's idea—you might make up probably a full school in this way—and another might then be established at the public expense for the children of those who are unable to pay much, or perhaps nothing.—I wish your letter in answer to this, may be explicit on this subject.[1]

"If you and your friends will complete the communications you were so good as to make to me in part, relative to the Indians with whose country you are familiarly acquainted, I shall be much obliged. From the questions I asked concerning the Menominees, & their country, you will know what I wish concerning the Winnebagoes (of whom I have your information in part) of the Sacs, Sioux, and any other tribes with whom you are acquainted—particularly their number, distinguishing men, women & children—the limits & situation of their territory, the soil & productions, the character, dispositions & habits of the Indians—means of subsistence &c.—If you, Sir, & the Gentlemen, will sit down, as we did, for an hour or two with Dr. Comstock, and let him put on paper your remarks for me, you will add much to the obligation I am already under to you.—

"I would have written you this before I left Green Bay—but I had expected a personal interview till it was too late to do it.

"We had a passage of 40 hours only to this place. In a few days we

---

[1] Apparently there was no school at Green Bay when Dr. Morse visited the place. However, there had been three or more, the first of which was established in the autumn of 1817. Of this and others that succeeded it, we shall hear later.

visit the Saut & back here for a few days more, & then shall go on to Detroit & home.

The situation of the inhabitants of your village has deeply interested my feelings, & I shall do what I can for your relief & welfare — With my regards to your associates, I am, Dr. Sir, with esteem

Your obdt Servt.
JEDH. MORSE."

Though a nobler destiny, as most will think, has come to Wisconsin than Dr. Morse planned for her, yet his was a benevolent design. It is evident from his report to the secretary of war that he wished the country west of Lake Michigan to be made a permanent home for the Indians. "Let regulations be made," he said, "to prohibit the introduction of white settlers within the limits of this territory,—that is, within limits bounded south by Illinois, east by Michigan, north by Superior and west by the Mississippi. Let this territory be reserved exclusively for Indians, in which to make the proposed experiment of gathering into one body as many of the scattered and other Indians as may choose to settle there,—to be educated, become citizens, and in due time to be admitted to all the privileges common to other territories and states of the Union. Such a course would probably save the Indians." The worthy doctor had also a plan for endowing a college in the proposed new Territory. "The funds belonging to Moor's Indian school, which is connected at present with Dartmouth college, together with funds in the treasury of Harvard college and of the society for propagating the Gospel among the Indians and others in North America might be appropriated in whole or in part to this institution." He even had hopes of making it an international institution, and thus securing also funds held in Great Britain for Indian education.

Mr. Sergeant also, the Stockbridge pastor, had his own philanthropic hope: "Means will now be used to obtain an act of Congress to exclude spirituous liquor and white heathen from Green Bay." There is heart-ache under our smile as we read the old man's fond dream. Spirituous liquor, we believe, has not been wholly excluded from Green Bay, though it is to be presumed, of course, that there are no white heathen there.

In 1830 the Indians told Mr. Colton, of whose visit to Green Bay we shall hear later, that Dr. Morse advising removal from New York to what was so soon to become Wisconsin said to them in all sincerity, things like these: "You will never again be disturbed. The white man will never go there. He will never desire those lands. They are too far off." From which it appears that a man might be an eminent geographer, as Dr. Morse was, and yet be mistaken as to the progress of settlement.

Efforts were made to secure land west of Lake Michigan not only for the Stockbridges and an allied tribe the Munsees,[1] but also for the remnants of the

---

[1] A branch of the Delawares (Leni-Lennappes). The Munsees seem to have been scattered in consequence of having taken sides against the colonists in the American Revolution. From homes in New York, Canada and perhaps Indiana and elsewhere, some came in later

Iroquois or Six Nations,[1] then living in New York. To this end three parties were working, Dr. Morse that the Stockbridges and others might have a home free from liquor and "white heathen" the Ogden Land Company of New York because they wanted the land held in that state, by the Six Nations; and Eleazar Williams, an Episcopal missionary among the Oneidas, who dreamed of establishing a great Indian confederacy in the West, of which he, presumably, was to be the head. His schemes accorded well with the plans of the Ogden company, but were finally baffled because the great majority of the Iroquois, unlike the Stockbridges, did not wish to leave New York.

This project of settling Indians from New York on lands in the Green Bay region had the hearty support of John Caldwell Calhoun, then secretary of war, who is more than suspected of having entertained the plan of turning the whole Wisconsin region into an Indian territory in order to reduce the number of possible free states. In his official report for 1818 Mr. Calhoun proposed the formation of two reservations for the Indians, one in the northern and the other in the southern part of the vast region then occupied by the various tribes. With this motive on the part of many of its members, Congress had enlarged Illinois beyond the requirement of the ordinance of 1787. It was thought that Wisconsin thus reduced in size, would never have population enough to claim admission as a state into the Union.

We have seen of what sort were the first white settlers in the Wisconsin region, and have recognized their unfitness and inability to lay the foundations of a state. It may be said of them that they were half-civilized whites hostile to the colonists and to the new nation called into existence by the Revolution; now treaties were made to provide for the coming hither of half-civilized Indians loyal to the United States.

"Previous to 1820, and in that year especially, the government of the United States took active and efficient measures to facilitate the purchase of a tract of land in the Northwestern Territory for the accommodation and future settlement of the New York Indians. This was done for the avowed purpose of carrying into effect beneficially, a compromise with the Stockbridge and Munsee Indians for lands on the White river, purchased by the Delawares and partly owned by the former; and to accommodate them and their red brethren of New

---

years to Wisconsin where they have united with the Stockbridges.

[1] These were the Mohawks, Oneidas, Onondagas, Cayugas, Senecas and Tuscaroras. Until the last-named tribe, defeated in 1712 and driven from their southern home, joined their northern brethren then or two—possibly three—years later, the Iroquois confederacy was often called the Five Nations. "Massawomekes" was the name given them by the Virginia and Southern Indians. With allied Hurons and Mississaquas (Algonquians from Canada) they were called Mingoes by the English. A name used among themselves was Ko nosh-o ni. They were proud enough to speak of themselves collectively as Ongwhonwe [Superior Men]. Iroquois is a French adaptation probably, says Charlevoix, of the native word *hiro*, used to conclude a speech, and *koue*, an exclamation. Possible derivations are from *ierokwa*, the indeterminate form of the verb to smoke, signifying "they who smoke;" from the Cayuga form of the word for a bear, *iakwai*; and from the Algonquian *irin*, true or real; and *ako*, a snake, with the French termination *ois*. Compare with this last Schoolcraft's derivation of Nadouc-sioux (page 3).

See "Report of the Bureau of Ethnology for 1885-6," page 77.

York with a permanent home remote from the vicinity of any white settlement and the temptation to the use of ardent spirits, that 'bane of Indian improvement.' It was a desirable object with the government to place these friendly Indians, who had made desirable advances in civilization and improvement, on a distant outpost where they might serve to check or harmonize the disaffected or hostile savages of that region. Their attachment to the American cause and the assistance they afforded in the late war was also avowed as an additional reason for the extension to them of the fostering care of the government."[1]

To secure land near Green Bay for the New York Indians was a long struggle rendered more difficult by the fact that most of them were well content to stay where they were. Nor was their coming desired by the few whites then at and about the Bay. To nip in the bud the whole plan of Indian settlement thereabout, and for other reasons, Colonel John Bowyer, Indian agent at Green Bay, bought of the Menomonees, for an annuity of $800, a tract of land forty miles square, "on both sides of Fox river, extending from the mouth of that stream upwards." Of this transaction Dr. Morse thus wrote: "We found the Menomonees of Green Bay distressed by an attempt of wicked speculators to defraud them of valuable lands." Aided by the Stockbridges Dr. Morse took an active part in securing the rejection of this treaty. President Monroe did not even submit it to the Senate.

In 1821, though at first,—influenced by the traders and the French,—the Indians of the Green Bay region,—Menomonees and Winnebagoes,—refused any concession whatever, an agreement, or "treaty," was made, August 18th, by which they ceded to the Not-ta-ways,[2] as they called the New York Indians, a strip of land four or five miles wide, crossing Fox river at right angles, with the "Little Chute" (now Little Kaukauna), as its center, and extending northwest and southeast as far as the Menomonees and Winnebagoes held the land. Solomon U. Hendrick[3] and four others represented the Stockbridges; Rufus Turkey (Indian name Katakosakont), the Munsees.

As more land was needed an effort was made next year to secure it. John Sergeant of the third generation was one of those who represented the United States government which, however, was party neither to this treaty nor to the one of the year before. Wawauquekoh, or "Last Night," was the Munsee deputy; Solomon U. Hendrick was spokesman for the Stockbridges. He addressed the Wisconsin Indians as "grandchildren," a relationship which was duly acknowledged. In their own languages, the Stockbridges and Menomonees understood each other.[4] The Winnebagoes utterly refused any extension

---

[1] Part of an official report of a council held in August, 1830, signed by Erastus Root and James McCall, two of the three United States commissioners. The third was John T. Mason. A grand-daughter of Mr. McCall's, Marie Miner, wife of Charles H. Richards, long of Madison, now of Philadelphia, is well known in Wisconsin.

[2] Meaning doubtless the Oneidas and other Iroquois. See note on page 55. The name Nottaway, or Nadowa, is not properly applicable to the Stockbridges. It is borne specifically by an almost extinct tribe in Virginia,—a tribe which may be an offshoot from the Tuscaroras.

[3] The "U" probably stands for his Indian name Uhhaunnowwaunmut.

[4] Both tribes are of Algonquian stock and language. Of different race and speech are

of the grant of the year before, and left the council. But, 1822, September 23rd, the Menomonees made the New York Indians joint occupants of their territory. This treaty was afterward disowned by them,—an act that made no end of trouble. However, before this was done the treaty was ratified by President Monroe with a reduction of the limits within which the new-comers might settle.

In speaking of the favorable terms given by the Menomonees in 1822, A. G. Ellis says: "These Green Bay Indians, especially the Menomonees, were greatly under the influence of the French inhabitants, with whom they were largely intermarried. The better class of these French people had come to set a high estimate on education; they were at that very time endeavoring to get English schools established in the settlement. * * The Indians as well as the French people comprehended the importance" of a proposition to establish schools; "and the latter especially noticed that many of the New York Indian deputies wore the dress of civilization; that they spoke the white men's language, and even some of them could read books and write on paper."[1]

In 1827, August 11th, a treaty was made with the Green Bay Indians by the United States government. By this treaty of Little Butte des Morts, as it is called, the Winnebagoes and Menomonees sold land to the United States without any regard to their former sales to the New York Indians, whose claims, however, were referred to the President for arbitration. But the Senate took care that "said treaty shall not impair or affect any rights" of the New York Indians.

An attempt at adjustment was made by a council which held an eight days' session beginning on the 24th of August, 1830. Commissioners Root, McCall and Mason represented the United States; John Metoxen, John W. Quinney, B. Konkapot, Jacob Chicks and Andrew Miller, the Stockbridges; William Dick, N. Towles and John Jonston, the Brothertowns; John Anthony, Daniel Bread, Henry Powles, Comly Stevens and N. Autsequitt, the Oneidas. Eleazar Williams assumed to represent the St. Regis tribe,—which was not then in the Wisconsin region and never intended to remove thither. Oshkosh,[2] then head chief of the Menomonees refused to acknowledge that the New York Indians had any right to land in the Green Bay region, adding that as they were here they might stay during good behavior. Mr. Colton was a witness of the proceedings of this council. His words of praise are for the New York Indians, who in "moral worth and good manners towered above everything around them, not excepting the white population. Among them I could be sure of exemption from anything vulgar, profane or indecent." Of one, already named, he thus speaks: "Metoxen is about sixty years of age, an exemplary Christian, of uncommon meekness, a chief ruler in the civil and relig-

---

the Winnebagoes who use a dialect of the Siouan (Sioux) tongue and are akin to the Dakotas.
[1] "Wisconsin Historical Collections," volume VIII., page 339.
[2] Who is mentioned in Dr. John H. Hanson's "Lost Prince" as "Oiscoss, *alias* Claw:"— a spelling and designation for which Eleazar Williams is probably responsible. In the treaty as printed the name is spelled Oakoshe. It was at this council that he was made head chief.

ious concerns of his tribe." Mr. Colton tells that the New York Indians said little, relying on written statements of the treaties already made. He gives, however, the following report of a speech by Metoxen.[1]

"Brothers: hear what I have to say. Thanks to the Great Spirit who has brought your faces to our faces in health and peace. * * May the chain of friendship which has so long bound us together, still bind us while the sun comes up in the Great Lakes and goes down in our forest.

"Brothers: you know we have always been friends of our great father the President who has promised to keep off our enemies, if we will help him keep off his enemies. * * Our father said we should keep the peace between him and the wild people of the Northwest, that he would gives us and our children this land forever, that he would never let his white children come among us to sell our people strong water, and cheat them and get away our land. * * We were glad at his words. We let his white children take away our lands, and we took our wives and our children in our arms, and came across the Great Lakes to live here on the Fox river. We lighted the council fire and made peace with our brethren, the Winnebagoes and Menomonees. We gave them money for lands. They said they were glad to have us come and live among them, and that we would all be one people. They promised to leave hunting and fishing and raise corn like us, and that their women should spin like our women. * * You see, brothers, the white man is here; he has brought the strong water to sell to our people. * * The Indian is good for nothing when he can get strong water. It makes him mad. He will not work, he will whip his wife and his child, and perhaps kill one to be sorry for it the next day when he can not help it. * * The white man tells our brethren that we are their enemies, * * that if they will get back the lands which they sold to us they can sell them again to the whites. * * Three years ago our brethren received a great bag of money from the city of Washington to buy these very lands on Fox river which they had once sold to us.

"Brothers: there is no longer peace between us and our brethren here."

In part this is a temperance speech. Who in Wisconsin spoke earlier on this subject?

On the last day of the council, says Mr. Colton, "John Metoxen (than whom a man of more exalted worth can not be found on earth) addressed himself to his brethren of the Menomonees and Winnebagoes in a strain most sublime and touching. By his language and manner he brought us into the presence of God so that we felt ourselves to be there." A part of his speech Mr. Colton reports to us in the following words:

"Brothers: I speak now both to my white and red brothers and to all who are here. I am an old man and my spirit will soon be with the spirits of my

---

[1] It is to be remembered that this and the other report given by Mr. Colton are merely from memory. He took notes at the time but did not have them when he prepared for publication his book.—"Tour of the American Lakes,"—from which these extracts are taken.

fathers. I have been at the head of my people for many years. I have been anxious for them. When I came before them from New York to Green Bay I thought that they would have peace. But I see that I must go down to the grave without comfort. It is not peace. All the doings in this council show that there is no rest for my people who came here for rest.

"I wish to say a word to the Winnebagoes and Menomonees. It is not good that the white man has stood between us and kept us apart. We told you that there was no more room for us among the graves of our fathers, because the white man had come there. You took us by the hand and said 'We are glad to see you. Here is our country. Come and live among us.' We said to you, 'Give us land that we may call our own, and we will pay you for it.' You did so, and we made a covenant. * *

"I speak again to my white brothers. * * We left our land in the east country and came here on the understanding of those treaties. * * You offer to make a new treaty in the name of our great father. Make the old treaty good, brothers, and then, if there be any need, we shall have some reason to trust in a new one.

"We have learned one good thing from the white man, to trust in the white man's God. We feel that we need to trust him now. We are injured, and I know not what new injuries await the destiny of my people. I shall go down to the grave thinking of the words of King David's son which I read in the book presented to my father's father by your father's father from over the big salt lake: 'So I returned, and considered all the oppressions that are done under the sun': and behold the tears of such as were oppressed, and they had no comforter; and on the side of their oppressors there was power; but they had no comforter.'

"God is witness of our engagements, God will reward us according to our deeds.

"Brothers I have done."

The best account we have of this council is to be found in the journal kept by Commissioner McCall. He attempts none but the briefest report of any of the speeches and of those by Metoxen he says nothing. Under date of August 27th, Friday, the journal says: "There are now 1740 Indians attending. * * Oushcoush arose and stated that the [Menomonees] had not sold the Wappinackies any land." On Saturday the Wappinackies [New York Indians] laid claim to a tract on Fox river " making about 748,800 acres." They were offered by the Menomonees and Winnabagoes "something less than one-third of the amount asked." The proposition of the commissioners "was to give the New York Indians about 295,000 acres, being nearly 120 acres to every soul interested among them." But, August 31st, "the Menominees and Winnebagos told us they would not give or let one foot more land than they had offered."

Mr. McCall complains that the "greatest part of the inhabitants of this place" were striving to prevent the Menomonees and the Winnebagoes "from agreeing to anything." As the New York Indians were Protestants, Roman Catholic influence at Green Bay was averse to giving them homes there. Another obstacle in the way of securing land west of Lake Michigan, for the tribes that needed and desired it, was that Williams and the Ogden land company had been trying to get homes there for those who did not wish to leave New York.

But those who had come to the Wisconsin region, — the Stockbridges (and Munsees), a large part of the Oneidas and the Brothertowns,—of whom we shall have some account,— were provided for by a treaty made in Washington, 8th February, 1831. To this treaty only the Menomonees and United States government were parties. The latter secured a large cession of land,[1]— 2,500,000 acres,— for white settlement; and 500,000 acres were assigned to the New York Indians. A supplementary article was added on the 17th of the same month, and the Senate made as a condition of ratification that three additional townships, on the east side of Lake Winnebago, — each of 23,040 acres,— be set apart; two for the Stockbridges and Munsees, one for the Brothertowns. Further conditions were these: That for their improvements at Statesburg[2] the Stockbridges, were to be paid a sum not to exceed twenty-five thousand dollars, while the Brothertowns were to receive for theirs (at Little Kaukauna) one thousand six hundred dollars. The tract of land assigned to the other New York Indians,—a part of the Oneidas,—was enlarged by adding two hundred thousand acres on the south-west side and diminished by an equal amount to be "taken off from the north-eastern side of said tract."

But it was necessary to get the consent of the Menomonees to the conditions made by the Senate. This was secured 1832, October 27th, by United States Commissioner George B. Porter.[3] All parties were satified save Eleazar Williams and the Ogden land company.[4] Williams could no longer dream

---

This tract was ceded to the United States." — A. G. ELLIS.
[1] "All the lands east of Fox river, Green Bay and Lake Winnebago, and from Fond du Lac southeasterly to the sources of the Milwaukee river, and down the same to its mouth.
[2] South Kaukauna.
[3] Perhaps one reason why the promises made the New York Indians by the Menomonees in the treaty of 1822 were not fulfilled, and why subsequent treaties were so difficult of negotiation, was the utter loss of confidence in Williams. His failure to carry out promises that he made in regard to schools is specifically mentioned, by Mr. Ellis, as one cause of the trouble. Yet that the majority of the Menomonees, or any considerable number of them, cared much about schools is rendered doubtful by a further statement for which Mr. Ellis makes himself responsible: That the treaty of 1831 made "provision for an extensive farming and educational establishment" for the benefit of the Menomonees; and that the plan "proved abortive, the traders and Roman Catholics persuading the Indians to reject all its proposed benefits." See "Wisconsin Historical Collections," volume II., page 437.

[4] This it was that furnished Williams with part of the money needed in the prosecution of his scheme and theirs. It is not certain that either of them originated it, though Williams claimed that he did. However, the Ogden company had been in existence since 1810 in which year it bought from its predecessor, the Holland land company, "the pre-emption right of purchase from the Indians to most of the land of western New York, having derived it from Massachusetts originally, subsequently confirmed by the state of New York" (A. G. Ellis). The Green Bay region, as a place to which removal might be made, was suggested, very possibly, by Dr. Morse, to whom John Sergeant, in a letter dated 1821, December 16th, credits the entire plan, as far as it related to the Stockbridges. These people, however,

of an Indian empire at Green Bay, with himself at its head, and the company could no longer hope to get possession of land in New York by removing the Iroquois to what is now Wisconsin. It continued operations, however, and at a later date attempted to secure the removal of the Iroquois then in New York to the region drained by the Little Osage river (southeastern Kansas). There a reservation was conditionally provided for by a "treaty" made 1838, January 15th, at Buffalo Creek, New York.[1] By this "treaty" there was assigned to the United States whatever right or interest,—if there ever was any,—that the New York Iroquois retained in the five hundred thousand acres of Wisconsin land above mentioned. Thus the title to said land was left in the Oneidas of Wisconsin, and these, by treaty made February 3rd of the same year, ceded to the United States all of this great possession save about sixty-two thousand acres. Thus was constituted the present Oneida reservation near Green Bay. Iroquois from New York had found homes near "that end of the world"[2] to which, in the time of Radisson, their ancestors had driven the helpless Hurons whom Menard sought, and in seeking gave his life.

claimed that they had a century-old invitation from their "grandchildren," the Menomonees of Green Bay, thither to come and there to make their homes.

[1] A suit that grew out of this "treaty" is now (June, 1894) pending in the United States court of claims. It is brought in the name of the Iroquois with whom, it is alleged, the Stockbridges and Brothertowns, while in New York, were duly incorporated. Though a few Indians from New York and still fewer from Wisconsin removed to the proposed reservation, it was never really occupied according to the terms of the "treaty." As before, the Iroquois of New York preferred to remain there, and the plans of the Ogden company were again defeated. Hence the proposed Kansas reservation never ceased to be public land. It was opened to white settlement when the Territory of Kansas was organized. In the rush of the whites for land, and in the fierce conflict about slavery, whatever claims the Indians had were lost sight of utterly, and the few of them who were there removed to Indian Territory, where they became incorporated with kindred tribes. The suit aforesaid is brought for the recovery of damages alleged to be due for the loss of this proposed reservation. Some of our Stockbridges are deeply interested in this action, and to the whole matter several of their numerous statesmen are giving close attention,—gentlemen who would much better be employed in hoeing potatoes or in raising pigs and poultry.

[2] See page 8.

CHAPTER VIII.

ONEIDAS AND THE BROTHERTOWNS.

The Oneidas are an Iroquois tribe which, unlike the most of the others of that confederacy, was, with the Tuscaroras, friendly to the colonists during the Revolution. This fact, in reasonable probability, was almost wholly owing to missionary influence from New England, especially that of Rev. Samuel Kirkland, a native of Lisbon (then Newent parish, Norwich), Connecticut, who in 1761 entered the famous Lebanon school, whence he went to Princeton college from which in 1765 he received — though not present — the degree of bachelor of arts. The autumn before he had aided in establishing a school among the Mohawks; 1765, February 7th, after a twenty-three days' journey with two Indian attendants, he reached Kanadesaga, the principal town of the Senecas, and began missionary work among them.

Of this an account was given, many years afterward, to Rev. Thompson S. Harris, missionary of the American Board among the same people, by some aged chiefs. "These men state," wrote Mr. Harris in the "Missionary Herald" for March, 1829, "that the first attempt they ever recollect to teach their people the gospel of Christ was a fruitless effort by the Rev. Samuel Kirkland about sixty-five or seventy years ago. He remained with them at their village (now Geneva), nearly two years; had begun to excite some attention among the Indians, and had opened a school for the instruction of their children, when the person with whom Mr. Kirkland lived, of whose hospitality he had always faithfully shared, suddenly fell down dead. The superstition of the Indians was such, at that time, as to lead them to account for this man's sudden death on the supposition that it was a judgment of heaven for harboring some wicked person; and they soon after passed a resolution that he, — Mr. Kirkland, — be expelled the village. He was afterwards accepted by the Oneidas."

Another account, probably by Mr. Kirkland himself, states that though he came near being murdered among the Senecas that fact did not drive him from them. But he thought the Oneidas a "nobler race," and after his ordination at Lebanon, 1766, June 19th, he began labor among that people. In this service he was the successor of Rev. Samson Occom, of whom we shall hear more in connection with the history of the Brothertowns.

On the day of Mr. Kirkland's ordination he received a commission from the Connecticut "Board of Correspondents" of an organization in Scotland entitled "the Society for Promoting Christian Knowledge." But before he received aid from that source he was put to great straits as is shown by the following extracts from a letter written in 1767:

"From week to week I am obliged to go with the Indians to Oneida Lake to catch eels for my subsistence. I have lodged and slept with them till I am as lousy as a dog. Flour and milk, with a few eels, have been my only living. My strength begins to fail. My poor people are almost starved to death. There is one family consisting of four persons whom I must support the best way I can, or they would certainly perish. Indeed I would myself be glad of an opportunity to fall on my knees for such a bone as I have often seen cast to the dogs. Without relief I shall soon perish. My constitution is almost broken, my spirits sunk, yet my heart still bleeds for these poor creatures. I had rather die than leave them alone in their present miserable condition." Mr. Kirkland's needs were promptly supplied, and in June, 1773, the Scotch society, in conjunction with the corporation of Harvard college, agreed to pay Mr. Kirkland's salary. The aid from Scotland was continued until 1797.

Mr. Kirkland had more than his share of the fight against liquor. His courage almost cost him his life. His loyalty to the cause of the colonists lost him the support of his former friend, Sir William Johnson, governor of New York, who, as an Episcopalian and a loyalist, came to oppose Mr. Kirkland both on religious and political grounds. During the war the village and the churches of the Oneidas were destroyed by the British. Mr. Kirkland served as chaplain in the American army. But his great service in the cause was done among the Indians. After the Revolution he resumed his missionary labors. For a time two Frenchmen, one a Jesuit, gave him serious annoyance. Governor De Witt Clinton wrote the Indians a letter warning them against these schemers. Mr. Kirkland died in 1808, March 18th. In the same year the Northern Missionary society of New York[1] provided as his successor an inefficient man named William Jenkins who was supplanted by the notorious Eleazar Williams. Thus it will be seen that Episcopal mission work among the Oneidas was a continuation of that of Mr. Kirkland, a Congregationalist, whose service began in July, 1766. His home was at Ga-no-a-lo-ha-le, now the village of Oneida Castle. He was virtually the founder of Hamilton college, Clinton, New York. Rev. John Thornton Kirkland, president of Harvard from 1810 until 1828 was his son.

Williams was a remarkable though most unworthy man. "In the Mohawk[2] he was a born orator." Thus he was perfectly understood by the Oneidas among whom he begun to labor as catechist and lay-reader probably in 1816 or the year following. He began his work by winning over to his own denomination those who had been trained in the mission begun by Occom and

---

[1] See page 47.
[2] His native language. He was of the St. Regis tribe, which, in race and origin, seems to be of the Mohawk "nation."

continued by Kirkland and Jenkins. These he represented as intruders, recalling the labors, among the Mohawks, of Rev. Henry Barclay (1735) and Rev. John Ogilvie (1756-62), missionaries of the church of England. We may anticipate a part of our narrative by remarking here that those whom Williams thus influenced became known as the first Christian party. Next he addressed himself to the pagans, and with such success that they soon became known as the second Christian party. Soon he began to promulgate those plans, to which reference has already been made, of a great Indian empire in the region of Green Bay. "I could but admire," says the late A. G. Ellis,[1] the comprehension [comprehensiveness], grandeur, even, of his scheme. Not the Oneidas only, but the whole Six Nations were to be included. The country west of Lake Michigan to the Mississippi, and perhaps further [farther], was to be mapped out, and a large area to be set off to each of the tribes — the St. Regis to occupy the mouth of Fox river and head of Green bay. A new form of government was to be adopted. The wisdom of the past was to be searched for a model; it should not be a republic, but some plan of empire, with one supreme head."

Williams's modesty was not so excessive but that he indicated clearly enough the person whom he thought best fitted for this exalted position. In furtherance of his plans he went West in the summer of 1821, but turned back at Detroit on learning of Bowyer's treaty. This, however, as we have learned, proved to be no obstacle at all to the settlement in the Fox river country of such of the New York Indians as wished to remove thither.

But Williams himself proved to be the most serious obstacle to the carrying out of his own schemes. By a continued course of advice and falsehood he had lost the confidence of nearly all the Indians, and both parties,— first Christian and second Christian or pagan,— among the Oneidas united 1821, November 21st, in a remonstrance against him, addressed to Bishop J. H. Hobart of his church and asking for Williams's immediate removal as a religious teacher among them. So far from doing this, Dr. Hobart sustained Williams, who was thus left free for the further development of his schemes. The next year, 1822, he came to Green Bay accompanied by Oneida "delegates" and followed in 1823 by others of the same tribe. The first Oneida settlement in this region was at Little Kau-kau-lin (Little Kaukauna; post-office, Little Rapids). There they came to number about one hundred fifty, and thence they removed when, in 1825, there came on of their people from New York a number larger than in any former year. On Duck creek, and about eight miles from Fort Howard, they formed a settlement, the present village, as I suppose, of

---

[1] Mr. Ellis came to be associated with Williams in November, 1820. The schemes of empire did not attract Ellis, but in 1824 he came to Green Bay and for about three years was assistant in the Episcopal mission of which Williams was nominally the head. See volumes II. and VIII. of the "Wisconsin Historical Collections." It should be said that the late Judge Morgan Lewis Martin of Green Bay thinks that Ellis is too severe on Williams. On the other hand the latter has received credit not due him. For example it is said that he translated the Episcopal prayer-book into the Mohawk tongue whereas his work thereon, though good, was one only of revision.

Oneida. At this place and at Little Kau-kau-lin among the Indians, at Fort Howard and elsewhere among the whites, Williams continued the exercise of his ecclesiastical functions,—a service which soon became as unacceptable here as it had been in New York. Of part of his homiletic material we have an account that takes us back to New England history of the seventeenth century, and to Williams's ancestry. Thus runs, in brief, the story:

Rev. John Williams, ordained pastor of Deerfield, Massachusetts, in 1688, and known as the "Redeemed Captive" from a narrative of which he was subject and author, had a daughter Eunice, a child of seven years[1] when the family were taken captive by French and Indians, 1704, February 29th. She was brought up among the Indians and married one of them. Though she afterward visited her kindred she adhered to the faith of the church of Rome in which she had been trained and returned to the Indian mode of life, lest she imperil her soul by staying among Protestants! Her family, according to a custom not uncommon among those of mixed blood, took the name of their white ancestor. About 1800 or later, her grandson Thomas, was persuaded to put his two sons John and Eleazar in school at Longmeadow, Massachusetts. Somehow Eleazar became possessed of sermons of his Puritan ancestors of which, says Mr. Ellis, he "had at least a barrel." A suspicious quantity! Some of these, after much tutoring by Ellis, Williams managed to preach at Green Bay. It is curious enough to think of the New England minister of the seventeenth and eighteenth centuries thus preaching to Wisconsin's early residents through the false lips of an Indian descendant,—Williams was a man of extraordinary mendacity,—baptized by a Romanist and ordained, though not till 1826 and then as a deacon, by an Episcopalian. "He connected himself with our church from conviction, and appears warmly attached to her doctrines, her apostolic ministry and her worship," says the journal of the diocese of New York for 1818. But in 1827 the Domestic and Foreign Missionary society of the Protestant Episcopal church, having lost confidence in Williams, appointed as their missionary in the Green Bay region Rev. Richard Fish Cadle. His work, however, was among the whites and the Menomonees rather among the Oneidas, and these people did not get rid of their incubus Williams, weary as all,— even those who had been his partisans,—had become of him, until 1832 when the "confidence and patronage" of his church were finally withdrawn from the crownless would-be emperor.

Years later Williams attempted to pass himself off as the son of Louis XVI. of France and Marie Antoinette. Incredible as it may seem he succeeded thereby in deluding a number of people who, so far I know, gave no other evidence of idiocy. Born at Caughnawaga (Sault St. Louis), Canada, about 1790, Williams died 1858, August 28th, at Hogansburg,[2] New York.

All the early Oneida emigrants to Green Bay were of the first Christian

---

[1] Eunice Williams's age at the time of her capture is variously given. I accept the statement in George Sheldon's "History and Genealogy of Deerfield."
[2] Both these places, however, are on the reservation belonging to the St. Regis Indians and lying on the St. Lawrence partly in New York and partly in Canada.

(once Williams's) party. After a time, the second Christian party, which had determinedly opposed removal from New York, divided, not only in regard to this proposition but, perhaps first, on church matters as well. About half of them came under the care of the Methodists, and this Orchard party, as it was called, "adopted the emigration policy and removed to Green Bay."

In 1832, July 21st, there arrived among them a man of fervent spirit, Rev. John Clark, a member of the New York conference of the Methodist Episcopal church. On the 16th[1] of the following September he dedicated a combined church-and-school,—"an unpretentious structure built of logs."[2] In size it was twenty-four feet by thirty and it "was the first Methodist house of worship west of Lake Michigan, and north of a line extending west from a point fifty miles south of Chicago to the Pacific ocean." The occasion was one of happy Christian fellowship. For in the congregation, worshiping with their Methodist brethren, and with them receiving the sacrament of the Lord's supper, were some of the Stockbridges among whom the American Board had established a mission where is now South Kaukauna, five years before.

On the day following the dedication, that is on Monday, 17th September, 1832, a school was organized. Of this a woman of the Stockbridge tribe, Miss Electa W. Quinney, was made teacher. Previously she had taught among her own people.

Mr. Clark was a true itinerant. That he might be free for the work of mission organization and superintendence, he put his Oneida flock in charge of one of their own number, Mr. Daniel Adams, who had been a preacher among them in New York. The mission thus begun is still continued, and that of the Episcopalians survived even Williams and also abides to this day. One established by Father Clark among the Menomonees at what is now Marinette did not prove to be permanent. Of his work among the Ojibways we shall yet have some account.

Mr. Adams won a wife in the person of Miss Quinney, and in 1835, or thereabout, the twain found a new home among the Senecas of Indian Territory. Among these people Mr. Adams continued his work as pastor and evangelist. Is he not Wisconsin's first missionary?

Among our Oneidas there continued to be somewhat of strife. The building in which the Methodists opened a second school was "razed to the ground," says Mr. Bennett, "by a mob composed of chiefs and others under the pastoral charge of the Protestant Episcopal missionary." Fortunately, however, ministers are not to be held responsible for the doings of all who may be, in a greater or less degree, under their pastoral charge, and we may charitably suppose that the evident quarrel among the Oneidas arose from quite other causes than

---

[1] The exercises may have begun on Saturday, the 15th.
[2] "History of Methodism in Wisconsin," by Rev. P. S. Bennett, A. M. Where did this building stand? At Grand Kau-kau-lin, Mr. Bennett seems to imply. I am sure it was not there; it may have been at Little Kaukauna. The Methodist church building at "Oneida West,"—the first, apparently, of that mission that was used exclusively as a house of worship, was dedicated, 1840, January 4th.

the difference in their religious training.

Of both parties among them there came to the Duck creek reservation,— their new home in the Wisconsin region,— about eleven hundred. According to the census of 1890, the Oneidas of the Green Bay agency, "including homeless Indians," numbered 1716. They have not become citizens, and therein have been wisely conservative. During the late war, ninety-six of their number enlisted in the Union army.

As a tribe, the Oneidas seem to have been unusually generous. To them James B. Jenkins[1] gives the credit of "adopting" the Tuscaroras who came, he says, "from South Carolina in 1715" [1714]. In 1774, October 4th, at Oriskany Creek, New York, they made, by formal deed, a gift of land to certain of their Indian brethren from New England and Long Island. These, ten years later, formed the Brothertown "nation." The chief settlement,— not made until years later,— in the new home of these united peoples was fourteen miles south of where is now the city of Utica, New York, and the land given comprised a tract ten miles square. Between givers and receivers the chief agents of communication were Samson Occom, the missionary, and David Fowler, a teacher.[2]

Occom was a Mohegan, born in 1723 at the place of that name on the western bank of the Thames in Connecticut. The settlement was founded by his father who "was known in his native tongue as Aukum (Aucum, Maucum, Mawcum) and subsequently Occom" (Occum). When the son was ten years old a missionary school was established in his native village. This school he probably attended but it was soon given up as a failure. "Man seeth not as God seeth." "Ministers from the region round about came, and the result was the awakening of a few in the tribe to a sense of their heathen condition. Samson Occum, then sixteen years of age, was one of these, and for six months he was struggling out of darkness toward the light. When he was seventeen he found the light, which roused anew his thirst for learning, and kindled a pity for his poor people." He was one of the converts in the "Great Awakening," as the great revival is called that under Jonathan Edwards and others swept over a great part of New England. In 1743, Occum came under the instruction of Rev. Eleazar Wheelock, D. D., pastor of the Second (Congregational) church of Lebanon, Connecticut. "It has been generally supposed," says Rev. William DeLoss Love, Jr.,[2] of Hartford, Connecticut, "that Rev. Eleazar Wheelock dug this diamond from the earth and polished it, but it seems to have been already glittering before Wheelock met with it. It was Occum who sought out Wheelock" with whom he spent four years and whom, apparently, he inspired to establish a school to educate other Indians, and also to train whites to be missionaries and teachers among the native tribes. It was

---
[1] Attorney for some of the Stockbridges and others before the United States court of claims in the suit mentioned on page 61.
[2] Son of the author of "Wisconsin in the War." The father was for many years pastor of the Grand Avenue (then Spring street) Congregational church in Milwaukee.

opened for the latter service in 1748 and more fully established in 1754. After receiving in 1755, July 17th, a certain gift it was called Moore's (or Moor's) charity school.[1]

"In November, 1749, Occom began a work as schoolmaster, counselor, judge and preacher among the Montauk Indians in Long Island, which lasted twelve years and was greatly blessed. About 1751 he married Mary Fowler, of the Montauk tribe." Two brothers of his wife, David, born in 1735, and Jacob, probably younger, became closely associated with Occom as his work extended, as did also one Joseph Johnson, who married Occom's daughter Tabitha. Probably during the early years of his work on Long Island, Occom received, from the Windham association, of Connecticut, approbation to preach, and in 1759 he was ordained by the presbytery of Long Island.[2] In June, 1761, Occom and David Fowler visited the Oneidas. Occom remained until autumn, Fowler returned in August taking with him to the Lebanon school three Mohawk youths, one of whom was the celebrated Joseph Brant[3] (Thayendanegea). Fowler continued his own studies until (March, 1675) he was "approved" as an Indian teacher or, more strictly speaking, as a teacher for Indians. On the 29th of April following he set out for the Oneida nation. There he opened a school at Canajoharie. But the famine of that year drove the Oneidas from their homes and Fowler back to New England.

Preceding Fowler's coming as a teacher, Occom had cared, as best he could, for the Oneidas by spending among them a considerable part of the summers of 1762, '63, '64, continuing the mission work that he had begun among them. This, as we have seen, was taken up in 1766 by Samuel Kirkland to whom David Fowler and Joseph Johnson became assistants.

The names of Occom and Jacob Fowler link the history of our Brothertowns to that of the beginnings of Dartmouth college. More's charity school needed money of course, and in company with Rev. Nathaniel Whitaker of Norwich, Connecticut, Occom was sent to England on what inconsiderate people sometimes call a "begging trip." Thither they sailed 1765, December 23rd. Occom was the first Indian to preach in Great Britain, and he aroused there a wonderful interest. "From February 16, 1766, to July 22, 1767, he preached more than three hundred times, and usually to crowded houses." He had even the honor of preaching before King George III. who gave £200 of the £12-000 raised in England and Scotland for the school which had educated such a prodigy. With its enlarged means there was planned for the institution a greater work. It was removed in 1770 to Hanover, New Hampshire, a place chosen despite the protests of both Occom and Kirkland. For one year, 1774-5, Jacob Fowler was preceptor of the school, which had already been virtually

---

[1] The giver, however, wrote his name Joshua More.

[2] The difference, then, between Congregationalists and Presbyterians was largely one of geography. The same man would be a Congregationalist in New England, and a Presbyterian elsewhere.

[3] Chiefly celebrated for two very unlike things: his supposed or real connection with the massacre at Wyoming, during the Revolution, and his translation into the Mohawk tongue of the Episcopal prayer-book; the translation afterwards revised by Eleazar Williams.

absorbed into Dartmouth college.

After Occom's return from England he "seems to have exercised a missionary's care over seven different places: Montauk, Long Island; Mohegan, Niantic, Groton, Farmington, Stonington, Connecticut; and Charlestown, Rhode Island. He it was, probably, who formed the plan of gathering into one community the Christianized tribes among which he was doing the work of an evangelist and pastor. But so active was David Fowler in carrying out the plan that his name, more than any other, seems to be held in remembrance by our Wisconsin Brothertowns.[1] It was he who started with Occom, 1774, July 8th, "to view the land offered by the Oneidas and settle its boundaries. They took back with them the deed of gift, an instrument which seems to have been drawn up by Occom himself with the purpose of keeping the New England blood pure and preserving a tribal unity. Then came the revolutionary war which interfered with the plans made. During the war Occom, the Fowlers and Johnson were the Indian heroes of New England." They deserve to be remembered also as the founders of Brothertown, New York. "About twenty families started for the Oneida country on May 8th, 1784." Some families had gone thither earlier. In the autumn of the next year Occom visited them, and was present when, 1785, November 7th, they organized their government and named their town.

The new "nation" came to include remnants of various New England and Long Island tribes: Narragansetts, Pequods, Montauks, Mohegans, Nanticokes (Nahanticks) and Farmingtons.

Through most of these tribes the religious history of our state is linked with that of Connecticut and of the settlements about Massachusetts bay. Though in their dealings with the Indians, the New England colonists were sometimes neither wise nor just, their record in this respect is, on the whole, better than that made by our American people in later years. In missionary service there were abundant labors. Upon the first seal of Massachusetts was a star (to suggest that of Bethlehem), the figure of an Indian, and the Macedonian cry "Come over and help us." The Indian and the star are upon the seal now in use. John Eliot preached the gospel even to Philip of Mount Hope. The Puritan "Society for Propagating the Gospel among the Indians in North America," was the first of organized missionary societies.[2] Thousands of In-

---

[1] See "Wisconsin Historical Collections," volume IV., page 291.

[2] It was incorporated in England, 1649, July 27th, by the famous "long parliament." In connection with the act of incorporation, it was "enacted that a general collection be made for the purposes aforesaid, through all England and Wales; and that the ministers read this act, and exhort the people to a cheerful contribution." This first-formed missionary board of Great Britain grew out of the labors of Eliot. Its charter was renewed when Charles II. came to the throne, in 1660. Under its patronage there was published the first entire Bible printed in America,—the translation made by Eliot into the language of the Indians among whom he labored.

For many years the eminent philosopher, Robert Boyle, served as president of this society (which must not be confounded with the existing "Society for the Propagation of the Gospel in Foreign Parts"). The older society "employed as its distributing agents and correspondents the commissioners of the United Colonies (first union; the one formed in 1643), so long as that confederacy lasted. When that arrangement came to an end, amid the politi-

dians received Christianity and a considerable degree of civilization. In entire tribes there was a larger percentage able to read than there is in Russia at the present day. Without the help of these Christian and other friendly Indians the whites would have found it difficult to maintain their position in New England. It may be that otherwise the colonies would have been blotted out. The punishment of those who murdered a Christian Indian for making known King Philip's plans was the immediate occasion of the war called by the name of that chief,—a war that in part was one of heathenism upon Christianity. Yet, notwithstanding the strife and disturbance of that time and the years following, we find that in all, or nearly all, the tribes whose names are given above converts were made to the Christian faith.

After the organization of the new "nation" at Brothertown, Occom spent his summers there. On "his journeys to and fro he preached and performed pastoral labors among the new settlements along the thoroughfare of emigration. He was known as the missionary of the wilderness. On November 28th and 29th, the Stockbridges and Brothertowns conjointly and formally called Occom to be their minister, and he accepted their call. A creed or confession of unusual interest was drawn up, which also declared their purpose in going into the wilderness. The church subsequently became Presbyterian, and Occom says it was the first ever organized among the Indians without the assistance of a white man." The Stockbridge church, however, had been organized before that tribe removed from Massachusetts. In 1789, the pastor-elect removed to New York and made his home first at Brothertown and then for a few months at New Stockbridge where he died on the 14th of July, 1792.

With a just enthusiasm Mr. Love calls Occum "the glory of the Indian nation." He has some renown as an author. The most famous temperance sermon of its time was one preached by him, 1772, September 2nd, at the hanging of Moses Paul, an Indian who, notwithstanding the authority of lawgiver and teaching of apostle suggested by his names, had committed murder. Perhaps no man is ever quite ready to be hanged, but this sermon, good as it is, has parts that must have made the unhappy wretch almost wish that the execution had come first and the sermon afterward. "Your grave is dug," says the preacher addressing him, "your coffin is ready." Yet something of this awful sternness is needed among "fools who make a mock at sin." A treatise by Occom on the Montauk language lay in manuscript for the greater part of a century, but within a few years has been published by the Massachusetts historical society. Part of his diary, begun in 1743, is now in the library of Dartmouth college. He was one of the editors of a hymn-book of which three editions were called for. Two of the hymns therein are from his own pen, and one that he wrote later, "Waked by the Gospel's Joyful Sound," appears in many of our modern books under the disguise, "Awaked by Sinai's Awful Sound."

---

cal disorders of 1086, 'Commissioners were especially appointed by the corporation, consisting of the principal gentlemen of the civil order, and of the clergy in New England,' with power to fill their own vacancies."

He was one of the original members of the presbytery of Albany, constituted in 1790. A century has passed since Samuel Kirkland delivered the sermon at burial of this Whitefield of the Indian race, and at length men are doing a tardy justice to the name and work of Samson Occom.

David Fowler died 1807, March 31st. His last years saw a lessening of the strife that embittered the dying of Occom whom it drove from Brothertown,—strife in which a part of the newly formed "nation,"—as is always the case among Indians,—took the part of interlopers who came among the Brothertowns to get land. Perhaps the beginning of the trouble was the desire on the part of some of the Oneidas that the Brothertowns yield to the common possession of both "nations" the tract that had been assigned to the sole use and ownership of Occom and his fellow-emigrants. Their exclusive title was confirmed, however, by a "treaty," made 1788, September 22nd. By this, the original tract assigned to the Brothertowns was reduced to one three miles in length by two in breadth.

But though white men could not own land in the Brothertown settlement they could get ten-year leases which some of the tribe were foolish enough to make to them. Under these circumstances disputes arose as a matter of course. Finally the entire reservation was divided into two parts equal in area. Choice of these was given to the Indians, and the whites on the selected area were compelled to remove. The other half was sold. Out of the sum thus realized, the whites were indemnified for their losses, and the remainder was deposited in the treasury of New York for the benefit of the Indians. Until 1841 they drew only the interest but in that year, the principal, amounting to about $30,000 was paid to them.

But even this somewhat heroic remedy of separation and division did not prove effectual. The legislative act by which (1795, March 31st) it was accomplished did indeed make it impossible for the individual members of the Brothertown "nation" alienate their lands. But in the ways in which a stronger and shrewder race can take advantage of one inferior in these respects, the whites got the better of the Indians until the latter were ready to try the universal American panacea for social and financial troubles. So the Brothertowns "moved West." Hither in 1823 came the first,—a small party that settled at Little Kau-kau-lin. Of the Brothertowns who were there in 1830, Commissioners Root and McCall say, under date of September 30th: "These are farther advanced in civilization and the arts of domestic life than perhaps most of the borderers on a distant frontier." The settlement, however, could not have been a large one inasmuch as the Senate proviso, appended for the benefit of the Brothertowns to the treaty of 1831, grants them only "one thousand and six hundred dollars for the improvements on the lands now in their possession on the east side of Fox river." And as no mention is made of other lands or other improvements we may conclude that there were none.

Emigration to the new reservation began, probably, in that year (1831). There they and, northward of them, their neighbors, the Stockbridges, were again the pioneers of civilization in the wilderness. "The first steamboat that ever graced the crystal bosom of Lake Winnebago, was built in our [Calumet] county by the Brothertown Indians under the superintendence of Peter Hoteling, who was a white man and the captain of said boat. Having no laws which they could enforce, for the protection of their lives and property, and having in all their ways, manner of living, appearance in dress, and [in] speech (not having spoken * * their own tongue for one hundred years), become perfectly assimilated to their white brethren, they concluded to petition Congress for citizenship. Their prayer was granted, and an act passed for their benefit on the third day of March, 1839. From that time they have lived under the laws of the state, have officers of their own in most cases, and have sent three of their own men as members of the legislature, to-wit: William Fowler, Alonzo D. Dick, and W. H. Dick." Thus wrote Thomas Commuck, a Brothertown, 22nd August, 1855. He added: "Already has intermarriage with the whites so changed the Brothertowns in complexion that three-quarters of them would be readily considered white where they were not known."

"Fifty or more"[1] of those having Brothertown blood in their veins enlisted in the Union army. "We have furnished ten teachers during the last thirty years."[1]

One of the first Methodist Episcopal churches in Wisconsin was established at Deansburg, the name given first to what is now Brothertown. That was in 1839 and the pastor of that early day has been followed to the present time by successors of his noble brotherhood.[2]

---
[1] Mr. E. M. Dick of Brothertown, Wisconsin.

[2] The data furnished by Mr. Love, from his forthcoming biography of Occom, led to a recasting of what I had written concerning the Brothertowns. Mr. Love's work possesses a definiteness that is wanting in what Commuck wrote on the history of his people. Incidentally, we observe here that, notwithstanding Dr. Draper's suggestion (Collections, IV., 298) that Commuck may have been murdered, there is no good reason to think that such was the case. Of Occom's life there is a good sketch in Dr. E. F. Hatfield's "Poets of the Church."

Some time since, a statement was made in the "Standard," a Baptist paper of Chicago, that the first church of that denomination, in Wisconsin, was one among the Brothertowns at Little Kaukauna in 1828. But I find no evidence of the existence of such a church, and a note of inquiry, addressed to the writer of the article in the "Standard," brought,—owing, perhaps, to his illness,—no reply.

CHAPTER IX.

THE MUH-HE-KA-NE-OK.

Under the name of Stockbridges we have had mention of a people who, in their own language, call themselves the Muh-he-ka-ne-ok.[1] According to their legendary history of the tribe, "a great people came from the Northwest; crossed over the salt waters,[2] and after long and weary pilgrimages (planting many colonies on their track), took possession and built their fires upon the Atlantic coast, extending from the Delaware on the south to the Penobscot on the north. They became, in process of time, divided into different tribes and interests; all, however, speaking one common dialect. This great confederacy, comprising Delawares, Munsees, Mohegans, Narragansetts, Pequots, Penobscots, and many others * * held its council once a year to deliberate on the general welfare. * *

"The tribe to which your speaker[3] belongs, and of which there were many bands, occupied and possessed the country from the sea-shore at Manhattan to Lake Champlain. Having found an ebb and flow of the tide, they said: 'This is Muh-he-con-new,— like our waters, which are never still.' From this expression and by this name they were afterwards known, until their removal to Stockbridge in the year 1730. Housatonic River Indians, Mohegans, Manhattas, were all names of bands in different localities but bound together, as one family, by blood, marriage and descent. * *

"Where are the twenty-five thousand in number, and the four thousand warriors, who constituted the power and population of the great Muh-he-con-new Nation in 1604? They have been victims to vice and disease which the white man imported. The small-pox, measles and 'strong waters' have done the work of annihilation."

In regard to the name and language of these people we have an authority that is both older and better than of Mr. Quinney. "When I was but six

---
[1] If I were to write this name as I heard it spoken by Henry Sprague and wife,— the former a Munsee, the latter a grand-daughter of John Metoxen,— I should change the spelling by using, in the last syllable, *a* with the sound as in *arm*. For further remarks on this subject, see appendix, and also the author's monograph, "Muh-he-ka-ne-ok: a History of the Stockbridge Nation." To that booklet this chapter is, in part, purposely made supplementary.

[2] "At the place where this and the other country are nearly connected," says the legend as given in Miss Electa Jones's history of Stockbridge, Massachusetts.

[3] These quotations are from a Fourth of July speech made at Reidsville, New York, in 1854, by John W. Quinney (Waun-nau-con), of Stockbridge, Wisconsin.

years of age," wrote the younger Jonathan Edwards,[1] afterward president of Union college, "my father removed with his family to Stockbridge [Massachusetts], which at that time was inhabited by Indians almost solely; as there were in the town but twelve families of whites, or Anglo-Americans; and perhaps one hundred and fifty families of Indians. The Indians being the nearest neighbors, I constantly associated with them; their boys were my daily schoolmates and play-fellows. Out of my father's house I seldom heard any language spoken, beside the Indian. By these means I acquired the knowledge of that language, and a great facility in speaking it. It became more familiar to me than my mother tongue." "Both at this time, and in after life," says his grandson and biographer, Rev. Tryon Edwards, D. D., "he was so familiar with the Indian language that he often dreamed in it." President Edwards continues: "I knew the names of some things in Indian, which I did not know in English; even all my thoughts ran in Indian; and though the true pronunciation of the language is extremely difficult to all but themselves, they acknowledged that I had acquired it perfectly; which, as they said, never had been acquired before by any Anglo-American. * *

"When I was in my tenth year, my father sent me among the Six Nations, with a design that I should learn their language, and thus become qualified to be a missionary among them. But on account of the war with France, which then existed, I continued among them but about six months. Therefore the knowledge which I acquired of that language was but imperfect; and at this time[2] I retain so little of it, that I will not hazard any particular critical remarks on it. I may observe, however, that though the words of the two languages are totally different, yet their structure is, in some respects, analogous, particularly in the use of prefixes and suffixes.

"The language which is now the subject of observation is that of the Muhhekaneew or Stockbridge Indians. They, as well as the tribe at New London, are by the Anglo-Americans, called Mohegans, which is a corruption of Muhhekaneew, in the singular, or Muhhekaneok in the plural. This language is spoken by all the Indians throughout New England. Every tribe, as that of Stockbridge, that of Farmington, that of New London[3] etc. has a different dialect; but the language is radically the same. Mr. Eliot's translation of the Bible is in a particular dialect of this language. The dialect followed in these observations is that of Stockbridge. This language appears to be much more extensive than any other language in North America. The lan

---

[1] He was born 1745, May 26th. The above quotations are made from his treatise "Observations on the Language of the Muhhekaneew Indians," published at the request of the Connecticut Academy of Arts and Sciences.
In the Appleton Cyclopedia (first edition) the remark is made that this treatise "led Humboldt to say that if he [Edwards] had not been the greatest theologian, he would have been the greatest philologist of his age."

[2] The first edition of President Edwards's "Observations" etc. was probably issued in 1788. In the same year it was reprinted in England in connection with the famous sermon delivered by Occom at the hanging of Moses Paul.

[3] By this, Dr. Edwards doubtless meant the tribe whose chief settlement was at Mohegan, Occom's birthplace.

guages of the Delawares in Pennsylvania, of the Penobscots bordering on Nova Scotia [which then comprised what is now New Brunswick], of the Indians of St. Francis in Canada, of the Shawanese on the Ohio, and of the Chippewaus at the westward of Lake Huron, are all radically the same with the Mohegan. The same is said concerning the languages of the Ottawaus, Nanticooks, Munsees, Menomonees, Messitaugas, Saukies, Ottagaumies, Killistinoes, Nipegons, Winnebagoes[1] etc. That the languages of the several tribes in New England, of the Delawares and of Mr. Eliot's Bible, are radically the same with the Mohegan, I assert from my own knowledge."

Dr. Edwards then gives authorities,—"Captain Yoghum of the Stockbridge tribe, and Carver's Travels,"—for his other statements, and proceeds with his dissertation on the Mohegan language. And notwithstanding his caution, he remarks of "the Mohauk, which is the language of the Six Nations," that it "is entirely different from that of the Mohegans. There is no more appearance of a derivation of one of these last mentioned languages from the other, than there is of a derivation of either of them from the English. One obvious diversity, and in which the Mohauk is perhaps different from every other language, is that it is wholly destitute of labials; whereas the Mohegan abounds with labials." It is this fact, presumably, that enabled Eleazar Williams to write his native language with the use of only eleven letters of the English alphabet.[2]

Notwithstanding Mr. Quinney's implied statement, it was not from the Housatonic but from the Hudson, wherein, after their long legendary journey, the Muh-he-ka-ne-ok first saw on the Atlantic coast the ebbing and flowing of the tide, that they received their name "River Indians." Yet when the attention of the Anglo-Americans,— to use Dr. Edwards's happy term,— was first drawn to these people, their home was in the upper part of the valley of the Housatonic, and, therefore, in western Massachusetts.

It is in early years of the eighteenth century that these people come into some prominence in the history of the Massachusetts frontier. Some of them may have borne arms for the colonists in "Queen Anne's war,"— the one known in European history as the "war of the Spanish succession." If not then, they probably took the side of the Anglo-Americans in the Indian or, more correctly, the inter-colonial war that was "resumed" in 1722 and ended in 1725, when a "treaty" was made, ending a war that had really lasted about forty years. Whatever was the service and whenever rendered, we find that in May, 1734, two Muh-he-ka-ne-ew chiefs, Konkapot and Umpachene, received at Springfield from Governor Jonathan Belcher of Massachusetts commissions in the British colonial militia, Konkapot that of captain; Umpachene, of lieu-

---

[1] In this, as we have seen, Dr. Edwards was in error. This of course may be an incorrect inference of his own or, for aught I know, there may be a mis-statement in Carver's "Travels." It is not likely that Yoghum, " a principal Indian of the [Stockbridge] tribe," would know anything about the Winnebagoes.

[2] Wisconsin Historical Collections, volume VIII., page 350.

tenant. Konkapot's home was at Wnahtukook (Stockbridge); Umpachene's at Skatekook (now Sheffield). These places the Indians had reserved for themselves when, by deed dated 1724, April 25th (May 6th),[1] they made a sale of land to some white men to whom the right of purchase had been granted 1722 June 30th (July 11th), by act of the general court (legislature) of Massachusetts. These early settlers came into a wilderness unbroken save by a few clearings made—"under the grant of the Livingston manor,"[2]— by Dutchmen from New York, between which and Massachusetts the boundary line was yet undetermined.

Ebenezer Miller, a humble parishioner of Rev. Samuel Hopkins of West Springfield, learned that Konkapot and his people seemed ready to receive instruction in Christianity. This fact he made known to his pastor who interested in the matter Colonel John Stoddard of Northampton and the Rev. Dr. Stephen Williams[3] of Longmeadow. Desiring to establish a mission among the Muh-he-ka-ne-ok,— the "River Indians," as they were commonly called,— Mr. Hopkins and his associates applied for aid to a "Board of Indian Commissioners" in Boston.[4] Aid was promised. Now for the needed man.

He was ready. A New Jersey boy, John Sergeant, born at Newark in 1710, had the misfortune, as it seemed at the time, to cripple his left hand by a cut with a scythe. That he might earn a living in some other way than by manual labor, he was sent to Yale college. "He proceeded Bachelor of Arts, *September* 1729, and commenc'd Master 1732, before which he was elected Tutor of the College, in which he had his Education. In that Post he continu'd four Years, to the Satisfaction of those who repos'd in him that Trust, and to the Advantage of those who were under his Instruction.

"By this Time he was determin'd for the Work of the Ministry, and tho' he was well pleased with the Business he was now in, and stood as fair as any Man *whatever*, for a Call & Settlement in any, even the best Parish, that might become vacant; yet he preferred a *Mission* to the *Heathen:* not from any Views he could have of Worldly Advantage from thence, but from a pious, generous and ardent Desire of being an Instrument in the Hand of God of Good to the Indians, who were sunk below the Dignity of human Nature, and even to the lowest Degree of Ignorance and Barbarity.

"There was something very uncommon, and which seems to have been from above, in the Disposition and Inclination there was in him to this self-denying Service: For before there was any Prospect of his being imploy'd among the *Natives*, his tender Mind was so affected with the Tho'ts of their perishing State, that it had been his Practice, for a long Time, to make Daily

---

[1] The use of the Gregorian (new style) calendar was not legally established in England and her colonies until 1751. Then it was enacted that the day following the 2nd of September, 1752, should be accounted the 14th of that month.

[2] E. W. B. Canning.

[3] Son of Rev. John Williams, the "Redeemed Captive." The son was taken prisoner with the others of his father's family.

[4] An organization to be identified, probably, with that mentioned on page 69 as existing in New England.

an article in his secret Addresses to God, that he would send him to the *Heathen*, and make him an Instrument in *turning them from Darkness to Light*, &c. *God granted him that which he requested;* for which he returned his grateful Acknowledgments to *him who heareth Prayer*. And of these Things he inform'd Mr. *Woodbridge*, his Fellow-Labourer, at his first going to Housatunnuk; but strictly injoin'd him to keep them secret, which he accordingly did till since Mr. SERGEANT'S Death."

The above is from a book that was new one hundred fifty years ago: a biography of Sergeant and an account of his work among the Muh-he-ka-ne-ok, by Samuel Hopkins, who thus became the historian as he had been a founder of the mission. The few copies of the book that are left,—possibly not more than six in number,—are among the choicest possessions of the libraries in which they are found. The man of whom it was written deserved the eulogy of his biographer and won the prize most to be desired by the noblest ambition,—a place among those who have turned many to righteousness.

When Konkapot and Umpachene came to Springfield to be invested by Governor Belcher with the insignia denoting the rank of each in British service, they were met also by Messrs. Hopkins and Williams who had been asked by the commissioners in Boston to try to get the consent of the chiefs to the establishment of the proposed mission. These, like men of good sense, referred the matter to their people, by whom under Konkapot's leadership,—despite the opposition of traders who had been accustomed to furnish liquor to the Indians, —the desired consent was given at a four days' meeting beginning 8th (19th) July, 1734, in what is now the town of Great Barrington, Massachusetts.

The way for his coming being thus prepared, Sergeant, who was still engaged as tutor in Yale college, visited the people among whom he purposed soon to make his home. He was accompanied by one of the neighboring pastors, Rev. Nehemiah Bull of Westfield. On the day after their arrival, Sunday, the 13th (24th) of October, 1734, they gathered a congregation in which were about twenty adults. Then or soon thereafter, Mr. Sergeant's interpreter, Ebenezer Poohpoonuc, desired to be baptized. After what seems to have been a very thorough examination,—inasmuch as the candidate was brought to declare that he would rather burn in the fire than deny the truth,—Mr. Bull baptized him 18th (29th) October, at a meeting held in the wigwam of Lieutenant Umpachene at Skatekook. From this confession of faith and baptism of an Indian convert, the old church of Stockbridge, Massachusetts, counts the number of its years.

The mission was first established in what is now the town of Great Barrington. Here on the 21st October (1st November), was begun the erection of a building which was to serve for church and school. So rapidly was the work pushed forward that the school itself was opened on Tuesday, the 5th (16th) of November. Mr. Sergeant himself was the teacher. Think of the college tutor, who had been giving instruction to such men as Joseph Bellamy, Aaron Burr, afterwards president of the college of New Jersey (Princeton), and

James Lockwood who was once offered the presidency of Yale,— think of him thus teaching Indian children the very rudiments of book knowledge!

This work was soon interrupted by service in behalf of another people. From his own diary we have the story:

"Monday, *November* the 25th [6 December, 1734]. I went to *Albany*, being desir'd by the Ministers of the Country, to inquire after the disposition of the *Mohawks*, and the rest of the *Indians* in friendship with the English, towards the Christian Religion; carrying a letter from the Rev. Mr. *Williams* of *Hatfield*, to the Hon. *Philip Livingston*, Esq; to desire of him Information in that Matter. Mr. *Livingston* told me there was a Probability that the Protestant Religion might, if proper Means were us'd, be introduc'd among most of those Nations; and he looked upon it [as] absolutely necessary in Order to preserve the Trade with them, and keep them in Friendship with the *English;* for the *French* of *Canada* were very industrious to gain them over to their Interest; and that they have *Missionaries* among them, who came as near to their[1] Government as they dare; that the *Indians* are drawn off more or less, every Year to *Canada*. Much the same Account other Gentlemen gave me. Mr. *Barclay*, an ingenious and religious young Gentleman, has been about a Year and a half among the *Mohawks*, and is learning their language, and designs to get *Episcopal* Ordination, to be a *Missionary* among them, if the *Society for Propagating the Gospel in Foreign Parts* will support him. * *

"Upon my Return from *Albany*, (which was on Saturday November 30th) I found Mr. *Timothy Woodbridge*, a young Gentleman very well qualify'd for the Business, sent up here, to take Care of the *School*, and to instruct the *Indians* in a Catechetical Way, when I should return to my Business at *College*."

Soon began the contest that every faithful missionary to the Indians is obliged to carry on with those who sell them intoxicants. The Indians were exposed to the evil influences of certain Dutch traders from New York who were "very industrious to discourage the *Indians* from being *Christians*, thinking it would lessen their Trade with them, or at least they should not be under so good Advantages to cheat and impose upon them. For they make vast Profit by selling them *Rum*, and making Bargains with them when they are drunk; and Drunkenness is a vice the *Indians* are extremely addicted to. These Traders tell them, that the *Religion* we are about to teach them, is not a good one; that we design in the End to serve ourselves by them, to make Slaves of them and their Children, and the like. They also took Occasion, from the law there is in this Province, against private Persons selling the *Indians* strong Drink, to prejudice them against the *Government* and *People;* as though we were not their *Friends*."

With a little,— and very little,— change how modern and familiar all this sounds! Upon the ignorant Indians it produced at first much the same effect as like talk produces upon unthinking white men at the present day. In combating these influences, Mr. Sergeant did not at first propose total abstinence,

---

[1] Ambiguous. Perhaps Mr. Livingston said "our government."

—if he ever did,—but showed the Indians that the restrictions on the sale of liquor under Massachusetts law were designed for their benefit; "that the Traders doubtless were the Men that intended to make a Prey of them, and their Children. * * With what I said they seemed well satisfied; especially *Kunkapot;* for he saw thro' the design of the Traders. * *

"Then I asked them if they would let two of their Children go and live with me at *New-Haven* the Rest of the Winter; and they agreed that the *Captain's* only Son *Nungkawwat,* and the Lieutenant's oldest Son *Etowaukaum,* (who by the Way is Grandson by his Mother to *Etowaukaum,* Chief of the *River-Indians,* who was in England in Queen *Ann's* Reign) should be the Children. * * And the next Morning, Monday *December* the 9th [20th], we set out for *New-Haven,* leaving Mr. *Woodbridge* in the School."

Evidently Mr. Sergeant was not one of the so-called "Christians" who act as if they think that people can be saved while they are held off at arm's length. He writes: "*December* 14th [25th]. We got to *New-Haven.* I took the Boys into my own Chamber at *College,* and sent them to the free School. * * They lived very contentedly, were made much of by every Body; for indeed they were a couple of very likely Boys, especially the Lieutenant's Son."

In a letter to "*Adam Winthrop,* Esq;" secretary of the Board of Commissioners, Mr. Sergeant shows the spirit that makes lovers, enthusiasts, missionaries and martyrs: "'Tis no small Satisfaction to me that *your Honour,* with the Rest of the Honourable and Reverend *Commissioners,* are pleased to entertain a good Opinion of me. I have had the Approbation of my Conscience in the Business I have undertaken, nor have I been at all discontented. Thro' the Blessing of God, the Design has hitherto succeeded full to my Expectation, excepting that I have not had quite so many Auditors as I hop'd to have (there being generally about 30.) There has been about 25 Scholars in the School, besides some older ones who took some Pains to learn the Letters; but I suppose their Patience will hardly hold out to learn to read well. They have always treated me with Respect & Kindness, in their Way. The Children in the School, I think, were fond of me, and they all seemed to put great Confidence in me, and what I believe you will think a sufficient Evidence of it, is, I have brought a Way with me too little Boys. * * The Lads had a great mind to come with me. * * They are two very likely Lads, and if I do not judge amiss, the *Indian* Children excell the generality of ours, in Pregnancy of Parts and good Humor. I am sure I could not have found an *English* School, any where, that would have pleas'd me so much. Capt. *Kunkapot* is an excellent Man, and I do believe has the true *Spirit* of *Christianity* in him. * * I found them generally possest with the belief of One supreme Being, the Maker and Governor of all Things, and that they acknowledged the Difference between Moral Good and Evil; that God regards the Actions of Mankind, in order to reward or punish them, in some future State of Existence."

"It is a Custom among the *Indians*," says Mr. Hopkins, "not to proceed in any Affair of Importance, till they have the Consent of the *several Clans* belonging to their *Nation;* and the *Indians* at *Housatunnuk*, having proceeded so far without the general Consent of their *Brethren*, were much concern'd lest they should be frowned upon at the approaching Meeting; and the more so, because they had heard, that the *Indians* of *Hudson's* River highly resented their receiving a *Minister* and *School-Master*, before they had gain'd the Approbation of the Rest of their *Tribe;* yea, there was a report that a Design was on Foot to poison the *Captain* and *Lieutenant*, on that Account; as also, because they had received *Commissions* from his Excellency Governor Belcher. Whether there was any just Ground for these Reports, or whether they were set on Foot by the *Dutch Traders* to discourage the *Indians*, at *Housatunnuk*, I am not able to say. But however that was, the *Indians* were so affected with these flying Stories, that they sent desiring some of the Ministers of the *County* would come to them, and be present at their *general Meeting*.

Accordingly, *January* 15th 1734,5,[1] the Rev. Mr. *Stephen Williams* of *Springfield*, and I, accompany'd by *John Ashley*, Esq; of *Westfield*, went to *Housatunnuk*." They were successful, evidently, in winning the confidence of the Indians who, as Mr. Williams wrote, "gave us Encouragement that they would as a Nation submit to Instruction."

This following paragraph and the next are by Mr. Sergeant: "It happen'd as soon as this Meeting[2] was over, that several of our *Indians* were taken sick; and two Men seiz'd with a violent Fever, died suddenly. This, with the Apprehension they had before of Mischief, design'd by some of the other *Indians* that came from the neighboring Government [New York], put them into a great Fright; and made them suspect that those Persons were poison'd. Tho', I believe, the Suspicion was groundless. For it is so far from being strange to me, that some are sick after such a Frolick, that I rather wonder they don't half [of them] die. For their *Dancing* is a most laborious Exercise. They dance round a hot Fire, till they are almost ready to faint, and are wet with Sweat; and then run out, and, striping themselves naked, expose their Bodies to the cold Air, and, if there be Snow upon the Ground, roll in it till they are cold, and then return to their dancing again, and when they are hot, and tired,

---

[1] Though the change from "old style" to "new style" was made in Scotland in the year 1600, England did not adopt the Gregorian calendar until 1752. With this change came the substitution of January 1st for March 25th as the date of the beginning of the new year. For a time thereafter the custom was followed by many of writing the dates thus transferred from one year to that following with the number of each of the years as Mr. Williams does above. The January in which he made the visit that he is telling us about was reckoned, at the time, as part of 1734; when he published, it was considered as part of 1735. His reckoning of days is probably old style, but he makes an error,—for which Williams who kept a journal of their proceedings is perhaps responsible,—in saying that "the *Indians*, who were expected from *Hudson's River*, came not till Saturday, which was the 19th of the Month." It was the 18th or the 29th according as we use the Julian calendar or the Gregorian.

[2] Mr. Hopkins here inserts, in brackets, the words "Drinking and Frolicking always conclude such Meetings."

cool themselves in the same Manner, and, it may be, repeat this four or five Times in a Night; concluding the Frolick with excessive drinking. And when they are drunk, often fall asleep in the open Air, perhaps buried in Snow.

"This general Meeting happen'd in a very cold Season, and when there was a very deep Snow upon the Ground. And I never could learn that there was any certain symptom of poison. However, the *Indians* were persuaded they were poison'd, and concluded to apply to some *invisible Power* for the Discovery of the Murderers."

It is evident that this invisible power was to their minds most immediately represented by their "Priests or Pawwaws." At an effort to make the desired "discovery",—a performance given by some of these gentry,— Mr. Woodbridge was present, as were also some of the Indians to whom he was giving religious instruction. These being warned by their teacher not to take part in such heathenish performances, "resolved never to do so any more."[1]

"Mr. Sergeant goes on and observes, that the Indians used to have a high Opinion of these Pawwaws, (whose Character answers pretty well to the vulgar Notions of Wizards and Conjurers) and tell Stories of the great Feats which they can do. However, they confess they have no Power over Christians. And concludes with these Words. 'There may be something, for ought I know, in what they say: But I am apt to think, they are very much imposed upon by such kind of Pretenders, as the Rest of the ignorant Part of the World is.'"

Let us remember that the witchcraft horror at Salem occurred but eighteen years before Sergeant was born.

Mr. Woodbridge's school was broken up in February by the going of the Indian children into the woods with their parents to make maple sugar. This leads Mr. Hopkins to suggest that the white people apply themselves to the same form of industry. He takes the trouble to tell how the sugar is made, and adds that it is "of a very agreeable Taste, and is esteemed the most wholesome of any. It might doubtless be made in great Plenty; and, I can not but think, to the great Profit of the Undertakers."[2] We wish we had not taken the trouble to suggest how "excellent *Rum*," as he supposes, could be made from the sap, but the fact that he did so suggests how difficult must have been the struggle which, as we shall see, our poor Indians soon began against their greatest enemy.

Under date of May 6th (17th), 1735 Mr. Sergeant wrote: "Came Capt. *Kunkapot*, Lieut. *Umpachenee*, his brother *Johtohkuhkoonaut*, and *Ebenezer* [*Poopoonuc*], to *New-Haven*, to wait upon me up, and to carry the Boys back who had been with me all winter. *Johtohkuhkoonaut* had been a very vicious fellow, and a very bitter enemy to the *Gospel*; but a little before this he came

---

[1] Is it not a most hurtful thing that, even in our day, certain people, for the sake of what is to their vicious and vulgar taste an entertaining spectacle, encourage the Indians in these and like displays that connect the poor creatures with the demonism of the past and make worthless dancers and jugglers the centers of attraction and interest?

[2] "To the Indians we owe maple sugar and the as-ku-ta-squash,- in English, vine-apple."- Miss Jones's "History of Stockbridge." Doubtless, Mr. Hopkins's suggestion proved useful.

strangely about, and was much in Favour of the *Christian* Religion; undertook to learn to read, and made extraordinary Proficiency in it."

"I entertained these men with as much Respect, and Kindness, as I could; showed them our Library, and the Rarities of the College; with which they seemed to be well pleased; and behaved themselves while they were there, well, and with much Decency."

The little company set out from New Haven on the 8th (19th) "and got to *Housatunnuk* on the 10th, at Night." Mr. Sergeant's stay was limited by his duties at college to sixteen days during which time "he and Mr. Woodbridge both kept School; one at one Place, and the other at the other, each taking his Turn a Week at a Place;" for "the *Indians* were parted again from the School-House; and lived some of them at *Wnahtukook*, and some at *Skatekook*;[1] for at those Places they planted their Corn and Beans, which is all the Husbandry they carry on. For the rest of their Living they depend upon *Hunting*."

Of this second visit to his people, Mr. Sergeant wrote an account to one of the leading members of the "Board of Indian Commissioners," Rev. Benjamin Colman, D. D., of Boston. Of his admirable reply only parts can be given: "You are high in the Heart of Governor Belcher, and all the [other] Commissioners. I have read your letter to him, but our publick Affairs will not allow us a Meeting presently.   *   *   I have taken leave this Morning, to insert in a Letter to a Gentleman in *London* [Isaac Hollis], a Copy of your's to me. The Gentleman, three Years ago, press'd me to receive from his Hand a Security of *Twenty Pounds Sterling*, per Annum, for ever, for a fourth *Missionary* to the *Indians* on our Borders. But as I could not see that the other three were likely to benefit the *Papisted Indians*. I refused him; giving my reasons. But I have now shown him an *open and effectual Door* at *Housatunnuk*, and said all I can to fix him and his noble Charity on the Mission thither [there]. If the Gentleman (who will not yet let me name him) come into my Proposal, it will please me much, and make our Way easier. But, if this fail, I trust we shall be able to support the good Work of God, begun by you."

In a letter written many years later (1743, August 22d—31st), Dr. Colman tells of the answer that he received from Mr. Hollis:

"It was about the Year 1731, 2' that Mr. *Isaac Hollis*, (Nephew to *Thomas Hollis*, Esq; the great benefactor to *Harvard College*, and soon after his pious *Uncle's* Decease) sent me a *Hundred Pounds* Sterling, with his particular *Directions* how to distribute and lay it out.   *   *

"In the Year 1734, when he had seen a printed Account of the *Ordination* of Messieurs *Parker*, *Hinsdel* and *Secombe*, and their *Mission* to the *Indian Tribes* on the *Eastern* and *Western* Borders of *New-England*; Mr. *Hollis* then made me a most generous Offer of *twenty Pounds* Sterling *per Annum*,

---

[1] It will be remembered that the first school house built under Mr. Sergeant's auspices stood at an intermediate place; in the town,—and perhaps on or near the site of the village,—of Great Barrington which "anciently bore the name of Houssatonnock."

for Ever, for the Support of a *fourth Missionary*; but in Faithfulness I advised against such a Disposition of his Money. * *

"Within two Years after this, I heard of a very promising Door opening for the Gospel among the *Indian* Tribe at *Housatunnuk*; * * Whereupon I immediately let Mr. Hollis know, that now I could freely and earnestly advise him to fix his twenty Pounds Sterling per An. for the Support of this Mission:

"In Answer to this Motion, November 19, 1736, I received from Mr. *Hollis* his Bill on Col. *Wendell* to pay 56 *l* Sterl. for the Education of twelve *Indian* Boys at *Housatunnuk*, under the Care of the Rev. Mr. *Sergeant;* and Aug. 15, 1738, I had a second Order from him for 343 *l.* our Money; and again May 17, 1740, a third Order for 447 *l.* 9 *s.*: (Errors excepted)."

Dr. Colman's second letter anticipates a portion of our narrative. Accordingly we return to Mr. Hopkins's narrative:

"*July*, the 1st, 1735, Mr. SERGEANT (having dismissed his Class at College) left *New-Haven*, intending to spend the Rest of the Summer, and indeed of his Life, with the *Indians* at *Housatunnuk*, where he arrived on the 5th, and the next Sabbath preached to the *English*, there being no Interpreter present. And he, with Mr. *Woodbridge*, went on to keep the School, as before; one above, the other below,[1] changing Place every Week.

"Lord's-Day, July 13th. Preach'd to the *Indians*, few in Number:—No Man present except *Kunkapot*, who was very much affected, weeping almost all the Time. The Men were gone into *New-York* Government, to reap for the *Dutch* People there."[2]

"The *Indians*' reaping for the *Dutch* does not turn to their Advantage, (tho' it might, if they had Prudence to save their Wages) but proves a Snare to them. For (as Mr. SERGEANT observes in his Journal) when the Harvest is over, the *Indians* at *Hudson's-River* drink up all their Wages. But he had the Pleasure to hear that *Wnampee*, one of his Hearers, on this Occasion, overcame the Temptation, and told the *Indians*, at *Hudson's River*, plainly, that he design'd to go to Heaven, and therefore must leave off such Wickedness. But some of them, to his great Grief, did not come off so well. Neither is it to be wondered at, that Men, who for a long Course of Years, have addicted themselves to Excess, should be overcome, when such Temptations are laid before them by their Brethren, and urg'd on by others for the sake of Gain.

"The Pains some of the *Housatunnuk Indians* have taken to cure themselves of this ill Habit, has been very great. And some instances there have been of Persons among them, who, when strong Drink has been offered them, have refus'd to *taste* of it, giving this as a Reason, *viz.* that if they *once taste* it, they are in the utmost Danger of exceeding the Bounds of Temperance."

Was not this the first total abstinence movement in America? It does not

---

[1] That is, above and below what is now called Monument mountain; or, in other words, at Wnatukook and Skatekook.

[2] The foregoing paragraph is evidently from Mr. Sergeant's diary.

seem to have occurred to Dr. Hopkins to recommend to whites a course that he evidently regards as good for Indians. But we should not blame a man for not being in all things in advance of his age, and we must give the Doctor due credit for zeal in founding missions and interest in making maple sugar.

In this matter of temperance the Indians soon took a farther step. About the 7th (18th) of December, 1735, "the Indians agreed to have no trading in *Rum;* which they remained by." In 1739, apparently the autumn or early winter, Mr. Sergeant and others interested in the good of the Indians proposed to them "to restrain those among themselves, who were wont to make Gain by bringing Rum into the Place." This proposal "the well disposed *Indians* freely came into; and agreed upon a penalty of Forty Pounds *York* Money[1] to be laid upon those who should do it. Those also who kept Taverns in neighboring Places, and had sold Drink to such Indians as were given to Excess, they reproved, and endeavor'd to dissuade them from a Practice which prov'd so hurtful to the Indians. But some evil-minded Persons among the *English* and *Dutch*, made a Handle of those Things to disgust the *Indians;* telling them that this was an unreasonable Enroachment upon their Liberties; that they were us'd worse than *Slaves;* that they were treated as if they were *Dogs*, and the like."

The Indians at Stockbridge were, it may be, strengthened in their own temperance resolutions by learning the effect that had been produced by some advice that they had given to their kinsmen, the Shawanoes. Let Mr. Sergeant tell the story:

"*May* the 12. Came hither *Jeremy Aunauwauneekhheck*, lately return'd from the *Showwanoos*, who brought with him three *Belts* and a *String* of *Wompum*, with the following Messages, viz. [those with the belts have no special interest]:

"The String of *Wompum* brought an Answer to what our Indians sent to them some Time ago.

"'Brother, I thank you for your Word of Advice, you told me drinking was not good. I now leave it off, and you shall not find your Brother drunk again."

"The Messenger added, that they actually had made a Law against buying any Rum of the Traders, and had broken some Cags in which they had brought it to them, and spilt the Rum."

When Mr. Sergeant came to live among his people nothing was more necessary for their good than that they should be brought into one settlement. That this might be done, the "general court" (legislature) of Massachusetts,

---

[1] "York money," says Professor Arthur Latham Perry of Williams college, "was issued at an avowed discount of twenty-five per cent." The people who want "cheap money" and a "flexible currency" might read to their advantage the following paragraph:

"That charitable and generous gentleman, Mr. *Hollis*, had been at the Expence of about two *Hundred and eight Pounds* Sterling, in the Space of about four or five Years, for the benefit of the *Indians* at *Stockbridge*, which was then upwards of one *Thousand Pounds* our Money."

This statement Mr. Hopkins puts in his narrative of the events of 1742.

"early in 1736, granted the Indians a township which in April was laid out in an exact square, six miles in length and breadth. This included the present townships of Stockbridge and West Stockbridge."[1] It is worthy of especial mention that just titles held by white men[2] to a large portion of this land had to be purchased, and some white settlers had to be won to consent to their own removal thus to make place for Indians. If there is another instance like this in American history, save one of the same sort in behalf of some of Eliot's converts, it has not come to my knowledge. In dealing with her Indians, as in almost all other matters, Massachusetts has a most honorable record.

Within the tract thus provided for the Muh-he-ka-ne-ok was the place where Konkapot lived, " *Wnahtukook*, alias the Great-Meadow." This received the name of the English village of Stockbridge from some resemblance in the situation and appearance of the two places.[3] To this new home of the united clans came Umpachene and the other Indians whose home had been at Skatekook. Their lands there were given up in partial payment for the enlarged area at Wnatukook whereon it was designed to gather not only the Muh-he-kane-ok but also as many of other tribes as might choose the way of civilization and Christianity, and wish to remove thither.

"As to *the Situation of the Place where* Mr. SERGEANT *settled*," Mr. Hopkins gave his readers the following interesting information: " I observed before, that *Housatunnuk* is in the S. W. Corner of the *Massachusetts Province*, butting upon *Connecticut Colony* South, and upon *New-York Government* West. For tho' by Charter the *Massachusetts Province* extends West to the South Sea, and must therefore Butt upon the Gulf of *California* near the North Part of it, yet the *Dutch* being previously settled upon *Hudson's River*, cut this *Province* in two, and at present we inhabit no further West than to the *Dutch* Settlements. *Stockbridge* lies at the North End of what goes by the Name of *Housatunnuk.*   *   *

"And as for *the Condition of the Country round it;*—South, upon *Housatunnuk River*, it has lately been purchased of the *Indians*, and is settled by Inhabitants of this *Province*. The name of the Town is *Sheffield;* it is divided into two Parishes, in each of which there is a Minister settled. East of *Stockbridge* there is a Wilderness of about 40 Miles extent, which reaches to the English Settlements upon *Connecticut River;* it is Mountainous, and loaded with immense Quantities of Timber, of almost all Sorts,[4] West is a Wood of about 20 Miles extent, reaching to the *Dutch* Settlements in *New-York Government*. And North lies that *great and terrible Wilderness*, of several Hundred Miles extent, which reaches to *Canada*."

---

[1] "Historical Sketch," by Rev. David Dudley Field, D. D., in the manual of the (Congregational) church of Stockbridge, Massachusetts.

[2] See (page 76) account of grant and purchase.

[3] Or the name was given first and the resemblance discovered afterward. Stockbridge, England, is on the river Test and in Hampshire.

[4] In *Stockbridge* Bounds, and in the adjoining Wilderness, is found Plenty of that famous East India Root, *Gin Sang*. In Summer, 1751, it was first found.—Note by Mr. Hopkins.

"In the Beginning of *May* [1736], the [Muh-he-ka-ne-ok] Indians all settled in their new Town; were greatly pleased with it. 'They gave very much into Husbandry, (says Mr. Sergeant) planted more this Year than ever they did before, by three Times at least.'" Thus in a manner honorable to both white men and Indians was laid the foundation of Stockbridge.

At Deerfield, in 1735, Governor Belcher had met the Indians and there, August 31st (old style), Mr. Sergeant had been set apart to be their pastor.

"As an introduction to the Ordination, the Rev. Mr. *William Williams* of *Hatfield* made a speech to His Excellency the *Governor*, in which he took notice of God's inclining the hearts of some generous Persons in *Great-Britain*, by their charitable Donations, to seek the Salvation of the benighted Heathen; and of its being submitted to the Direction of an honourable *Corporation*[1] *there;* and that by them a Number of Honourable and Reverend *Commissioners* (of which His Excellency is at the Head) were here appointed for the same End; and of their having found a suitable Person for the Instruction of the *Indians,* of which those at *Housatunnuk* were desirous: And humbly asked, if it were His *Excellency's* Pleasure, that the Pastors then conven'd should proceed to set him a-part for that Work.

"To which His *Excellency* manifested his Approbation."

To do well the work of a bishop to which he was thus called and set apart, Mr. Sergeant applied himself to learning the language of his people. In this he made such progress that on the 18th (29th) of February, 1736, he used it in public prayer. He was then absent with his people who were on their annual sugar-making expedition. During or about April of this year "the honourable *Samuel Holden,* Esq; of *London,* directed the Rev. Dr. *Colman* to bestow *one Hundred Pounds* of his Money for the benefit of the *Indians* at *Stockbridge,* which Mr. SERGEANT, with Dr. *Colman's* Approbation, thought best to expend for the benefit of the *Females;* seeing Mr. *Hollis's* Donation was confined to the *Males.*"

On the 7th (18th) of August, 1737, Mr. Sergeant for the first time, preached to the Indians in their own tongue. He had previously translated into that language Watts's catechism for children, and also a marriage service. To these he added, in time, nearly all of the New Testament and a great part of the Old. What proportion of these translations passed out of manuscript into type, I do not know. It was probably small.

He did not confine his pastoral labors to Stockbridge. On the 11th (22nd) of September, 1737, he preached to the Indians at Kaunaumeek. "I had prepared a sermon in *Indian* for the Occasion. They heard me with great Attention, and said they understood me." Here in 1743, the illustrious David Brainerd began his missionary labors, and in the following year, by his advice, the Indians of Kaunaumeek removed to Stockbridge, and he himself sought more distant fields of labor among the Delaware and other Indians of Penn-

---

[1] Probably either the same society that aided Eliot or a successor to its funds and its work.

sylvania and New Jersey. In this he was carrying out a plan originated very probably by Mr. Sergeant who, three years before (1741), "according to his Purpose, set out on his Journey, accompanied by some of his *Indians* to the *Shawanoos, May* the 26th.¹ *June* 3d he arrived at *Sasquahannah. June* 7th he preach'd to the Indians living on *Delaware-River,* as he returned from Sasquahannah."

"I found," he wrote, "that they had strong and invincible Prejudices against Christianity, at least the Protestant Religion; derived, it would seem, from the *French,* and confirmed by their own Observation of the Behaviour of that vile Sort of Men the Traders, that go among them; for they said (which I believe is an unhappy and reproachful Truth) that they would lie, cheat, and debauch their Women, and even their Wives, if their Husbands were not at Home. They were further prejudiced against Christianity from the inhospitable Treatment they had sometimes met with from those who call themselves *Christians.* They said the *Sinnicas* (a tribe of *Indians* much under the Influence of the *French*) gave them their Country where they now live; but charged them withal never to receive Christianity from us.

"The *French* spread their influence far and wide, and indeed I believe (which I was not so much aware of before this Journey) that they have scatter'd their Poison among all the *Indians* of *North-America,* and have been the Means of stirring up that Jealousy and Suspicion among our *Indians,* which has made us so much Difficulty in dealing with them. * *

"When I returned to [the] *Delaware,* I got the Indians inhabiting there, together, and preached to them in our Dialect, which they could understand without an Interpreter. The whole Tribe is about 400 in Number; but is much dispersed, having no Accommodation of Land; but I have engaged some Gentlemen to endeavour to provide for them in that Respect; which, if it can be effected to their Satisfaction, there is hopeful Prospect of a successful Mission among them."

But no plan of Mr. Sergeant's has had wider or better influence than that of the boarding-school that he founded, which in many respects anticipated the methods of the institutions at Hampton and Carlisle. "I began to keep the 12 *Indian* Boys on Mr. *Hollis's* Foundation. I took them into my own House, and under my own Instruction." Thus he wrote 1737, January 11th (22nd). Soon other labors compelled him to find homes in English families for as many of these boys as could be persuaded to leave Stockbridge. The others stayed at home, were clothed by Mr. Hollis's bounty, and attended the school taught by Mr. Woodbridge.

It was on the 4th (15th) of June, 1738, that Mr. Sergeant first celebrated with his people the sacrament of the Lord's supper. There were eleven Indian communicants. On Thanksgiving day, 1739, November 29th (December 10th), the little congregation worshiped for the first time in a meeting-house

---

¹ "I found the Place about 220 Miles distant from us, about 50 from any *English* Inhabitants, and the Road to it exceeding difficult."

built for them by the colonial government.¹ The site of this old bethel,— house of God,— is now marked by a memorial tower erected by the late eminent lawyer, David Dudley Field, whose father was for many years the pastor of the Stockbridge church.

Soon the new meeting-house contained an interesting audience. On the 20th (31st) of January, 1740, Mr. Sergeant "preached to a large Auditory, consisting of many Strangers, who were gathered together here with a Design to promote, and confirm, a League of Neutrality among the several Tribes of *Indians* in *North-America*, in case there should be a War between *England* & *France*, which was then expected. This Tribe had, about two Months before, receiv'd a *Message*, which then came directly from the *Scattekooks*, which imported that the *French* and *English Mohawks* had already consented to stand Neuter. And this *Tribe* were now desired to come into the Projection. They therefore prepared three Belts of Wompum, with distinct Messages to each."

The first of these messages is a reminder of former and continued friendship. The second is decidedly practical, and has a suggestion of grim humor:

"*Brother at* Wtanshekaunhtukko. *By this we may know we are Brethren, because we have one Father in Heaven, the Lord of all. Let us have a tender Regard to our Families. The white People, with whom we respectively live in Alliance, are about to enter into a War. We only destroy ourselves by medling with their Wars. They are great and strong, and reach to the Clouds.*

"*Let us sit and look on when they engage. Don't let any of your People assist in their Wars. And while they fight, let us sit and smoke together.*

"*Therefore three of your Brethren send you this Message, from the Highlands,* Mohekun, *and* Skatekook.²

Third belt:

"*Brother at* Naunauchoowuk.³ *Though you had begun a War with the English, you would regard us, if we should desire you to leave off. You will without Doubt not intermeddle if we insist upon it. May be, the English think the Indians prevent their conquering their Enemies the French; therefore let us sit and smoke together, and see who will be Conquerers.*"

"A very just and rational Scheme this," says Mr. Hopkins, "and, had it succeeded, would have been much to the Advantage of the *Indians*, as well as to us. But there is little or no Prospect of such a Neutrality taking Place, so long as the *French* have such an Ascendent over many of them."

Thus amid wars and rumors of wars, Mr. Sergeant pursued his work.

---

¹ In Puritan and correct usage the "meeting-house" is the place where, in a special sense, God meets man,— not simply, as some ignorantly think, where men meet each other. Compare the expression "Tent of Meeting," as used in the Revised Version of the Old Testament.

² That is, three tribes, not three individuals. The Indians carefully preserved the traditions of tribal relationship. It will be remembered that when the Muh-ho-ka-ne-ok came to what is now Wisconsin that our Menomonees recognized them as "grandfathers."

³ "The same I suppose which is generally in *New England*, call'd *Norridgewock*," says Mr. Sergeant.

Upon petition of the Indians themselves, the general court, May session, 1739, ordered that the tribal land be divided to them in severalty. At the beginning of the Stockbridge settlement a few white families had been brought in to settle among the Indians to be, in a measure, models of industry and right living. The number of white families gradually increased after the Indians had power to sell their land, and thus most of the tribe were dispossessed of their former homes. The change was wrought in the generation that succeeded the first settlers,— those of 1736 and the next few years thereafter.

But Mr. Sergeant did not live to see it. Indefatigable in labor he established the Indian boarding-school on broader foundations, planned for a like institution for girls at Stockbridge and had it in mind to go among the Mohawks to try to persuade them to send thither some of their children. In this design, he had reason to expect aid from Mr. Barclay who still continued his missionary labors among the Mohawks but was also chaplain "in the King's Garrison at *Albany*, and oblige'd to spend half his Time there, 40 Miles distant from them."

But these two friends were not to meet again on earth. Mr. Sergeant was taken from his people 1749, July 27th (August 7th), in the thirty-ninth year of his age. He was one of the men who make it easy to believe in God.

The record of his work makes us wonder that he lived as long as he did. "He was obliged to compose four Sermons every Week, two for the *English* and two for the *Indians;* his Congregation consisting of both. Those he prepared for the *Indians*, he first wrote at large in English, and then translated into the Indian Tongue, as he did also a Portion of Scripture to be read to the *Indians* on the Sabbath; and notwithstanding he had so many Sermons to make, they were well studied excellent Discourses. * *

"He had a most laborious Task to perform every Lord's-Day. His Manner was to begin the Publick Exercise in the Morning, with a short pathetic Prayer for a Blessing on the Word, in both languages. Then he read a Portion of Scripture, with explanatory Notes and Observations, on such Passages as seemed most to need them, in both. All his publick Prayers and the Communion Service were in both Languages; and it was his steady Practice to preach four Sermons every Lord's-Day, two to the *English* and two to the *Indians;* except in the short Days and cold Season of the Winter he preached but three, one to the *English* and two to the *Indians*. And besides all this, it was his constant Custom, in the Summer Season, to spend about an Hour with the *Indians*, after Divine Service was over in the Afternoon; instructing, exhorting, warning and cautioning of them in a free, familiar and pathetic Manner in their own Tongue. The *Indian* Language['s] abounding in Gutturals renders the Pronunciation of it a most laborious Exercise to the Lungs; that, therefore, with his other Exercises, so exhausted Mr. SERGEANT'S Spirits and Strength, that he was scarcely able to speak when they were over."[1]

---

[1] The wonder is that the poor man could speak at all. Here is the first paragraph of his

Mr. Sergeant left three children, one of whom was the grandmother of the late President Hopkins of Williams college, an institution that bears the name and perpetuates the memory of Mrs. Sergeant's brother. One of the three, an unconscious babe bearing the father's name, was destined, in the providence of God, to continue his father's work among that father's people, and a John Sergeant of the third generation was to accompany them to new homes within what is now Wisconsin.

A pity it is that they ever had to leave the old one. There about the time of Mr. Sergeant's death they had come to number two hundred eighteen in fifty-three families. Mr. Sergeant had baptized one hundred eighty-two, of whom one twenty-nine were living. Forty-two were communicants. One of the deacons of the church was an Indian, Peter Pau-quau-nau-peet. The village school (attended by both whites and Indians until 1760) had at this time an enrollment of fifty-five. Living in peace and good-will with their Indian neighbors were twelve families of whites.

The boarding-school, then under charge of a Captain Martin Kellogg, had made an interesting history. In 1743 (August 1st, old style) Mr. Sergeant stated his plan at some length to Dr. Colman of Boston, by whom public attention was called to the matter and considerable interest aroused on both sides of the Atlantic. "Thomas Coram, gentleman;" of London, who, as his " humble Petition [to the Prince of Wales] most humbly showeth, * * in the Reigns of King William, and Queen Anne transacted Affairs of Commerce in His Majesty's Plantations, in North America, where he resided many Years," became so much interested as to attempt to secure subscriptions for the work. Through Rev. Dr. Francis Ayscough, "Clerk of the Closet and first Chaplain" to the father of King George III., Frederick, Prince of Wales, Captain Coram was able to present his petition for aid in the undertaking to his royal highness. The response was a gift of twenty guineas. An equal sum was given by the Prince's brother, the Duke of Cumberland, victor at Culloden. Other titled persons also gave, and a man better than the whole of them put together, good old Dr. Watts, the hymn-writer, sent; though perhaps not at this time, as a gift made by himself and friends, not less than £ 70.

But Captain Coram received a rebuff from a "certain Gentleman and

---

" Prayer before Sermon:"

" Oe Taupaunnumeauk Pohtumınauwaus, maukhkenun, quauwauntam, wonk, knoi Keyuh keshehtouwaunoop wauweh ohquauekeh, wonk kaukhhunnouwauntuminun mauweh ohquoiekeh. Keyuh kesheh keyaukoop kruppauntummuh neen nhokkaunaun. Konomptumnuh mauweh oquoiekeh. Quauwehtaunuh neen ndohnaun oinenaunquokh, waunehk pshooq ktohchoowauntum, kshekenummun ne mautchk."

The " Morning Prayer,"— perhaps the one whose first use is mentioned on page 86,—presents an appearance even more formidable. Here follow the first two sentences:

" Oe Keuh maukhkenun Pohtummouwaus, Keuk kesheh touwunnoop ne spummuk wonk no Hkeek. Ktinneh weenwumnoohhannuh pnouwenaunuh ne spummuk woocheh; Kuttummaukaunummenaunuh, nwauwehtaunaunuh ktaupeh aum eshtoh, kuttumınaukaunummuhannuh, ktaupeh aum ommuchehoonnoohhannuh, ndinnahtannaunuh yhokkaunaun waucheh aum taupeh mummukhhuhwenouwuhheauk hannummeweh ne mtantowenauk tanneh, neek ndauhunaunk mummutsoowuh mautchk pshooq uhwauntummauk neen ndoinoienaunaun, maumutihkeh neen shekenummunneh kuhnuh kmaumucheh annehhoonhannuh."

Lady" who in some way were greatly affronted at something the worthy captain, with no thought of offense, had done or failed to do. And thus the amateur soliciting agency came to an end. Perhaps, however, it helped prepare the way for Occom's later and more successful mission.

But the school,— regarding it as an outgrowth of the work supported by Mr. Hollis,[1] — was continued, and in 1748 a building still standing, was put up for it at Stockbridge. After the dispersion already mentioned, the recipients of his bounty were a second time brought together, and were put under the care of Captain Kellogg, of Newington, Connecticut. Teacher and pupils, at Mr. Sergeant's request, came to Stockbridge in April, 1749, and, it would seem from the narrative, remained there.

After Mr. Sergeant's death the position of missionary among the Muh-he-ka-ne-ok was offered to Rev. Samuel Hopkins of Great Barrington, nephew of the historian of the mission. Destined himself to be one of the world's great teachers of unselfishness, he declined the offered position, with its larger salary, in favor of his friend and instructor Jonathan Edwards, who was installed pastor at Stockbridge, 1751, August 8th (19th). To him the comparative retirement of the Indian mission gave opportunity for the production of some of his greatest works, among them the famous treatise on the "Freedom of the Will."

A wonderful command this man must have had over himself thus to give his mind to metaphysical subtilities in the midst of the alarms of war. In the preceding struggle, commonly called "King George's war," Mr. Sergeant had written (1744, July 2nd, or 13th), "We are situated upon the Borders of the *Massachusetts Province*, open to the *French* Settlements, and in the Road where the *French* and *Indians* us'd to make their Irruptions. My House is garrison'd; a Number of Soldiers are sent into the Town." Nor was the danger soon over. We find entries like these among others in the diary of the younger Hopkins: "November 22 [1745]. Some time after midnight there came a man to my lodgings, and cried out with all earnestness, saying that Stockbridge was beset and taken by the Indians. But the report was false. This day the most of my people moved off into forts. * * Tuesday, August 26 (September 7th) 1746. The Indians killed five men and a girl at Deerfield yesterday. * * Sunday, September 28 (October 9th). Have been strongly urged to go into the woods with a scout of a hundred men. Stockbridge, Monday, September 29. Came here to-day from home with the design to go in the scout if Mr. Sergeant should advise to it, and with his advice have concluded to set out with them. September 30. Set out in the afternoon with a scout of one hundred white men and nineteen Indians."

Though this narrative belongs to the time of Mr. Sergeant, yet it serves here a double office as showing the dangers,— described not less vividly by the same pen,— that, in the French and Indian war, surrounded Mr. Edwards. He was urged to seek a place of greater safety than Stockbridge. But as his

---

[1] In 1747 (January 27th) Mr. Hollis agreed to support twelve more "*Heathen* boys;" a total of twenty-four. All were to be of heathen parentage.

flock, not less than himself, were in danger, he refused to leave them pastorless.

His people were steadfast friends of the colonists and the English. Almost every man among them, capable of bearing arms, went with Governor Shirley in 1755 on his expedition against Niagara. They rendered most efficient service. For the protection of the settlers of western Massachusetts, the little Indian settlement at Stockbridge was better than a fort.

Another source of anxiety Mr. Edwards had, greater, probably, than that occasioned by the war. One of his parishioners,— Ephraim Williams,[1] we are sorry to say,— sought to secure the management of the Indian boarding-school and to make it,— and in this he was partly successful,— the opportunity of pecuniary gain to himself and to what in modern parlance would be called a "ring." The school had been, in some measure, successful. Sergeant "being dead yet spoke" with the persuasiveness of his holy purpose, and some of the Mohawks moved by his invitations and those of his people, had removed to Stockbridge. Of these new-comers, there were in the winter of 1750-51, "about ninety."

Apparently, however, Mr. Kellogg did not give satisfaction as master of what I am inclined to call the industrial rather than than the boarding-school.[2] Probably, also, Williams was then busy with his knavish schemes. This, however, is merely an inference from the following statement, condensed from an English edition of President Edwards's works:[3]

On Tuesday, 13th,(24th) August, 1751, the chiefs of the Mohawks came from their two principal settlements to Stockbridge, and met there the "commissioners of the province,"— representatives, probably, of the board of Indian commissioners at Boston. The chiefs expressed a very strong desire that their children should be educated, but objected to removal to Stockbridge on the ground that the affairs of the Mohawks there were left in the utmost confusion, that no regular school was established, and no thorough means taken for the education of their children. The commissioners agreed to get another man in place of Kellogg, and the chiefs agreed to send their children to the school. The council seems to have been in session for a full week, or even more. In reporting its proceedings to Hon. Thomas Hubbard, speaker of the Massachusetts House of Representatives, Mr. Edwards spoke of the agreement to encourage the education of the children of the Mohawks,— who evidently had a special interest (shared by the Oneidas and some of the Tuscaroras), in the advantages thus offered to all of the Six Nations, whose friendship, in the then

---

[1] His was one of the first four white families that settled in Stockbridge. These, as already stated, were to be models and exemplars to their Indian neighbors. This Williams must not be confounded with his son of the same name, the founder of Williams college.

[2] And should be more inclined to do so had not the word been almost spoiled by the silly sentimentalists who have succeeded in getting it applied to the state homes for the correction of young hoodlums who need, in about equal proportions, the bath-tub, the Westminster catechism, and the activity of a good hickory switch.

[3] The American edition that I have at hand,— that published in four volumes by Leavitt & Allen in 1843, seems to be expurgated as far as this matter is concerned. There seems to be no sufficient reason for its suppression now, and no one can be harmed by knowing what it was that brought to naught much of the best planning and work of Sergeant and of Edwards.

existing crisis, it was most necessary to secure. Mr. Edwards mentioned the hostile movements of the French in the West, recited their " machinations to seduce the Six Nations from the English interest," and pointed out the "religious and literary instruction" of the Indians as the only means of securing their attachment to the British cause, and detailed the measures necessary to be pursued at Stockbridge to promote these great objects.

To do the enlarged and better work promised by the commissioners they employed as Kellogg's successor, a graduate of Yale college, Gideon Hawley, of the class of 1749. He came to Stockbridge, 1752, February 5th (16th). His work there seems for the most part to have been among "Mohawks, Oneidas and Tuscaroras from Kanajohary and Onohoghwage." To the kindred of these people, Iroquois in New York, he paid a visit in September, 1752. Apparently he determined to establish a mission among them. His leaving Stockbridge may have been occasioned by the mischievous conduct of Williams who "took on arrogant airs, renewed his quarrel with Mr. Woodbridge, went into the boarding-school * * and, usurping its direction, conducted himself in such a manner as to disgust the Oneida parents, who removed their children and returned to New York."

Mr. Canning who tells us of these evil deeds and the natural consequence thereof, does not give the year of their occurence, nor that of the commissioners' summons to Mr. Edwards to meet them in Boston,— an opportunity which he used to such good purpose that the schemes of Williams and his accomplices were subverted. Soon thereafter the chief mischief-maker removed from Stockbridge. But the school had been hurt beyond remedy. The Oneidas refused to return, "the Mohawks lingered a little longer and then left also."

These events seem to have led to the final breaking-up of the institution for which Mr. Sergeant so long labored and prayed. Again,—perhaps on account of the war,—boys were sent from Stockbridge to be taught. Thus, writing to Mr. Edwards under date of 31st May, 1756, the famous theologian of Bethlem, Connecticut, Joseph Bellamy, makes report concerning some Indian boys in his own family.

The troubles mentioned above continued, doubtless, through several years. Some of them, it may be, occurred in 1754 or even later. However, Mr. Hawley's second departure for New York took place on "Tuesday, May 22nd, 1753,[1] when Mr. Woodbridge, myself and company set out from Stockbridge for the Indian country. Our departure upon so great an errand as the planting of Christianity in the wilderness about a hundred miles beyond any settlement of Christian people drew the attention of the whole town. And the Rev. Mr. Edwards, his wife and others accompanied us a considerable distance into the woods toward Kinderhook." The end of their journey seems to have been "Onohquaga"[2] on the Susquehanna (now Windsor, eastward from Binghamton).

These men found among the Indians a wish for a prohibitory liquor-law.

---

[1] It is interesting to notice that Mr. Hawley here uses the new-style mode of reckoning.
[2] Probably the "Onohoghwage" named above.

Mr. Woodbridge represents[1] Indians as desiring to say to the governor, "My brother, I would have you tell the great men at Albany, Skenectetee and Skohary not to bring us any more rum."

Mr. Hawley's stay in New York could not have been a long one. "I was ordained in the Old South meeting-house (Boston) 31st July, 1754." Immediately thereafter he removed again to Stockbridge.

Then may have occurred the conflict described above. Let that be as it may, Mr. Hawley, starting in April, 1755, and taking with him Mr. Edwards's son Jonathan, returned to "Oughquauga,[2] by way of Canajoharie. Owing to the distractions and dangers of war their stay there was but a short one, and Mr. Hawley became "chaplain in the army marching against Crown Point."[3]

How great was the influence that in all these and other ways went from the mission established among the Muh-he-ka-ne-ok, a people who were to aid in laying the foundations of civilization in Wisconsin, no one can measure.[4] The Christianization of the Mohawks was, no doubt, effected in part, at Stockbridge.[5] Sergeant, Edwards and Hawley opened the way for Occom and Kirkland. Thus of the churches existing among our own Oneidas at the present time the foundation was really laid in old Stockbridge. Not in vain did Sergeant find a home and a grave among a once barbarous people, not in vain was Hawley driven into a more distant wilderness. Now we know why it was good

---

[1] In a letter to Governor Sir William Johnson, dated at Albany, 1753, June 20th. "Schonectady" and "Skoharie" are forms more familiar to us than those used by Mr. Woodbridge.

[2] Probably the "Onohoghwage" named above.

[3] In a "narrative" enclosed in a letter by Major General Charles Lee, dated 1758, September 16th, we have reference to service by Iroquois,—among whom Sir William Johnson was then the great leader,—and Stockbridges in behalf of the British and the colonists:

"On the 5th of July we embarked on Lake George with an army of Fifteen thousand men, consisting of 9 thousand Provincials, 5000 Regulars & 1000 Rangers, all in perfect health & spirits.

"We here took one Prisoner, who informed us that the Enemy had near four thousand Regulars at Tikenderoga, very few Canadians & no Indians. The same morning we moved on in Columns thro' the wood towards the Fort.

"(July 6th) Our troops were numerous & in vast spirits. both men and officers the French by all appearances in the extreamest confusion and panick. They without a single Indian, We with a most formidable body, for at this place we were joined by four hundred of the choicest warriors of the six nations (a greater number than ever we cou'd assemble together before) we had likewise one hundred choice Stockbridge Indians."

[4] "Such was the influence of this mission upon other tribes that the French Papists of Canada, while they sedulously shut out the light from their own countrymen were compelled to open schools for the Indians to prevent their secession to the English."—Miss Electa Jones's biographical notice of Konkapot.

No doubt, Miss Jones wrote from a somewhat prejudiced point of view. However, it is well known that the Roman Catholic church bestirs herself in the matter of popular education chiefly when it is evident that if she do not take some action of the sort the children of her homes will attend schools which priests can not control.

[5] It will be remembered that missionaries from England had labored among the Mohawks, and that they were much under the influence of Sir William Johnson. Hence it is not a matter of surprise that they espoused the cause of the British as against the colonists in the Revolution. Thus it was that they lost their possessions in New York. It is to the honor of Great Britain that she does not forget those who have done her service, and the Mohawks were provided for in what is now Ontario. Joseph Brant (Thayendanegea) was then their leader.

The familiar name of these people is derived from the name "Mahaquas" given them by the Algonquians. Another name,—perhaps the one in their own speech,—is Agmegue, or Gagmegue, derived, it may be, from a word that signifies "she-bear."

that, among men of his own race, Edwards lost parish and popularity and was put into the seclusion of a frontier hamlet of Indians. There he did the work that has enrolled his name in the short list of the world's most profound thinkers, and won for him the presidency of one of America's greatest colleges. By a council that took action 1758, January 4th, he was advised to accept the call to Princeton. On the Sunday before (January 1st) he had preached from the text "This year thou shalt die." The foreboding was literally fulfilled in his own person. Scarcely had he assumed the duties of the presidency when, March 22nd, there came to him the end of life.

His successor at Stockbridge, Stephen West, afterward doctor of divinity, —that title had meaning then,— was "introduced to the town" or, what is the same thing, to the parish,—the two were then, in Massachusetts, merely the civil and religious aspects of the same institution,—in November, 1758, and was ordained on the 13th of the following June. There were then, says Dr. Field, "about twenty log huts in Pittsfield [Massachusetts]; but with that exception the whole country northward was a wilderness to Canada. To the West there were some Dutch settlements near the Hudson and on the Mohawk; but westward, there were no English settlements quite onward to the Pacific ocean, and but few French settlements and those distant from each other. Wild men and wild beasts held dominion over almost the whole of this vast region." Stockbridge still continued to be part of the frontier.

But there the wilderness did not master the colonist.[1] The emigrant thither found the Christian home, the church and the school. The persuasiveness of the white man's money made peaceful conquest of Indians' land. Soon the Arabian story of the camel that got his nose into the tent, found in the case of the Muh-he-ka-ne-ok another application. The white population of Stockbridge became more numerous than the Indian. The old church divided into two congregations, and John Sergeant, the younger, assumed the pastoral charge of his father's people. He could speak their language,—a thing President Edwards and Dr. West never learned to do.[2]

At the beginning of the ministry of the younger Sergeant to the Stockbridges, they were called upon to take up arms, for the fourth time, in support of the colonists. Of all causes that have combined to harm the Muh-he-ka-ne-ew "nation," it is probable that no other was so hurtful as the Revolutionary war. Bingham's "Columbian Orator" preserves a speech made by one of their chiefs to the Massachusetts legislature in offering to the colonists the services of his people. On the 30th of June of this same year (1775) letters and speeches from the Stockbridge Indians were laid before Congress and read. The committee on Indian affairs was directed to prepare "proper talks" to the different tribes of Indians. It was also resolved "that the securing and preserving the friendship of the Indian nations appears to be a subject of the ut-

[1] Expression adapted from Professor Turner's "Significance of the Frontier in American History."
[2] The English edition,—already referred to,—of Edwards's works states that Sergeant had expressed the opinion that his successor would better not attempt this task.

most moment to the colonies." In the memorable year 1776, August 7th, Washington wrote to Timothy Edwards, then commissioner for Indian affairs, on the subject of employing the Stockbridges in the service of the United States. Some of them "fought through all the war, threaded the wilderness with Arnold to Canada, aided in compelling the surrender of Burgoyne and made the Jersey campaigns with Washington." "The Stockbridges," says the British Lieutenant-Colonel John Graves Simcoe,[1] writing of an affair in which more than thirty of them lost their lives, "about sixty in number, excellent marksmen, had just joined Mr. Washington's army." They were under command of one of their number, Daniel (or Abraham) Ninham, who fell with his men. This skirmish or, rather, slaughter, took place 1778, August 31st, near White Plains, New York, where "Mr." Washington was then commanding. A large proportion of their most promising young men were killed in battle.[2] Perhaps the tribe has never recovered from losses of men, homes and character then suffered. We should remember this if we are inclined to think of its present condition almost with contempt. Nor should we forget that too often then, as in later years, drunkenness was made easy for them. At the close of the war, apparently after the warriors had returned home, a barbecue was prepared for them by command of Washington. Whisky was furnished, we are sorry to add, even though their pastor presided at one of the tables. This suggestion of what camp and social life then was, prepares us for the sorrowful statement that many of those who survived the dangers of war fell victims to the habits of idleness and intemperance. In these ways many got into debt to their white neighbors and lost their lands.

So the tribe sought a new home. They removed to a tract of land in New York,[3] part of which is now in Madison county and part in Oneida. Hither they came at the invitation of the Oneidas, whom, it is said, they had once saved from a powerful enemy. This place,—a tract six miles square,— was secured to them, perhaps, when, 1774, October 4th, the Oneidas gave land to those who afterward took the name of Brothertowns. More likely, however, the gift to the Stockbridges was made in 1783. Be this as it may, the Muh-he-

---

[1] Afterwards first governor of Upper Canada, now Ontario.
[2] In the catalogue of the portrait gallery, belonging to our Wisconsin state historical society, we find the following:
"98. Moshuebee.
"A very aged woman of the Stockbridge tribe who died about 1867, supposed to have been one hundred and twenty-five years of age. She is said to have had three sons engaged in the Revolutionary war, one of whom lost his life in the service, and she was a camp-follower of the patriot army."
Unfortunately the catalogue does not tell who indulged the supposition concerning the woman's age, nor who made the statement about her sons.
[3] Some, who must ultimately have been absorbed into other tribes, had found, at an earlier time, another home. Mr. Sergeant (the father) tells the story in a letter to Thomas Coram; a letter dated at Stockbridge, 1747, January 22d (February 2nd):
"Our Number increases from time to time by the Addition of new Families, especially of those who are kindly dispos'd to Christianity. It is probable, we should have had more of them before now, if there had not come some *Moravian* Preachers among some of them near to us. I do not pretend to so much Acquaintance with that Sort of People, as to pass any positive Judgment about them; the converts they have made, are, I think, Enthusiastick &

ka-ne-ok who did not remove to New York until after the Revolution. Then the little band of ninety, with whom the elder Sergeant began his missionary labor, had increased to four hundred[1] or four hundred twenty.[2] A very few remained at Stockbridge, the home once so carefully provided for them, but kept for less than half a century.

Near where Kirkland had so long taught and preached, nearer the place where Hamilton college was to be built, and nearer yet to the settlement of the Brothertowns, the Muh-he-ka-ne-ok built New Stockbridge.[3] Little enough, we may fear, did they have to bring with them, and apparently there had been a division of sentiment as to whether they should go at all. The years 1783 and 1788, mark, probably, the beginning and virtually the end of the emigration. The greater portion of the tribe made the removal, we have reason to think, in 1785. For in that year, according to the good custom followed more than once in New England history, a church,— of sixteen members,— was organized of those purposing to become settlers in the new town.

Mr. Sergeant made what, after this lapse of time, seems to be the mistake of not going with the emigrants of 1785. The next year when he did go he found, it would seem, that Samson Occom was ministering to his people, and had gained favor with many of them. Then followed, as we have seen, the organization of a church composed in part of Brothertowns, in part of Stockbridges,— the one which in 1787, November 28th and 29th, called Mr. Occom to its pastorate.[4] To this office he could not have given his full time until 1789. The united parish had "two places of worship, one in Brothertown at David Fowler's and the other in Stockbridge at Hendrick Aupaumut's or Captain Hendrick, as he was usually called. This relation continued to Occom's death, the Stockbridgers going to Fowler's and the Brothertowns to Hendrick's on alternate Sundays."[5] Meanwhile Mr. Sergeant "regularly spent six months yearly"[6] with the people of New Stockbridge. Let us hope that he and Oc-

---

Bigotted. They have rendered themselves so much suspected in the Governments of *New-York* and *Connecticut*, that they would not tolerate them within their Bounds. They refused to take the Oath of Allegiance to *King George*, or even the Quakers['] solemn Declaration. What was the meaning of this I can not tell. They drew off a number of *Indians* from these Parts, and some from this Place to *Pennsylvania*."

"Enthusiastic," as then used, commonly bore the meaning of "visionary" or "fanatical." It is very likely that some of the Moravians of that time, excellent people as they were, did measurably possess that characteristic. Such was the case certainly with the earlier Quakers.

"Mr. Sergeant was no *Bigot*," says Mr. Hopkins, "but of a most *generous & catholick* Temper. *Bigottry* was what he had a great Aversion to; and he was far from the rigged and narrow Spirit those are of, who confine Salvation to themselves, with those who think just as they do."

[1] According to Mr. Canning.
[2] The number given by a local historian as of those who removed to New York.
[3] The "New" has been dropped from the name, and it is now simply "Stockbridge." The little village is in Madison county.

In the town where the Muh-he-ka-ne-ok made their settlement there was born, 1836, October 10th, to a Methodist clergyman, a son, William Dempster Hoard, lately governor of Wisconsin, and more honored in his defeat in 1890 than two years before in his election.

[4] See page 70, where, unfortunately, the year of the "call," 1787, is omitted.
[5] Rev. William De Loss Love, Jr.
[6] Dr. Field.

com each made his work supplementary to that of the other. After Occom's death the church to which he had ministered passed out of existence, and the Stockbridge branch of it united with their brethren of the older church that was formed before the tribe left Massachusetts.

During their stay in New York, the Muh-he-ka-ne-ok and the Brothertowns seem to have become regarded, through union with the Oneidas, as part of the "Six Nations." "In accordance with your views [I] estimate the Stockbridges as a part of the Six Nations," says Commissioner T. H. Crawford in a report approved 1843, February 3rd, by John C. Spencer, secretary of war. Iroquois and Stockbridge delegates together visited President Washington in 1792, that, in the words, probably, of his message of invitation, "measures might be concerted to impart such of the blessings of civilization as might suit their condition."

As was the case years later in nascent Wisconsin, so when central New York was receiving its first strong current of emigration, the mission among the Muh-he-ka-ne-ok was a fountain whence flowed the water of life to surrounding communities. One narrative of many that might doubtless be given is found in the history of the (Congregational for seventy years, now Presbyterian) church of Clinton, New York, the spiritual home in successive years of so many hundreds of the students of Hamilton college.

Here we may stop to note the fact that this region "was originally granted by the mother country to the colonies of New England. The conflicting claims of New York and Massachusetts to this territory were settled by the grant of pre-emption right, on the part of New York, to the state of Massachusetts. This pre-emption right was purchased of Massachusetts by New England men, Messrs. Phelps and Gorham;[1] and by them the Indian title to a large portion of the soil was extinguished; so that it was at an early day advertised and offered for sale in New England. * * Hence, most of the early settlers of this region were New Englanders, and brought with them their New England preferences."[2] Thus it came naturally to pass that before there was time to put even a roof on the home in which they met, the first settlers of Clinton gathered for the public worship of God.[3] Such men as these are the ones who found communities that are worth living in.

"Only occasionally was Clinton, during 1787-88, visited by a clergyman. Samuel Kirkland was at Oneida. John Sergeant was with the Stockbridge Indians over the West Hills. Now and then these brethren came to Clinton and preached to the people. Sometimes, too, they had the privilege of hearing that famous Indian preacher, Rev. Samson Occom, whose gifts and eloquence were not inferior to [those of] any of his white brethren." When the church of Clinton was organized (August, 1791) the younger President Edwards presided at the service, and John Sergeant and Samuel Kirkland were members of

---

[1] This was the origin of the Holland, later the Ogden, land company. See note 4, page 60.
[2] "Congregational Quarterly," volume I., page 152.
[3] 1787, April 8th. One year, lacking a day, before the settlement of Marietta.

the council that, on the 18th of September, 1793, helped to install its first pastor.

We come now in our narrative to the "journal of John Sergeant, the missionary to the Stockbridge Indians, living in the vicinity of Oneida, from the society for Propagating Christian Knowledge in Scotland, from the 22nd of November, 1793, to " And the place was left blank forever. Had he been endowed with prophetic vision he might have written "1824, September 7th."[1] For then this labor and his life ended together.

The society from which Mr. Sergeant derived the support that the Indians were unable to give is still extant, and has its headquarters in Edinburgh. A letter of interest and inquiry from its president, George Drummond, Esq., was answered by the elder Sergeant 1741, April 29th (May 10th), and on the 23rd of the following June (July 4th) he made report to Mr. Drummond in regard to his visit to the Delawares and "Showanoos."[2] Two years later Dr. Colman sought to secure a portion of the society's beneficence for the industrial school at "Housatunnuk."[3] To neither school nor mission came anything from that source during Mr. Sergeant's life-time.[4] But said society was the chief support of Mr. Edwards during his residence at Stockbridge. It continued to aid the Stockbridge church in supporting Dr. West until its help was needed in providing a stipend for the younger Sergeant. This was withheld during the Revolutionary war, but, at the close thereof, arrearages thus incurred were paid, according to the honorable customs of our British brethren. This society continued to give some aid to the Stockbridge mission until the withdrawal therefrom of Rev. Cutting Marsh in 1848.

Again we turn to Mr. Sergeant's diary, and reproduce some of the more significant portions:[5]

"November 22nd. 1793.—This day set out to visit my people at New Stockbridge." Perhaps he uses the term "visit" because his home was still at Stockbridge, Massachusetts, whence he did not remove to the field of his pastoral labor until 1796.

"24th, Lord's Day.— Intended to preach this day at Guy Park (so called), where I arrived last evening, but being sick put up at an inn.

"25th.— Continued my journey; the roads very bad.

"28th.— Arrived at New Stockbridge.

---

[1] Yet it is probable that had he filled the blank it would have been with the last date in this particular portion of his journal,—1794, February 9th.

[2] See page 87.

[3] He tells of this in his letter of 22nd (31st) August, 1743.

[4] This seems to be a safe inference from the following remark by Mr. Hopkins: " I find no Return he [Mr. Sergeant] ever had from Mr. *Drummond*, or any other Member of that Society, nor any further Correspondence with it; except a letter Mr. SERGEANT wrote to the *President*, for the Time, of that *Society* of *May* the 18th 1749, desiring, if it fell within their sphere, that they would assist in promoting the *Boarding-School*, then begun at *Stockbridge*. Whether Mr. Sergeant's Letter fail'd by the way, or what else happened to prevent a friendly Correspondence, I am not able to say."

[5] Certain contractions used by Mr. Sergeant might perplex many readers. Accordingly for the purposes of our narrative it seemed best to treat his manuscript as he himself would have wished to do had he been preparing it for the press. A transcript of the original can be found in the library of the state historical society.

"December 1st, Lord's Day.— Preached from Acts III. 19. From these words endeavored to show the nature of repentance and conversion.

"2nd.— This day went to Oneida to visit Mr. Caulking who, I understood, was about to leave the place and business because he had no school house provided for him. I visited some of the chiefs, exhorted them to make provision for the school. They encouraged me they would attend to it.

"5th.— This day my people agreed to set apart as a day of public thanksgiving. Accordingly we met at 12 o'clock at the church where I exhorted them to the duties of the day by repeating to my hearers the many reasons they had for devoting this day to praise and thankfulness. Mentioned among other things that God had not forsaken them, but continued the gospel among them. That it was owing to the goodness of God that they had advanced in religion and a civilized life far beyond their ancestors, &c.

"After the assembly was dismissed I was invited to dine with a part of the tribe who were collected at one house, where a table was spread sufficient to accommodate about thirty or forty persons. We were served with puddings, boiled meats and a variety of pies. Our drink was good, wholesome spring water. After dinner our chief in a long address to the company, among other things, said: 'My friends, we have reason to be thankful that we have, through the goodness of God, been carried through all the trials that we have experienced the year past, that we are brought to see this happy day, that we have now been allowed to sit together in love and peace, and partake of the bounties of heaven; that in eating food we might have obtained [it] from white people, our neighbors, which was our state of dependence in the country where we came from, but we have now been fed by such things as we have obtained by the labor of our own hands; this is matter of thankfulness.'

"The provisions that were left were given to the old and poor who went away rejoicing.

"8th, Lord's Day, A. M.— Concluded my subject from Acts III. 19. [In the afternoon] after I had dismissed my people [I] delivered a short discourse to the Tuscaroras and Oneidas present.[1]

"14th.— This morning sent for to visit one of the strangers who lately came from the westward[2] with Cant Nendrol,[3] found her very sick,— let a little blood, since have heard she is a little recovered.

---

[1] Mr. Sergeant's constant spelling is "Oniedas and Tuskaroras."

[2] I think it very likely that these "strangers from the westward" were Munsees. This little tribe is a branch of the Delawares (Leni-Lennappes). The Munsees seem to have been scattered in consequence of having taken sides against the colonists in the American Revolution. From homes in New York, Canada and perhaps Indiana and elsewhere, some came in later years to Wisconsin, where they have united with the Stockbridges.

From Brown's "History of Missions" we have the following most uncomplimentary reference to the Munsees:

"While several of the Indian tribes joined either with the English or the Americans, and committed the most shocking outrages on their enemies, the chiefs of the Delaware nation, determined to maintain a strict neutrality. The Monsys, indeed, one of the Delaware tribes secretly resolved to separate from the body of the nation, and to join the Mingoes, a gang of thieves and murderers."

[3] The best reading that I can make of a very poorly written name.

"17th.— This day visited another of the strangers who came from the westward, a widow with four children. I asked her many questions upon the subject of religion; told me she had never heard preaching in her life, but would attend the next Lord's Day.

"This day also several of our young men returned from hunting."

But probably at no time during their life in New York were the Stockbridges dependent upon hunting for their means of living. It must have been soon after their removal thither that they divided the tribal land so that each family had its particular possession but, probably, without the right of disposing of it to any one outside of the tribe.

"20th.— This day evening a conference meeting at my house at which I gave my hearers an exhortation upon the nature of religion. That it consisted much in humility. For any one to commend himself and speak much in his own praise was a sign of spiritual pride. There having been some separate Baptists in town the day before from Brothertown (so called)[1] and preached up their sentiments, I thought proper to explain some passages of Scripture with a design to show [the] folly of some of their doctrines. After this many questions were asked and answered.

"22nd, Lord's Day, A. M.— Read and expounded upon that passage of that Scripture recorded in Matthew XVIII. from the first to the sixth verse, in which I endeavored to hold up the doctrine of humility.

"P. M. Took my text from the seventh verse of this chapter. After meeting, a number of the Tuscaroras and some Oneida chiefs came in to see me; when I repeated my sermon to them by an interpreter. They appeared to go away rejoicing that they had heard the word of God.

"27th.— This evening a conference meeting, at which several questions were asked, (viz.); If any one entertains revengeful feelings toward his neighbor, whether it is not, in the sight of God, murder? Answer: In a degree.

"29th, P. M.— Preached from Psalm XXXVII. 37. From thence endeavored to prove the future happy state and condition of the righteous.

"After I had dismissed my people, repeated my subject to the Tuscaroras by an interpreter.

"January 10th.— A conference meeting at which several questions were asked, (viz.): What is the reason Indians always come so short — they appear for a while to prosper in spiritual concerns and their temporal, and then fall into a state of poverty? Answer: That it arises in a great measure from the

---

[1] It will be remembered that Brothertown was then a place of sharp contention. Probably,— such is the weakness of human nature and the wickedness of sectarianism,— the division extended to church matters also. Without this, it is not likely that Occom would have been driven from his home to New Stockbridge,— which, as we have reason to believe, was virtually the case.

Of course we can not now tell whether or not Mr. Sergeant was justified in his somewhat severe remarks. But I am free to say that I don't like them. The presumption is certainly against any who intrude upon mission work among an unstable people, whether the intruders are " separate " Baptists,— whatever they are or were,— or, as is quite as commonly the case, bear some other name. And "separatism" of the kind suggested though too often found in the church is yet oftener found outside of all churches.

prejudices of their education from their childhood, contracting bad habits, &c. Question: What was the occasion that Christ after his resurrection repeatedly asked Peter whether he loved him? Answer: It was likely meant as a gentle reproof for his bold declaration of attachment to his person at the time he was taken the evening before his crucifixion. Question, by a woman: Is it their duty to meet together by themselves for prayer to implore the divine interposition in a time of great darkness and inattention to religion? Answer: It is no doubt an important duty.

"19th, Lord's Day.— Read and expounded on the XV. chapter [of] Matthew from the 1st to the 3rd verses. After I had dismissed my people, preached by an interpreter to a considerable number of the Tuscaroras and Oneidas present.

"25th.— This day an Oneida chief came to my house with a number of young people, and informed me that he was sent with a young man and woman to request me to join them together in marriage. After examining the relations on both sides,— found no objection could arise, — I performed the ceremony. After this I instructed them into the duties of the marriage relation, &c. The chief thanked me for my instructions, and said he would use his influence to enforce my instructions upon that young married pair, that they never may lose this pleasant path of friendship which you have just marked out to them.

"26th. Lord's Day.— Forbade the young people the practice of hollowing nights. Also announced the sacrament of the Lord's supper to be administered here the next Lord's day. Spoke by an interpreter to the Tuskaries and Oneidas as usual.

"31st.— Attended a sacramental lecture.

"February 1st.— About twenty of the Oneidas came to my house with a desire that I should marry a couple of young people. After I had performed the ceremony agreeably to desire, I instructed the young people into the nature and importance of the marriage covenant. The parents thanked me and promised to enforce my instructions when they returned to their habitation.

" 2nd, A. M.— Baptized two children and administered the Lord's supper. Before I dismissed the assembly, invited all the men who had any concern about their own souls, and wished for a reformation, would [to] meet at my house for prayer; the women to meet at another house for the same purpose. In the evening all the principal men in town came, to the number of fifteen or twenty. We spent the evening in prayer and conversation. All agreed to use their utmost influence to restrain the young people from every bad practice.

"I understood the women universally met and made two or three prayers. Agreed to use their utmost influence also to reform the young women in particular. I thought both meetings were tokens for good.

"Note.— Since I solemnly warned the young people of the bad, heathenish practice of hollowing, &c., out [on] the streets nights, have this satisfaction that it appears to be entirely dropped.

"7th.— This day set out agreeably to invitation and promise to visit the

Tuscaroras and Oneidas, and preach the following Sabbath at the Oneida Town.

"Held a conference meeting on my way with the Tuscaroras about noon. Thence proceeded with my friend Cushik for an interpreter towards Oneida. Called at the first village, about ten houses. The people gathered at one house, when I endeavored to set before them the importance of religion. They appeared to be very attentive, and thanked me on parting. Then we proceeded on. I visited two other houses. Night coming on, I put up at [the home of] Shonandon, a worthy Oneida chief. We spent the evening in agreeable conversation upon religion. He thanked me that I was so kind to begin this friendly visit; [said] that I was heartily welcome to his house. Note: This man has a numerous family, very industrious, raises all kinds of grain, has a good number of horses, cows, hogs, &c., owns a sleigh and wagon. Understood the last year he raised nearly one hundred bushels of wheat. We had a supper of tea, good wheat bread and butter. Cushik returned home this evening. But as all the young men who understood English and [whom I] had heretofore made use of as interpreters were not in town, and without an interpreter I should lose the usefulness of my visit, I requested him to return the next day and tarry with me till after the Sabbath, and I would request the society at Boston to give him something for his time and service, to which he agreed.

"8th.— Saturday noon Cushik returned. We then proceeded on our visit. Called to see the widow of the famous Indian known by the name of Good Peter.[1] She received me with the greatest possible tokens of joy, told me they were all asleep as to religion; had heard no preaching for three months. I proposed a conference meeting in the evening, to which she heartily agreed. I had time to visit but eight houses more, two where there were sick with whom I conversed freely. Prayed with the sick. In the evening put up at [the home of] one Seuranis (?), a very good family who came from Ohnaquango and [are] members of Mr. Crasbury's[2] church. Here we held our conference meeting.

"9th, Lord's Day.— A full meeting, house about twenty feet square. Many stood at the door and windows, could not get into the house. I preached from the same words I had lately done to my people, viz., O that they were wise, that they understood this, that they would consider their latter end.

"At the conclusion of my sermon observed that they had told me they longed for the constant instruction of God's word, that their church affairs might be regulated, that they might enjoy the privilege of the sacrament of the Lord's supper, that a reformation might take place in their town, that a stop might be put to excessive drinking and polygamy,[3] that if they really desired these things they must pray for them, that God expected his children would cry for spiritual blessing. I then exhorted them to meet in prayer once a week

---

[1] "'Good Peter,' catechist and teacher, and the most eloquent man among the Six Nations, was Mr. Kirkland's assistant."—Miss Electa Jones.

[2] Or "Crasburg's."

[3] This reading is in accord with a suggestion made by Secretary Thwaites. Whatever the word, it is probably misspelled, and is really indecipherable.

for these blessings. After this, baptized a child. After the assembly was dismissed a number, both men and women, took me by the hand, thanked me for my advice [to] them, [and promised] that they would set apart certain seasons for prayer, agreeably to my advice, &c.

"Before I left the house, one of the chiefs desired me to inform the society that although Mr. Caulking had left them through their neglect, yet they hoped the society would not think they rejected this great gift, that they should early in the spring erect a school house and call the master back. For they considered a good school in their own town to be much more beneficial to them than to send only a few of their children to be taught in a school among the white people. Note: They sent a sleigh with me about half-way. [I] returned home before dark; my people came in. I then gave them a particular account of my proceedings. We spent the evening in religious conversation and prayer for the outpouring of God's Spirit. The women also met this evening for the same purpose."

This report of the work of a winter that passed a century ago would probably serve, except in mere date and detail, for the service done in many another season.

The supposition to which reference has been made, that, while in New York, the Stockbridge tribe was considered as forming part of the Iroquois confederacy seems to be strengthened by the fact that on the 11th of November, 1794, when the United States government made a treaty with the "Six Nations" the Stockbridges also were made a party thereto, and received a proportionate share of annuities paid out of the national treasury.[1]

At Stockbridge, Massachusetts, there was published, in 1795, doubtless under Mr. Sergeant's auspices, a little manual of religious instruction containing two catechisms: the one commonly called "shorter,"—merely by comparison with another, also put forth by the Westminster assembly,—and one for children, by that good old bachelor, Dr. Watts. On page 31 of this little pamphlet, the printed matter ends with the words: "The foregoing is Printed in the Moheakunnuk or Stockbridge Indian language." There may have been an earlier edition, though I doubt it. These translations were doubtless made by the elder Sergeant and his assistant,—perhaps John Quinney, whose son, as we have seen, was made chief of the tribe in 1777.

In 1796 Mr. Sergeant and his people had a visit from Dr. Jedidiah Morse, then one of the trustees of the still existing (Boston) "Society for Propagating the Gospel among the Indians."[2] At that time the population of New Stockbridge was about three hundred, a number soon increased. None were professed pagans, though only about thirty were members of the church. About two-thirds

---

[1] Under this treaty they continued to receive gifts or payments until 1830, inclusive. These varied in different years, being commonly $350 but sinking in 1827, 1828, and 1829 to $261. Payments on this account were made as lately as 1836 and 1842.

[2] The organization, in 1787, of this society, which now co operates with the American Missionary Association, is one of the evidences of the vitality of our churches in that unhappy time.

of the men and nine-tenths of the women were considered industrious. In this year a white man was convicted of bringing liquor into the "nation," an act contrary to tribal law. Soon after, through Mr. Sergeant's influence, the legislature of New York passed an act forbidding the sale of liquor to these Indians. For his action in this matter the worthy pastor was bitterly persecuted. A term, "white heathen," which he uses more than once, probably acquired vivid significance at this time. His people were tempted and ill-treated. While Indians sought to keep the Sabbath, white men violated it. Articles would be pressed upon the Indians in the way of sale, and later those who supposed themselves to be honest purchasers would be arrested as thieves and the possession of what they had bought would be used as evidence against them. It may be, as old President Dwight of Yale states in his journal of "Travels," in a letter that gives account of a journey begun 1798, September 16th: "The body of them have, in many respects, sustained a very imperfect character." Yet, when we remember the good man's high standard of character, and read his other statement, that "several of them have been eminent for their understanding and more for their piety," we do not doubt that they compared favorably with their white neighbors.

Several other of Dr. Dwight's remarks give information in regard to matters that have already interested us: "At the last interview which I had with Mr. Sergeant he informed me that his own people were increasing [in number]; not by accumulations from other tribes, but in the ordinary course of population." This was not the case during the life-time of his father, as the elder Sergeant himself tells us. Of Brothertown, President Dwight says that those who came thither had been resident chiefly in Montauk and Farmington, and were in number about one hundred fifty. He is lead to speak of the possessions of the Holland land company. These are in the states of New York and Pennsylvania, he tells us, and in area equal Connecticut.

The missionary spirit that we have seen in Mr. Sergeant's service to neighboring tribes must have communicated itself to his people, for in 1802 we find them sending a delegation to the Delawares, whom, after an Indian fashion, they called their grandfathers, and to some other tribes, to urge them to receive the gospel. Of this Mr. Sergeant writes:

"A council was held at Wappecommehkoke on the banks of the White river [Indiana], by Delawares and the delegates of the Moheakunnuk nation. The former then accepted all the proposals made by the latter, among which was civilization, of which, said the chief (Tatepahqseet)[1] 'we take hold with both hands.'"

Poor Tatepahqseet! He was then an old man doomed to perish soon and in a most barbarous manner. In February, 1806, a Shawano witch-finder came

[1] Spelled Tettepachsit in Brown's "History of Missions." This orthography, it is probable, comes to us through the narratives of the Moravian missionaries, and these were Germans. In some respects, the German alphabet is a better medium than the English for the transliteration of Indian words.
In the narrative given in Brown's "History" we find mention of "Woapikamikunk." It is safe, I suppose, to identify this with Mr. Sergeant's "Wappecommehkoke."

among his people. This villainous heathen accused the poor old man of dealing in poisons. Accordingly he was bound to two posts and his accusers began to roast him over a slow fire. Unable to stand the torture he was driven to say that he kept poison in the house of a Christian Indian, named Joshua. But when the latter was seized and brought to him Tatepahqsect acknowledged that the charge was false and was made only to escape torture. To make the dismal story as short as possible, the heathens murdered both, throwing the unhappy chief on the fire before life was extinct, and also burning to death a Christian woman. These ferocities led to the breaking up of a Moravian mission that had been established in the neighborhood.

In June, 1806, Mr. Sergeant visited the Onondagas. In reply to his address one of their chiefs "said that they designed to follow his advice, to cease from working on the Sabbath, to meet together to worship God, to labor diligently on their lands * * and to abandon the use of spirituous liquors." * * The narrative from which this is taken[1] thus continues (but without date): "There appears some prospect of the establishment of a school, the introduction of Christianity and the progress of the arts of civilization, among some of the western tribes by means of several of the Stockbridge Indians who have been sent to settle among them for these important purposes."

The foregoing statement may refer to the beginning of the movement by which, in time, the entire tribe was transferred from New York. At the time of the visit of the Stockbridges to President Washington in 1792, one of the delegation, Captain Hendrick (Aupaumut), was chosen by Major-General Henry Knox, secretary of war, to go on a mission to the western tribes. Hendrick had been a soldier in the Revolutionary war, was present at the surrender of Burgoyne and, it is said, had received from Washington himself a commission as captain.

The time of his first service in the West was that between the terrible defeat of the Americans under St. Clair (1791, November 4th) and the victory of "Mad" Anthony Wayne (1794, August 20th).

The success with which Hendrick discharged the duties of his mission to the West shows that Mr. Kirkland (by whom he was brought to the notice of the secretary) did not overrate the abilities and fidelity of the Stockbridge chief. He was one of the most effective opponents of Tecumseh and his brother Elskwatawa, the "prophet," in their great scheme of organizing an Indian confederacy designed to crush American power in the West. By his advice and exertions the Delawares and others were kept aloof from this mischievous scheme. He took personal part in the war in which Major-General William Henry Harrison won the military reputation, that, in 1840, helped make him President of the United States.

Soon came the war of 1812, and in this also Hendrick, with others of his people, took the part of the United States against Great Britain.

No doubt this war, like that of the Revolution, was an injury to the Stock-

---

[1] Brown's "History of Missions," I., 90.

bridge "nation." Probably, also, it prevented their getting a home on the White river. Before what we may call the Tecumseh war began, Hendrick had formed the plan of leading his people to a new home in the West. More than a century before, the Miamis had given land there to the Muh-he-ka-ne-ok, and, at some time, to the Delawares also. Settlements of these people in the White river region numbered, in 1818, about eight hundred souls. The title of the Stockbridges to what was probably part of the Miami grant, was, in a carefully guarded manner, attested by President Jefferson 1808, December 21st. In this transaction Hendrick was the representative of his people. In 1810 he and his son Abner were in the White river country and purposed to settle there. There is good authority for saying that it was Captain Hendrick who "formed the plan of collecting all the eastern Indians in that region, where they might live in peace with the whites, and in fellowship with each other and, he hoped, be no farther wasted."[1] We have seen how this project was interrupted.

But though it remained in abeyance during the war and for some years thereafter it was not forgotten. But in the spring of 1817 the Stockbridges were made uneasy by the report that the land to which they had a claim, had been sold by the Delawares. But these, in answer to a letter of inquiry, denied the charge, adding: "When we rise in the morning, we have our eyes fixed toward the way you are to come, in expectation of seeing you coming to sit down by us as a nation."

Accordingly, some of the Stockbridges prepared for removal. Two or three families went that year. In June, 1818, Mr. Sergeant thus wrote to Dr. Morse: "About five families of my people will start for White river in three weeks. But they are still troubled by reports that the state government of Indiana intends to purchase the Indian lands."

Others were added to the number of those proposing to emigrate. Mr. Sergeant collected the whole tribe on Friday, 24th of July, of that year, "with the view to have them present at the forming of a church from their tribe" of those "who, with a number of others of the tribe, were about to remove and form a new settlement. According to a good Puritan custom, a church was organized of those who were preparing to make the removal. In the following December Mr. Sergeant wrote: "The families left in August, consisting of a third part of my church-members, and a quarter part of the tribes,— in all from sixty to seventy souls from Oneida." The "tribes" are doubtless the Stockbridges and Munsees. None of the Oneidas, so far as I know, removed to Indiana, and the agitation among them by Eleazar Williams in favor of emigration westward had scarcely then begun. Yet this movement of the Stockbridges could hardly be without effect upon their neighbors.

But between the two there was this great difference. The Stockbridges had left the land of their fathers, and were in a country that to them had scarcely ceased to be new and strange. One removal often prepares the way

---

[1] Miss Electa Jones.

for another. But the Oneidas and the other Iroquois were in their ancestral home. Among these, the persuasions of Eleazar Williams produced, outside of his own congregation, little effect; opposed, as they were, by the pagan faith that still prevailed among the majority of the Iroquois, and by the influence of their proud tribal traditions. Moreover, they had land enough, and that by no one's gift. But, among the Stockbridges, it would seem that all the influences favored removal. Hendrick (Aupaumut) had formed the plan, it is said, as far back as 1809. In favor of it, there seems to have been a feeling virtually unanimous. For this, there were many reasons. Notwithstanding the worthiness of perhaps a decided majority of the white settlers in the surrounding community, men of the evil class that is always to be found about Indian reservations were doing mischief and bringing corruption. No doubt, the then late war had increased the tendency to drunkenness. At the same time, the Muh-he-ka-ne-ok's faithful service therein had made the United States government desirous of using them in the West as a barrier against barbarous and hostile tribes. The state government of New York was more than willing to have them go. Their Brothertown neighbors were ready for removal. Both of these little tribes would find Algonquian kindred in the West; their Iroquois neighbors in New York were of alien speech and blood. Among the Delawares or Menomonees the little Stockbridge church could do a service that was impossible in New York. No doubt there was a genuine missionary spirit in Mr. Sergeant's flock, and he believed that in sending his people forth into the wilderness he was sending teachers of civilization and Christianity.

Thus was made the beginning of a movement that was to add many pages of exceeding interest to the history of Wisconsin.[1]

---

[1] The excerpts from the diary of the elder Sergeant, from the letters of Dr. Colman, and other documents of that time, are chiefly if not wholly from Hopkins's "Historical Memoirs." In whatever has been taken from that source, there has been an attempt to follow the peculiarities in the usage of the printers of a century and a half ago, except in regard to the use of catch words and an antique style of type. Certain failures to observe this rule should be noted: On page 82, the name "Woodbridge" appears in Roman when it should be in italic; and, on page 83, the name "Sergeant" (in the extract from Dr. Colman's letter) is in italic when it should be in small capitals. On page 85 the words "alias the Great Meadow" should be in parentheses, and on 89 the "e" in "oblige'd" is superfluous.

The punctuation of Mr. Hopkins's most interesting book is not only of a sort now obsolete,— as, for example, the semi-colon after "Esq;"— but shows some manifest omissions. These I have not felt it my duty to supply nor has it been deemed best even to correct one or two evident errors of orthography.

The portion of the younger Sergeant's diary herewith given, has, so far as I know, never before appeared in print. For the use of it, and for other favors, I am indebted to his granddaughter, Mrs. Mary E. Niles, of Trumansburg, New York. It will interest many to know that the late Henry Sergeant West, M. D., missionary physician of the American Board in Asiatic Turkey was a brother of Mrs. Niles, and that a daughter of that good lady, Mary West Niles, M. D., is a medical missionary in Canton, China.

Some doubtful readings in Mr. Sergeant's diary are marked, and it may be that more should have been. "Cushik" may be "Cusik," or even "Cussick." In certain places where Mr. Sergeant says that "several questions were asked" there has been given only the one that seemed of special interest.

Mr. E. W. B. Canning (Williams college, class of '34) to whom I owe much in the way both of impulse and information, died 1890, August 11th. He was a church clerk who appreciated the importance and dignity of his office.

To the Rev. Professor Arthur Latham Perry, D. D., LL. D. I owe thanks for special favors.

CHAPTER X.

STATESBURG AND STOCKBRIDGE.

Before the westward bound party of the Muh-he-ka-ne-ok could reach their destination they heard that the land upon which they were intending to settle had been bought by the United States government.[1] "What deception somewhere!" exclaims Dr. Morse in mentioning this transaction, and contrasting it with the rights claimed by the Stockbridges and the assurances held out to them before beginning their journey. But the Delawares who had given the invitation could not prevent the sale even of their own homes and another grief was added to the long catalogue of their sorrows. From the time of the visit of the elder Sergeant, their history and that of the Moravian missions, so closely connected with it, is one of shame to almost every one who is mentioned therein, save the Christian Indians and their gentle teachers whom Sergeant misunderstood rather than misjudged. Yet it seems to be true that these too often acted as if the command to be wise as serpents were not as much a divine requirement as the one that bids us be harmless as doves. It is pleasant to know that their work and that of Sergeant had blended together even in the little company of Muh-he-ka-ne-ew emigrants from New York whose leader, John Metoxen, had been educated in a Moravian school at Bethlehem, Pennsylvania.[2]

On hearing of the loss of the land some of the company turned back, but Metoxen and others, perhaps forty in number, pushed on. We trace their course, in part, by notices concerning their little church. "In May, 1819, James McCockle wrote to Mr. Sergeant from Piqua, Ohio, saying that the papers of the church-members had been received at that place with cordiality, and a communion service appointed on their account. The pastor of the Piqua church[3] frequently preached to them. They had spent the winter in that vicin-

---

[1] By the treaty of St. Mary's, 1818, August 8th. Apparently this contained no reference to the Stockbridges. Says Commissioner W. Medell in a report to Secretary Marcy (1840, January 23rd): "I have examined the treaty with the Delawares, made in 1818, for a cession of their lands in Indiana, and can find nothing that would lead to the remotest idea that the Stockbridges had any interest therein."

[2] Also prominent in this movement was Austin E. Quinney. The "E." is probably for his Indian name: Eo tow-o kaum, as given in Catlin's "North American Indians;" or, E-tow-wah-koon (accent on last syllable), as given by Mrs. Frances Jane Pendleton, of Stockbridge blood, Shawano, Wisconsin. The meaning is said to be "On both sides of the river."

[3] The old church is probably the one that is now in the United Presbyterian body, and if so, was then, I suppose, connected with the Associate Reformed synod.

ity, and generally been ornaments to their profession."[1] They regularly maintained meetings of their own in which the reading of Scott's Commentaries took the place of sermons. This continued until (long after their coming to the Green Bay country) they again enjoyed the services of a settled pastor.

Sickness weakened the little band and death lessened its number. We may be reasonably sure that they waited eagerly to hear what Dr. Morse might accomplish for them at Green Bay. Thither a hundred years before, they had been invited to come, if we can trust a tradition that Metoxen fully believed, by the Outagamies and the Sauks. That must have been when these were disputing with the French for the mastery of the region between Lake Michigan and the upper Mississippi. There, too, were "grandchildren" of the Stockbridges, the Menomonees, from whom, evidently, favors were expected.

All these reasons make it probable that as soon as Metoxen and his party heard that a new home had been provided for their people they would set about getting there as soon as possible. But their journey must needs be delayed until the cattle could feed by the way, and perhaps until food could be raised for themselves. For these reasons, we may conclude that it was summer or autumn of 1822 when the little company turned their backs upon the region where poor Tatepahqsect had been burned and murdered by the ferocious Shawano witch-hunter.

On their way, after reaching Lake Michigan, the Stockbridge emigrants went in part by canoes upon the water and in part on foot upon the land. "They drove their cattle along the shore, camping where night overtook them. They swam their cattle across the streams. They had great difficulty in getting them to cross the river at Chicago, but finally one large animal, bolder than the rest, plunged in and the others followed."[2] It would be a bold ox that would swim the Chicago river in these days!

"The small immigrant party of some fifty of the Stockbridges, which came on this year, located late in the fall at the Grand Kakalin, on the east side of the Fox river." The site thus occupied is that of South Kaukauna; the year 1822. Mr. Ellis from whom I quote this remark, seems to assume that these immigrants came from New York. Certainly a party did come thence in 1822, for on December 21st of that year (the third) John Sergeant has among the items of the report of his mission to Green Bay a charge of $1,670.99 "to expenses in maintenance, transportation and supplies for the colony left at Green Bay." Was it he who chose for his father's people the marvelous site of South Kaukauna? It is quite as likely that the choice was made in 1821, under the leadership of Solomon U. Hendrick (Aupaumut), the son of the Revolutionary hero, for the narrow tract[3] secured that year included the place where there was made in 1822 the first settlement of Stockbridges in what is now Wisconsin. Probably, however, the selection was made by many rather than by one; perhaps by the party from Indiana, who may have come earlier than

---

[1] Miss Electa Jones.
[2] Miss Helen C. Storm, Stockbridge, Wisconsin.
[3] With the Little Chute,—which is *not* Little Kaukauna,—as its center.

"the small immigrant party" of which Mr. Ellis speaks,—though I have been inclined, without sufficient reason, perhaps, to identify the two. And notwithstanding his express statement that "the next year [1823] the White river band of Stockbridges, headed by John Metoxen, came through by land to the Bay," I feel sure that, on this point, he is in error. For Rev. Cutting Marsh, who from 1830 to 1848 was missionary pastor of the little church among the Stockbridge Indians, calls the sojourn in Indiana "a period of three or four years. * *   Whilst there, three of their number died." He is speaking, apparently, of members of the church, and thus continues: "In 1822 they removed to Green Bay with the rest of the remaining colony." This accords with what we might expect.[1] For when the Delawares sold the White river land they reserved the right of occupancy for three years only, and therefore the limit expired in 1821. The pressure of white emigration then pouring into that region would make it exceedingly difficult for the Stockbridges to remain there, however, much they might desire to do so. By the change in ownership of the land on which they had sought to settle they had become trespassers rather than tenants at will. Soon, we may be sure, the little church of the pilgrimage, with its attendant band, would be compelled, even if they did not desire, to turn their faces northward toward the promised home of all their people.

Thus came to Wisconsin its first Puritan church. There was here neither minister nor priest. But these spiritual children of Sergeant and Edwards did not, in the wilderness, forget their God. "They kept up their meetings here also."

They had a worthy leader in Metoxen whose knowledge of Scripture is shown in a letter written 1823, December 2nd, from "Cades, Green Bay" (probably Grand Kaukaulin), to John Sergeant, his old pastor. Mentioning the arrival of a new band he says: "Our brethren appear to be quite different from what they were when I first saw them. I trust that some of them are choosing God for their portion, remembering that he is the only source of true happiness for the immortal soul, and grieving because they had forsaken the only King of the universe. * * * * It is true, indeed, that the soul was made for God,—it came from God and can never be happy but in returning to him again.[2] Thus we may have reason to believe that the Spirit of the Lord is moving upon them, saying, 'Arise ye and depart, for this is not your rest. If ye then be risen with Christ, seek those things which are above, where Christ sitteth on the right hand of God.' "

Special significance is given to this letter by the remark: "He and Mrs. Metoxen found their backsliding brethren in deep waters. They had exposed themselves to err by the use of ardent spirits."[3] What temperance work in

---

[1] It is no disparagement to Mr. Ellis,—certainly one of our best authorities on early Wisconsin history,—to believe that of the two Mr. Marsh was likely to be the better informed on this particular point.

[2] With this remark of Metoxen's it is interesting the famous saying by St. Augustine: "Fecisti nos ad te, et inquietum est cor nostrum, donec requiescat in te." "Thou hast made us for thyself and restless is the heart until it rests in thee."

[3] Even some of the delegation of 1821 were guilty of drunkenness.

Wisconsin is of earlier date than that of these Indian Puritans, John Metoxen and his wife? With them the struggle against intoxicants was part of the gospel.

"Previous to the arrival of the Rev. Mr. Miner as missionary, Mr. Metoxen was in the habit, as his wife relates, of officiating as a religious teacher among the tribe, when they had good meetings and were much engaged in religion."[1] Surely this first of Wisconsin's deacons "served well and gained to himself a good standing and great boldness in the faith which is in Christ Jesus."

Years afterward Metoxen was honored,— probably all unknown to himself,— with this fine tribute from his pastor, Rev. Cutting Marsh: "In points of general intelligence, manliness and integrity of character, he will not suffer in comparison with any white man."

Deservedly was this man made chief, or sachem, of his tribe "about 1823." He was chosen to this position after the death of Solomon U. Hendrick, who in 1817 had taken the place formerly held by his father. The elder Hendrick, it grieves us to know, had become one of the countless victims of drunkenness. He lived on but was no longer fit for the duties of his former office. His service had been one of many years. "In 1771 Benjamin Kok-ke-we-nau-naut, called King Ben,[2] being ninety-four years of age resigned his office of sachem, and requested his people to elect a successor. Solomon Un-paun-nau-waun-nutt was chosen. But Solomon died in February, 1777, while Ben lived until 1781, dying at the age of one hundred four. After the death of King Solomon, the government, it is said, devolved upon Joseph Quan-au-kaunt *   * now generally spelled Quinney. He divided his power more equally with his counselors, Peter Poh-quon-nop-peet, Captain Hendrick Aupaumut and Captain John Konkapot."[3]

It was no mock government that these men maintained. Pastor Sergeant, the younger, drew up a code of laws for his people while they were in New York. The legal authority of the tribe was not dissolved in that state until 1827. Thus for a time there was tribal rule both in New York and in what is now Wisconsin.

But white men were beyond their control. The ever-present evil of intemperance called forth a letter from them to Governor Cass of Michigan Territory. They complained of "the alarming ravages of spirituous liquors. It is an evil we wished to be free from, and came into this distant clime with the

---

[1] From "The Last of the Mohicans," by Levi Konkapot, Jr., in volume IV. of the "Wisconsin Historical Collections."

[2] This "King Ben" could not, of course, be the one whom John W. Quinney calls "the last of the hereditary chiefs of the Muh-he-con-new Nation." For this "King Ben was in his prime in 1645," when "a grand council was convened of the Muh-he-con-new tribe, for the purpose of conveying from the old to the young men, a knowledge of the past." Of this "knowledge" we have a portion at the beginning of the last chapter.

[3] Miss Jones's "History of Stockbridge." This John Konkapot was probably son or nephew of the old captain. Poh-quon-nop-peet graduated from Dartmouth college in 1780, was often called "Sir Peter" and was son of the deacon named on page 90.

hope of finding a resting-place, and the hope of being greatly useful, by our examples, toward civilizing that portion of our Indian brethren with whom we should have intercourse; but we are sadly disappointed in this." Cass called the attention of the government to the matter, and writing under date of 1826, December 9th, expresses the wish that Congress would act in the matter "promptly and efficaciously. Unless they do so," he adds, "vain are our efforts to improve the condition of the Indians, and false and delusive will be our hopes."

The following year must have been one of keen disappointment to the Muh-he-ka-ne-ok. For, by the treaty of Little Butte des Morts,[1] the land on which they were living was sold to 1827, August 8th. To their claims and rights, as had been the case in Indiana, there was paid practically no attention by those who framed the treaty.[2] How the Senate secured their rights we have already learned. This just action on the part of that body was taken, partly no doubt, in consequence of "a petition and appeal" made by the Indians interested,—both those in the Green Bay region and their brethren in New York. In this matter, John W. Quinney seems to have represented all the "New York Indians" then living in what is now Wisconsin, and for a number of years he was the principal business agent of his people.

Notwithstanding the treaty of Little Butte des Morts the Stockbridges remained at Grand Kaukaulin, which sometime during the years of early occupancy came to be called Statesburg. Indian emigration from New York continued. "The plan of removal was by detachments,— one to go each year until all were removed."[3] Means were provided by the sale of the reservation given them by the Oneidas,—the state of New York being the purchaser. The first sale, thus made, was of four thousand five hundred acres in 1813. Other purchases were made by the state in 1822, 1823, 1825 (when for the first time, according to Mr. Quinney, the New York legislature paid an Indian tribe full value for its land), in 1826, 1829 and 1830. Even in 1842 and 1847 agreements in regard to the transfer of land were executed by the New York land-commissioners and the Stockbridges.

The "Winnebago war" of June, 1827, gave the Stockbridges and Oneidas an opportunity of showing their allegiance to the United States. Sixty-two of them joined a company raised by "General" William Dickinson and "Colonel" Ebenezer Childs. The "war" was scarcely more than several atrocious murders in the vicinity of Prairie du Chien. There is reason to fear that association with "Colonel" Childs would offset much teaching on the subject of temperance and almost every other virtue. Those who wonder that Christianity has accomplished no more for the Indians should remember that in its work for them it has had to contend with the vices of civilization as well as with those of savagery.

---

[1] See page 57. Also on page 24, an account of the massacre of Outagamies by Marin.
[2] Governor Lewis Cass and Colonel Thomas L. McKinney, on the part of the United States. They treated with the Menomonees and Winnebagoes only.
[3] John W. Quinney.

But the year 1827 was not, to the Muh-he-ka-ne-ok, one simply of misfortune. In July of that year Mr. Sergeant's successor at New Stockbridge, Rev. Jesse Miner came to Statesburg, under the auspices of the American Board. He was evidently considering the question of removal westward with the people whom he had been serving in New Stockbridge. He spent some weeks with the little pilgrimage church that had been pastorless ever since its organization in 1818. Thus began,— if we except Williams's work, and the winter's stay (1824-1825) of Rev. Norman Nash,[1]— the first Protestant pastorate in what is now Wisconsin.

After his return to New York Mr. Miner made ready to remove his family, and engaged the late John Y. Smith, so well known in Wisconsin history, to come West "to erect or work upon the mission buildings." Of the two, Mr. Smith was the first to come, next spring, to Green Bay where he arrived on the 18th of May, 1828. That was Sunday, and, we may be reasonably sure that a strict Presbyterian, like Mr. Smith, would go no farther that day, if he could avoid doing so. His passage had been paid by Mr. Miner, who also furnished him with twenty dollars to buy tools. But when the young missionary-carpenter started from Utica he had only a dollar and a quarter in his pocket. No doubt he would get at work as soon as possible. In Librarian Durrie's sketch of the life of Mr. Smith[2] it is said that "his first employment was on the mission-house near Green Bay, and afterwards at Kaukauna, among the Stockbridges." The reverse of this much more likely to be true. Mr. Durrie wrote merely from a somewhat indistinct recollection of what Mr. Smith told him.[3] Mr. Miner was soon to bring on his family and a house would be needed for their reception. For all these reasons we may conclude that Mr. Smith's first work in unnamed Wisconsin was at Statesburg.

Nor would he build in wood alone. This reader of Milton and of Edwards strove no doubt, to please his Indian neighbors "for their good unto edification." He had been chosen because of the character that was in him as well as for the skill of his hands.

The home that he built for Mr. Miner may have been the second framed house in Wisconsin. It was a story-and-a-half structure and stood on or near the present site of the railway "round-house" at South Kaukauna. Distant three-fourths of a mile, or thereabout, stood, or was soon built, a church that was used also as a school. This was of logs, and may have been built, at Mr. Miner's suggestion, the summer before. However, it is never safe to presume of a body of Indians that they will be in haste to engage in any work of this kind or show much perseverance in finishing it. A living witness,[4] who was brought as a child to Statesburg in 1829 seems to remember the building as standing when he came. Afterward he attended school in it. Whether built in 1827

---

[1] See chapter on the history of Green Bay.
[2] "Wisconsin Historical Collections," volume VII., page 452.
[3] As he stated in conversation with the writer hereof.
[4] George Thomas Bennett, born at Cedar Hill, Albany county, New York, 22nd of August, 1823.

or in 1828 this building was, for a time, the only house of worship in Wisconsin. For the combination church-and-school which the Roman Catholics began at Shantytown in 1823 had been burned.

Mr. Miner arrived at his new home (probably) on the 20th of June, 1828. Strengthened by the work of the summer before, his people had proved faithful. "During the preceding winter, when no missionary or teacher was among them, they kept up religious worship on the Sabbath, the monthly concert for prayer, Sabbath school, weekly conference, female prayer meeting, and meeting of young people for reading the Scriptures."[1] There are some churches that do no better than this even when they do have a pastor.

There probably never was a genuine Puritan church without a school close at hand. One was established at Statesburg, in 1828. It was taught by Miss Electa Quinney[2] who had spent six years in the famous foreign-mission school at Cornwall, Connecticut, and had been a teacher among her own people in New York. Thus Statesburg has the honor of establishing what was practically the first of American free public schools in the region between Lake Michigan and the Mississippi; and Miss Quinney herself, with one possible exception,[3] was our first schoolmistress,—the first teacher, indeed, of a free school.

An assistant missionary, Augustus T. Ambler, who is called a physician in the "Missionary Herald" for January, 1829, arrived at Statesburg, 1828, November 4th. It may be that he came to do school work, but if so, the state of his health forbade it. A change of field did not long preserve his life. Going southward he died in 1831 at one of the missions among the Choctaws.

The winter of 1828-29 was one of special interest in the re-organized mission. A letter from Mr. Miner published, without date, in the "Missionary Herald" of June, 1829, gives the subjoined narrative: "The good work of God is still going on in this place, and I hope with increasing power. Eight of the natives were added to the church the first Sabbath in this month;[4] also two of my sons, and one mechanic laboring at this station, making the whole number added since my arrival twenty-five. About fifteen others are indulging hopes, some of them, I believe, on good grounds. Meetings are solemn, still, refreshing. Most of the youth are seriously concerned, or hoping. Meetings are full on the Sabbath." This was doubtless the first religious revival in Wisconsin.

But the hand that sent the glad tidings was even then forever still. His pastorate had ended with his life on the 22nd of the preceding March. Near where he labored in life his people made his grave. "I am sorry," writes Mr. Miner's daughter,[5] that I can tell you so little of my father. An old Indian woman whom I met six years ago, who had belonged to his church, said that he was like a father to the Indians and they loved him much. They gave him an

---

[1] "Missionary Herald," January, 1829.
[2] Indian name: "Wuh-weh-wee-nee-meew;" or, "Woh-weh-wee-nee-meew."
[3] "In 1828 the five American families at Shanty Town, now a part of Green Bay, erected a log school house and imported a young lady teacher from the East—Miss Caroline Russell." — REUBEN GOLD THWAITES, in "History of Education in Wisconsin."
[4] February, perhaps. But the winter mails of that time were few and irregular.
[5] Mrs. M. A. Whitney, Grand Crossing, Illinois, 26th of May, 1891.

Indian name, Wah-nuh-wah-meet, which means 'very true man.'[1] He died at the age of forty-seven. The Indians had these words placed on his tombstone: 'He shall gather the outcasts of Israel together.' He had translated many of our hymns into their language, forming quite a hymn-book, from which they sang at his funeral. My father lies buried in the cemetery at Kaukauna, to which he was removed from the old mission burying-ground.[2] Metoxen was loved of my father and revered of my elder brothers."

In the spring of 1829, Mr. Quinney, who had been in New York and Washington to protest against the ratification of the treaty of Little Butte des Morts, "collected the poor of the Stockbridge nation, who were unable to remove themselves, to the number of thirty souls, and returned home with them." This was virtually the end of the tribal emigration, though our warrior-friend, Captain Hendrick (Aupaumut) did not leave New York until the following September.

On the 24th of the same month Cutting Marsh, a missionary for the Stockbridge tribe, was ordained in the famous Park-street church of Boston.[3]

The early closing of navigation that year prevented Mr. Marsh from reaching his field of service until spring. He spent the winter,— profitably as he thought,—with friends at an Indian mission station, Maumee, Ohio. "Thursday, April 9th," he writes in his diary, "took my leave of the mission friends at Maumee. The Sabbath following, was at Monroe [Michigan], and preached. * * The next Sabbath was at Detroit, and Tuesday following, April 20th, set sail for the Bay; passed four days at Mackinaw very pleasantly, and arrived at the Bay, April 30th. May 1st, Saturday, went on board a boat at the Bay, for Statesburgh, and arrived about half past ten that evening, in safety, though much fatigued. May 2nd, Sabbath, preached for the first time to an Indian congregation. Was struck with the order which prevailed in the house of God, the attention with which they listened, and their apparent solemnity." * * * *

Good order has always been noted as a characteristic of the religious meetings of these people. Of this fact and others, we have an interesting witness in Mr. Colton, who reported for us his recollection of the speeches made by

---

[1] Without doubt Mrs. Whitney is in error. It is probable that what she sought to transliterate is the Muh-he-ka-ne-ew term "Wah-weh-nuh-maht," "This true man." Literally it may be "This true one," for the word for "man" is "mon-naow."

[2] This was done chiefly by the reverent thoughtfulness of Herbert Battles Tanner, M. D., of South Kaukauna.

The stone now at the grave bears the inscription (with errors):

IN MEMORY OF
JESSE MINER,
BORN SEPT. 26, 1781.
COMMENCED THE MOHEAKUMUK MISSION
AT THIS PLACE, JUNE 20, 1828.
DIED MARCH 22, 1829.
AGED 49.

[3] The occasion must have been one of peculiar interest. Fifteen others were ordained at the same time, one other for service among Indians, two for work in foreign lands, three to become agents for benevolent institutions, and nine to be home missionaries. The services were under the direction of the presbytery of Newburyport.

Rev. Cutting Marsh.

John Metoxen at the council of 1830. Writing under date of August 16th of that year, Mr. Colton gives a most entertaining account of the Stockbridge settlement on Fox river, at "Grande Kawkawlin" as he calls it. He explains that "Kawkawlin" means "falls" or "rapids," adding that "Grande" is French and needs no explanation. "I am now writing," he says, "from the mission house of the American Board. The Stockbridges number about three hundred fifty souls, and have probably made greater attainments in the English language and manners, and in the useful arts of civilized life, and also in the Christian religion, than any other tribe of the aborigines on the continent; except that the Brotherton Indians have so long used English as to have lost their mother tongue. But in the moral state of society and in general improvement the Brothertons are far behind the Stockbridges."[1] The day before was Sunday and Mr. Colton had attended service. Amid over-hanging trees there was a well-built log church, used also as a school. It would seat a congregation of three hundred. There was a Sunday-school with Indian teachers and a white superintendent (probably J. D. Stevens). All the congregation were "neatly dressed in a costume about half way between the European habit and that of the wild tribes." This, to Mr. Colton's mind, suggested the degree of their civilization. "The men seldom wear hats." There were differences in dress indicating, as among whites, "social standing, degree of respectability, and domestic wealth." The afternoon sermon was "interpreted for the benefit of the small portion of the tribe who do not understand English." The singing is highly and, I doubt not, deservedly praised. It was probably in both languages.

"The staff and office of parish beadle"[2] particularly interested our traveler. He thinks it probable that the office, with its peculiar duties, originated in the time of John Sergeant, and makes no mention of the probability that it was merely a transference to an Indian church of a custom,— that of choosing a tithing-man,— existing at that time among their white neighbors. "The staff in the present instance was a green switch about ten feet long which the functionary had cut from the wood as he came to church." This was used with such vigor about the ears of at least one disorderly boy that they must have burned, Mr. Colton thinks, the rest of the day. A sleeping adult was roused by hitting, with the heavy end of the "switch," the stove-pipe until it rang, the beadle meanwhile crying out in Indian, "Wake up there!" This official is spoken of as severely and strictly impartial, and our traveler does not doubt that even a stranger would be duly admonished if there should be need. On this particular occasion, though the preacher was manifestly disturbed, the congregation remained unmoved, taking the whole proceding as a matter of course. The drowsy one gave good heed to the rest of the sermon, and the fact is noted that the congregation was very attentive.

Another thing that especially interested Mr. Colton was the fact that after

---
[1] Not so now, whatever may have been the case in 1830.
[2] Mr. Colton's book was meant for British readers.

the benediction the congregation sat down, giving those nearest the door an opportunity to retire. Others then followed without confusion.

The next entry in Mr. Marsh's diary is dated on the Sunday after Mr. Colton's visit, August 22nd. "On the whole I have passed the time agreeably." He has been led to believe that he is somewhat esteemed by his people, but speaks of the astonishing fickleness of many of them. "I seem almost to be amongst the children of Israel who one day sing God's praises and perhaps the next murmur against him." There had been one case of discipline,— for intemperance. He continues:

"In respect to these Indians, a dark cloud seems to be gathering over their future prospects. Notwithstanding all their precautions, government seems determined, if possible, to drive them from this, their supposed last, retreat. They seem to be in trouble and hardly know what to do. * * *

"August 29th (Sabbath). Things outwardly appear dull and discouraging. Almost all of my dear people, both men and women, absent at the Bay attending the treaty with the agents of government. Oh! when will they become more stable, and less attracted by what is new or of a public nature. When will they feel that providing for their families both food and clothing, taking care of their crops and farms, are objects of the greatest temporal importance, or more [important] than running where they are not asked and can accomplish no real good! No preaching; the number so small; but [I] occupied the time in the morning, after reading the CIII. psalm in making remarks, together with Mr. Stevens."

With this entry it is interesting to compare those made about the same time by Commissioner McCall. We have had[1] a part of his record,— a part that pertains to the business for which the council was called together. Additional portions here reproduced make known some of the utterly demoralizing features of the occasion, and show to what sort of influences the Indians were exposed from nearly all their white neighbors at the vile, mongrel Green Bay of sixty-four years ago. "At night,"— August 27th,— says Mr. McCall, "a band of the Winnebagoes appeared, painted all coulors — not only their faces but their bodies — before the door of the house where we boarded, incouraged by some and Treated by others with whiskey. They held the war dance and kept it up until 10 o'clock at night, with all their disfigured and distorted countenances — naked except Breech clouts. All, with some kind of warlike weapon and horrid yell, made them resemble so many infernals." On Saturday, the 28th, "after we adjourned about 70 Pottowatimies came in — all to git rations, as they had no concern in the treaty or council. At evening the Winnibagoes held another war dance in which the head chief, Four-Legs, displayed great activity.

"29. Sunday. Laid by. About 9 o'clock Four-Legs came to the house and asked if we wanted them to dance. We told them it was Sunday, or day to worship the Great Spirit. He said white man sent him Telling him we

---

[1] On page 50.

wished to have them dance, as there would be no councel. No doubt some person did it for To make sport."

The heathen Fore-Legs! Were he only living now he would find many "Christians" ready to dance with him,— and, for that matter, to get drunk with him,— on Sunday; some of whom would be moved to the deepest indignation at the denial of religious liberty involved in the proposition that the state may justly require the use of its official language in the instruction of the children of its own citizens.

Had Commissioner McCall been of the sort that many officials are, he would have had "Four-legs" and his company dance, have given them whisky, and then, on his return home, been ready to express the opinion that it is impossible to civilize or Christianize the Indians.

"I have forgot to mention," says Mr. McCall in his entry for the next Tuesday, "that a drunken soldier posted near the Indian encampment to guard a field of potatoes & corn, stabed a Menominee chief — a harmless old man — by the name of Big Soldier. The soldier was put under guard and probably will be punished for getting drunk on his post and for improper conduct as a soldier." We wonder if Mr. McCall smiled when he wrote next day, "To the Indian wounded by the soldier yesterday we presented one bbl. pork, one barrel of flour and 3 bushels of corn, and then the councel Broke up" (September 1st.)

"Without accomplishing the object for which it was called together," he might have added. Reasons for this we have already learned: There was the natural desire of the Menomonees and the Winnebagoes to keep their land. To be sure they had more than they needed and had accepted from the New York Indians payment for part of it. But those who may have authority to make a contract do not always have the continuance of life and power to carry it out. Such was the case in this instance, Mr. J. W. Quinney tells us. Moreover, in every community there is always a dishonest party, and the Menomonees and the Winnebagoes knew very well that what they could keep from the New York Indians they could sell to the United States. That was what the Americans at Green Bay wished them to do. This class of whites desired to get rid of the Indians already there rather than to have any more come. To throw all obstacles possible in the way of further Indian immigration was a work that required a knowledge not possessed by the ignorant Menomonees and Winnebagoes, and there were not wanting means by which payment could be secured for such service. As to the French of Green Bay they, of course, would be inclined to take sides with the Menomonees among whom they had so many kinsmen. Religion, too, which like so many other things, serves, according to its quality, one extreme or the other, was in this case, if Mr. Ellis has rightly informed us, brought to bear among the Roman Catholics of Green Bay against the coming of the New York Indians because they were Protestants. Then we must not forget the preposterous schemes and broken promises of Eleazar Williams, nor the extravagant claims of the New York Indians themselves,— more than three hundred four acres of land to "every soul interested."

After the breaking up of the council, the Indians who had been impudent in their refusals as related to the "Wappinackies," or New York Indians, became equally impudent in beggary for themselves. Mr. McCall tells the story:

"In the afternoon [of the day when the council finally adjourned] the com'rs were invited to attend at the agent's house to hear what the Indians had to say to him.[1] After their usual formalities they began by stating they were poor and ignorant creatures, and they wanted to know where all the commissioners' instructions came from and no presents. That they were going home to gather their rice and they had no Tobacco to smoak, and instead of a pipe they had to put a stick in their mouth. That they wanted 2 days' rations to help them home. That they wanted powder & shot to assist them to procure meat for their children. Besides, the current was strong to push against and they wanted to suck one of their father's breasts — that milk would make them strong — meaning a keg of whiskey to suck at. Then paused a little and said that they had heard of their great father the president, and wanted to go and see him, but was so poor that [they] could not go without his help, and wanted the agent to write to the president to furnish them with clothing and expenses, and for the agent or some other person to accompany them with an interpreter. Also to go to washington. *A fine Job for two or three to make money.* A plan got up by Judge [James D.] Doty and the Grigions to rob the Treasury of some eight or ten thousand dollars."

On the next Friday "the wounded Indian came with two or three others, as our interpreter informed us, To take his leave of us and to ask for a blanket, a shirt and some Tobacco which we gave him, and to 3 others gave each a shirt — being the last of what 4 ps. of Blue callico made, as it has been a fashion to give every one a shirt that comes to dine. Towards evening the old man was as drunk as any of them."

What wonder that Mr. Marsh lamented that so many of his people had gone to form part of such a throng as Mr. McCall pictures to us! The motley crowd had to be fed by the commissioners, and by the greatest number[2] of rations issued in any one day,— 1872,— we have a datum from which to estimate the largest attendance.

Two of the commissioners, Mr. McCall and Mr. Root,[3] believed in the substantial justice of the claims made by the Stockbridges, the Oneidas and the Brothertowns. The third member of the commission, Mr. John T. Mason, did not "concur in the position taken in relation to the claim of the New York Indians." But his colleagues seem to be supported in their views by the terms of the treaties on which said claim was based. The first,— that of 1821,— sold a tract, the boundaries of which are thus given: "Beginning at the foot of the rapids on the Fox river, usually called the Grand Kakalin; thence up said river

---

[1] Samuel C. Stambaugh was then in charge of the Indian agency.
[2] "Greatest number 1,445 M.— 75 Win,— N. Y. 191— Chip. 161, per day," is the way Mr. McCall gives the statement.
[3] See note 1, page 56.

to the rapids at the Winnebago lake, and from the river extending back in this width on each side to the northwest and the southeast equidistant with the lands claimed by the said Menominie and Winnebago nations of Indians." Mr. Ellis describes the tract as having "the Little Chute as a center."[1] He further tells us that "after much deliberation, and a good deal of hesitation, it was concluded, on the advice, chiefly, of Hendrick, the Mo-he-kun-nuck chief, to accept the grant."[2] For this the New York Indians paid two thousand dollars.

"The acquisition by this treaty," say Messrs. McCall and Root in continuing their report, "did not give perfect satisfaction to every portion of the New York Indians. * * They were therefore prompted to solicit the Government for its aid in procuring an extension of the cession. * * The Government efficiently aided them in the accomplishment of their object * * and appointed an Agent [John Sergeant, Jr.] to superintend the negotiation on the part of the United States. Thus encouraged and sustained, they concluded a treaty with the Menominie nation * * at Green Bay on the 23rd of September, 1822. By this treaty the Menominies ceded, released and quit claimed to the New York Indians all their right, title, interest and claim to a large tract of country containing at least five millions of acres, rather, undefined, but limited southwesterly by lands ceded to them the year before, by the Winnebagoes and Menominies, and by the Mannawahkiah (supposed to be the Minnewawkie) river,[3] easterly and northeasterly by Lake Michigan and the Bay des Enock,[4] northerly and northwesterly by the height of land between the waters of Lake Superior and those running into Green Bay and Lake Michigan. This cession was made in consideration of three thousand dollars."

This is the treaty that the Menomonees afterward so vehemently repudiated. But the New York Indians strenuously insisted on the rights. What there were was referred by the next treaty,—that of Little Butte des Morts, — to the President for arbitration, and it was to aid in determining the questions involved that the commission of 1830 was appointed. Its work was not wholly in vain, though the Stockbridges and Brothertowns were not able to keep the places where they had made their homes. Again Mr. Quinney was called upon to represent at least the former in business then pending at Washington. For the scheme so indignantly denounced by Mr. McCall was in some measure carried out though not, so far as appears, by the men whom he named. Acting-Agent Samuel C. Stambaugh, who had been a leading marplot in defeating the aims of the commissioners, soon made ready to go to Washington taking with him some fourteen of the Menomonees. This party left Green Bay on the 8th of November, 1830.

We learn from Mr. Marsh's diary that he was fully in sympathy with his

---

[1] See page 56, where, to my great regret, the "Little Chute" is mistakenly identified with the Little Kaukaulin, or Little Kaukauna.
[2] "Wisconsin Historical Collections," volume II., page 426.
[3] The Milwaukee river.
[4] Either the Big or the Little Bay de Noquet, Escanaba, Upper Michigan, in on the former.

people. Under date of October 28th, he wrote: "Went to Green Bay in company with Mr. Metoxen, Saturday night. Stayed at the Rev. Mr. Cadel's [Cadle's], and was very kindly and hospitably entertained. Sunday, A. M., heard him preach. Sermon upon the death of Bishop Hobart. In the afternoon, [I] went to the garrison and preached to the soldiers. About 100 present, and all gave good attention.

"Monday, November 1st. Just one year from the time I landed at Detroit. Parted from J. W. Quinney and Mr. [Robert] Stewart [Stuart] from Mackinaw who sailed in the Mariner, Captain Johnson. Tuesday, 2nd. Returned to Statesburgh.

"Wednesday, 10th. Went to Green Bay and passed the remainder of the week; but, alas, little satisfaction can be taken there: all is discord and confusion. Hardly knew what to do in respect to the affairs of the Indians; their state is indeed precarious and involved in uncertainty.

"November 25th, 1830. The day set apart for Thanksgiving and prayer. * * Solemnized a marriage, it being [of] a couple who had lived together in an unlawful manner. The manner in which the marriage covenant is treated here [is] truly a great evil, and in consequence, society is very much disorganized, and it is but one of the lamentable evils that abound here.

"Sabbath, December 5th. Spoke against parents' interfering in marriages of adult sons and daughters. So far as I understand the Bible, children are not under obligation to obey their parents in this respect * * [though] their consent should be asked, and, if possible, obtained. The interference of parents * * has caused great confusion among this people. * * In the evening, a meeting at Mr. Metoxen's [at which he notes that Austin E. Quinney spoke in English].

"Sabbath, January 2d, [1831]. Mr. and Mrs. Whitney from Green Bay attended the meeting. 6th. Went up to Smithfield, and made some calls and addressed a few at Mr. Smith's. [On the 11th, he went again to Smithfield, which, I am inclined to think, was an Oneida settlement that he is soon to tell us about. A hymn that he gave out they sang in Mohawk.]

"Saturday, January 22nd. In the forenoon went [from Green Bay] to Duck Creek. Passed the night and Sabbath at Mr. Beard's who belongs to the church. Immediately after my arrival, received a message from some of the leading men that they had received orders from Mr. Williams not to hear any minister preach of another denomination, and so I must not preach. O how unlike the spirit of Jesus Christ. [He attended service as a hearer.] Found perhaps sixty or seventy present, of all ages. The [Episcopal] church service was read and accompanied with singing twice, and a short portion of Scripture was read from one of the Gospels and then the services were concluded, in all occupying perhaps half or three-quarters of an hour. Alas, how jejune, and how little calculated to enlighten and instruct the ignorant are such services! In the evening, attended what was called a prayer meeting. When I arrived, found the meeting had commenced, and after I arrived they sang about a dozen times, and then read a prayer, the same they had in the day time, and the meeting broke up. Felt poorly paid for walking a mile to attend a meeting where there seemed to be neither the life nor the power of godliness. Still I hope that I am unfeignedly thankful that God has cast my lot among a people where it is entirely different,— where there appears to be much of a spirit of genuine piety, and where our social meetings are often highly interesting and spiritual.

"Was very hospitably entertained in the family of Mr. Beard who is a member of the Episcopal church. His appears to be a spirit of genuine kindness, unmingled with ostentation, or without expecting a reward. His family consists of a wife and three children — one of them able to read in the New Testament, which is the case with very few of the Oneidas.

"Monday, 24th. Returned to the Kakalin. Tuesday, 25th. Went to Smithfield, and attended to the Sunday-school there.[1] On the way, called at Metoxen's and saw his infant child die.

"Tuesday, February 3rd.　*　*　Mr. Stevens absent at the Bay. *　* In his absence, am teaching the school. *　* Had but just commenced my school when word came that Abram Abrams had frozen to death in a drunken fit! *　* At two o'clock, went and attended the funeral of a young man, Dolly Isaac's son, at Smithfield. Saturday, 12th. Eclipse of the sun. Commenced a little after 10 o'clock, A. M. The whole obscuration [lasted] about two and one-half, or perhaps, two and one-fourth hours."

On the 2nd of May, 1831, Mr. Marsh made report to the "venerable society" in Scotland, "having been certified by the Rev. Dr. John Codman, secretary of your Board in Boston, of my appointment *　* as missionary among the Indians.

"The settlement of the Stockbridge Indians is situated upon the south-east side of Fox river, near what is called the Grand Kacalin or Big Rapids, *　* and extends along the river about four miles in length, and from one and a half to two in breadth.

"About one hundred of the Oneida tribe who left the state of New York last summer have joined the Stockbridge Indians; [have] settled down on the Fox [river], two or three miles above them." When Mr. Marsh made his report, he and Mr. Stevens were holding meetings, once each Sabbath, with these Oneidas. Other services, and a Sunday-school of twenty-five or thirty pupils, they maintained by themselves.

This settlement is probably Mr. Marsh's "Smithfield." We may be sure that these Oneidas were of the "Orchard" or Methodist party,— the people to whom Mr. Clark came in the following year (1832). Here it was, no doubt, that he built the first Methodist chapel in the vast region between Lake Michigan and the Pacific ocean.[2]

---
[1] "Bible school," or "school for religious instruction," is, I suppose, what Mr. Marsh had in mind.
[2] See page 66. After the printing thereof, I had opportunity by the favor of Rev. A. V. C. Schenck, D. D., of Madison, stated clerk of the Presbyterian Synod of Wisconsin, to examine and to use Mr. Marsh's diary. This is conclusive on some points of our early Wisconsin his-

[1831] Thursday, July 7th, Attended a wedding at Mrs. Hendrick's. Samuel Miller and Harriet Jehoiakim were united in the conjugal relation. On account of difficulties which have hitherto been occasioned by method adopted in marrying, resolved to adopt a new course, viz.: to ask the individuals if it is their sincere desire to marry, &c.

"At Mrs. Hendrick's." Perhaps the widow of the old soldier.[1] Hendrick himself died some time the summer before. Mr. Marsh was with him in his last illness and made report of his death to the "Missionary Herald." Notwithstanding his great sin, Kaukauna may well be proud to count him among her founders. Not only was he a soldier; if Mr. Pilling is right he was a translator as well,— one who edited what is likely to prove the last book issued in the Muh-he-ka-ne-ew dialect. That, like the one published at Stockbridge, Massachusetts, in 1795, is a manual of religious instruction. It contains the shorter catechism, Dr. Watts's catechism for children, the first twenty-one verses of the third chapter of the gospel of John, the first twenty of Matthew V. and all of Matthew VII. save the last two verses. There are also metrical translations of four of the psalms or parts thereof. These, I doubt not, are made from corresponding English versions by Dr. Watts. The entire compilation closes at the bottom of page 34 with the words: *The foregoing is printed in the* MOHEAKUNNUK, *or Stockbridge Indian Language.*

Of this book "the first twenty-five pages," says Mr. Pilling, "contain an exact reprint of the edition of 1795; the remainder was probably translated by Captain Hendrick, at the suggestion of Rev. John Sergeant who died in 1824. The exact date of its publication has not been ascertained; but from the appearance of the paper and typography, it would seem to belong to the period of the removal of the tribe from New Stockbridge, New York, to Indiana in 1818, and to Wisconsin in 1822. Mr. Sergeant wished to have his people well supplied with books before their departure. 'My people,' he writes, March 30, 1818, 'can read their own language very fluently, when they pronounce English very indifferently. This will always be the case, so long as they speak their own language in their families.' In another letter, dated December 16, 1821, he says: 'I am in hopes to obtain copies of Elliot's Bible in the Indian language, and am of opinion, that this Bible will be understood by a good part of the natives in the N. W. Territory.'"

In regard to the booklet with which he connects the name of Captain Hendrick, Mr. Pilling gives, interrogatively, Stockbridge, Massachusetts, as the place, and 1818 as the time, of publication. I doubt that he is quite right in his opinion that Hendrick was the translator of the last nine pages. Brainerd, while at Kaunaumeek in 1743-44, translated "*sundry psalms*" into the language of his people. I find no mention in Mr. Hopkins's "Historical Memoirs" of like service among Mr. Sergeant's varied and abundant labors. But that his people,— among whom Mr. Brainerd's little flock came to dwell in 1744,—

---

tory. His reports to the society in Scotland are of almost equal value.

[1] Or the wife, or widow, of a son.

sang psalms, and in their own language, I have no doubt. The Muh-he-ka-ne-ok are now and always have been fond of singing.

Moreover, the Scripture lessons contained in the passages mentioned above are doubtless among the very first that Mr. Sergeant employed in the instruction of his people. Certainly they are all included in the translations that he made. The selection of particular portions would probably be made by his son and he, I presume, chose also the versified psalms that his people liked best.[1]

Though for the reasons given, I doubt that Hendrick was the translator of any portion of the book of 1818, yet he may have been the editor or reviser thereof. Nor would it be fair not to give the statement found in a manuscript note in a copy of the booklet; a copy now in the Boston Athenæum, and at one time in possession of Henry Rowe Schoolcraft, by whom perhaps, said note was written:

"This translation was made by John Quinney and Captain Hendrick who received his commission from General Washington. Little else has ever been translated into the Stockbridge language besides this."

With this it is interesting to compare a statement made by Rev. Cutting Marsh in a letter written 1838, August 23rd.[2] "The Stockbridge language has never been reduced to a system, and but little has been attempted at translations into it. The only translation"—perhaps Mr. Marsh did not know of the book of 1795, perhaps he regarded the two as virtually one—"is a very small book (of which I send a copy) containing the assembly's shorter catechism, Dr. Watts's do. for children, and some small portions of Scripture, and three or four select psalms. This book is little used except by the old people, because hardly any of them are able to read their own language, although they sing the psalms fluently." He does not say by whom the work of translation was done.

Yet, on the 2nd of September, 1832, only six years before he wrote this letter, Mr. Marsh made entry in his diary: "At the evening meeting Deacon [Jacob C.] Chicks prayed in English, which is not usual for the members of the church." Good men pray and bad men swear in the language they learned in childhood.

Whatever part, if any, Hendrick may have had in the making of this book, it will always possess peculiar interest for bibliographers of Wisconsin.

---

[1] How any one can sing them seems, judging from their looks, to be a marvel. But it is a pleasure, not simply a matter of curious interest, to hear these harsh-looking verses sung by the few Muh-he-ka-ne-ok who still are able to use the language of their fathers. I subjoin psalm IV. It is written in long meter:

1 Lord ptou we muh ween wom non nuh;
   Hunnaumeweh tnantippaunmeh;
   Neyuh quaukhoon kaunwehkommauk,
   Nquaukhetommon mautaunuhkaun.

2 Thuhkeh aunnaukhemoohhiyuh,
   Wonk thuhkeh ounaukhemeyuh;
   Weekchaupoquot maumsaunonneh
   Quehnuwweh nuh duh wonk keyuh.

3 Ktennemmaunen Caupohtommun;
   Yuhhuh kesunnuhkiyau neh,
   Great God! nuhkauwthowaukonneh
   Htauwkkuktammaukaunwaukonnuk.

4 Neh aunkokhaut neh, neyuh duh,
   Nmaukennuh, nkeesquon kawwenauk;
   Kauehetoneh, wuhkommauweh,
   Kukhkhonnuwwaunmeh kauwyauneh.

[2] To George Boyd, then Indian agent at Green Bay.

It was for the use of a people who became our own, and hither, probably, were brought nearly all the copies ever issued. Few of these are left, and the men and women who can read the language of Hendrick and Metoxen can, almost literally, be numbered on one's fingers. I doubt that it is now the language of a single home.

Even Hendrick himself, it would seem, preferred to write in English. "During his residence at New Stockbridge," says Mr. Pilling, "Captain Hendrick compiled and wrote in English the traditional history of the 'Muh-he-connuk Nation.' Some fragments of this curious and interesting work have been preserved in Dr. Dwight's *Travels* (New Haven, 1821-22), and in Jones's *Stockbridge* (Springfield, 1854)."

Of Hendrick's Revolutionary service, Mr. Marsh, in the letter quoted from above, gives some particulars. It should be said, however, that the old warrior's name is not to be found in the list of Revolutionary officers at the department of state. Yet President Jefferson, in his qualified attestation of the Stockbridge title to part of the Miami grant,[1] calls Hendrick "captain." But we turn to Mr. Marsh's narrative:

"Captain Hendrick, who received a captain's commission from General Washington, was actively engaged in various ways during the war. He was in the battle when General Burgoyne was taken at [Saratoga]. On one occasion General Washington employed him * * to go and treat with the Ottawas who then lived on the Maumee river, in [what is now] Ohio. The task was not only difficult but dangerous, yet he executed it with honor and satisfaction concerned, although the Indians violated their engagements. General Washington offered him any assistance which he would ask or number to go with him. He replied: 'No, I only want some gold to put in my belt, which I wear around me, and one friend whom I shall choose;' this, of course, was granted.

"Of his singular adroitness, an instance may be mentioned while on this important agency. When he arrived among the Indians he told them of his errand. They wished time for consultation, &c. There were three British officers around who were stirring up the Indians to make war upon the frontier settlers, and were suspected by Captain Hendrick of using their influence to thwart his purposes. The Indians replied: 'You say that you are our friends; we are glad and hope that you are, and, if so, we want you to go with us and help destroy these white people (Americans) who live near us and are intruding upon our lands, and then we shall know that you are friends indeed.' Captain Hendrick replied: 'We are your friends and are willing to help you all we can, but the path is very long in which we have come, and our feet are sore; now if you will go and cut off those troublesome intruders at a distance, we, in the meantime, will kill those that are about here (meaning the British officers). The next morning not a British officer was to be seen, for every one had ab-

---

[1] See page 107.

sconded during the night. After this, Captain Hendrick found no difficulty in bringing the Indians to terms and accomplishing his object."

Evidently it was no ordinary man whose body the men of Statesburg buried in a now forgotten grave on that summer day three score and four years ago.

There appears now in Mr. Marsh's narrative a man who thirty years later was to be at the head of a short-lived but most famous confederacy. "Wrote [1831, July 25th] to Lieutenant [Jefferson] Davis, Fort Winnebago. Contents of the letter: First, the bill of the Bibles &c. Second, urged the importance of his inquiring whether he could not do something for the moral renovation of the soldiers at the Fort. Love and gratitude to the Savior should induce it immediately. Although alone, he should not feel [that] a sufficient excuse for declining to make an effort. David went alone against his foe and the defier of the armies of Israel, but in the name of the Lord of hosts, and he conquered. God has without doubt something for you to do in thus bringing you, as you hope, to the knowledge and to the acknowledgment of the truth as it is in Jesus. It was but a few years ago when Christians began to make the inquiry respecting seamen as a very few do now respecting our military posts, and behold the result!

August 5th, Friday. Went to Green Bay. * * Saw swarms of flies hopping up out of the water, which appears[1] like flakes of snow in a stormy day. * * Says Mr. Metoxen as we passed along. 'Moo-chau-now sh-woon-ah-ah-kun.'[2] 'Look like foggy."

Before closing our narrative for 1831 we turn again almost to its beginning to observe that, writing under date of January 11th, Mr. Stevens gave the number of the tribe as two hundred twenty-five. Thus it is almost certain that Mr. Colton's "three hundred fifty" of the preceding summer was an over-estimate. There were in the church fifteen men, twenty-seven women. It is pleasant to read in a later communication from Mr. Stevens that "on the last Sabbath in January, 1832, Rev. Richard F. Cadle, superintendent of the Episcopal mission at Green Bay, administered the sacrament." Mr. Cadle's worth redeemed the mission that he had in charge from the reproach that the mendacious Eleazar Williams had brought upon it. In the autumn of 1833 Mr. and Mrs. Stevens left Statesburg. Soon they began work among the Sioux, and in 1835 established a mission at Lake Harriet, within the present limits of Minneapolis. This was part of the beginning of the great work that has practically changed the character of the tribe, known from the time of Marquette as ferocious and dangerous enemies;[3] a work that, begun on the upper Mississippi, has place now in Nebraska and the Dakotas by the turbid waters of the Missouri.

We turn again to a report by Mr. Marsh. It was made to the society in

---

[1] I can not but think that Mr. Marsh meant to write "appear."
[2] Perhaps for "kun" I should have read "keen."
[3] Among whom the Jesuits established no missions.

Scotland, and bears date 1833, August 1st: "This church was organized in New Stockbridge, New York, July 24th, 1818, and consisted of eleven members, four males and seven females."[1] The membership when he made report was fifty-nine, of whom twenty-four were men or boys,—"males," as he calls them. "Forty-five [of the church-members] are married. In twenty-four of these families there are family prayers, morning and evening." What Wisconsin church of the present day can show, in this respect, as good a record?

"All get a living by agriculture," says Mr. Marsh, "and some of the men are skilled in the mechanic arts. The women all understand sewing, and some of them spinning, weaving, etc. Three have taught school, and one female has been engaged for some years in teaching, and a few weeks ago was married to a Mohawk Indian from Canada, whom the Methodist Episcopal society sent out last year as a missionary to the Oneidas in this region." Mr. Marsh writes also of the annual meeting of a temperance society, probably the first in all this region. It was organized soon after he came to Statesburg. The newly married missionary and his wife are no other, of course, but our friends Rev. Daniel Adams and the teacher who was Miss Quinney.

On the morning of the memorable 13th of November, 1833, Mr. Marsh "was awakened between four and five o'clock by an alarm which a neighbor, part Indian (Mr. G.), had given, that the stars were falling. * * Being somewhat frightened, he came to call me, and said that if it kept on they would all fall. * * One thing appeared very remarkable, and was that the greater part of them appeared from a point near the zenith."

On the 28th of the same month Mr. Marsh makes note of the "annual Thanksgiving." This institution his people were doubtless the first to establish and honor in what is now Wisconsin. Christmas, too, they observed in a religious manner "of their own accord," as we learn from the record made by Mr. Marsh in 1832. He held religious service in the morning, and a temperance meeting in the afternoon. The "annual fast" also, as formerly kept each spring-time in Massachusetts, the people of Statesburg remembered and observed after the manner of the New England Puritans of the eighteenth century. In this they have found no followers, and even the old Bay state herself is seeking to recognize legally the change that has made a time of merriment out of the day that was meant to be one of self-denial and of worship. Mr. Marsh notes that he held a preaching service on the 1st of May, 1834, a day that he calls the "annual fast." A few days before this (April 14th), "a number of Menomonees, very decently clad and in a very orderly manner, came up to hold a council with the Stockbridges respecting putting a stop to the sending of ardent spirits to their people." Was not this the first temperance convention in unnamed Wisconsin? What a measure of eternal condemnation men of the

---

[1] He gives their names and ages: John Metoxen, deacon, fifty-two; Robert Konkapot, fifty-six; Joseph Quinney, dead; John Bennet, absent and standing not good; Esther Thowhusquh, seventy-nine; Margaret Quinney, dead; Elizabeth Bennet, sixty-four; Hannah Konkapot, fifty-two; Catherine Metoxen, forty-six; Dolly Now-ottokhunwoh, (dead ?); Mary Konkapot, age not given.

white race have brought upon themselves in dealing intoxicants to the easily tempted Indians!

The time was drawing near when the Muh-he-ka-ne-ok must give up their chosen home on the banks of the Fox. For their improvements "they received a reasonable compensation," wrote Mr. Marsh. The sum paid by the United States government.— $25,000,— certainly does not seem to be excessive. We may turn back to Mr. McCall's narrative to notice what had been done at the time of his visit. Under date of 1830, August 13th, he made entry: "Across the river up to the lower end of the rappids of the Grand Kakalin, where the Stockbridge tribe settlement begins, unloaded our boat and hired our load carted up over land to the head of the rappids and a little above the Mission house, and sent our Boat to that place. Hired 5 Indians, making eight hands. Stopped at ——— Gardners, an Indian on the bank of the river. There are 7 islands in this great Rappid which falls about 30 feet. The Stockbridge tribe have a saw Mill and are preparing to [build] and [put] the frame up for a grist mill on one of the branches of the river.

"Satterday morning. Rained all the fournoon. Staid and Breakfasted at the Mission House."[1]

No wonder that the Indians were unwilling to leave this favored place that they had chosen as their own, and in whose earth they had already hidden the bodies of some of their honored dead. In a letter[2] written 1833, October 14th to the American Board, they had expressed "much solicitude on the subject." "The effects and consequences of removal will be disastrous," wrote Mr. Marsh under date of 1834, February 1st. His Oneida friends had already gone, for on the 28th, perhaps of the preceding month, he "went to Duck Creek, about twenty miles distant, to visit a band of Oneidas who had lately moved there, and who formerly lived near the Stockbridges. Some have lately built their houses, and others are now building." Thus what seems to be the first Methodist church in unnamed Wisconsin found a new home.[3]

The story of 1834 is continued in a letter by Chauncey Hall, dated July 2nd, of that year, at Statesburg, but postmarked "Grand Cakalin." It was addressed to Mr. Edmund F. Ely of the Ojibway mission at Sandy Lake, in what is now Minnesota. The postage, eighteen and three-fourths cents, reminds

---

[1] It was on their return that the commissioners "came down to the mission house [August 17th, Tuesday], and according to appointment when we went up met the chiefs and head men of the stockbridge Tribe in council; gave them our hands, and presented them with a short written address and a copy of extracts from our instructions as far as related to them, to prepare their minds against their meeting us in council on Tuesday next. They appeared pleased and closed our business for this Time. In the meantime Mrs. Stephens had prepared an excellent dinner of which we partook and then started our boat down the rappids, And we went on by land to the foot of the rappids, where we joined the boat and returned to the Bay about 10 o'clock at night."

[2] It was signed by Jacob Cheekthaukon, John Metoxen, Austin E. Quinney, Thomas T. Hendrick, Andrew Miller, Timothy T. Jourdan, Cornelius S. Charles, John W. Quinney, Samuel A. Miller and Josiah W. Miller.

[3] It seems to me that Mr. Marsh's evidence shows conclusively that this was virtually, if not formally, an organized church more than a year before Mr. Clark came to Green Bay.

us that certainly in some things the former days were not better than these.

"When Rev. Mr. Green[1] was at Mackinaw last summer, an arrangement was made for my future labors which made it probable that I should in the course of the coming fall or early in the spring leave Mackinaw for the place from which I am now writing. This station was occupied by the Rev. Mr. Marsh and Mr. and Mrs. Stevens. Mr. Stevens and wife left last fall, but it was not consistent for me to leave till spring.   *   *   We [himself and wife] left Mackinaw on the 21st of May at 2 o'clock P. M., Monday, and arrived at Green Bay on Wednesday evening. Our passage was in the steamboat Oliver Newbury and, though we were detained by fogs, was very pleasant.

"We left Green Bay on Friday at 12 o'clock, and proceeded up the Fox river.   *   *   We reached the mission-house at 3 P. M., had time to get our baggage, etc., from the landing (one and one-half miles distant in consequence of the rapids) and get very comfortably settled before evening. Rev. Mr. Marsh gave us a very cordial reception. He had been alone since last fall, much of the time without any one to attend to his domestic concerns, and he was truly glad to receive fellow-laborers. We found in him what we expected, a kind and warm-hearted Christian, much devoted to his work, and enjoying to a great degree the love and confidence of the people for whom he labors.   *   *   The condition of the Indians among whom we dwell presents much that is truly encouraging to the missionary, and methinks a view of them as they collect together for the worship of God, or talk of His love in their dwellings, would make the heart of one destined to labor among the uncivilized Indians, where no gospel has extended its benign influence, to rejoice in view of what the Lord has done, and encourage him to pursue his labors assured that He who has done so much for these Indians is able also to extend the work and will do it through the instrumentality of His children. The church among the Stockbridge Indians consists of sixty or seventy members. Most of them adorn their profession. Several who had wandered from the path of duty have recently returned with apparent penitence, and, as far as I know, their lives give evidence that it is sincere. The church is a temperance church, agreeing to abstain from the use of all strong drink, not excepting wine, strong beer and cider. Most of the tribe are members of a temperance society which exerts a salutary influence. At their last annual meeting, a few weeks since, they resolved to give up the use of wine, strong beer and cider. (The resolution had before existed but in the church.)

"Perhaps from what I write, you will conclude that we are among a people so civilized that we have nothing to remind us that we are on missionary ground. Truly we are among those for whom 'the Lord has done great things.' Yet had I time and room I could tell you with all that seems to be cheering much that would lead you to feel that, if we are not in the midst of heathenism, we have enough to remind us of heathen wretchedness, enough to call forth the compassion of feeling hearts, enough to call forth our unwearied labors and

---

[1] Rev. David Greene, secretary of the American Board, 1828-1832.

to lead us to ask with sincerity for an interest in your prayers.

"I mentioned the absence of the Rev. Mr. Marsh. He left with five of the principal Indians on the 12th of June. In the 'Missionary Herald' for April, 1834, is a letter from the chief man of the Stockbridge Indians which will explain to you the object of this journey. Much interest has been and is still manifested by the Indians in the mission to their benighted neighbors. On the Sabbath previous to their departure, Mr. John Metoxen, the head chief of the tribe, addressed his people at the evening meeting. He was one of the delegation, and he reminded his friends in a feeling and dignified manner, that they were soon to be separated: that perhaps this was their last meeting upon earth. Then he spoke of the contemplated journey to their neighbors west of the Mississippi, and he appeared deeply to feel the importance of the errand on which they were going.

"He said it was the first time their people had undertaken to tell the 'glad tidings' to their brethren in darkness.[1] He expressed his sense of the blessings which had been conferred on them through the gospel; of the preciousness of their privileges, and the obligation which rested upon them to improve them, as well as to discharge their duty to their wretched brethren. With much feeling he spoke of the condition of the heathen, and particularly of the Indians, while destitute of the gospel. His heart seemed to feel for their wretchedness in this life, but the burden of his sorrows seemed to be the hopelessness of their condition in the future world while destitute of a saving knowledge of Jesus. He assured them of his attachment to home and his desire to return, but expressed the most cheerful resignation of the will of his Heavenly Father respecting this. His counsel to his people who were to remain was faithful and affectionate, earnestly desiring their prayers for a blessing upon this embassy.

"The absence of Mr. Marsh and the chief men takes from the Indians those who have been their counselors, and we are not without our fears respecting the effect, particularly as this will be a season of much temptation, as the Indians are to receive their money for their improvements and are much unsettled in consequence of removing. Our hope is that He who has promised that 'they who water shall be watered' will watch over us. We have had cheering indications that the Lord was with us for two or more weeks past. Christians have been evidently revived, and two or three individuals have publicly expressed anxiety for the salvation of their souls, and asked for the counsels and the prayers of Christians. Our meetings are well attended and our Sunday school is interesting. About half the people have moved to the new station about twenty miles from us and forty from Green Bay, the nearest white settlement. We expect to remove there in a few months as well as the remainder of the people; have yet to remove the timber and erect a dwelling."

This missionary journey of Mr. Marsh, Metoxen and others beyond the Mississippi was an event of rare interest. The Muh-he-ka-ne-ok were "grand-

---

[1] We wonder if Mr. Metoxen was not misunderstood. The statement, as it stands, is of course totally erroneous.

fathers" to the Sacs and Foxes. When the latter, by the injustice of the whites, were driven into the war of 1832, the Muh-he-ka-ne-ok exposed themselves to some suspicion by refusing to take up arms against them. Theirs was a nobler course than that of the miserable Winnebagoes. The Sacs and Foxes sent an embassy asking their "grandfathers" not to strike them. Loyal as the Stockbridge tribe was and always has been to the United States, the pledge asked for was given and kept.[1] The year following the defeat of Black Hawk, 1833, seems to have been, on the part of the Muh-he-ka-ne-ok, one of special interest in his people. "The Sacs and Fox and Delaware tribes of Indians are our friends and relatives, and a delegation from our people intend visiting them next season." We have seen how this purpose was carried out. "Can we not tell them the great benefits we have received from being taught the gospel?" continues the letter.[2] "Can we not tell them that your society is ready to send them teachers if they are willing to receive them? Can you not appoint a missionary to accompany us? Fathers, if you think there is any way we can do good in our visit to our poor brethren beyond the Mississippi, we wish you would give us some instructions."

This letter seems to have found a ready response. A sense of justice prompted the offer of a mission to the Sacs and Foxes. Moreover, it was at that very time that the foundations were being laid of the wonderful missions among the Sioux. For this work, Mr. Stevens, so lately at Statesburg, received, in 1834, his commission from the American Board. The summer of the same year Thomas Smith Williamson, M. D., spent in "an exploring tour among the Indians of the upper Mississippi, with special reference to the Sacs and Foxes." It was also an object "to collect what information he could in regard to the Sioux, Winnebagoes, and other Indians." He was then in the mission service.

And now Mr. Marsh tells the story of his summer's pilgrimage:[3]

"Set out on the 12th of June (1834). Upon the 14th encamped for the Sabbath, having in full view to our right the Big Butte des Morte, which had taken its name from the slaughter of an entire Sac village by the French and Menominees about one hundred years ago.[4] As we pursued our journey we occasionally saw lodges of Winnebagoes along upon the banks but no corn fields or vegetables of any kind which they had growing. Whenever they saw us coming they would * * beg as if half starved. Col. Cutler informed me that * * they were the most indolent, thieving tribe that he knew of. He had known as many as three or four hundred drunk at one time. * * The Cumberland Presbyterians have a mission among them near Prairie du Chien. The Catholics are making some effort to proselyte them and numbers are Catholics at the present time.

---

[1] Alexander J. Erwin was commissioned to raise two or three hundred Oneidas and Stockbridges for the Black Hawk war. This he failed to do, as the Indians would not go.—Statement of James M. Boyd, "Historical Collections," vol. XII., page 278.

[2] The one already referred to,—that addressed to the American Board, 1833, October 14th.

[3] In a report dated at Stockbridge, 1835, March 25th.

[4] See page 25.

"The second Sabbath, June 22nd, we passed at a place called the Pine Bend on the Wisconsin, about sixty miles from Portage, where was a small settlement. A few Indians were present and attended religious worship with us. We arrived at Prairie du Chien on the 25th and finding that Dr. Williamson had left we made no tarry. Saturday evening, the 28th, we arrived at Rock Island. Dr. Williamson had left this place also the day previous.

"Mr. Metoxen had an interview with Black Hawk who was returning from Rock Island to his village, which Mr. Metoxen had just been to visit.

" Black Hawk went on to tell how kindly he was treated by the white people wherever he went when on his tour. 'In no place,' says he, 'did I see white men and white squaws drinking together the same as our people do. When I passed through your place it was just so, and I want to have my people just like those good white people, for I see where they do not drink they do better and live better. Now what do you think is best about receiving missionaries?' ' By all means receive them,' I replied,' says Mr. Metoxen, 'for they will do you good.' Black Hawk: 'But the trader, Mr. Davenport, told me not to have anything to do with them for they would only make you worse.'[1]

"Our attempt to establish a mission amongst the Sacs and Foxes entirely failed of success.

"I went to visit old Ke-o-kuck's village soon after my arrival. He told my interpreter that he knew what I had come for but he wanted to learn nothing about it.[2] The head chief, called the 'Stabber,' said the same thing to my interpreter when I went to his lodge. As they had no previous notice of my visit, and inasmuch as their mode of treating the subject was so contrary to the rules of Indian etiquette, I do not hesitate to say that they had particular instructions previously.

"After a few days the Stockbridges met with the 'Stabber,' who is considered by the Sacs as the head chief, but not by the white people. They proposed to the 'Stabber' to make the intended visit to his people. At first he objected, but consented after they had told him that they had provisions of their own. They went and stayed about five days, but having no interpreter could converse but little with the Sacs and so the latter understood little of the object of the visit. Still I had reason to believe, from what I afterwards ascertained, that a favorable impression was made on the minds of the Sacs by the visit. After this the Stockbridges set their faces towards home. I had gone down the river to visit one of the most remote bands upon the river Des Moines.

"The deportment of the Stockbridge delegation during the whole tour was such as to do honor to themselves and to the cause of missions. Many white

---

[1] George Davenport, born in Lincolnshire, England, 1783, enlisted in the United States army in 1805, and served for ten years. With the soldiers who came to build Fort Armstrong, he landed on Rock Island 1816, May 10th. In the autumn of 1835, he became one of the founders of the city in Iowa that bears his name.

[2] Ke-o-kuk continued to be so much of a heathen that, as already stated, during or about 1840, he had a squaw put to death for the alleged reason that she bewitched one of his children. Mr. Catlin says the name Ke-o-kuk means "the running fox."

people where they went had never seen a civilized or Christian Indian before. Often the most singular inquiries would be made, as 'Do they belong to the church?' 'Can they speak English?' etc. On their return they were of course alone and they came by land part of the way. In the mining country, not far from Galena, the Sabbath overtook them and there they stopped until it was passed. I returned the same way and heard it remarked by some of the people 'that they sang hymns all Sabbath day.' This seemed not only new but strange to those who make no distinction between one day and another when traveling.

"The appearance of John Metoxen, his conversation, etc., were universally spoken of with admiration, particularly by Christians.

"My connection with Dr. Williamson was short. Together we visited Ap penoose's village, one hundred twenty-five miles from the mouth of the Des Moines. After Dr. Williamson left to return to his friends in Ohio I was attacked with dysentery. I returned about one hundred miles down the Des Moines river to the house of a trader, Mr. William Phelps, where I was sick one week.

"Mr. Phelps, though a professed infidel in sentiment, still was friendly to my object. He declared that if something were not done soon for the Sacs, etc., they would all be swept off. He treated me with great hospitality. He and a brother of his are trading in opposition to the American Fur Company and it rather operates to our advantage than otherwise."

"A tour by land and water of over 1,300 miles;" "absence of three months and some days," are among Mr. Marsh's comments on his journey.

"Take the American Fur Company in the aggregate," General Zachary Taylor once remarked, "and they are the greatest set of scoundrels the world ever knew."[1] For their purposes, civilized Indians were of little use. Hence, and for other reasons even less creditable, most of the traders opposed such missions as proposed to turn the Indians from hunters into farmers.

But though evil influences thus prevailed among the Sacs and Foxes, effective work was begun among the Sioux. Of these, there were at this time some within the present limits of Wisconsin, and in 1836 missionary work was undertaken for them. We may pardon the short digression that tells the story.

Two men, perhaps from the St. Crishona seminary though more probably from the mission training school (both) at beautiful Basel in Switzerland, where the swift Rhine turns northward on its course from the Alps to the sea, came to the upper Mississippi region. Amid the mountain-like bluffs near the present village of Trempealeau, not far from where Nicholas Perrot spent the winter of 1685-6, if not on the very spot, one of these men, Rev. Daniel Gavin, with an associate, Louis Straum, whom he found at Prairie du Chien, made the first modern settlement within the limits of Trempealeau county. His Swiss colleague, Rev. Samuel Denton, in the spring of 1835, established a mission where is now the village of Red Wing, Minnesota. Rev. Alfred Brunson, who saw

---

[1] "Minnesota Historical Collections," vol. VII., part 2, page 239.

both these missionaries on his first trip up the river above Prairie du Chien (1837) thinks that the Red Wing establishment was founded in 1834. Both movements were unsuccessful, as was also an attempt by Rev. J. D. Stevens to found a mission at Wah-pa-sha's village, now Winona. The chief named was hostile to all these missionary efforts, and as they were neither French nor Romanist the traders gave them no favor. In 1837 the Sioux transferred to the United States government the land on which stood the Trempealeau mission, and in the following year Mr. Gavin abandoned the field. He then joined his colleague who had married Miss Persis Skinner of the Mackinaw mission. He himself in 1839 married Miss Lucy C. Stevens, niece of J. D. Stevens, and this missionary quaternion found other homes among the Sioux and, in connection with missionaries of the American Board, continued labor with them.

Among the Muh-he-ka-ne-ok, the year 1834 was a memorable one not only for the westward missionary journey of their pastor and some of their leading men, it was the time of their "nation's" third removal within less than fifty years. It was also the centennial anniversary of the consent given by the tribe to the establishment of a Christian mission among them, and of the first coming of the elder Sergeant to the people to whom he was to give his life. Perhaps these facts were quite forgotten; I find no allusion to them.

To the "new station" mentioned by Mr. Hall was given the old name Stockbridge. There "a good building for the school and for religious meetings" was erected,[1] principally by the Indians themselves,[2] and thither the mission establishment was removed in the autumn of 1834. By the next year it could be said that "numbers of them have cleared and fenced large tracts for themselves, have erected comfortable houses, and are laboring industriously on their new lands." Not a bad record for a people who twice,—and some of them three times,—within a dozen years had been called upon to battle with the difficulties of subduing a wilderness. At Statesburg "they had begun to live quite comfortably," says Mr. Marsh, and at Stockbridge "they hoped that

---

[1] It still stands, though at some distance from the site whereon it was built. The old structure suggests the fact that, probably more than any other place in Wisconsin, Stockbridge reproduced some of the features of a New England town of the eighteenth century. The "meeting-house" was used, not only for religious service but for other public gatherings. This old building, after serving as a Congregational church until 1869, December 19th, became successively a school, a printing-office and a blacksmith shop. It has had in it, probably, more silver money than has been at one time in any other house of worship in Wisconsin,—making no exception for Sundays when special collections have been taken for missions, either home or foreign! At one payment (1849, probably) the Indians received therein eighty thousand or more silver half-dollars. The use of the same building for purposes both of church and state,—merely different aspects of the same Christian commonwealth,—was judged right by the Puritan, and did not imply any unbecoming use of the house wherein he worshiped God. He had little use for the term "secular" in its present meaning. It is probable that the tribal meetings of the Stockbridges, like the town meetings of the olden time and some of the present, in New England, were opened with prayer.

Two tithing-men or "beadles," to use Mr. Colton's term, were chosen at the annual church meeting to keep good order during service. We may suppose that this included the prevention of "gazing about, sleeping, smiling and all other indecent behavior,"—the words on this subject of the Presbyterian "Directory for Worship."

[2] Report at the annual meeting of the American Board, September, 1835.

they had found a place where they might long enjoy peace and a permanent resting-place."

Mr. Hall, who, by reason of the financial straits of the American Board, was compelled to leave the Stockbridge mission in the autumn of 1838, bore at a later time this fine testimony to the virtues of the people among whom he made his home for more than four years:

"I have been well acquainted with the early settlements of the whites in Wisconsin and Illinois, yet never knew a people who in their early settlement manifested so much attachment to the ministrations of religion. It has never been our privilege to dwell with a people so distinguished for this, and so moral. The Sabbath was universally kept sacred; meetings on that and other days were well attended; intoxicating drinks were prohibited from being brought upon their lands; the women had started meetings for prayer, besides the maternal association and a meeting for improvement in sewing, &c. Fast and Thanksgiving days were always observed as in New England. The men lived upon their farms, and regarded hunting and fishing as uncertain employment. A church member who sought direction from his Bible once said to me, 'I thought about going a-hunting; I thought of Esau; may be I come home hungry.' The rifle was laid up, and he went to his field."

But scarcely were the Stockbridges settled in their new homes when another removal was proposed. "Even now," says the annual report to the Board for 1836, "when the Indians have hardly put up their houses and cleared and enclosed their fields, the proposal has been made to take them from their homes again, and transport them to a country west of the Mississippi river. Their minds are beginning to be agitated on the subject. The perplexity and discouragement to which the missionaries are subjected from this source are very great; but not to be compared with the disheartening and deteriorating influence exerted on the Indians by being so often obliged to abandon the houses and fields which they were just beginning to enjoy, and to prepare for themselves other homes of which they may be despoiled as soon." Of their condition otherwise at that time the narrative adds, "Temperance, industry and attention to religious instruction, have been more general than for the preceding two or three years. Temptations have beset the people from the white settlers who are crowding in around them. Some painful cases of defection have occurred. Others have resisted temptation so as to excite the admiration of unprincipled men."

Whatever may have been the origin of this proposed removal beyond the Mississippi, some of the Indians themselves heartily favored it. Hence, and doubtless for other reasons also, a division arose among them. Their pastor opposed removal. To Agent Boyd he thus wrote under date of 1838, August 23rd:

"The Stockbridge, or Muh-hee-kun-neew Indians (*i. e.*, River Nation, or skilled in going over the waves),[1] have so long resided in the vicinity of the

---

[1] I doubt not that this is an erroneous translation. However, I find the following in Cat-

white people, and have so long since abandoned most of their Indian habits and customs, that little can be said of them that is peculiar to Indians. All now subsist by cultivating their lands and, if properly encouraged, and if they can remain permanently on their present reservation, [they] will, in a few years, have good farms cleared up, and live as comfortably as their white neighbors."

But some did not wish to remain "on their present reservation," and 1839, September 3rd. there was made a treaty "by which these two townships were split in two north and south, and the east half was receded to the United States, the west half of each of the two townships remaining as a reservation." Having received, doubtless, their share of the proceeds of this sale, a party of between fifty and sixty removed to what is now Kansas. Their ultimate destination was, I suppose, the proposed Osage river reservation[1] but "they were allowed to settled temporarily upon the lands of the Delaware Indians five miles below Fort Leavenworth on the Missouri."[2]

This removal seems to have rid our Wisconsin Stockbridge of a disturbing element. But there speedily rose a new cause of dissension,— the proposal to follow the example of the Brothertowns and become citizens of the United States. It seems to have been some time, however, before this became a cause of bitterness.

Meanwhile tribal authority continued to be exercised in full vigor. On the 17th of February, 1840, Mr. Marsh heard of the murder of Peter Sherman by Isaac Littleman. With a promptness that puts to shame the courts of the present day, the trial,— which was by "the nation,"— was concluded on Saturday, the 22nd of the same month. March 13th, the murderer was hanged. "If it can be so ordered," wrote Mr. Marsh, "I desire never to witness another execution." "The sheriff," of whom he speaks, was an Indian, Peter Littleman, who is said to have been a cousin of the murderer. Among the Wisconsin Oneidas there have been two cases of capital punishment by tribal authority.

In 1840 what is now Calumet county "contained about two hundred thirty Stockbridge, and about three hundred Brothertown Indians, and only about three whites,"[3]— if, among whites, men alone are to be counted. A civil organization of Calumet county was, nominally at least, both effected and dissolved that year (January 6th and August 6th, respectively).

Three years later Mr. Marsh was able to give this hopeful statement of the condition of his people:[4]

---

lin's "North American Indians" (London edition): "Mo hee-con-nouks, or Mohegans (the good canoemen)." But I do not trust Mr. Catlin's translations. Thus J. W. Quinney's Indian name, which our author spells Waun-naw-con, he translates as "the dish," the true Mohegan for which is "Waun dath" (*a* as in *dath*, as in the English word *arm*). Mr. Catlin gives portraits of both the Quinneys. Austin E. is said to be "very shrewd and intelligent man, a professed and, I think, a sincere Christian." Mistakenly he calls J. W. Quinney "a Baptist missionary preacher," and adds that he is "a very plausible and eloquent speaker."

[1] See page 61. The leaders of this party were Thomas Hendrick and Robert Konkapot.
[2] Miss Jones's "History of Stockbridge."
[3] Thomas Commuck. The three whites were a tavern-keeper named Westfall, Rev. Cutting Marsh and Moody Mann, a mill-wright, afterward county judge.
[4] In a letter to "Julius P. B. McCabe, Green Bay," written 1843, January 3rd.

"Although the evils of intemperance are far from being banished from the nation, still the good accomplished can never be estimated in this world in the marked improvement of the health, habits and morals of the people. It is an interesting fact that there is not half the sickness and but about half the number of deaths now in the nation that there were twelve years ago; while the number of births, which, at that time, was only about equal to the number of deaths, for two years past has been just double the number of deaths.

"There is also a Congregational church which numbers fifty-five members in regular standing; there is a Sunday-school also which is attended by both young and old.

"The situation of the Reservation on the east side of Winnebago lake is delightful, and well suited, in every respect, to agricultural purposes. It is well watered by numerous springs which come out of the limestone ledges.

"Schools have been taught in the nation a greater part of the time since they removed to this country, and they were for a number of years aided by the funds of the American Board in sustaining them until the pecuniary embarrassments commenced, and since then none has been afforded.

"For two or three years past their schools have greatly languished for the want of funds to support them in consequence of the officers of the general government withholding the money due under the treaty of September 3rd, 1839, for reasons which they do not see fit to give, and which are inexplicable to the Indians."

Mr. Marsh speaks of "schools." One was a continuance of that begun at Statesburg. Of the second, Mr. Marsh wrote 1838, August 23rd:[1] "Another school, it is expected, will go into operation as soon as a house which they [the Indians] have commenced can be completed. The children are taught reading, spelling, writing, arithmetic, geography, English grammar and composition. Latterly, one half day in each week has been appropriated to teaching the small girls to sew. Our school has been kept up the year round excepting vacation at the close of quarters, or in the spring when the traveling is very bad, and during the short season in harvest time when the parents want their children at home.

"In general the children appear quite as tractable and make as good proficiency in their studies, according to their advantages, as the children of white people.

"A majority of the people can speak and read the English language intelligibly, and many fluently, and the use of English in giving instruction and in common conversation is becoming more and more in vogue and soon, I hope, all interpretation will be superseded." This, we remember, was in 1838.

"As the Indians have taken their schools under their own direction," says the annual report of the American Board for 1840-41, "Mr. Marsh has forwarded no account of them during the year."

As nearly as I can determine, the Stockbridge tribe has had in this region

---

[1] In his letter to Agent Boyd.

west of Lake Michigan no happier years than those from 1835 to 1842, inclusive.

On the 3rd of March, 1843, an act was approved making the Muh-he-ka-ne-ok citizens of the United States. This measure was strongly opposed by what seems to have been the better portion of the "nation,"—Metoxen, the Quinneys, Samuel Miller and others. Henceforth the story is one chiefly of strife and conflict within the tribe itself. Thus of a council held 1843, March 24th, at Mr. Metoxen's, there is this record in Mr. Marsh's diary: "Accomplished nothing, on account of the objections made by the citizen party to my assisting." Somewhat more than a year afterward (1844, April 13th), J. N. Chicks, a leader of that party, "came before the church [in answer to a summons], but it was to read a paper of a slanderous character which he had drawn up against myself."[1]

If the impression I have received from living witnesses is the correct one, Mr. Marsh sought to avoid identifying himself with either party. He had probably looked forward to American citizenship as the ultimate condition of the Muh-he-ka-ne-ok, and he may at first have favored the Congressional act of 1843 in regard to his people. But if he did, he doubtless came soon to see that the measure was premature and so unwise. I doubt that the opposition scheme of the tribal party,—"to remove forthwith to some region beyond the Mississippi,"[2]—met his approval. It is almost certain that much that was said and done by men of both parties was to him a source of great mortification and grief. In the report at the annual meeting of the American Board in 1844, it is said: "Such has been the state of the church that the missionary has not felt at liberty to administer the Lord's supper during the year." It seems, however, that both parties continued to attend church.

I come now to paragraphs that I wish I did not feel called upon the write. That I may be just, I will give certain statements from "Thirty Years in the Itineracy," by the late Wesson Gage Miller, D. D., a very worthy and a very useful man, I have no doubt. He is speaking of the beginnings of his ministerial service in Wisconsin. "But we had hardly got our home work [at Brothertown] fully in hand, when there came an invitation from Stockbridge, several miles below, to extend our labors into that settlement. There had been a Congregational mission among the Stockbridge nation for many years, but its condition was not very promising. * * [It] was now in charge of Dr. Marsh, a gentleman of education and ability. He divided his time, however, between the ministerial and medical professions, and, as a result, the spiritual interests necessarily languished."

It was not brotherly of Mr. Miller thus to write. We have seen sufficient reason why "spiritual interests languished" among the Stockbridges. These interests were destined to "languish," yet more, and his own work, I have no

---

[1] Though the offender,—for such he seems to have been,—was excluded from the church, these men seem to have become reconciled, for 1848, June 10th, Mr. Marsh "attended the funeral of an infant child of J. N. Chicks."
[2] Letter of 1844, May 1st, signed by Austin E. Quinney, John Metoxen and J. W. Quinney, and addressed to "his excellency Governor Doty, superintendent of Indian affairs."

doubt, contributed to this result. Mr. Marsh's attendance upon the sick was merely incidental to his missionary work. This Mr. Miller should have said or been silent. There is for him this measure of excuse, that with a warm and, I doubt not, a good heart, he had but a boyish and biased judgment. In 1845, probably April, he began a series of meetings in Mr. Chicks's barn. Mr. Miller "gushes" to a surprising extent over this man whom he calls the "head chief of the Stockbridge nation."[1] This could not have been the case, for Chicks was a leader of the "citizens' party" in whose view,—and indeed, according to the then unrepealed statute of 1843,—there was no Stockbridge nation. In regard to this matter, Mr. Miller seems to have been, in his mature years, as uncritical in his writing as in his youth he was inconsiderate in his action.

No doubt this unhappy religious movement increased the division that was not healed by the repeal 1846, August 6th, of the act that had made the Stockbridges citizens. The tribal organization, which its supporters had not permitted to lapse, was able to resume at least a limited degree of authority. But it could not rule the white men who had bought homes on the reservation, and who soon came to out-number the Indians. There was the old and easy and ruinous remedy,—sale and removal. Whatever lands had not been allotted in severalty were sold by the tribe to the United States government by a treaty made 1848, November 24th.

But a little time before, Mr. Marsh, their constant friend and faithful pastor, had been constrained to leave them. One of the tribe, Jeremiah Slingerland, seems to have taken up the work for so much of the time as he spent among his people.

The faithful memory of one still among the living has preserved for us a picture of the condition of the Muh-he-ka-ne-ok just before this time of hurtful change. Nearly all the homes of the people were of logs, but there were a few frame houses. For years Mrs. Marsh had been a teacher of good housekeeping to the women and many followed, at least in some measure, her example. But there was a considerable number who did not properly guard against dirt and vermin. Naturally there were sneers for those who tried to fashion their apparel after the manners of the whites. The women of the progressive party wore at church and other public places beaver hats shaped somewhat like the silk hats so commonly worn by gentlemen. The other women wore neither hat nor bonnet. Men and women alike, to the number of perhaps

---

[1] I am much afraid that even in his "conversion,"—real or pretended,—at this time, Chicks acted the part of a deceiver. Mr. Miller reports him as saying "Me great sinner." I don't doubt the entire truthfulness of this statement but I don't believe that he needed to say it in broken English. He had been at school among the whites, probably at the Oneida Institute, New York, and almost certainly at Hanover, New Hampshire, where he was, I have reason to believe, enrolled as a student either in Dartmouth college or in Moor's "Charity school" (see pages 67 and 68). What he acquired among the whites was, apparently, chiefly an unfitness for the conditions of life then existing among his own people. Had he never returned to them it would doubtless have been a blessing for both. He was one of the factors in bringing about the removal of the Indians from Stockbridge,—an injury from which the tribe can never recover,—and he himself died a drunkard.

half or more of the tribe, wore "blankets." These were commonly of blue broadcloth, and were worn in public. The men all wore pantaloons and shirts. But the order in which were worn the parts of these garments that are next to each other does not accord with our ideas of propriety. The want of suspenders was manifest by the constant "hitching" needed to keep the pantaloons in place. The women did most of the work, even of that in the field. Yet there were men who had accepted enough of Christian teaching to know that this kind of work was especially their duty and to act accordingly. Some of the families lived at a considerable distance from the school but all the children received therein more or less training. Nearly all the tribe attended church. Their Sabbath, as in former years, began at sunset on Saturday evening. Mrs. Benson remembers a peeled stick used to keep order and secure wakefulness in church. There must then still have been a "tithing-man." So many of the tribe understood the language of their fathers that Mr. Slingerland occasionally preached in it. This Mr. Marsh did not think necessary. Some of the young men had been educated in Eastern colleges. These, with the possible exception of Mr. Slingerland, did no credit to their training. They married half-civilized women and lapsed into something worse than their former mode of life. Mrs. Benson's work among this people, like that of Mr. Marsh, came to an end in 1848. Then the American Board gave up its mission. This seems now and is judged by Mrs. Benson to have been a serious mistake.

By the treaty of 1848, "the Stockbridges belonging to the tribal organization stipulated to remove west of the Mississippi.[1] It was proposed to form a reservation for them on the Crow river, Minnesota, "but the removal of the Indians was delayed by the Government['s] not succeeding, until 1852, in purchasing lands from the Sioux."[1] Then the Stockbridges refused to go, and soon the Crow river lands were occupied by white squatters.

Preliminary, perhaps, to this proposed removal what seems to have been a census of the Muh-he-ka-ne-ok was taken in May, 1851. The total enumeration was two hundred thirty-five, of whom twenty-five or thirty were in the Kansas region.[2]

Of the condition in which the Muh-he-ka-ne-ok were living in the spring of 1852, we have these recollections from Mrs. Mary A. Niles, a grand-daughter of John Sergeant, the younger:

"We found the Indians living very comfortably, in very good houses, New-England fashion, on one long street. One of them invited us to dinner and served us very handsomely on a table, set according to our own ideas, with blue china, and every thing neat and nice. The Indian woman waited and served us very handsomely."

But soon the Indians seem to have drifted into the sadly demoralizing condition of living on the proceeds of the sale of their lands rather than upon the

---

[1] House Mis. Doc., No. 14, Forty-sixth Congress, Third session.
[2] Most of those who removed thither died within a few years or returned to Wisconsin See also note 1, page 61.

products of their labor. Presumably a town government was set up soon after the enactment of 1843. Between this and tribal authority somewhat of conflict was inevitable. There came to be three times as many whites as Indians upon the old Stockbridge reservation. Again the camel drove the Arab from the tent,[1] and on the 5th of February, 1856, a treaty[2] was made assigning to the Muh-he-ka-ne-ok two townships of land in Wisconsin, "near the southern boundary of the Menomonee reservation." The land that from promises made them they had a right to expect is that lying on and near the southern shore of Lake Shawano. But this was too good to set apart for Indians,—though the Lake Winnebago reservation which the Stockbridges had given up is one of the finest regions in Wisconsin,— and so the tract assigned them consists of land inferior both in quality and location. However, it contains a small lake, and through it, over a bed of red granite, and broken at places into rapids, courses the Red river, a tributary of the Wolf.

Following the course of these streams and of the Fox, or going over the horrible roads of that time, the wronged tribe sought its new home. Removal began in 1856. Some went in October. I have been told that most of the tribe made the change in 1857. The last to remove "came two years after the treaty was made."[3] Some Indians from New York,[4]—about eighty in all, I have been told,—joined the Muh-he-ka-ne-ok at the time of this last removal.

---

[1] In spite of the efforts of the Indians to have the township on Lake Winnebago restored to them. By a treaty agreed to 1855, June 1st, by the commissioner of the United States general land-office and signed by the Indians "almost unanimously" it was provided that such restoration should take place. But Francis Huebschmann, then Indian superintendent, recommended that this treaty be not submitted to the Senate for ratification. His advice was followed, and the Indians lost their home.

It may be added that in 1854 Samuel Miller was a member of the "Presbyterian and Congregational Convention of Wisconsin." He presented the case of his people, and the Convention appointed a committee to "memorialize the proper department of the government, in our name, in behalf of the Stockbridge tribe, setting forth their grievances, and petitioning for the restoration to them of their lands." How nearly successful this movement was, has just been stated.

[2] The Muh-he-ka-ne-ok have suffered no greater wrong than this treaty of 1856. I have little doubt that Dr. Huebschmann acted most arrogantly and unjustly in procuring thereto the alleged consent of the Indians. He assumed authority to depose the tribal chief, Austin E. Quinney, and the councilors who served with him. To fill the places thus made vacant, Huebschmann ordered a special election. The favor of the "citizens' party,"—and, it is alleged, of others who were not, and never had been, of the Stockbridge-Munsee "nation,"—was secured by allowing them to vote and promising them equal shares in whatever was due the tribe or might be given to it. Perhaps other means even less creditable were employed. The sachem thus elected,—Ziba T. Peters,—and the new councilors, were of course favorable to the proposed treaty, which all of both parties were invited to sign. This Austin E. Quinney and others of the Indian party,—in all, perhaps, a majority of the true "nation," as distinct from the "citizens," refused to do. But, counting both parties, Huebschmann probably secured a majority. This done, his supporters found that they were his dupes. For it was not "nominated in the bond" that the tract they expected was the one they should get. Huebschmann saw to it that the white man was to have the turkey and the Indian might take the owl. Slingerland, Chicks and their ilk found a trickery and cunning that more than matched their own.

[3] Mrs. Sarah Irene (Seymour) Slingerland. For thirty years she was associated with her husband in teaching the government school among the Stockbridges. She won a measure of esteem that was given to her husband only by those who did not know him well. It is due, however, to both to say that the wife,—a white woman,—had full confidence in her husband and the highest regard for him. Mrs. Slingerland died 1892, August 15th.

[4] Representative Munsees from that state were allowed to sign the treaty of 1856.

But, as in Massachusetts and New York some of their own number remained in the old home.

Among these was Austin E. Quinney. He indeed made a brief sojourn at the Red river settlement but returned to Stockbridge, where he died 1864, August 17th.[1] We are glad that of the other two leaders in the Wisconsinward migration of their people neither was called upon to leave the home to which they had led their people. John W. Quinney died at Stockbridge, 1855, July 21st. There was reason at that time to entertain the hope that the Lake Winnebago reservation might be restored to the Stockbridges. This project is said to have been his own.[2] Upon a marble slab, in the old Indian cemetery near Stockbridge, is the legend, "John Metoxen, died April 8th, 1858, aged 87 years." We have a right to claim as our own this son of Massachusetts. Let his name stand first in the list of Wisconsin's honored laymen. Aside from Dr. Morse, he was probably the first to hold public worship on Wisconsin soil according to the simple rites of the Puritan. And he was the first, after the departure of the early French Jesuits (who are so much overpraised and whose work is so much overvalued by sentimentalists and sectarians) to maintain here regularly the public worship of Almighty God.

Almost immediately after removal the tribe adopted a new constitution.[3] This superseded one drawn up by J. W. Quinney in 1833. Probably the two were much alike. I understand that the constitution adopted in 1857 has since been laid aside and another adopted. The name first given to the new reservation was "Moh-he-con-nuck," an historic designation and one worth keeping. But the place,— there is neither village nor post-office,— seems now to be called "Red Springs." The central part of the reservation where is the poor old church-building, the manse and the cemetery bears the name "Stockbridge."

By act of 1871, February 6th, three-fourths of the "Red Springs" reservation was sold and, it would seem, all of the pine that was fit for lumber. Also under this act citizenship was bestowed upon a number of the tribe who desired it. These form the "new citizens' party," and have gone forth from the reservation. At least a semblance of tribal organization is still kept up by the "Indian party" between which and what is left of the "old citizens' party" the chronic quarrel still continues.

Again the deaths among these people out-number the births. The logging camps where most of the young men of both the Stockbridge and Menomonee tribes spend the long winters and the delayed springs of northern Wisconsin are poor schools for the development of right character, or even for training in habits of steady industry. The white neighbors of these people are, for the most part, not of a sort to teach needed lessons of temperance. The frequent removals of the Indians, and the practical socialism in which they are living, have made it impossible for a man to feel sure that if he made a good home he

---

[1] He was born 1780, January 1st, and served in the war of 1812.
[2] See "Wisconsin Historical Collections," volume IV., page 310.
[3] See "Muh-he-ka-ne-ok," page 48.

could leave it to his children. Indeed, there are on the reservation farms that in equity ought to belong to the children of the men who cleared and improved them, but that are now in possession of intruders. Men who have no right to any share in tribal property crowd in upon the reservation or claim tribal relationship so as to get, if possible, a share of the common property when the division, believed to be not far off, shall be made. Indeed the question now at issue is not so much, Shall this be done? as it is, Who are entitled to share the proceeds? As a socialistic experiment we have here a most wretched failure. Nearly all the people on the reservation are poor and dispirited. They do not use to advantage even the few opportunities they have. And the most serious effect is that made upon habits and character.

Most painfully is manifest the lack of effective pastoral oversight.[1] Mr. Miller's work was short-lived and better adapted to the inclinations than to the needs of this somewhat fickle-minded people. It was doubtless a factor, though probably a minor one, in bringing about the removal of Rev. Cutting Marsh from the position that long experience had enabled him to fill so well. It may be said now,— for both men are in their graves,— that Mr. Marsh had no confidence in his successor or, rather, supplanter, Jeremiah Slingerland. He had been, it is said, somewhat of a ladies' pet both at Dartmouth and Bangor.[2] By William Parsons, "United States special Indian agent," he is described as "a speculative and dishonest Stockbridge Indian." However, Mr. Parsons's report[3] is one of great, though I dare not say undeserved, severity,— a severity that spares neither white man nor Indian. Even of certain men high in political standing he writes as if he believed that they would take and keep what did not honestly belong to them!

To influences proceeding from an unfavorable location; from a soil that offers the agriculturist but a poor reward; from a debasing environment; from a practical socialism,— and even that ill-organized; from hateful disputes thence and otherwise arising; from unwise abandonment of missionary work; from a mistaken sectarianism; from unworthy leaders; from grasping white men in high positions and low; and from the ever-present evil of drunkenness; — to all these influences there has been opposed no adequate resistant. The

---

[1] No church was organized preliminary to removal, as was done in 1785 and 1818. Nor did the emigrants follow the example set by their fathers at the time of the removal from Statesburg and take with them the old organization. Mr. Slingerland became a local preacher in the Methodist Episcopal body, and, later, joined the Presbyterians. A church of that order was organized 1867, September 18th, and still exists. It has been mistakenly put under the care of the Home Mission board. But churches of the Indians and of other weak races need, for their proper oversight and care, an organization specially adapted to just that kind of work — such, for example, as the American Missionary Association.

There is now no resident pastor on the reservation. Rev. Jacob Van Rensselaer Hughes, of Shawano, does what he can, in feeble health and limited time, for this otherwise pastorless people.

[2] "Jeremiah Slingerland, (Indian), Moor's Charity School, Hanover, New Hampshire; Indian teacher, [Lake] Winnebago and Green Bay, Wisconsin; died 1884, June 4th, Neshina, Wisconsin." The foregoing is from the general catalogue of Bangor seminary, "class of 1845." For "Neshina" we are to read "Keshena," and we should notice the fact that Mr. Slingerland did not teach at Green Bay, but on the present Stockbridge reservation.

[3] Dated 1888, January 16th.

mission among the Muh-he-ka-ne-ok was not a failure, but the want of one has been a failure most unmistakably.

In the old days of the Hebrew commonwealth a woman who in giving life lay dying named her son Ichabod, saying, "The glory is departed." Thus it is with the people whose ancestry made so noble a history, the greater and better part of which seems, even by their descendants, to be forgotten. But the great state that the Muh-he-ka-ne-ok helped to found has reason to remember with honor and gratitude the spiritual children of John Sergeant and Jonathan Edwards. The mighty impulse that these men gave their people reached us in the making here of Christian homes, in the founding of churches[1] and other religious institutions that still abide,[2] in the establishment of schools, in a valiant struggle in behalf of temperance, in prohibitory legislation as regards intoxicants, in anti-slavery sentiment and in continued loyalty to the United States government.

During the late war the Stockbridges furnished thirty-eight volunteers for the Union army, more than one-tenth of the entire tribe.[3] Not one deserted. But their losses were heavy, especially by disease. Far from home, no doubt, most of those who died in the service had burial. And in the little cemetery on the reservation there are nine soldiers' graves.

The people who, for us and for our fathers, gave these men and their kindred of former generations to the silence of death, have made their distinctive history. Let it not be unread nor unheeded. For though it has much that is to their shame, and more that is to ours, the story of the nation named for "the waters that are never still" is one that makes for righteousness.

---

[1] At Stockbridge (Wisconsin), they received whites to the membership of their church, which thus lived on, was re-organized in 1860, and continues at the present time its unbroken life and uninterrupted service. The whites who formed the (so-called) Presbyterian church of Green Bay, the First Presbyterian (now Immanuel) of Milwaukee, a church among the soldiers at Fort Winnebago, and one long since extinct at Calumetville, sent to Stockbridge for the help of the pastor there in the work of organization. The Indians aided in the support of Rev. O. P. Clinton when he was doing his early and effective missionary service in the region about Lake Winnebago.

[2] Somewhat of their direct relation to the establishment of missions in the region west of the upper Mississippi, we have already learned. Their church was the first, not of the number that formed the organization, to join the Presbyterian and Congregational Convention of Wisconsin. It was received at a meeting held, by commission, at Green Bay 1841, January 2nd. John Metoxen was the delegate of the church, which, when local conventions were organized became successively a member of those bearing the names of Milwaukee, Beloit, Madison and Winnebago. The Madison Convention, Austin E. Quinney helped to organize.

Nor should it be forgotten that in the early time of few settlements and of long journeys, many a weary traveler found shelter at Stockbridge.

[3] Report of the commissioner of Indian affairs, 1864.

CHAPTER XI.

AMONG THE OJIBWAYS.

Notwithstanding the flight of the Hurons and the Ottawas from Chequamegon bay in 1671[1] the Sioux (Dakotas) did not become masters there. The strong and determined enemies of that tribe, the Ojibways, either had not then arrived or could not be displaced. These, according to their own tradition, "first reached Point Sha-ga-waum-ik-ong" about 1490. There "for many years they concentrated their numbers in one village. They were surrounded by fierce and inveterate enemies whom they denominated the O-dug-aum-eeg (opposite-side people, best known at this day as the Foxes), and the A-boin-ug (or roasters), by which significant name they have ever known the powerful tribe of the Dakotas."[2]

Pressed by these enemies, the Ojibways removed to the adjacent island of Mon-ing-wun-a-kaun-ing (the place of the golden-breasted woodpecker), now called Madelaine. But through some superstitious fears increased if not caused by their magicians, commonly called "medicine men," who in many respects correspond to our "spirit mediums," this place was afterward so utterly abandoned that an Ojibway would scarcely venture to set foot upon it.

From this legendary history which almost certainly errs in assigning to the Ojibway occupancy of Chequamegon bay too early a beginning, but otherwise

---

[1] See page 13.

[2] The meaning of their own tribal name is suggestive: "To roast till puckered up"; from "o-jib," "puckered up;" and "ab-way," "to roast." Both names, Ojibway and Abohnug, probably originated from the practice of putting captives to death by torture with fire.

Another name Saulteaux or Sauteurs "the people of the falls," properly used only of the part that remained at Sault Ste. Marie, is used sometimes apparently of the whole tribe.

"Chippewa" the Gallicized form of "Ojibway," or as Schoolcraft writes it "Odjibwa," is familiar to all.

William Whipple Warren, already named, to whom we are indebted for most of these statements concerning the Ojibways, states that the present tribal name has been in use "certainly not more than three centuries, and in all probability much less. It is only in this term of time that they have been disconnected as a distinct or separate tribe from the Ottawas and Potta-wat-um-ies. The name by which they were known when incorporated in one body is at the present day uncertain. The final separation of these three tribes took place at the straits of Michilimackinac from natural causes."

From these straits "the Potta-wat-um-ies moved up Lake Michigan and by taking with them, or for a time perpetuating, the national fire, which, according to tradition, was sacredly kept alive in their more primitive days, they have obtained the name of 'those who make or keep the fire,' which is the literal meaning of their tribal cognomen."

Those who remained eastward of both divisions of their kindred came first in contact with the French and thus, as their name signifies, became "Ottawas;" that is, "traders."

seems to be substantially correct, we turn to the fragmentary narrative of the time that follows the flight of the Hurons.

A few years after the great council at Sault Ste. Marie in 1671, the French began to take practical possession of the Lake Superior region. The missionary did not return, but the explorer and the trader did. Daniel Grayson du Lhut (Du Luth), Pierre Le Sueur and others made bold explorations and erected military and trading-posts. On the lake shore, a few miles above Kah-man-a-tig-wa-yah (Pigeon river), Du Lhut established, perhaps in 1679, the first permanent station held by white men within the present limits of Minnesota.

Some years later, apparently in 1692, or 1693, Le Sueur built some sort of a structure on Madelaine island, probably at the south end of it, a place which was long held by his countrymen. It is the site known now as that of the "old fort."

It was at this time, according to Rev. E. D. Neill, that "the Ojibways began to concentrate in a village upon the shore of Chequamegon bay." Rev. E. P. Wheeler, of Ashland, also differs in opinion, on this subject, with Mr. Warren and writes:

"The Ojibways, I think, can not be shown to have known anything about Chequamegon bay before 1660 when from a point toward Green Bay they were going up there to trade. Neill seems to me to be safer by far to follow than Warren. The second-growth trees which Mr. Warren instances as showing the early occupation of La Pointe can easily be accounted for by the fact that in 1762 a French trader was known to have summered there not because there were Indians there but because they were on the opposite side. Following down from 1762 to 1791 when John Johnson summered there and the Cadottes also came to the island, there were occasional traders who found it safer to trade from over across the channel on La Pointe island than at Bayfield and vicinity where the Indians were congregated. These transient traders at La Pointe would account for the second-growth timber which existed at the time of his early recollections as a boy (born in 1824)."

Whatever is the fact in regard to the coming of the Ojibways to Chequamegon Bay the trading-station on Madelaine island is one of the oldest in the Wisconsin region. There is no record of continuous occupancy by the French, though doubtless their traders, at least, kept coming and going. The last officer of that nationality at Chequamegon Point was Hertel de Beaubassin who left there in 1756 with Ojibways as allies for the French in the war then raging between them and the British (with whom before the American revolution the colonists are to be counted). Nine years later when the whole country had passed under the sway of King George Alexander Henry, the English trader and author who so narrowly escaped with his life at the time of the massacre at (old) Fort Mackinaw, 1763, June 4th, re-established the Madelaine island trading-post. To this place the name of La Pointe was applied some time during the present century, a name afterwards transferred to the "new fort" built by the American Fur Company two miles farther north, when, on account of the use of steamers in the Lake Superior trade, a deeper harbor became a necessity. Thus when we see the name La Pointe we need to remember that it once meant the mainland west of Chequamegon bay, then the southern end of Madelaine island and last of all the village that still bears it.

From Henry the trade seems to have passed to the brothers Cadotte, Jean Baptiste and Michael, descendants of a Mons. Cadeau who, it is said, came to the Lake Superior region in 1671, in the company of the French deputy already named, Simon Francis Daumont, the Sieur de St. Lusson.[1]

In 1818 a young man, Lyman Marcus Warren, a native of Berkshire county, Massachusetts,[2] came with his younger brother, Truman Abraham, to the Lake Superior region "to engage in the fur trade. They entered the service of Michael Cadotte and soon became great favorites with the Ojibways." "They married daughters of their employer and succeeded to his trade which they carried on at first in rivalry to the American Fur Company but afterward in connection with it." In 1825 Truman died while on a voyage from Mackinaw to Detroit. He left a son, James Henry who, even as these pages are in course of preparation (October, 1891), has retired from a service of twenty-seven years and three months as the Congregational Home Missionary superintendent for California.

To the elder brother were given more years of life. Of his conversion at Mackinaw we have already read. His eager zeal for the good of the Indians and others with whom he lived led to the establishment of the first mission at La Pointe on Madelaine island. He was obliged to wait four years for the fulfillment of his cherished desire. But at last the mission that he so earnestly pleaded for was begun. The object for which Mr. Stevens came west had not been forgotten, and we now return to him and his work.[3]

In 1828 he visited Sault Ste. Marie, Green Bay, the Stockbridges and the Oneidas. He made the acquaintance of Lewis Cass, then governor of Michigan; of many officers of the United States army; of Rev. Alvin Coe, who had come west under under the auspices of the Presbyterian Board; and of Henry Rowe Schoolcraft, known both as an explorer and a student of Indian languages and customs. Late in the autumn of 1828, the condition of Mr. Stevens's health compelled him to go back to New York. Rest and change gave him strength and he "began to cherish the hope of soon re-entering upon mission work in the great northwest. Late in March, 1829," he writes "we were greatly and agreeably surprised to meet the Rev. Alvin Coe, whose acquaintance we made at Sault Ste. Marie. In company with Dr. Ely, secretary of the Presbyterian Board of missions, he had visited Washington for the purpose of laying the subject of evangelizing the North American Indians before the

---

[1] A son of Cadeau's whose name is written Jean Baptiste Cadotte, resident at Sault St. Marie, was the father of the two named above. Their mother was an Ojibway woman, a lawful wife. The marriage was celebrated by a priest of Rome. W. W. Warren, a great-grandson, gives us these statements.

[2] Born 1794, August 9th.

[3] See page 49.

president [John Quincy Adams] and obtaining the sanction and protection of the government in prosecuting the work. The programme of the Board was to send out two men to explore the country between the Mississippi river, Green Bay and Lake Superior, ascertaining the different tribes, their locality, number, disposition toward the Americans and the needs of each; and select a few prominent sites for the establishment of mission schools if the outlook should be favorable to the enterprise. Bro. Coe and myself were commissioned to make this exploration the following season and make our report to the Board. In the meantime the Mackinaw mission had been transferred to the care of the American Board and re-enforced. I immediately wrote to Mr. Everts, secretary of the American Board, and received the approval of the executive committee- and further [was informed] that the Rev. David Greene, one of the assistant secretaries, would meet me and Bro. Coe in June at Green Bay for consultation on the proposed tour."

As far as rapidity of transportation is concerned, the modern age began in this century. Abraham could travel as fast as Washington. The then newly invented steamboat was all that gave Mr. Stevens an advantage in speed over the Apostle Paul. Says our Wisconsin missionary: "No railroad in the United States yet. From Buffalo by the lake to Green Bay, reaching there by the 14th of June. Death had entered the mission family with the Stockbridge Indians, the family whom I left the last November, and removed the Rev. Mr. Miner from his labors. Bro. Coe and Bro. Greene arrived in a few days. Matters were soon arranged and preparation made for the bereaved family to accompany Mr. Greene down the lakes to New York, and for Bro. Coe and myself to start on our work of exploration. We procured horses to take us to Fort Winnebago near the Wisconsin river. Thence we traveled by canoe down that river to the Mississippi at Prairie du Chien. There we spent some [about] two weeks. Between three [thousand] and four thousand Indians, Winnebagoes and Menomonees, were assembled here to treat with the government for the sale of their lands east of the Mississippi river. All these lands were at that time ceded to the United States. The Indians were to have five years to remove to the west side of the Mississippi.

"About the middle of August we proceeded up the Mississippi in bark canoes rowed by four Menomonees, thirteen days *en route*. Spent several days at Fort Snelling,[1] and in visiting the several villages or bands of Dakota (alias Sioux) Indians. At our request several hunters came to the council house at this place and we told them through our interpreter the object of our visit: To extend to them the hand of friendship; to invite them to participate in all the good things the Great Spirit had bestowed upon us. The good book the Great Spirit had given us to guide us in the straight path was as good for the Red

[1] In September, 1829, Rev. A. Coe and J. D. Stevens arrived at Fort Snelling. Agent Taliaferro (Major Lawrence Taliaferro of the United States army) treated them kindly and offerred the old mill and buildings at the Falls of St. Anthony for a Presbyterian mission school for the Dakotas, as well as the Indian farm opened at Calhoun and called Eatonville.—"History of Minnesota," by Rev. Edward Duffield Neill.

man as the White, and it required us to carry it to all people, both the Red and the Black as well as the White. Many of you are becoming old and gray-headed, and your eyes are becoming dim and will never learn to read this book. But your children may be taught to read it, and you can hear from them the sweet words of love which will make you wise and happy here and in the country of spirits where all our fathers have gone and to which we shall soon go. We want you to consent to let us come and live with you, and learn your language, and make books in your language, and teach your children to read them. This is what we have to say.

"The old chief Shonka-shan[1] (Red Dog) arose and said: 'We have listened to your words. The Great Spirit loved his white children better than his red children and gave them this book, and they are wise and happy. Now we are glad to hear that he has pity for us and has sent you to us to speak to us these words and give us this book to make us wise and happy that we may have warm houses and fine clothes and plenty to eat like his white children. This was what he had to say.'"

From Fort Snelling our travelers started toward Lake Superior. Their Dakota friends gave them the use of two horses, and two of the Indians went along as guides. "The third day," continues Mr. Stevens, "we came to a small river. The Indians said the name was Sunrise river. Here we camped for the night and our guides told us that when they had slept one night they should leave us and go back to the Dakotas; they were afraid to go farther in the Ojibway country; if we followed down that river"— it flows northward — "we should come to the St. Croix river, then following up the St. Croix, we should find the Indian trading-post. No offers we could make could induce them to go any farther."

Near noon the next day the guides started homeward, taking with them the horses, the shot-gun and a large part of the provisions of the party. The missionary explorers were thus left in a dense wilderness defenseless and alone "We peeled some bark, made our blankets and the provisions we had left into packs, hung them upon our backs and proceeded down the river. It flowed through a tamarack and cedar swamp which was almost impassable. Before noon of the next day, Bro. Coe became exhausted and could not proceed I proposed leaving the river to find better traveling. He proposed constructing a raft and floating down the river. This last plan was adopted. Six days we poled and floated slowly down this serpentine stream without seeing or hearing a human being. Our rations were growing short and when we were going get new supplies who could tell?"

Becoming impatient of their slow progress, Mr. Stevens left the raft to see if they could not do better by walking. Avoiding bends in the river he went farther down and awaited the coming of his friend. "I sat down on the high

---

[1] Mr. Stevens writes the name Shonka-shan, the n in both cases being nasal. The last is not proper. It is a mis-pronunciation when the sound is heard. As we spell now, we would write the name Shunka Sha, which is Red Dog. Red Dog's village was only a short distance above Fort Snelling.— A. L. Riggs, D. D., Principal of the Santee Normal Training School.

est point of the bluff, and watched and sang, and hallooed long and loud to the going down of the sun, but no response. No raft came. The shades of night were rapidly approaching, and I felt as much alone as though there were not another being on the face of the whole earth. What had befallen Bro. Coe? I sprang to my feet and made rapid strides up the stream, calling loudly lest I should pass him and be hopelessly separated. The stars came out one after another, but there came no response or indication of another human being upon the face of the whole earth. The dark, turbid, narrow stream, overhung by the tall grass upon its banks, was nearly concealed from my sight as the shades of night stealthily crept over me, so that I found it difficult and dangerous to follow its course. The marshy ground was full of holes and frog-ponds and bogs, that I could not see to avoid. One moment I was stumbling over the bogs, the next sinking deep into the mire or about to slip off a steep bank into the river. I had no apparatus for striking fire"—this was before the days of matches— "and kindling up a beacon light upon the bluff that could be seen from the river. Bro. Coe had these and, if some terrible calamity had not befallen him, he would certainly before this have struck up a light to indicate his whereabouts. As these thoughts were passing through my mind, I cast my eyes across the river toward the opposite bluffs and there, to my great surprise, I saw a bright light upon the top of the bluff. The awful solitude in a moment was gone. There were other human beings in the world besides myself. Hope gave new energy to my feet, and although a wide marsh, covered with high grass and bogs, and a deep stream were to be crossed amid the darkness of the night, I had not a doubt that I should soon be enjoying the fellowship of a companion in travel and a fellow-laborer in the kingdom of Christ." The raft had been broken in pieces upon a rock in a slight rapid.

Mr. Stevens's narrative was never finished. The hand, tremulous with age, laid down the pen forever.

Somehow the explorers made their way from the little Sunrise river to the shores of Lake Superior. Doubtless they went to La Pointe on Madelaine island where the American Fur company then maintained an establishment. There they would find a friend in Mr. Warren, the superintendent, whose entreaty for the establishment of a mission at La Pointe had seemed to the laborers like a call from God.[1]

Mr. Stevens's journey of exploration finished, the autumn of this year, 1829, saw him in Mr. Ambler's place as teacher at the Stockbridge mission.

In the summer of 1829, when Mr. Warren made his annual trip to Mackinaw he took a boat for the special purpose of bringing back with him a missionary. No one could go that year, but in 1830 Fredrick Ayer, returned with him, opened a school,—attended at first only by white children—studied the

---

[1] Mr. Warren was a most helpful friend to the mission. He rests in death where he labored faithfully in life, at La Pointe. (Died 1847, October 10th.) A son, William Whipple Warren, now dead, is the author of a "History of the Ojibways," published by the Minnesota Historical society. A daughter, Mrs. Mary (Warren) English, labors in the Episcopal mission at Red Lake, Minnesota.

Ojibway language, and made the beginning of a mission at La Pointe on Madelaine island three miles across from the site of the present village of Bayfield. At that time there was no other mission on Lake Superior. There was neither minister nor priest,— Mr. Ayer was not yet ordained,— west of Sault Ste. Marie. The Ojibways were in the rudest state of savage life."[1]

The next year the mission was strengthened by the coming of Rev. Sherman Hall and wife, with an interpreter, Mrs. Elizabeth (John) Campbell. The mission family left Mackinaw on the 5th of August, 1831, in company with Mr. Warren and arrived at La Pointe on the 30th of the same month. Under the former date Mr. Hall wrote as follows:

"The manner of traveling on the upper waters of the great lakes, is with open canoes and batteaux. The former are made in the Indian style, the materials of which are the bark of the white birch, and the wood of the white cedar. The cedar forms the ribbing, and the bark the part which comes in contact with the water. These are made of various sizes, from ten to thirty feet in length. The largest are sufficiently strong to carry from two to three tons of lading. They are propelled by the paddle, and when well built and well manned, without lading, will go from eighty to one hundred miles in a day, in calm weather.

"Batteaux are light-made boats, about forty feet in length and ten or twelve feet wide at the center, capable of carrying about five tons' burden each, and are rowed by six or seven men. They have no deck. Upon articles of lading with which the boat is filled, is the place for the passengers; who have no other seats than they can form for themselves, out of their traveling trunks, boxes, beds, etc. On these they place themselves in any position necessity may require, or convenience suggest. Such is the vehicle which is to convey us to the place of our destination. In the small compass of this boat we have to find room for eleven persons.

"At night our tent is pitched on some convenient place on shore."

This company took care not to travel on the Sabbath. Their first Sunday, August 7th, was spent at Sault Ste. Marie, "where they were received with Christian hospitality by the Rev. Abel Bingham, Baptist missionary there." Rev. Jeremiah Porter began his work at Sault Ste. Marie this year, but not until about Thanksgiving.

Mr. Hall's journal for August 14th shows how the second Sabbath was honored: "We commenced the day with our private and family devotions. The heat was very oppressive, but we raised a canopy. A large proportion of those in company with us are French Catholics, and do not understand the Eng-

---

[1] Of an earlier time than this, Mr. W. W. Warren, a warm friend of missions and a faithful Christian, wrote in 1851 or 1852.

"The Ojibways were more deserving of respect in those days while living in their natural state, and under the full force of their primitive moral beliefs, than they are at the present day, after being degenerated by a close contact with an unprincipled frontier population."

This last remark suggests the fact that the great question for us to consider in connection with mission work among the Indians is whether that race shall have good from our people or only evil.

lish language. In the morning our service was in the French language, consisting of a chapter from the Bible and a tract read by one of the clerks. A few of the men attended. We also had a service for the Indians, attended by a few. In the evening we held a prayer-meeting."

A wind from the north the next Sunday rendered overcoats a necessity. "On our arrival at this place [then called Petit Marais] last evening, we found the traders of the Fond du Lac[1] department encamped here, they having come to the determination not to travel on the Sabbath. There were therefore fourteen boats in the harbor together to-day, and not less than two hundred persons camped on the shore. At half-past ten, A. M., we had a service in English. In the afternoon we had a service in French which was conducted by singing, prayer, reading the Scriptures and a French tract. A much larger number attended than was present last Sabbath. In the evening we had a prayer-meeting. Thus has the gospel been preached in this wilderness to-day."

On the following Sunday a French service was held, attended by a "large number of men." The Tuesday thereafter the long voyage of more than four hundred eighty-five miles came to an end.

The La Pointe to which the missionaries came was very different from the deserted village that still bears the name. It was the "old" fort on the southern end of Madelaine island soon to be supplanted by the "new fort," or Fort Ramsey,[2] two miles northward. Each in turn was the chief place of trade on Lake Superior. "The first sermon ever delivered at this place by a regularly ordained Christian minister" was by Mr. Hall on the afternoon of the Sabbath after his arrival. He had held a meeting in the morning attended by a considerable number of Frenchmen. It is pleasant to read his acknowledgement of "kindness received from Catholic families."

About the first of September the school averaged twenty-five. "The instruction given has been wholly in the English language on account of our having no books in the language of the natives. Some elementary Indian books are very much needed. Some of the children begin to read in the English Testament. A Sabbath-school exercise has been held on Sabbath mornings with the children." Meetings for adults also were held at which a few verses were often read from a small Scripture tract prepared by Dr. James[3] of the United States army. The hymn-book used was one published for the use of the Methodist missions to the Ojibways in Upper Canada.

From La Pointe we return to Sault Ste. Marie where during the following winter 1831-32[4] Rev. William Thurston Boutwell was making special prepar-

---

[1] Fond du Lac: source of the lake. This Fond du Lac is in Minnesota, near Duluth.
[2] A name little used, apparently, and but for a short time.
[3] Though not at that time a professed Christian, Dr. James aided, as we shall see, in establishing the first Sunday-school in Wisconsin. Later he became a member of the Baptist church at Sault Ste. Marie. He accompanied, in 1819-20 Major Long's expedition to the Rocky Mountains and three years later published an account of it.
[4] During this same winter (March, 1832), Rev. Jeremiah Porter, himself a Congregationalist, organized at Sault Ste. Marie a church that was in name Presbyterian though never in connection with any presbytery. Henry Rowe Schoolcraft was one of the founders of this

ation to join the Ojibway mission. Of what sort this preparation was we learn in a letter dated 1831, October 13th: "I regret one thing—that I had not come here immediately after the subject was first proposed, in which case I should have been nearly, if not quite, three months' advance in Indian of where I now am. I am satisfied that it is not a difficult, though it may be somewhat of a laborious task to acquire the language. As yet I have devoted the major part of my time to the variation of the verb which is, comparatively speaking, endless, both in the affirmative and the negative form. And here I wish you to give all who have undertaken to learn Indian to understand that no one will do for a missionary to Lake Superior who shrinks from apparent difficulty at the outset—here is only the beginning of sorrow." In the same letter he writes for his "Greek Lexion, Greek Grammar, Ernesti on Interpretation, Woods on Baptism, Family Monitor, one of the blank account books and the little Memoirs of Nathan Dickerman."[1]

Years later Mr. Boutwell wrote the subjoined narrative:

"Dr. James, on a visit to the officers at the Fort at Mackinaw, made a brief call at the mission and learned from Rev. Mr. Ferry that I was anxious to learn the Chippewa language. I was called and introduced. As he was leaving he made this proposition to me: 'If you will accept a bed, and a plate at my table, you shall be a thrice welcome guest on this one condition, give me one hour a day in the study of Hebrew. In addition, you shall have the use of my office and my Indian interpreter who, when a mere lad, was taken captive, and adopted by an old squaw, and speaks the language like an Indian.' Such an offer was too valuable to be declined.

"From Mackinaw, ninety miles to the Sault, I passed my first canoe voy-

church and an elder in it. Captain, afterward Major, D. La Fayette Wilcox, commandant at Fort Brady (Sault Ste. Marie), entered into Christian covenant first with this church, and the wife of his successor, Major John Fowle was also a member. Pauline Adelaine, then a babe in arms, daughter of Major Fowle, is known to the world as herself a benefactor of Wellesley college and the widow of its founder, Henry Fowle Durant.

In a letter begun 1833, May 4th, at Sault Ste. Marie, and finished on the 14th of the same month at Chicago, Mr. Porter, in speaking of the former place, tells us that "about seventy have expressed hope in Christ since I first reached there. May 5th I preached in that favored spot for the last time. Eight were admitted to the church." He gave his reasons for leaving. Most of the church were connected with the garrison, and that had been ordered to Fort Dearborn. Mr. Schoolcraft, his patron and faithful friend, expected soon to remove to Mackinaw though he did not go until 1839. At Sault Ste. Marie there was a Baptist minister and an Episcopal. A third, a Methodist, was expected soon. Chicago needed a minister. Major Fowle invited Mr. Porter to go with him and his command. They embarked May 6th. "I hope we have brought in our colony military church the leaven of the gospel." It became the mother of the First Presbyterian church of Chicago, organized by Mr. Porter, mostly out of Congregational material, Wednesday, 26th June, 1833. One of its ruling elders was Major Wilcox who, in about a month after Major Fowle's arrival, relieved him in command of the fort Major Fowle was transferred to West Point as professor of military tactics.

Mr. Porter was the first resident Protestant pastor in Chicago. "A Papal priest [John Mary Irenæus St. Cyr] reached this place from St. Louis a fortnight since," adds Mr. Porter. Jesse Walker, a Methodist, had been coming in once a month or thereabout to hold meetings. Father Kent of Galena, who seems to have made a Pauline tour this spring was glad to find Mr. Porter at Chicago, a village which he thought would grow as rapidly as any in this Western country. Mr. Porter thought that it would soon be large enough to support a minister.

[1] This letter was written from "Saut de St. Marie" to Mr. Abel D. Newton at Mackinaw. It is dated 1831, October 13th.

age in silence, save that, as oft as its remembrance occurs, I thank God that my bones and those of the crew are not at the bottom of Lake Huron.

"At the table Christmas morning Dr. James said to me, 'Mr. Boutwell, when among the Romans you must do as the Romans do. Now visit every family in the village; kiss every female you meet on the way and wish her a merry Christmas; accept a cake and a sip of wine from each hostess.' Puritan blood flushed my face. I replied: 'If such is your Christmas I take none of it.'

"At ten A. M., I ventured to step outside, and take a look up and down the street. Squads of ten and twenty, men, women and children, of all tinges, from the pure native to the white French, were toggled in their best, going the rounds for cakes and cookies. The nights were made hideous by Indians, half-breeds and French in drunken revelry. Such was my first Christmas in this country."[1]

In the spring of 1832 Mr. Schoolcraft organized an expedition with the purpose of ascertaining the true source of the Mississippi, and making other geographical and scientific discoveries. Accompanying this expedition, Mr. Boutwell came to La Pointe, June 20th. Thence the party went westward by way of Fond du Lac. The first sermon ever preached at this old trading-post, now a station on the Northern Pacific railway, was by Mr. Boutwell, probably on Sunday, June 24th. "On the following Sabbath the rain and the mosquitoes rendered it impossible for us to have divine service."

Under date of 13th of July Mr. Boutwell wrote: "At two P. M., we reached Elk lake" (now called Itasca). Before that time Cass lake had been regarded as the source of the Mississippi. Apparently not satisfied with "Omoshkos,"[2] the Ojibway word for "Elk," Mr. Schoolcraft desired, for the lake of new renown, what he awkwardly calls a "female" name. Not being himself a classical scholar, he asked Mr. Boutwell the Latin words for "true" and "head." As "verum" did not seem to be suited to his purpose, Mr. Schoolcraft took the kindred noun "veritas," and from its two last syllables and the first of "caput" formed "Itasca."[3]

---

[1] During the writing of these pages Mr. Boutwell has passed from earth (1890, October 11th). He was born in Hillsborough county, New Hampshire, 1803, February 3rd. He received his education at Phillips (Exeter) academy, Dartmouth college and Andover seminary. In school life he was associated for nine years with Sherman Hall, with whom for so many years he shared the labors of the Ojibway mission. In 1847, feeling that he could thus be more useful, he abandoned work among the Indians and began home missionary service among the lumbermen in and about Stillwater, Minnesota.

[2] The o in *mosh* is printed in Mr. Schoolcraft's book after the fashion of a German o with an umlaut.

[3] The writer was one of a party of fourteen who, during the month of August, 1891, under the leadership of Captain Willard Glazier, explored the region of Lake Itasca.

Itasca was found to be a lake consisting of three narrow arms; at their point of meeting lies Schoolcraft Island. The greatest length of the lake is about four miles. The outlet is at the end of the north arm; at the end of the southwest arm, within one-fourth mile of each other, enter the two principal feeders of the lake. The more westerly and larger of these, Nicollet creek, drains a tamarack swamp. It is a fine stream of clear, cold water. It has several small tributaries: near its head are two ponds of three and twelve acres in extent. The source of the creek is springs. The total length of the creek is one and two-fifths miles. The other creek entering Itasca, the one commonly called Elk, is about half as large. It is but one-fifth of a mile long and affords an outlet for the waters of the lake known variously as

Mr. Boutwell returned by the same route which, probably, Mr. Stevens had traversed three years before, the way of the St. Croix (270 miles) and the Bois Brule (100 miles).[1] The entire distance traveled by him is estimated at 2400 miles. During the course of the journey, which occupied about sixty days, he visited "twelve or fifteen bands of Indians embracing about 3000 souls."

A mission-house, still standing but unoccupied, was built at La Pointe about half-way between the old fort and the new. Besides affording a place for worship and teaching, it became the home of all the missionaries who labored on the island. It was erected and occupied in 1834.

Again a pioneer of pioneers, Mr. Ayer, in the autumn of 1832, pressed farther into the wilderness on a tour of missionary exploration. He visited Sandy Lake and Leech Lake. The former lying "on the great portage route[2] from Winnepeg. by way of the St. Louis river to Lake Superior, has been a noted point on that route for two hundred years." Very near the confluence of the lake's short outlet with the Mississippi, was the home and trading-post of William A. Aitkin, for whom a Minnesota county has been named. Mr. Ayer wintered with him, taught school and finished an Ojibway spelling-book, begun at La Pointe. Early in the spring, with eighty dollars paid by Mr. Aitkin, who also furnished an experienced guide, Mr. Ayer started on foot for Mackinaw, bound for Utica, New York, to get his book printed soon enough to make it possible for him to return to Lake Superior that season with the traders. That was a journey for a hero, and very nearly cost him his life. Once, having broken through the ice, he would have been drowned but for a long pole which prudently he was carrying.

The missionaries of that time were not strangers to long and hard journeys. Nor were these always undertaken in summer. "It requires an athletic constitution," write Messrs. Hall and Boutwell from La Pointe, 1833, February 7th, "to shoulder one's pack and march five or six days in succession through the uninhabited wilderness, perhaps with a pair of snowshoes on the

---

the Elk or Glazier, which is situated one-fifth of a mile south of this southwest arm of Itasca. The greatest length of this lake is one and one-fourth miles. its width about half its length, its area two hundred fifty-five acres, its depth forty-five feet. It is fed by four creeks. The respective lengths of these are: one-fourth mile, one and one-fourth miles, one and one-fourth miles, one and five-eighths miles. On one of them is a pond of nine and one-half acres, on another a pond of two and one-half acres. They all drain tamarack swamps. The total distance from Lake Itasca to the longest of these is two and three-fifths miles. It is the opinion of the writer and I think of all of our party, that this lake (Elk or Glazier) fulfills the greatest number of conditions for being the source of the river.—ALBERT WURTS WHITNEY, Beloit, Wisconsin.

[1] During the second glacial epoch the eastern end of what is now Lake Superior was probably filled with ice. The lake thus reduced in area stood at a surface level at least four hundred twenty-five feet above that of the present day and found an outlet into the Mississippi through the Brule-St. Croix valley. Therein is now a low portage of only two miles.

[2] This route must not be confounded with another between the same lakes, one shorter and more used,—that by way of Grand Portage and the Pigeon river. See page 147 for a reference to the founding of Grand Portage. This place was the destination of the first British expedition that,—" in the latter part of May, 1762," under command of Lieutenant Thomas Bennett,—sailed the waters of Lake Superior. The words just quoted are those of Thompson Maxwell, a native of Massachusetts, and afterward one of the famous " Boston tea party." See " Wisconsin Historical Collections," volume XI., page 213. His fuller narrative is published in the " Essex Institute Historical Collections," volume VII.

feet, and at night to encamp in the open air with only a blanket or two for a covering." With men who would thus endure hardness as good soldiers of Jesus Christ, the mission was sure to do good work.

The first organization of a Congregational church within the present limits of Wisconsin took place at La Pointe, 1833, August 20th, Tuesday, in connection with this mission.[1] The first record-book of the church, recovered during the preparation of this narrative, thus tells the story:

"LA POINTE, Aug. 20, 1833.

"The re-enforcement of the Chippiwa Mission having arrived, and all the members being present, together with several other professors of religion, it was thought best that a church should be organized before those who were destined to other stations should leave this place; accordingly a meeting was held this evening for this purpose. After appropriate devotional exercises, a confession of faith, and Covenant were read by Mr. Boutwell and formally consented to by the members present. Mr. L. M. Warren was elected Clerk. It was thought inexpedient to elect other officers at this time.

"The individuals present who gave their consent to the Confession of faith and Covenant, were Rev. W. T. Boutwell, Rev. S. Hall, Mrs. B. P. Hall, Lyman M. Warren, Edmund F. Ely, C. W. Borup, Mrs. E. Borup, Mr. John Campbell, Mrs. E. Campbell, Mr. F. Ayer, Mrs. E. Ayer, Misses Delia Cook & Sabina Stevens."

This church maintained its Congregational character until after the transfer of the mission to the Presbyterian Board in 1870. It was re-organized, according to Presbyterian polity, 1876, August 6th, Sunday.[2]

In the autumn of 1833, Mr. Ayer sought a new field. September 16th, he went to Yellow Lake and at its outlet established a branch mission. "This," says W. H. Folsom, in his book "Fifty Years in the Northwest," "was the first actual movement in opening the way for white settlements in the St. Croix valley." Here was the gospel first preached within the limits of what is now Burnett county, Wisconsin. A school was begun there 1834, September 24th. On the third of October, 1833, Mr. Boutwell arrived at Leech Lake, near the head of the Mississippi, and there established a mission, the first west of that river and in what is now Minnesota. To this, the Seneca Indians of New York made a contribution. On his way to Leech Lake, one of the dark places of the earth, Mr. Boutwell stopped at Mr. Aitkin's where Edmund F. Ely had become Mr. Ayer's successor, arriving 1833, September 19th, and beginning his school September 23rd.

One other branch station, Fond du Lac, had a beginning the following year, as noted in the report of the mission for 1835:

"La Pointe: Sherman Hall, missionary, and his wife; Joseph Town, farmer and mechanic; Delia Cook, teacher. Yellow Lake: Frederic Ayer, catechist

---

[1] It will be remembered that the Stockbridge church had been organized before its first members left New York.
[2] Unwisely, this too, like the Stockbridge Indian church, has been put by the Presbyterians in charge of their Home Mission board. See note 1, page 144.

and teacher, and his wife; John L. Seymour, teacher; Sabina Stevens, assistant. Leech Lake: William T. Boutwell, missionary, and his wife. Fond du Lac: Edmund F. Ely, teacher and catechist.

"Mr. Ely removed from Sandy Lake to Fond du Lac in the summer of last year; the latter place, which is at the western extremity of Lake Superior, affording, in his opinion, a more promising field for permanent missionary labor. Since his removal he has had a small school, in which he was more successful than he anticipated, has held various meetings for giving religious instruction, and visited and conversed with the people. An ordained missionary is much needed at this station."

Of this "small school," at Fond du Lac (of Lake Superior), Mr. Ely, under date of 1835, October 23rd, thus wrote:

"I am much engaged in my school. * * It is on the whole very interesting. Some are making good progress. I think that a class of five or six will be able to read and write intelligibly in the spring. We have some inconveniences. For instance, family, school, cooking, baggage and beds are put into a house sixteen and one-half by fourteen, and about sixteen square feet of that is occupied by the chimney, but this is so much better than no school room that we rejoice instead of murmur. I trust that we shall be provided with a convenient room in due time."

We turn again to the mission report made in 1835:

"Mr. Boutwell still remains at Leech Lake. More than a year since he was united in marriage with Miss Hester Crooks,[1] heretofore a teacher at Yellow Lake. He is received and kindly treated by the Indians, large numbers of whom reside in the vicinity, but his instructions seem to make little impression on them. His remoteness from the white settlements exposes him to many inconveniences, and compels him to depend for subsistence almost entirely on the fish of the lakes, and the wild rice gathered in the marshes and creeks; and these afford but a precarious supply.

"At Yellow Lake the scarcity of provisions compelled the Indians to disperse in various directions in search of food, which, as all the children left the place, caused the school to be suspended for some months. The whole number of pupils there has been about thirty, and the average attendance twelve. As game is every year becoming scarcer, and their wild rice so frequently fails, the Indians will soon be driven to the alternative of cultivating the land or perishing by famine.

"During the last winter the school at La Pointe increased to the number of thirty daily attendants, the pupils and their parents manifesting more interest than at any former period. Most of the pupils are taught in both the English and Ojibway languages. Two public religious exercises are held at this station

---

[1] Mrs. Boutwell was a daughter of Ramsey Crooks, of whom Irving writes in his "Astoria." Crooks was a member of the American Fur Company. Mrs. Boutwell's mother was of Indian origin. The first dwelling of Mr. and Mrs. Boutwell after their marriage was a lodge of bark. At Leech Lake such provisions as they got from white settlements had to be brought from Fort Snelling, part of the way on men's backs. The Indians at Leech Lake did not long treat them kindly.

on the Sabbath: one in English and one in Ojibway language. As the number of persons speaking the English language is already considerable at La Pointe, and is likely to increase (since that place has become the principal depot for the business of the American Fur company in the Northwest), it is highly important that regular public religious services should be maintained in that language. The number of Indians who attend meeting has considerably increased, though most of the men still stand aloof and some ridicule and oppose."

A second mission, one of the Roman Catholic communion, was begun by Rev. Frederic Baraga, a native of Austria, who arrived at La Pointe 27th July, 1835. In the year of his arrival he caused to be built what Rev. Chrysostom Verwyst calls a chapel. Six years later some logs of this building were used in the construction of the present church, dedicated 1st August, 1841. This is the church over which, in spite of what Messrs. Warren (W. W.) and Verwyst both have written, some ill-informed people, supposing it was erected by Marquette, indulge in much wasted sentiment.[1] In it hangs a pleasing though not a great picture, a Descent from the Cross, probably by some Italian painter or copyist. The story given in some guide books that this painting was brought to America by Marquette is preposterous and absurd. If it had been in Marquette's mission,—which it will be remembered was not on Madelaine island at all,—he would doubtless have taken it with him when he and his people were driven to "Missilimackilnac." If, on this subject, any doubt is left, it will surely be removed by the subjoined letter, perhaps the last ever written by the late Captain John Daniel Angus, of La Pointe:[2]

Jan 27th 94

Dear Sir

Yours of the 18th is at hand and I hasten to Answer it I have Lived at La pointe the most of the time since 1835. Bishop Baraga brought picture as stated in 1840 from Rome I know, for I assisted him to unpack the same and he told me at the [time] that the pope presented [it] to him and at the time that he did not know its age. at the same time the Bishop's sister the Countess de Hefferon came with her brother and remained one [year] and then returned home to berlin She was a widow about 45 years of age and possessed of A Large fortune. No Marquette never Saw that picture unless he saw it in Rome Hoping that this find [you] well while

I remain yours

J D. Angus.[3]

---

[1] An innocently meant, but droll inscription upon a tombstone in the cemetery adjoining the church is here reproduced:

To The Memory
of
Abraham Beaulieu
Born 15, September
1822.
Accidently Shot
4th April 1844.

As a mark of affection from his brother.
[2] The dispatch announcing his death, is dated (1894) February 15th.
[3] Of course, a statement of the fact will make, to many, not the slightest difference. Our

Close by the lake shore, on the right-hand side of the landing-place, stands the church begun, perhaps, in 1839, and finished, says Rev. E. P. Wheeler, "early in the summer of 1840." It was built by subscription by the Protestant mission and congregation. According to Captain Angus there was a difference of only a few days in beginning work on this building and that belonging to the Roman Catholics. He does not remember which was begun first. The Protestant church was built on land that, in spite of the claim of the mission, the government years afterward offered for sale. Notice of the proposed sale did not reach the missionaries and the site was bought by a Jewish trader. Indians and whites had both left La Pointe and it was not thought worth while either to buy his claim or dispute his title.

In our narrative we return to Yellow Lake whence the mission force removed to Pokeguma lake, on the west of the St. Croix, arriving there in May, 1836. Though they were thus beyond our proper field, it may be noted that a church numbering at first only seven members, three of whom were Indians, was organized there by Mr. Hall in February, 1837. He baptized eight persons, and married two couples. These services were the first of the kind in the St. Croix valley. Some understanding of the difficulty of the mission work, at least in its beginning, may be gained from the following statement: "The motives of the gospel, in themselves considered, have no more influence over the Indian than over the deer he follows in the chase." The missionaries, therefore, first encouraged the Indian to work, and always purchased of him his spare provisions.

The mission at Leech Lake was less successful. The Ojibways there were of the band fitly known as the Pillagers. On an August day in 1836, Mr. Boutwell heard shouts and noises across the lake. Having rowed across, he found Jean N. Nicollet, a distinguished French astronomer, who, in the service of the United States government, had come to determine the latitude and longitude of various places about the head waters of the Mississippi. The Indians, totally unable to understand what he was doing with his mysterious instruments, and vexed because he made them no presents of tobacco or anything else, were giving him serious annoyance. The meeting of these missionaries of religion and science was a mutual pleasure. In his official report Mr. Nicollet acknowledges "kind attentions" from Mr. Boutwell, and expresses his personal "affection and gratitude" toward him.

In the following December, the Leech Lake Indians murdered the agent of the American Fur Company.[1] But not until they poisoned one of his children,— without, however, causing death,— did Mr. Boutwell leave them. In

---

true Marquette devotee is on that particular subject of her admiration, simply irrational; and the insincere one is playing a game to win Roman Catholic votes.

[1] It may be that this agent and he whose burial is spoken of in the subjoined note are one and the same:

"This afternoon I followed the remains of poor Alfred Aitkin to the grave. The wretched father arrived with them yesterday. It is impossible to see and not to pity him. He is the picture of distress and almost of despair. By his request the [Episcopal] church burial service was read at the house. The scene at the grave was impressive and affecting."—DELIA COOK, Fond du Lac, 25th February, 1837.

the summer of 1838 he removed to Pokeguma Lake, and Mr. Ayer went thence to Fond du Lac.

For a time, the work at Pokeguma was one of great promise. "We have reason to bless God for what our eyes are permitted to behold at this place. We believe that Christ has set his seal upon some here, and that the Holy Spirit is now leading others to him. * * Three, we believe, have the seal of Christ in their hearts."[1]

But soon there was a change. The heathen Indians became openly hostile: "At Fond du Lac and Pokeguma they have been much tried this summer with the Indians. They have killed several cattle at the latter place for the mission, and one at Fond du Lac. Some have appeared otherwise hostile. What the Lord intends to do with us and the Indians, I do not know. I have no further anxiety than to be ascertained of his will. At present, I do not see any reason why we should not persevere in efforts to save these wretched heathen."[2]

The next year Mr. Hall was able to say:[3] "The station at Pokeguma appears more promising than it did last summer." Of Fond du Lac whence, it seems, the Indians had meanwhile removed,—whether voluntarily or by compulsion I do not know,—he wrote under date of 1839, September 5th:

"Our station at Fond du Lac has been given up and the missionaries [have] removed to Pokeguma."

But the Pokeguma mission was not to escape violence. The Ojibways had reason to expect an attack from the Sioux. But these, Indian-like, had surrounded the mission settlement and had a force on the opposite side of the lake, in all one hundred and eleven warriors, before the Ojibways suspected their arrival. The plan of the Sioux was to slay their enemies when at work. But, fearing an attack, the Ojibways had been spending their nights on an island in the lake half a mile from the shore. So they were late in getting to the gardens which they were learning to cultivate. Meanwhile three of their young men rowed across the lake on their way to warn another portion of their tribe. Two of the mission school-girls, about twelve years old, went with them to bring the canoe back. The warriors who had been stationed on that side of the lake to cut off the escape of the fugitives fired, prematurely for the carrying out of their plan. The three young men on the shore got off safe, but the Sioux, in whose code of warfare the slaughter of a child is as honorable as the killing of a warrior, followed the girls, who were attempting to row back to the mission, and killed both. Thus the alarm was given and a fierce fight followed (1841, May 24th).

The Sioux were driven off after a two or three days' struggle, but the victory of the Ojibways was marred by the cannibalism of some of their pagan warriors. In contrast with this heathen feast was the Christian service at the

---
[1] John L. Seymour, Pokeguma, 1837, February 6th.
[2] Rev. Sherman Hall, La Pointe, 1838, October 13th, to his friend and former mission-associate, Mr. Abel D. Newton, Green Bay.
[3] Under date of 1839, March 11th.

burial of the poor girls, the first victims of the massacre. As soon as possible, Mr. Ely went in search of the bodies of his murdered pupils. Struck into the brain of each was a tomahawk. A tragic ending for a school-girl's life! "The Indians were scattered," writes Mrs. Ayer, "and dared not return." For two years they were thus kept from their homes. The Pokeguma church removed for a time to Fond du Lac. But "when the spring of 1843 came, the fear of their enemies had so far passed away that many of the old settlers at Pokeguma returned, pagans as well as Christians, and again cultivated their fields and occupied their houses."[1] But soon the coming of white settlers displaced the Indians. Pokeguma as a missionary station was abandoned in 1845 and, by the removal of its people, the Indian church there became extinct.

The fight at Pokeguma was but one of the occurences of a war that ultimately broke up not only the mission station at Pokeguma, but that established at Lake Harriet by Mr. Stevens and a third, of which we shall learn more, that was at Little Crow's[2] village, Kaposia.

A winter journey in 1843 took Mr. Ayer to Leech lake, west of the Mississippi, and to Red Lake whose waters flow northward into Hudson's Bay. At Red Lake, a mission was begun 1843, April 17th, probably by Mr. Ayer himself[3] and Mr. Ely. Though this field also is outside the limits of our state, yet an account of it shows that the work of the missionaries whose history we have been following was confined within no narrow geographical lines. Nor has their influence and following been limited to the operations of one missionary society or of one denomination of Christians. At Red Lake the Episcopalians now carry on the work.[4] In the first establishment of this station, we notice with the familiar names of Ayer and Ely a new one, that of David Brainerd Spencer. At this time he was the representative of a new movement, though at a later date he labored for a time under the auspices of the American Board.

As early as 1837 or 1838 part of the intensely evangelistic spirit of Oberlin was turned toward the Indians as objects of missionary work. About this time Professor, afterwards President, Finney said in his characteristic way that no man was fit to be a missionary who could not take an ear of corn in his pocket and start for the Rocky Mountains. Filled with this spirit, earnest

---

[1] S. R. Riggs, D. D.

[2] Father of the Little Crow who became so notorious in the massacre of 1862.

[3] "Mr. Ayer spent a few years at Red Lake and, in the winter of 1848-9, settled on the borders of the newly purchased Territory. In due time he opened a school for the more promising children in different parts of the Indian country. This school was kept up for several years, and when Belle Prairie was sufficiently settled to have an organization, they joined with us. We worked together till the commencement of the civil war." Thus writes his wife, Elizabeth Taylor Ayer. It should be added that Mr. Ayer was ordained at Oberlin in 1842, and when he returned to his work Mr. Spencer came with him. Mr. Ayer was a member of the constitutional convention which, sitting from the 13th of July until the 29th of August, 1857, framed the present constitution of Minnesota. Born at Stockbridge, Massachusetts, 1803, he died in the service of the American Missionary Association and was buried at Atlanta, Georgia, 1st October, 1867.

[4] For reasons satisfactory to themselves,—mainly, it is believed, financial,—the Congregational church[es] relinquished their mission at Red Lake in 1877, and, in 1879, their school at Leech Lake, and both places have been occupied by Bishop Whipple.—S. R. RIGGS, D. D.

young men and women sought distant fields, and among them were some who came to the Minnesota region. At that time the places of labor which these chose as their own were, as ex-President Fairchild remarks, perhaps more inaccessible than is any mission field on earth at the present day. Thither were two routes, presenting almost equal difficulties, one by way of Lake Superior the other by way of the Mississippi. On both were stations of the American Board where, as a matter of course, these recruits for the Master's work found a welcome,[1] and at some of which, as at La Pointe and elsewhere, they enjoyed opportunities for learning the language of the people among whom they proposed to labor. Thus the old missions became the fostering sisters of the new.

But at this time there were those at Oberlin and elsewhere who expressed, sometimes in fervid language, their distrust of the Board on the subject of slavery, and in turn many of the supporters of the Board, and others, looked with grave suspicion upon "Oberlin theology." And as President Finney's statement was found to require very great modification when reduced to actual practice, there was organized, 15th June, 1843, by the Western Reserve (Congregational) Association, the Western Evangelical Missionary society, which supported the missionaries spoken of above until 1848, when it gave up its distinctive life and work to the American Missionary Association which had been oranized two years before.

From this digression we turn to a later date and follow Mr. Spencer to a more distant field, St. Joseph's, in what is now North Dakota, in the Red River region, not far from the international boundary. Here in 1852 Benjamin Terry, a young Baptist missionary, began labor. But before the close of the summer he was, like St. Sebastian according to the legend, "shot full of arrows." The hostile Sioux did the murder and scalped their victim. It was with difficulty that his associate secured permission to bury the body in the "consecrated" earth of the Roman Catholic cemetery. As if a burial place could have a truer consecration than to receive the dust of one slain in carrying Christ's message to souls in darkness!

To the place thus marked with blood, came Revs. Alonzo Barnard and D. B. Spencer, already named, their wives and children. With them came an elderly associate. The party arrived, 1853, June 1st. "They came thither," says the narrator,[2] "in carts from the vicinity of Cass and Red Lakes, Minnesota, where for ten years they had labored among the Chippewas as missionaries of the American Board.[3] They removed to St. Joseph (now Walhalla) at the earnest request of Governor Alexander Ramsey, of Minnesota, and others familiar with their labors and the needs of the Pembina natives. Mrs. Barnard died 1853, October 25th, of quick consumption, as the result of ten years of suffering and exposure for the welfare of the Indians."

---

[1] Under date of 1843, July 21st, Rev. P. Y. Sprout wrote from La Pointe: "Mr. and Mrs. Ayer are here. They are going on to Red Lake, and with them a reinforcement of missionaries." These may have been a party sent out from Oberlin, for thence to Red Lake there came that year Rev. Alonzo Barnard and wife, and S. G. Wright.
[2] Rev. R. J. Creswell, in the "New York Observer."
[3] An error: The American Missionary Association.

"Late in 1854 the hostile Sioux were infesting the Pembina region. Mrs. Spencer arose at night to care for her sick babe. She heard a noise at the window. She withdrew the curtain to discover the cause. Three Indians stood there with loaded guns and fired. Three balls took effect, one in her breast and two in her throat. She neither cried out nor fell, but, reeling to the bed with the infant child still in her arms, knelt down, where she was soon discovered by her husband when he returned from barricading the door. She lingered several hours before she died. When the neighbors came in in the morning, they beheld a most distressing scene. Mr. Spencer sat as in a dream, holding his dead wife in his arms. The poor babe lay in the cradle near by, his clothing saturated with his mother's blood. The two elder children stood near by, terrified and weeping. The friendly half-breeds came in and cared for the children, and prepared the dead mother for burial. A half-breed dug the grave and nailed together a rude box for a coffin; then, with broken voice and bleeding heart, the poor man assigned to the friendly earth the mortal remains of his murdered wife." The babe thus baptized in his mother's blood is now a Congregational minister in Illinois.

From these scenes of blood we turn to a happier subject, the creation of a literature in a language in which men can not blaspheme the name of God. "There is no word in the Ojibway language expressive of a profane oath," says Mr. Warren. In the report of the mission given at the [Hartford] meeting of the Board in 1836, we have given the names of five books printed in the Ojibway language during the year." The list does not include "the gospel of Luke translated into the Ojibway language by Mr. Hall, assisted by a native young man" [Henry Blatchford]. This is spoken of as "now ready for the press." Mr. Hall carried on this work of translation until he had made from the Greek an excellent version of the New Testament. In this work he had the advantage of the prior but less accurate translations made by Dr. James. The story of publication is thus told by Secretary Edward W. Gilman, of the American Bible Society:

"The Annual Report of this Society for 1844 announced that this work [the Ojibway Testament] which had been translated with much pains by the Rev. Mr. Hall and others, missionaries of the American Board near Lake Superior, was in course of publication under the inspection of Mr. Hall. The Report for 1857 said that a new edition of the Testament had been printed, which had been revised and carried through the press by the Rev. Sherman Hall, of Minnesota, who was for many years a missionary among the Ojibways. Another edition was published in 1875, but I am not aware that any material change was made in it.

"Among other Scriptures in Ojibway, or Chippewa, I note these: Matthew, York, 1831. Genesis, Toronto, 1835. New Testament, Toronto, 1854. The Chippewa Testament printed at Albany in 1833 is said to have been made by Edwin James, assisted by John Tanner. The Toronto Genesis was Peter Jones's, and his Matthew is said to have been reprinted by the American Board

in 1839, Luke is said to have been issued by that Board in 1837, from a version made by George Copway and Mr. Hall. It is impossible to tell how far any one individual contributed to the grand result."

In 1841 Rev. Leonard Hemenway Wheeler and wife, Rev. Woodbridge L. James and wife, and Abigail Spooner came to the La Pointe mission. Mr. and Mrs. James did not long remain. Miss Spooner rendered years of service. It is no disparagement to the other laborers there to say that Mr. Wheeler was the first among equals. "It is safe to say," writes Edwin Ellis, M. D., of Ashland, who personally knew him, "that no man was ever more thoroughly devoted to the work of rescuing the Indian from barbarism, vice, and degradation, than was Mr. Wheeler. His primary object was to preach Christ, but he saw clearly that the Indian must be civilized or exterminated. When unscrupulous and grasping men were to rob and wrong the Red men, his watchful eye and sound judgment saw the danger and, like the old cavilier without fear and without reproach, he raised his voice and used his pen for their defence. His intercession in their behalf was usually productive of essential good, for those that knew him knew that truth and justice were at his back, and that it was not safe to take up the gauntlet against so unselfish a champion. It was not for himself that he pleaded but for those who could not defend themselves."

They needed a defender. In 1842, when the value of the copper deposits on the southern shore of Lake Superior began to be known, the Indians of that region made a treaty with the United States government, selling their land, but reserving their right of occupancy. It would seem that both they and the government commissioner, Robert Stuart, Esq., long an honored member of the church at Mackinaw and sincerely their friend, thought the whites would want nothing of the country save the right of mining in it. It appears that the Indians thought that this was all they granted, and for a time nothing more was asked.

During these years of tranquility the work of the mission made good progress. As is everywhere the case, the missionaries had a great variety of duties. Thus Rev. Alfred Brunson, well known in connection with the history of Methodism in Wisconsin, who for a time was Indian agent, tells of medical care done by Mr. Wheeler to the needy people among whom he labored.

Here, in our story of honorable service, we may link Mr. Brunson's name with that of Father Clark, whose work among the Indians has been already ment. But to know well what they did we turn back to the record of a work that antedates their own. "In 1819, John Steward, a free colored man, commenced a successful religious and educational work among the Wyandots, on the upper Sandusky. The influence of this effort extended over into Canada, to others of the Hurons. John Sunday and Peter Jones, of the Ojibway tribe were converted and became active helpers. This was in 1823. In 1830, and onward, we find John Sunday and George Copway and others, going on missionary tours on Lake Superior. In 1833, they established a successful and permanent mission at L'Anse, on Keweenaw bay, in Michigan. Here was commenced a civilized and Christian community — the Indians laying by their annuity money, after 1842, to enter their lands as white men. Of these and of other missions, Rev. John Clark, whose headquarters were at Sault Ste. Marie, was the superintendent."[1]

Under Mr. Clark's direction, George Copway and two associates, John Tounchy and Peter Marksman, were sent to what is now the Lac Court Oreilles reservation. This movement was not immediately followed by the establishment of a mission. "The next summer (July, 1836), Mr. Clark visited the place himself, was treated very kindly by the chief, Moo-zoo-jeele (Moose Tail), and accomplished his object. He left Copway and Tounchy in charge of the mission, and made his way to the Mississippi, about two hundred miles above Prairie du Chien. Here he met Rev. A. Brunson, who,"— and here I turn from the narrative of Mr. Bennett[2] again to that of Dr. Riggs, "had become interested in the Indians of the Northwest by reading Lieutenant Allen's account of his voyage with Schoolcraft, when in search of the head of the Mississippi. He communicated this interest to the Conference at its meeting in July, 1835, and, receiving an appointment to the work, he immediately set out on horseback and traveled through the states of Ohio, Indiana and Illinois, and up to Fort Crawford, at Prairie du Chien." Under Mr. Brunson's supervision a mission among the Sioux was established at Little Crow's village, Kaposia, on the west side of the Mississippi, "six or eight miles" below Fort Snelling. To man this station he drew upon the one established by John Clark at Lac Court Oreilles. In this service we find again the names of George Copway and Peter Marksman. The third was a John Johnson.[3] "The Sioux could hardly believe that they were Ojibways, for they worked, they said, like Frenchmen."[4] From this mission at Kaposia dates the history of Methodism in Minnesota. It was not sustained, financially, as it should have been, but in time, with transfer of place, became the beginning of a work among the whites. Mr. Clark left the upper lake region in 1836, and some years afterward (1841) went to Texas to engage once more in frontier missionary service.

In becoming an Indian agent, Mr. Brunson did not cease to have a hearty interest in mission work. However, he was not judicial in his cast of mind, and his manuscript reports of service as agent are prolix to a degree that is discouraging to the one who remembers the brevity of human life. He complains (1843, September) that government money (tribal annuities) was unfairly distributed among the schools of the different missions, those of the American Board with 91 pupils receiving $1000; those of the Methodist with 121 pupils

---

[1] Stephen Return Riggs, D. D., "Minnesota Historical Collections," volume VI., part 2, pages 135, 136.

[2] "Methodism in Wisconsin," pages 17, 18.

[3] Mr. Johnson, whose Indian name was Enmegahbowh, afterward entered the ministry of the Protestant Episcopal church and engaged in mission work under direction of Bishop Whipple.

[4] Dr. S. R. Riggs. The remark which he quotes, was probably meant for a compliment, though, considering what class of Frenchmen the Sioux had met, it seems like a somewhat dubious one.

receiving only $750, and the Romanists with no pupils receiving $250. But as this money was tribal annuities it was probably due in varying amounts to the different bands of Indians. What statement others, from a different point of view, would have made, I can not say.[1]

When Mr. Wheeler came to La Pointe "the Indians spent their time in hunting and fishing and, as Mr. Wheeler mingled among them and studied their customs, he became thoroughly convinced that no permanent good could be done the Indians until these roaming habits were broken up."[2] Moreover, the long reign of the fur-trader in the old Northwest was drawing to an end. Of the change that followed the opening of the mines in the Lake Superior region, Dr. Riggs thus writes: "The influx of white settlers brought evil more than good to the Ojibways. The men who came to work the mines were neither religious, nor very moral, as a class, and their influence upon the Indians was, in the first instance, debasing. At every point plenty of fire-water came into the country, and thus the red men were tempted too strongly on their weakest side." It was desirable that the Indians leave La Pointe and, apart from the whites, found an agricultural community.

Across the south channel of Chequamegon Bay from La Pointe is a tract of land which on account of its rich bottom, large rice fields, extended "sugar bushes," abundant fisheries and remoteness from white settlements, Mr. Stuart noticed, in 1842 as possessing advantages for an Indian reservation that no other point in that region had. Mr. Wheeler believing that for Indians,— and white men as well,— industry is a necessary part of Christianity, determined to found an agricultural settlement. This he established on the Mushkesibi,[3] or Bad river, and named "Odanah," an Ojibway word meaning "village." Thither he removed 1845, May 1st. Mr. Hall remained at La Pointe until 1853 when he removed to Crow Wing, on the Mississippi.

Among the Indians in this new settlement Mr. Wheeler established civil government. He aided in the same service among the whites, holding, after La Pointe county was organized, various offices which increased his responsibilities rather than his income. Nor did he forget the spiritual needs of the whites. He was the first to preach at Ashland, and probably at Bayfield. We quote again from Dr. Ellis who wrote in 1874. "Amid all the trials and discouragements of Ashland's early settlers, he was ever ready to offer words of encourment and cheer. In its darkest periods he prophesied of Ashland's final suc-

[1] We are Mr. Brunson's debtors for a table of distances that suggests one of the difficulties in the work of all the Ojibway missions:
From La Pointe to Fond du Lac, 90 miles.
From Fond du Lac to Sandy Lake, 150 miles.
" " " " to Crow Wing, 150 miles.
" " " " to Pokeguma, 150 miles.
" " " " to Chippewa Falls, 150 miles.
From Chippewa Falls to La Pointe, 250 miles.
Evidently these figures are approximate rather than exact.
[2] "Bibliography of the Algonquian Languages," by James Constantine Pilling.
[3] From *mushkeeg*, a marsh, and *seebi* or *zeebi*, a river. In pronouncing, give the letter *i* its short sound.

cess, and his words were influential in including some of us to hold on when otherwise we should have given up in despair. He was a frequent visitor among us in those early days, and his social influence was purifying and ennobling. He participated in the first public celebration ever held in Ashland, July 4th, 1856. He was a man of much mechanical ingenuity; and during his residence at Odanah he invented a wind-mill which has since been patented under the name of the Eclipse Wind-Mill, a very useful invention, which is now extensively used all over the United States and to some extent in Europe."

Soon after Mr. Wheeler's removal to Odanah, perhaps the following year, a log school house was erected which was used also as a place of worship until a commodious chapel was built in 1853.

About 1850 came a determined effort to compel the Indians to remove west of the Mississippi. Their annuities for that year were paid at Fond du Lac,[1] whence Mr. Ely had removed in February of the preceeding year.[2] Mr. Wheeler could not advise the Indians to refuse to do what the government commanded but he did not conscientiously advise removal. "They appear to be fully determined," he wrote at a later date, "to remain on the shores of Lake Superior, and even forego their annuities, if the government choose to withhold them." This for two years they were obliged to do.

In the winter of 1850-51 "Mr. Wheeler, being on a visit to New England, went with one of the secretaries of the Board, Rev. S. B. Treat, to Washington, to represent to the Commissioner of Indian Affairs the desirableness and propriety of permitting these Indians to remain on the shores of Lake Superior. On his return to Bad River [Odanah] in the spring, he could not give the Indians any assurance that the government would comply with their request to remain; but he could tell them that the only possible conditions on which they could stay were that they should adopt the dress and habits of white people.

"This information and advice had a good effect. The Indians were put on their character. They planted more. They did not make dances. They sent their children to school, and they themselves came to church. And they greatly abstained from intoxicating drinks."

And yet in 1851 the pressure to compel removal was made stronger than before. It need scarcely be said that there was a corrupt "Indian ring" back of this effort, and it will cause no surprise to say that a man who afterward held the office of United States senator from Minnesota was a member thereof. In this year Messrs. Hall and Wheeler made a tour of exploration in the country to which it was proposed that the Lake Superior Ojibways should go. They left La Pointe June 5th and returned July 11th. Mr. Wheeler returned with the conviction that it would be a deed of mercy on the part of the government to shoot the Indians rather than to send them to the new region assigned them where they would be exposed to the fury of their relentless enemies, the Sioux.

---

[1] Dr. Riggs says "at Sandy Lake," and adds: "Some went and some did not; and those who went fared the worst, as the provisions were scanty and poor."
[2] It would seem that Fond du Lac had again been made a mission station.

In 1852 the dismal struggle continued. The United States agent promised the Indians that he would support them for one year at the expense of the government if they would remove to Fond du Lac. He permitted gambling and violation of the Sabbath by men under his control. To destroy liquor held in violation of law, he sent men who themselves got drunk upon it.

A letter written at La Pointe 1853, July 11th, by Mrs. Wheeler to her parents draws to the following gloomy picture:

"The last winter was one of the most dreary, lonely and trying ones we have ever spent in the country. The breaking up of the mission here and the unsettled and confused state of Indian affairs threw a gloom over the future. Often did I flee into my bed-room to hide the tears I could not control. The heat and burden of the day press heavily upon my dear husband. He has grown old fast since we returned from the East and I sometimes look anxiously forward to the future. He is obliged to attend to all the secular affairs of our station, and has charge of the property of the Board here, oversees all our own and the Indians' farming,—giving out their seed, plowing their ground, etc. He is doctor for both places [Odanah and La Pointe] chairman of the board of county commissioners, besides numberless other things too small to mention perhaps, but which nevertheless break in upon his time and divert his mind from his more appropriate work. To human appearance our people were never in a better condition to profit by the preaching of the gospel. We think there is hardly a possibility of removing them. They are fully determined not to go. They have lived two years without their payments and find that they do not starve or freeze. Indeed I doubt very much whether there is a band of Chippewas beyond the Mississippi, with all their annuities, that are as well fed and clothed as ours are."

Again Mrs. Wheeler writes from the same place:

"October 20th, 1853.—Will you believe me when I tell you that we are just in the midst of the bustle and excitement of payment? America does not contain a happier company than is congregated on this island to-night. I have been out this eve to some of the lodges of rejoice with those who rejoice. The payment is one of the best that has ever been made. It took us all by surprise."

"October 29, 1853.—I will add [it is Mr. Wheeler who writes] a few lines before the boat leaves. We are expecting to leave for Bad river to-morrow where we shall spend the winter. It is now almost certain that no farther attempts will be made to remove our Indians. There is little doubt that the old order of things will be restored; that the farmers, carpenters, blacksmiths will be given back to them, and missionaries be encouraged to go on with their labors as formerly. The late efforts to remove the Indians have not only proved a failure, but are now clearly seen by the Department at Washington to have originated with a few designing men who wanted the Indians removed that they might get their money. An astonishing amount of fraud has been discovered and the former agent is now under arrest to answer for some of his villainous conduct. The Lord reigns."

It will be noticed that these letters are written from La Pointe. Mr. Hall with family and assistants, removed in June of that year (1853) to Crow Wing, Minnesota, whither they arrived in the following month. Promises made by one agent were not fulfilled by his successor and this movement proved a failure. Mr. Hall entered home missionary service among the whites.

As a suggestion of the need that still existed of missionary work I quote from a letter written from La Pointe, 1853, August 31st, by Mr. Wheeler's eldest son, then a boy of ten:

"I was going to tell you about an Indian funeral. Julia was writing about it, but she did not tell what the Indians said in their speeches to the dead child. I understood them, so I will tell you some as near as I can remember. Old Buffalo, the first chief, made his speech first and told the child it would take him two days to get to the spirit land, and before he got there his friends would would come to meet him, and that the fishes would jump into his canoe and would be his food, and when he got to the mouth of the Bad river he would hear the roar of the guns of the spirit land and his friends would come and meet him and would be his playmates. One of them said, 'Once I shot a Frenchman and blowed his brains out. Then I cut off a piece of his flesh and eat it, and it was very good and you may have the same for your food on your journey.' " Perhaps this is the last trace of genuine cannibalism in Wisconsin.

The medical resources of the mission were taxed in February and March, 1854, by an epidemic of small-pox. However, this enemy proved to be a comparatively easy one to grapple with.

Mr. Wheeler's ideas of justice toward the Ojibway Indians were substantially embodied in a treaty made with them, 1854, September 30th, by which three reservations were provided for,— at Odanah, where he had made a settlement so many years before, at Lac Court Oreilles and at Lac du Flambeau. The action of Agent Henry Gilbert, who framed the treaty, was approved by Commissioner Manypenny who came to Odanah the following season. Both were honest men, and preferred the counsel of the missionaries to that of the Indian traders. The commissioner soon found himself honored with the ill-will of the latter class. "Mr. Wheeler," he said on one occasion, "these traders would like to hang us both." To have the government give the head of each Indian family eighty acres of land, and to induce the Indians to settle upon farms and improve them, were favorite projects with Mr. Wheeler. In short, he anticipated what enlightened public sentiment now demands as the only just and sensible method of dealing with the Indians.

From the first establishment of the mission, much was made. of school work. At Mrs. Wheeler's first coming to La Pointe, her direct service to the mission was in the line of teaching. From her school Mr. Baraga, afterward "bishop," was at the pains, on two separate occasions, to have the children of Roman Catholic families removed on account of religious exercises, the chief feature of which was the use in common of the Lord's prayer. But it was hard to keep the children away and their mistaken spiritual guide did not fully succeed in doing so. Notwithstanding his action, the missionaries of the two creeds remembered that they were all Christians, and the two bishops,—such in truth they were,—Baraga and Wheeler, met more than once even in prayer.

For years it was a cherished plan with Mr. Wheeler to establish a boarding-school into which children could be gathered from wigwam life. Part of the story of his success, and some account of the labor involved in the school, is thus told by Rev. D. Irenæus Miner, now of Hayward, Wisconsin:

"In May, 1859, Miss Jennie L. Cooley and I were united in marriage and, about the first of June following, started by steamer from Cleveland, Ohio, to join the mission forces at Bad river, Wisconsin. The missionaries then on the ground were Rev. and Mrs. L. H. Wheeler and Henry Blatchford. The building for the boarding-school was taken going up, and was completed that summer, so that we commenced taking in boys and girls as boarding-scholars in the fall of that same year. My duties from the first were teaching the school and looking after the work of the boys out of school hours till evening, when Rev. D. B. Spencer, who joined us about the opening of the fall term, took the boys under his care. Mrs. Miner had charge of the manufacturing of the clothing for both boys and girls, had the task of instructing the girls in sewing, and the entire care of the girls out of school hours, except while they were working in the kitchen, until Miss Rhoda Spicer joined us as assistant teacher."

As the burden proved to be too great for Mrs. Miner, she and her husband, in June, 1861, gave up their work at Odanah. This Wisconsin missionary family has sent in later years a daughter to the work in China. Mr. Spencer in the spring of 1863, sought another field of labor and in 1864 the mission had a bit of romance in the marriage of Miss Spicer to the young man who as a boy gave an account, ten years before, of an Indian child's funeral.

For many years the Odanah boarding-school afforded the best educational facilities that the Wisconsin Ojibways have yet enjoyed. It was judged worthy of governmental recognition and aid.

But with the realization of his cherished hope came an ominous change in Mr. Wheeler's health. A hemorrhage from the lungs in the spring of 1859 warned him that he must never again sleep out of doors in the bitter cold of a Lake Superior winter night with the thermometer at twenty-eight degrees below zero. He must take no more journeys that would bring him home with feet bleeding from cuts made by the thongs of his snow-shoes. Yet his work was not done.

The years of the war were years of anxiety and danger. The little mission church of Odanah made its offering of precious life. The rascality of certain officials in dealing with the Indians threatened serious disturbance. Mr. Wheeler went to warn the government of impending danger. While he was gone the Sioux outbreak occurred in Minnesota (August, 1862) and an embassy came to stir up his own people to revolt. But these remained loyal to the influence and teaching of the missionaries. They wished even to raise a company to help the Great Father in Washington subdue his enemies, with the particular thought, it may be, of making war upon their own traditional enemies, the Sioux. But it was not thought best that they should engage in warfare or be led to believe that their Great Father could not do without their help. An Ojibway delegation visited President Lincoln in 1864 and were much gratified by his evident interest in them and their cause. When his great heart was still in death no tears were more sincere than theirs.

"Why was he at that play-house? Why did his young men let an enemy come so near him?" These were their lamentations repeated again and again.

After serving, for a quarter-century, those whom so many despise and wrong, Mr. Wheeler's special labors in their behalf came to an end in October, 1866. The wasting of consumption compelled removal and left him but six years of life. These were spent at Beloit in establishing the manufacture of the wind-mill already referred to. It was invented the spring before his removal while he was crippled with a broken wrist and while his eldest son who aided him in the work was lame from an injury to the knee. This invention provided support for his family and education for his children.

Up to the time (1869) of the re-union of the old-school and the new-school branches of the Presbyterian church the latter division did its foreign missionary work through the American Board. Thereafter this work was done through the Presbyterian Board to which, in justice, certain missions were transferred, among them, in 1870, the one at Odanah. The missionary then and still in charge, Henry Blatchford, is an Indian of mixed race, educated in the mission school at Mackinaw and named in honor of the father of the vice-president of the American Board. We have heard of him as one of the translators of the Ojibway Testament. He thus wrote under date of March 1st, 1890:

"When this church was first organized,[1] the membership was up to 75 members, but in about two years from the time it was organized some began to drop off by joining an Indian dance, and some have died. Our people are not here the year round, they have to go and work in the logging camps. But when they are all here we have a full attendance. I am getting old and am troubled with the congestion of the brain and am weak. I am now on my seventy-seventh year. In June next I will have reached my seventy-eighth year. And I have been connected with this missionary field fifty-five years without cessation."

Some years ago the Presbyterian Board sold the mission school property upon which Mr. Wheeler bestowed so much planning and labor. By another purchase this fell into the hands of the Roman Catholics who have so much of the benefits of Mr. Wheeler's judgment and foresight. Their mission is now apparently the more prosperous of the two and, out of the gift made by Miss Catherine Drexel for Indian education, is certainly better supported.

---

[1] He refers to the re-organization already noted. This letter is remarkable for the steadiness and legibility of the hand-writing. The peculiarities of expression I leave unchanged. He gives the membership at that date as forty-seven, the population between five hundred and six hundred.

Father Baraga, having been made first bishop of Marquette, Michigan (consecrated 1853, November 1st), withdrew personally from the Odanah mission years before his death. This occurred 1868, January 19th. Of this worthy pastor, but without reference to his death, the late James Parton thus wrote:

"I have had the pleasure, once in my life, of conversing with an absolute gentleman: one in whom all the little vanities, all the little greedinesses, all the paltry fuss, worry, affectation, haste, and anxiety springing from imperfectly disciplined self-love,—all had been consumed; and the whole man was kind, serene, urbane, and utterly sincere. This perfect gentleman was a Roman Catholic bishop, who had spent thirty years of his life in the woods near Lake Superior, trying (and failing, as he frankly owned) to convert rascally Chippeways into tolerable human beings. 'I make pretty good Christians of some of them,' said he; 'but *men?* No: it is impossible.'"[1]

It would be interesting to know how much this confession of failure has been affected by Mr. Parton's interpretation.

We return in our narrative to follow Mr. Wheeler to his final rest. To him the end of life came on the 22nd of February, 1872. On Sabbath, three days afterward, the wasted body of this faithful missionary of the cross was borne beneath the cathedral-like arches of the great First church in Beloit whence so much precious dust has been carried to the grave.

"Mr. Wheeler," says Dr. Ellis, "was beloved almost equally by white men and red men, by Protestant and Catholic. In the delirium of death he was among the members of the native church at Odanah praying still for their preservation from the dangers to which he knew full well they would be exposed. Time will not fully disclose the value of the results of his labors. Those who have known the Indians twenty-five years will agree with me that very great progress has been made, and Mr. Wheeler, I believe, more than any other man, has contributed to this result, and aided by his labors to raise thousands from a condition of low and degraded heathenism, if not to a state of high civilization, at least to a state far above that in which he found them."

"God buries his workmen but carries on his work." The great results of all missionary and church work are written only in the Book of Life. But upon the pages of history, even as men write it, there is honorable place for the record of twenty-five years' labor among a once barbarous people, the establishment of civil government among them, the development of improved plans of missionary and educational work, the training of laborers for other fields, the founding of a town and the establishment of a successful business carried on in the spirit of the Master.

We may fitly close this portion of narrative with the English form of the solemn "covenant" of the churches connected with the Ojibway mission:

"You do now, in the presence of the heart-searching God, and before angels and men, choose the Lord Jehovah, Father, Son and Holy Ghost, to be

---
[1] "[A]tlantic Monthly," April, 1868.

your God; the supreme object of your affections, and your portion forever. You cordially acknowledge the Lord Jesus Christ in all his mediatorial offices, Prophet, Priest and King, as your only Saviour and final Judge;—and the Holy Spirit, as your Sanctifier, Comforter and Guide.

"You humbly and cheerfully devote yourself to God in an everlasting covenant of grace. You consecrate all your powers and faculties to his service and glory; and you promise to take the Holy Scriptures as the rule of your life and conversation: and that, through the assistance of His Spirit and grace, you will cleave to Him as your chief good, and that you will give diligent attention to his Word and ordinances, to family and secret prayer, to public worship, and to the conscientious observance of the Sabbath;— that you will seek the honor of his name and the interests of his Kingdom, and that henceforth, denying ungodliness and worldly lusts, you will live soberly, righteously, and godly, in this present world.

"You do now cordially unite yourself to this church as a church of Christ, promising to submit to its discipline, so far as conformable to the rules of the gospel, and you solemnly covenant to promote its edification, purity and peace, and to walk with its members in Christian love, faithfulness, circumspection, sobriety and meekness. All this you promise to do with humble reliance on the grace of God, and with an affecting belief that your vows are recorded on high, and will be reviewed in the day of judgment.

"Thus you solemnly covenant, promise and engage?"

Response in behalf of the church:

"We do now receive you into our communion and fellowship, and we promise to watch over you with Christian affection and tenderness, ever treating you in love as a member of the body of Christ, who is head over all things in the church. This we do, earnestly imploring the great Shepherd of Israel, our Lord and Redeemer, that both you and we may have wisdom and grace to be faithful in his covenant, and to glorify him with that holiness which becometh his house for ever. Amen."

CHAPTER XII.

BY THE MIZI SIBI.[1]

In the structure of colonial intercourse that the French built in North America, the Fox-Wisconsin route may be described as the key of an arch, one of whose abutments rested on the Gulf of St. Lawrence, the other on the Gulf of Mexico. Accordingly the early history of this region stands related not only, as we have seen, to that of New France, or Canada, but also to that of Louisiana. Apparently the line of demarkation between these provinces was not well defined and the authorities of the two came often into somewhat of conflict.

White settlement on the lower Mississippi had almost its beginning in John Law's knavish scheme. Nor did the new colony escape the curse of slavery. This was permitted and regulated by a decree of Louis XV. "given at Versailles, in the year of Grace one thousand seven hundred and twenty-four."

While most of this decree is taken up with matters regarding to slavery, —in which respect it seems to be neither better nor worse than its time,—it contains certain other commands that make the expression "year of Grace" seem like bitter irony. The "precise orders"[1] given by Louis XIII. "that no Huguenot should settle in New France"[2] find their counterpart in this decree issued almost a century later by his great-great-grandson.

Here is the bidding of "his Most Christian Majesty,"—"the eldest son of the church," etc.:

---

[1] "The Indians never speak of the Mississippi as the *Father of Waters*, but invariably refer to it as *the Big River*. The Winnebagoes called it *Nee koonts Hah-ta kah* - the former part of that compound word meaning river, and *hah-ta-kah*, large. The Sioux called it *Wat-pa-Ton ga*; *wat pa*, river, and *ton-ga*, large. The Sauks designated it as *Me-chu-Sa po*; the Menominees, *Me-che-Se paa*; the Kickapoos, *Me-che-Se-pe*; the Chippewas, *Me-ze-Ze-be*; and the Ottawas, *Mis sis-Se pi*. *Me-cha, me-che, me-ze*, and *mis sis*, all mean the same thing – large or big; and *sa po, se paa, se pe, ze-be* and *se-pi*, all mean river."—B. W. BRISNOIS, *Hist. Coll., IX.*

Ignorant as I am of the Algonquian language, in the Ojibway or any other dialect, I am convinced that "Mississippi" does *not* mean simply the "great river," but that Mr. W. H. Wheeler of Beloit is substantially correct in translating it as the "everywhere river." This he affirms from his own knowledge of the language. But any one of us can get an Ojibway Testament. In reading this, we are to remember that the vowels are used according to the French or German, rather than an English, system of orthoepy. Thus *mizi* is pronounced *mee-zee*, with the last syllable shortened perhaps, in time of utterance. This word seems to have the meaning of "every" in relation to place. We find it in Luke IX. 6, where the locative sense is apparent, and in Philippians IV. 12, where the translators of the Ojibway Testament may have followed the Authorized Version in its rendering of the Greek *en panti. Mizine* (mee-zee-way) in the sense of "everywhere" is found in Acts XVII. 30 and XXVIII. 22; in I. Cor. IV. 17, and II. Timothy II. 8. *Kiji* is the Ojibway word for "great" or "large."

[2] See page 15.

"ARTICLE I.— We enjoin the directors general of said company,[1] and all our officers, to remove from said country all the Jews who may have taken up their abode there — the departure of whom, as declared enemies of the Christian name, we command within three months, including the day when these presents are published, under pain of forfeiture of their bodies and estates.

"ARTICLE III. [First Part].— We prohibit any other religious rites than those of the Apostolic Roman Catholic church; requiring that those who violate this shall be punished as rebels disobedient to our commands."

With the colony thus inauspiciously begun, the western part of what is now Wisconsin, had easy communication by way of the Mississippi. This in the early time was not regarded as a line of division. Thus it was on the east side of the Great River, at Post St. Antoine,[2] that Nicholas Perrot, who in 1685 had been appointed "commandant of the West,"[3] formally took possession 1689, May 8th. in the name of the French king, of the entire region drained by the St. Peter or Minnesota, the St. Croix and the upper Mississippi. Seven years previously,—1682, March 14th, and April 9th,—La Salle had taken possession of the lower Mississippi region. Indeed, he then laid claim to the whole country "along the river Colbert or Mississippi, and rivers which discharge themselves therein from its source." So that Perrot's *proces-verbal* was, in a sense, merely supplementary to the more extensive claim made by La Salle.[4]

Thus early and in this interesting way is the history of the western part of Wisconsin connected with that of Louisiana,— the vast Louisiana that was but an official name for the valley of the Mississippi,— a name not restricted to the region on the westward side of the Great River until after the treaty of Paris in 1763.

But early explorations in the upper part of this vast region,— those of Radisson, Joliet, Perrot and others,— were made by parties that descended the Wisconsin rather than by those that ascended the Mississippi. Soon both routes came to be commonly used and France possessed in North America, a waterway the extent of which equaled the breadth of oceans,— a water-way that, as we have seen, offered, in the interior, more courses than one to the trader and explorer. Of these, none was traversed more frequently than that by way of the Fox and the Wisconsin. Hence, after their long and disastrous war with the French, it was "with characteristic sagacity," as Mr. Hebberd remarks, that the Outagamies selected the site of Prairie du Chien as that whereon they could still use most effectively whatever of power was left them.

Of this place Captain Jonathan Carver gives some account in his famous book, "Three Years' Travels throughout the Interior Parts of North America."

---

[1] The "Company of the Indies," established 1717, August, under the management of the famous John Law.

[2] The site of which is on the Wisconsin shore of Lake Pepin and between the villages of Stockholm and Pepin.

[3] The winter following he spent at an encampment near the majestic bluff that has given name to the village of Trempealeau See page 134.

[4] We must remember, however, that Perrot held his commission, not from La Salle, but from the authorities of New France.

Thus begins his "Journal:" "In June, 1766, I set out from Boston, and proceeded by way of Albany and Niagara to Michillimackinac,[1] a fort situated between the lakes Huron and Michigan, and distant from Boston 1300 miles." This place he left on the 3rd of September, and "on the 18th arrived at fort La Bay. * * On the 20th of September I left the Green Bay. * * On the 25th I arrived at the great town of the Winnebagoes, situated on a small island,[2] just as you enter the east end of the lake Winnebago. Here the queen who presided over this tribe instead of a Sachem, received me with great civility, and entertained me in a very distinguished manner, during the four days I continued with her.[3] * * On the 7th of October [we] arrived at the great Carrying Place [Portage], which divides it [the Fox river] from the Ouisconsin. * * On the 15th of October, we entered that extensive river, the Mississippi." We may presume that on the same day he arrived at Prairie du Chien. Thither the people had come, they told him, about thirty years before from a place not far distant which had been their home but which the Great Spirit, speaking in an audible voice, had told them that he wished for himself. Carver supposes that the Indians were victims of some trick played by French or Spaniards. "The people soon after their removal," he continues, built a town near the Ouisconsin at a place called by the French La Prairie des Chiens, which signifies the Dog Plains; it is a large town and contains about three hundred families. I saw here many horses of a good size and shape. This town is the great mart where all the adjacent tribes, and even those who inhabit the most remote branches of the Mississippi, annually assemble about the latter end of May, bringing with them their furs to dispose of to the traders. But it is not always that they conclude the sale here; this is determined by a general council of the chiefs, who consult whether it would be more conducive to their interest, to sell their goods at this place or carry them to Louisiana, or Michilimackinac. According to the decision of this council, they either proceed further, or return to their different homes."

Before the permanent settlement of Prairie du Chien by whites, American colonial troops may have come thither. We have already had a report, in Sinclair's letter, of the British expedition which returned to Mackinaw probably in May, 1780. From that place in the same year a second expedition was sent, perhaps in June, to secure furs left at Prairie du Chien by the traders. Captain J. Long, a British Indian-trader, was in command. In their nine canoes he and his men carried off about three hundred packs of furs. Sixty packs more they burned, probably by setting fire to the buildings[4] in which the furs had been stored. The reason for this is easily inferred from Long's statement that "about five days after our departure we were informed that the Americans

---
[1] Carver's "Michillimackinac" is the "old fort" on the southern side of the strait.
[2] The island lying between Neenah and Menasha.
[3] In reference to note 1, page 75, it should be said that Carver noticed the radical difference between the Ojibway language and that of the Winnebagoes.
[4] This store-house and the old French "fort" are probably one and the same. The "fort," however, may have been a similar structure of logs built earlier, perhaps as soon as 1745, for a like purpose.

came to attack us; but to their extreme mortification we were out of their reach."

Notwithstanding the popular impression that "Prairie du Chien is as old as Philadelphia," no evidence appears of permanent settlement there by whites prior to 1781. As Prairie du Chien was on one of the great water-courses from the Upper Lakes to the more distant interior, traders and others from New France were often there before any whites made a permanent settlement in the place. Some may have remained even for years.

The first official report by any United States officer in regard to Prairie du Chien is by Lieutenant (afterwards Brigadier-General) Zebulon Montgomery Pike. On the 9th of August, 1805, he left St. Louis on an exploring expedition toward the headwaters of the Mississippi. He reports that, with three houses on the west side of the river, there were in Prairie du Chien and vicinity thirty-seven in all, "which it will not be too much to calculate at ten persons each. * * This calculation will not answer for the spring or autumn as there are then at least five hundred or six hundred white persons."

Under date of 1811, February 2nd, Nicholas Boilvin, an Indian agent already spoken of, made a report to William Eustis, secretary of war: " Prairie du Chiens is an old Indian town which was sold by the Indians to the Canadian traders about thirty years ago, where they have ever since rendezvoused, and dispersed their merchandise in various directions. The Indians also sold them at the same time a tract of land measuring six leagues up and down the river, and six leagues back of it. The village contains between thirty and forty houses, and on the tract just mentioned about thirty-two families, so that the whole settlement contains about one hundred families. The men are generally French Canadians, who have mostly married Indian wives; perhaps not more than twelve white females are to be found in the settlement."

British and Canadian influence continued to be supreme at Prairie du Chien until after the war of 1812. We have already had mention of Robert Dickson and Lieutenant-Colonel McKay, honorable men both, who as far as possible, restrained the Indians from outrages against their American enemies. On the return of peace the place was evacuated by the British 1815, May 24th. But it was not until the 21st of June, 1816, that the fort which the Americans had named Shelby and the British called McKay was re-occupied by United States troops. These were under command of Colonel Thomas A. Smith, brigadier-general by brevet. He and his men were most unwelcome. They occupied and repaired the old fort, thereafter known as Fort Crawford in honor of William Harris Crawford of Georgia, then secretary of the treasury. In the spring of 1817 Colonel Talbot Chambers succeeded Smith. Complaint is made that he treated the inhabitants as conquered people. Probably there was reason for his doing so. With the subsequent commanders save one, Colonel Zachary Taylor, afterward President, we have no special concern. He succeeded Major Stephen Watts Kearney in 1829, probably in June.

The old fort stood on low ground as described hereafter. One of stone was erected on higher land. This was begun in 1830, occupied by part of the troops in 1831, and completed in 1832.

Colonel Taylor remained in command until the autumn of 1836 when he was ordered to Florida to take part in the Seminole war then raging.

Among the subordinate officers at Fort Crawford was the late Jefferson Davis, whose service here was interrupted by that at Fort Winnebago. A garrison was kept at Fort Crawford until the 9th of June, 1856.

With the secure possession of the place by United States troops came thither an American population. Among the first was James H. Lockwood. "On the 16th of September, 1816," he says, "I arrived at Prairie du Chien, a traders' village of between twenty-five and thirty houses, situated on the banks of the Mississippi on what, in high water, is an island. The houses were built by planting posts upright in the ground with grooves in them, so that the sides could be filled in with split timber or round poles, and then plastered over with clay, and whitewashed with a white earth found in the vicinity, and then covered with bark, or clap-boards riven from oak. [Mr. Lockwood himself in 1826 built the first frame house].

"Indian traders, as a class, possess no enterprise, at least none that is of any advantage to the settlement and improvement of a country. They are enterprising in going into the unexplored Indian country to traffic, and collect furs and peltries; but I have never seen a man who made money in the Indian trade apply it to the ordinary improvements that foster and encourage the growth of a country.

"Of all the foreigners that came to this country, the Canadians of French extraction seemed to have the least idea of the privileges of American citizenship. It appeared almost impossible to instill into their minds anything of the independence of self-government, and this was not confined entirely to the uneducated, but would apply more or less to the partially educated classes.

"The *coutume de Paris* [French law] so far prevailed in this country generally, that a part of the ceremony of marriage was the entering into a contract in writing, generally giving, if no issue, the property to the survivor; and if they desired to be divorced, they went together before the magistrate and made known their wishes, and he, in their presence, tore up the marriage contract, and according to the custom of the country, they were then divorced. I was once present at Judge Abbott's at Mackinaw when a couple presented themselves before him and were divorced in this manner. When the laws of Michigan were first introduced at Prairie du Chien, it was with difficulty that the justice of the peace could persuade them that a written contract was not necessary; and some of them believed that, because the contract of marriage gave the property to the survivor, they were not obliged to pay the debts which the deceased owed at the time of his death.

"In speaking of the early settlers and their marriage connections, I should perhaps explain a little. In the absence of religious instructions, and it becoming so common to see the Indians use so little ceremony about marriage, the idea of a verbal matrimonial contract became familiar to the early French settlers, and they generally believed that such a contract of marriage was valid without any other ceremony. Many of the women married in this way believed, in their simplicity and ignorance, that they were as lawfully the wives of the men they lived with, as though they had been married with all the ceremony and solemnity possible.

"In the spring of 1817 a Roman Catholic priest, from St. Louis, called Pere Priere,[1] visited Prairie du Chien. He was the first that had been there for many years, and perhaps since the settlement, and organized the Roman Catholic church, and disturbed some of the domestic arrangements of the inhabitants. He found several women who had left their husbands and were living with other men; these he made by the terror of his church to return and ask pardon of their husbands, and to be taken back by them, which they of course could not refuse.

"The first Sunday-school established in the place was by my first wife, Mrs. Julianna Lockwood.[2] Mrs. Lockwood was raised among the Presbyterians or Congregationalists of New England, and early imbibed the strong prejudices of those people against the Roman Catholics, but afterwards, having lived in Canada two or three years, and having become intimately acquainted with several ladies of that faith, who were apparently good pious people, she concluded that there were good and bad among all sects, or denominations, calling themselves Christians, and her early prejudices in great measure wore off. We were married in the summer of the year 1824, and came to Prairie du Chien in the autumn. There was not at that time any church or meeting to attend on Sunday. Even the Roman Catholics had a priest visit them only occasionally, and Mrs. Lockwood, having been accustomed to see the children collected in Sunday-schools, and seeing a large number playing about the streets on the Sabbath, concluded it would be doing them a good service to gather them into a Sunday-school, and proposed to Miss Crawford, a young lady raised in the place, who spoke English and French fluently, and who had a good education, to assist her. To this she agreed at once, and they influenced Dr. Edwin James, surgeon of the United States army, then stationed at Fort Crawford, and John H. Kinzie, Esq., formerly of Chicago, then quite a young man, in the employment of the American Fur Company at Prairie du Chien, to assist

---

[1] Under date of 1893, April 26th, the Rev. H. Van der Sanven, chancellor of the [Roman Catholic] diocese of St. Louis, wrote: "The priest after whom you inquire can not be any other than the Rev. Paul de St. Pierre, * * of whom Shea says that he belonged to the Carmelite order. * * Prairie du Chien, in my collection of documents is mentioned for the first time on September 29th, 1832."

"By the way," writes Secretary R. G. Thwaites, under date of 1894, January 13th, "referring to the matter of Father Priere, or Pierre, in *Wis. Hist. Colls,* v. ii., page 127, I obtained in Prairie du Chien yesterday, the baptismal, marriage, and burial records of the Catholic church there, for the years 1817-1825, and they are now before me. The name of the officiating priest is given for 1816-17 as M. Dunaud; for the other years, there is no priestly signature. Doesn't this rather upset, at least the year, of Pierre's arrival as given by Lockwood?"

[2] Sister of L. M. Warren of La Pointe. "She was a noble-hearted as well as a queenly-looking woman," writes her nephew, Rev. J. H. Warren of San Francisco.

them. They collected the children, and commenced their school in the spring of 1825, and continued it until the winter following, but not without opposition. As this measure did not originate with Mr. Roulette,[1] he felt bound to oppose it. He took what he thought would be the most effectual mode of suppressing it, by going to the mothers of the children who attended the school, and representing to them that it was the design to make Protestants of the children. To counteract Mr. Roulette, they introduced and taught the children the Roman Catholic catechism, finding nothing to their minds very objectionable in it; and as I said before, they continued their school until winter, during which time Dr. James was ordered to some other post. In the spring of 1826, my wife and myself went to New York; Miss Crawford accompanied us as far as Mackinaw, where she remained until she was married. Mr. Kinzie went also to Mackinaw, during which time he received an appointment in the Indian department under Governor Cass, and went to Detroit to reside. The Sunday-school was not again resumed, nor was one again attempted in the place until about 1830, when the members of the different religious denominations united in forming the Union Sunday-school. This continued a few years, until the Methodists, becoming by far the most numerous class, assumed the management of it, since which time they have claimed it as a Methodist Sunday-school."

With a possible exception noted in the history of Green Bay, the Sunday-school by Mrs. Lockwood appears to be the first in Wisconsin. We know who, in those days, were "the Presbyterians or Congregationalists of New England." The work done by Dr. James in connection with the Ojibway mission has been mentioned.

Not only does Prairie du Chien have the honor of the first or second Sunday-school in Wisconsin, one of the first day-schools was hers also. The teacher was a Willard Keyes who seems to have come from southern Illinois, and who probably did nothing more noteworthy in his life than to establish this school. He thus speaks of it in a letter dated 1818, June 7th, and addressed to Dr. Samuel Andrew Peters:[2]

"On the 25th ultimo I commenced a school in this village; have about thirty scholars, mostly bright and active, at two dollars a month. I board with your old landlord, Mr. Faribault,[3] but have to regret the loss of your company. I have engaged for three months, and before the expiration of that time I trust your business will be amicably settled with the Indians."

Under date of January 3rd, 1820, the ex-teacher again addresses Peters:

"I remained at Prairie du Chien till May, 1819, when, despairing of hear-

---
[1] An enemy, or at least a rival, of Mr. Lockwood.
[2] "Samuel Peters, D. D., LL. D., Clerk in Holy orders," as he signed his name to the record of two marriages at which he officiated at Prairie du Chien. Naturally enough this story vilifier of Connecticut was on a swindling scheme. He affirmed that Carver, whom he calls "an Anabaptist [Baptist] in religion" had a valid claim to a vast tract of land extending from the Falls of St. Anthony * * [to] the mouth of the Chippewa river, thence eastward one hundred miles, thence northward one hundred twenty miles, and from thence in a straight line to the Falls of St. Anthony." Certainly this was a tempting plum and Peters and two grandsons of Carver had come to this distant land to pick it.
[3] For whose son Faribault, Minnesota, was named.

ing from you, and believing it to be of no use to remain longer in this expensive place, I came down the river. and am now in Madison county, state of Illinois."

Years were to elapse before either church or school were permanently established at Prairie du Chien. Laymen are often, as they ought always to be, true home missionaries, and one such, apparently, was Joseph Montfort Street who, in October or November, 1827, came to Prairie du Chien as an Indian agent to succeed Mr. Boilvin whose life had come to an end,— perhaps by drowning,— the summer before. Mr. Street was a Presbyterian of the Cumberland branch of that church, which was then not in very high favor with the more conservative portion.

In 1829, as we have learned, Mr. J. D. Stevens and Rev. Alvin Coe, passing through Prairie du Chien, spent two weeks at that place. The latter may have made at least a second visit and it is he, probably, of whom Mr. Lockwood writes thus disparagingly:

"In 1830, a man by the name of Coe, who claimed to be a minister of the Presbyterian church, and missionary to the Indians, passed through the country and remained over Sunday at Prairie du Chien, and made an attempt at preaching; but he was a very illiterate man and not over-burdened with common sense.[1] I must here relate an anecdote of this man. He made several trips to the upper Indian country, and on one occasion took passage on a keel-boat, and arrived within about thirty miles of Fort Snelling on Saturday night; and as the boat would start early in the morning, and he would not travel on the Sabbath, he went on shore without provisions, and encamped over Sunday, and on Monday made his way to Fort Snelling, hungry and nearly exhausted."

If this was Mr. Stevens's companion we may doubt his illiteracy. Whoever he was we cannot but honor his endurance of hunger, loneliness, fatigue and danger for conscience's sake.

As this event is not in Mr. Lockwood's narrative connected in date with the "attempt at preaching" we cannot but wonder if the latter may not have taken place in 1829. If in 1830, it is remarkable that we have no allusion to it in the narrative of Rev. Aratus Kent, the first who labored in this part of the world under commission from the American Home Missionary society. In July, 1830, he held religious service in Prairie du Chien. Let us have the story in his own words:

"I started July 5th for Paairie du Chien by request of General Street, fulfilled several appointments on my circuitous route, and after great fatigue arrived in time to meet my engagement to preach there on the 11th at the meeting of the council with the Indians, of whom three hundred of different tribes

---

[1] Since writing the above I have become convinced that Mr. Lockwood was exceedingly unjust to Mr. Coe. The following transcript is made (by kindness of Rev. O. E. Boyd of the Presbyterian Board of Home Missions) from the minutes of the synod of Pittsburg:

"1817 Presbytery of Grand River (Western Reserve, Ohio) report Alvin Coe licensed for four years. At the request of the Connecticut Missionary society, the presbytery ordained Mr. Alvin Coe as an evangelist on the 10th of June and admitted him as a member of presbytery." Such a request would have been neither made nor granted in the case of a "very illiterate man."

were present. My congregation of two hundred presented as great a variety of the human family as was perhaps ever addressed at the same time by an ambassador of Christ."

It seems that the honor of holding the first Protestant service in Prairie du Chien belongs either to Mr. Coe or to Mr. Kent.

From this time until a resident minister came thither Mr. Kent seems to have regarded Prairie du Chien as a part of his parish. Of one of his visits, made probably in the autumn of 1831, he writes: "I came at a late hour where many were gathered together praying." Like "square dealing" people,— to use a Western and very expressive term,— Mr. Kent's hearers paid his expenses. Before he left they also made an offering of $11 for the work of the American Home Missionary society. We may doubt that there was one of earlier date than this, for said object, within the present limits of our state. And, if there was, we can readily believe that Mr. Kent made the appeal in response to which it was given. On the Monday of this visit of Mr. Kent to Prairie du Chien, there was observed what was relatively better known among our churches (the more's the pity) in former days than now,— the monthly concert of prayer for the conversion of the world. The little congregation voted to continue it, and appointed a committee to report mission news both foreign and domestic.

Perhaps good Brother Kent took a little satisfaction in adding to his account of this visit to Prairie du Chien: "The Methodists have not been there yet." He says also: " In going and returning I preached at Cassville."

An agent of the American Home Missionary society, Rev. D. W. Lathrop, who made a trip in the West in the summer of 1831 wrote of Prairie du Chien as a place that "needs a minister." He adds that it has "a population of eight hundred, one-half of whom are French."

"Some time in the year 1832," says Mr. Lockwood, "a student of divinity of the Cumberland Presbyterian sect came here and taught school for about six months, and on Sundays attempted to preach." Whether or not any of these attempts were successful Mr. Lockwood does not tell us. He thus continues his narrative :

"In some of the treaties with the Winnebagoes, provision had been made for an Indian school near Prairie du Chien, and in the year 1833 the Rev. David Lowrey, of the Cumberland Presbyterian denomination, came to the place as superintendent of said Indian school. But it was about a year thereafter before suitable buildings were erected on the Yellow river[1] in Iowa, and Mr. Lowrey remained in Prairie du Chien and preached on Sundays; and, during this time, collected those professing religion of the different denominations into a society."

Mr. Lowrey himself gives us an interesting narrative of his coming to Prairie du Chien and his early work there. Bringing his family, he came overland from Nashville, Tennessee. This movement he calls "leaving his native land." He arrived at Prairie du Chien, 1833, September 7th. The Indians

---

[1] Three or four miles above Prairie du Chien.

were unwilling to remove west of the Mississippi. Accordingly the execution of the order to erect buildings for the school had been suspended. "It is a great pity," wrote Mr. Lowrey that most of the intercourse kept up between the white people and [the] Indians is by men of dissipated character, traders, whose sole object it is to make money, and who frown on every attempt to improve the condition of the poor Indians, for they know if they [the Indians] turn their attention to agriculture and civilized habits, the fur trade with them would be seriously injured."

True to his calling Mr. Lowrey at once began to hold preaching services. "I never saw a place where the gospel was more needed. Settlements forty and fifty miles distant are very desirous of preaching. Schools are greatly needed and would be well supported could suitable teachers be obtained. I have recommended an itinerant plan of school keeping until teachers can be procured for every neighborhood." He recommends young men of piety and enterprise to teach. "I know of no country where money is more plenty than it is here." It would need to be, one would think, for he tells us that "corn and wheat bring $1 per bushel. Fifteen dollars and boarding are given per month for laborers on a farm."

He rejoices that "no slavery can be admitted here." Writing under date of 1833, December 7th, he says: "The cause of temperance on yesterday achieved a very important victory. I delivered an address to a very large audience mostly of officers and soldiers, and secured sixty pledges to abstain." The letter was delayed a week. Meanwhile "fifty-five more signatures were obtained; total, one hundred fifteen: more than half the garrison!"

Further mention of Mr. Lowry's work is to be found in Butterfield's "History of Crawford County:" "In 1834 the Rev. David Lowrey organized the first Protestant society in Prairie du Chien: it afterwards was merged into the Congregational society."

General Street as he is commonly called,— he did efficient service in the Black Hawk war,— was one of the founders of the church. Another was one who yet abides with us, ex-Judge J. T. Mills, now of the Lancaster church.[1] A native of Paris, Bourbon county, Kentucky, he nevertheless early became a temperance man and an opponent of slavery. These "abolitionists" from the South were, more than any others, the men who made southwestern Wisconsin strongly anti-slavery. Wiser than the sharp-tongued followers of Garrison they did not believe in disunion. From Illinois college, whither he had been drawn by the name of Edward Beecher, president there from 1830 until 1834, young Mills came to Prairie du Chien. On his way he saw Black Hawk, then a captive. The young collegian became tutor in the family of Colonel Taylor and later in the home of General Street. It was with some misgivings and questions of duty that this sturdy Kentucky abolitionist became one of the brotherhood of this church. For one of its members, Andrew Cochran, held slaves in Missouri.

---

[1] Since the above was written, he has become a resident of Manitowoc.

In about a year Mr. Lowrey's official duties prevented his rendering the church more than occasional service. "There is a Presbyterian church, of twenty-five or thirty members in the place," says Rev. Stephen Peet speaking of Prairie du Chien in the "Home Missionary" for September, 1838, "supplied half the time by a Cumberland Presbyterian minister who occupies a station a few miles above." Rev. Isaac Erving Heaton still living[1] in honored age at Fremont, Nebraska, removed about October, 1839, from Belmont, one of Wisconsin's early capitals, to Prairie du Chien.

He writes: "At Prairie du Chien I preached only occasionally to supply a vacancy. My occupation there was teaching. For one year, partly before I went to Prairie du Chien, Rev. Mr. Bonham[2] was the pastor. He was a young man, I think, from Tennessee. He was a Cumberland Presbyterian." Thus, as Father Kent was by preference a new-school Presbyterian, Mr. Heaton was probably the first Congregational minister to preach at Prairie du Chien. He soon removed to Mineral Point, and at that place was one of the first to have charge of its public school.

Mr. Stevens, who came to Prairie du Chien first in 1829, removed thither from his mission among the Sioux, and in December, 1841, began work as pastor of the church organized by Mr. Lowrey in 1834. Mr. Stevens filled this office until September, 1843.

Long years afterward (1866), Jeremiah Porter came from army service to take the pastorate of the same old church that virtually had its beginning in 1830 and 1831 under his friend and associate, Father Kent.[3] From Prairie du Chien Mr. Porter went once more to the South,—this time to Brownsville, Texas, and soon thereafter a son and a daughter became missionaries in far-off China where they yet abide.[4]

Another sturdy pioneer was Rev. Alfred Brunson who, as we have learned, came Prairie du Chien first on a tour of missionary exploration in the autumn of 1835. Continuing his work of mission superintendence, he came West the next summer, arriving at Prairie du Chien 1836, July 16th. He brought with him from Meadville, Pennsylvania, by canal, French creek and the Alleghany river to Pittsburgh, thence eighteen hundred miles by the Ohio and the Mississippi a keel-boat with four families, including his own, and a dwelling-house ready to be put together. The cost of towage from Pittsburg by steamboats was $650 of which $400 was the charge from St. Louis to Prairie du Chien.[5]

---

[1] While the greater part of this narrative was in course of preparation. He died at Fremont 1893, September 18th.

[2] B. B. Bonham, as he has been identified by Chancellor N. Green of Cumberland university, Lebanon, Tennessee.

[3] Organized as a Cumberland Presbyterian church, in the year given above, it dropped the "Cumberland" in 1842 and became Congregational in 1856.

[4] It may be that even as the pen writes these lines (1894, September 11th) Miss Porter,—having paid a tribute to the memory of her mother, and rendered to her father the last service that earthly love can give,—is traversing the Mediterranean sea or the Red on her return to continue the work from which she was taken for a time only by the call of filial piety.

[5] The first steamboat to make its appearance at Prairie du Chien,—the Virginia of St.

Mr. Brunson was a unique gift of Connecticut to the West and to Methodism. Whether, on a night journey, singing hymns to drive away wolves that seemed ready to devour him and his horse, fighting his opponents in Conference, proposing additional articles of faith for the Methodist church, or demolishing Calvinism, Campbellism and the glacial theory,—all of which he seems to have held in about equal abhorrence,—he was the same self-reliant, aggressive, determined man, often mistaken, sometimes unjust, but a true soldier of the church militant.

It is interesting to know that Duncan Graham, captain in the British Indian service, who in 1815 thought of Prairie du Chien as such a forlorn place,[1]—which no doubt it was,—became a resident there. He was one of those who had charge of "three Mackinaw boats, manned with six hands each, [and] loaded with wheat, oats and peas,"—boats that on Saturday the 15th of April, 1820, "left Prairie du Chien for Selkirk colony [Pembina] on Red river,"—a settlement that in its beginning seems to have found its base of supplies at Prairie du Chien. In 1827, at the time of the Winnebago outbreak, Graham was the means of ridding Mr. Lockwood's home of marauding Indians who, in the husband's absence, had come thither with the intent, probably, of taking the life of Mrs. (Warren) Lockwood or that of any one whom opportunity might put in the way of their guns or scalping-knives.

Again and again the hopes of those who expected a great city at Prairie du Chien have been disappointed. In 1857 the old village was wakened for a little time to new life by the coming thither of the first railway that crossed the state of Wisconsin. That was a generation ago and even now when men hear the name of Prairie du Chien,—the Kipisagee[2] of the Ojibways and other Algonquians,—they think not of the future but of the past.[3]

Louis,—came in 1821. "It was a stern-wheeler, and a man with a pole was stationed on the bow to aid in steering."

[1] See page 43. A sketch of Captain Graham's life is given by Secretary Draper in volume IX. page 299 of the "Wisconsin Historical Collections."

[2] "Meaning the place of the jet or overflow of the [Wisconsin] river, The word appears to be based on the verb *kipa*, to be thick or turbid, and *sc.uge*, outflow; the river at the floods being little less than a moving mass of sand and water."—H. R. SCHOOLCRAFT.

In 1822 there was very high water in the Mississippi. The parade ground of the old fort was flooded to the depth of three or four feet. The garrison was compelled to remove to the higher land back of the slough. See Durrie's "Annals of Prairie du Chien."

[3] And yet I hope that time may disprove the remark of Charles J. Latrobe, an English traveler who visited Prairie du Chien in 1833: "The place seems destined to remain under the same spell as others of a like origin." Yet it is noticeable that whatever American communities were early afflicted with a preponderance of Romanism have been relatively unprogressive. Compare Green Bay with Milwaukee, St. Louis with Chicago, New Orleans with Philadelphia, Quebec with Boston.

Of a still more distant past than that known to whites, Mr. Latrobe gives hint when he tells us that from "an Indian mound round which the new buildings [of the fort] were constructed * forty-eight bodies, some enclosed in wooden or bark coffins, were removed." "Ancient mounds and fortifications" at Prairie du Chien are described in Major Long's journal perhaps of 1817.

CHAPTER XIII.

AMONG THE MINES.

The southwestern part of Wisconsin is peculiar geologically from the fact that its surface bears no evidence of the glacial action that has marked so unmistakably all the rest of the state. Including the extreme northwestern part of Illinois, and a narrow strip along the Mississippi in Iowa and Minnesota, this "island in a sea of drift" has an area of about ten thousand square miles. In it is the Galena lead region.

Here, where the denudation made by the storms and floods of unnumbered years had left masses of ore lying almost upon the surface of the ground, there was needed for the "discovery" thereof nothing more than a pair of eyes even though they were as keen as those of the ordinary Indian are supposed to be. And heat no greater than that of a camp-fire would turn this substance into the material of bullets. Indeed the soft ore itself could be cut or beaten into the desired form. If this was done,— as is probable enough,— by Indians, it would not take them long to conclude that, in addition to furs, they had something that the Frenchman would value.

Mines were always an object of the explorer's search. It must have been with peculiar interest that Perrot, while journeying on the Wisconsin river, perhaps in 1692, received from some Miami Indians[1] a specimen of lead ore. Search for the place whence it was brought led him, perhaps, to the site of the mines that, almost a century afterward (1788) were wrought by Julien Dubuque. On the opposite side of the Mississippi, probably not far above the mouth of the Galena river, Perrot, it is said, built a trading-post. Yet of all this, his own statements say nothing.

In our story of La Pointe, there appears the name of Pierre Le Seuer. His building of a "fort" on Madelaine island was done not only to secure the trade of the region round about, but also, with another, to command the Brule-St. Croix route between the Great Lakes and the Mississippi. This second post Le Seuer built,— in 1695 ?— on an island near Lake Pepin. Soon we find him in France claiming that he had discovered, "at the source of the Mississippi, mines of lead, copper, blue and green earth," and seeking a license to work

---

[1] With the Mascoutins (see page 2) there seem to have been in 1669 some Miamis. A part of the tribe La Salle found in 1680 on the St. Joseph's river (Michigan or Indiana). There and on the Wabash and the Maumee all the Miamis seem by 1721, to have found a home.

them. This he obtained, and in 1699 started for Louisiana. In the following summer, he made his way up the Mississippi, and on the 25th of August, 1700, came to what he called "the river of the mines," known to us as the Fever or the Galena. This river he was the first white man to explore, and on its banks he found lead mines wrought in a crude way by Indians. There, and on or near the site of Dubuque, and also in what came to be known as "Snake Hollow" (Potosi), he set to work the thirty miners whom he brought with him from France. Their work in "Snake Hollow,"— so-called when the Americans began coming thither,— brought Le Seuer and his men within the limits of what is now Wisconsin, and they were probably the first whites to work therein for lead,— the first, perhaps, to know of its existence there. But this opening of mines only a few miles from those already known can hardly be called a discovery.

The warlike Outagamies seem to have prevented the French miners from accomplishing much in this region. Whatever the Miamis also may have done there,— which was not much,— soon came to an end, and the Outagamies won, in the lead region, a mastery strengthened rather than weakened by the change of tribal home that their long war with the French forced upon them. In time, however, the southwestern part of what is now Wisconsin seems to have passed, though, apparently, not by conquest, into the possession of the Winnebagoes. In 1788 at a council held at Prairie du Chien, the Outagamies made to Julien Dubuque a grant of land fronting the Mississippi on its western bank for twenty-one miles. But they came to hate the Americans, and when Colonel James Johnson and his men first came to Fevre river,— about the 5th of July, 1822,— the Outagamie and the Sauk Indians would have forcibly resisted their landing had not the utter folly of such action been made manifest by the presence of United States troops.

In 1811 Nicholas Boilvin recommended that the United States government encourage the Indians to become lead-producers instead of fur-gatherers. "This would put an end to the subsisting intercourse between the Canadian traders and the Indians." He adds that "during the last season they,"— he is speaking of the Sacs, Foxes and Iowas,— "manufactured four hundred thousand pounds of that article" (lead). It would not be at all like the Anglo-Saxon race to leave in possession of barbarians a region so rich in mineral treasures. Indeed by "treaty" made at St. Louis, 1804, November 3rd a vast tract including the lead region had already been sold to the United States[1] government. That the chiefs who made the sale had the right to do so was afterward denied by a large part of the tribe,— the Sacs and Foxes,— in whose name the deed was done. By the terms of the treaty, the united tribe was received into the friendship of the United States, and placed under the protection of our government. But a portion, if not a majority, of the tribe seem to have trusted for protection chiefly to themselves.

It was natural, under the circumstances, that those dissatisfied with the

---

[1] Governor William Henry Harrison afterward president, represented the United States.

seek alliance with the British, to whom they had given
1812. The leader of this "British band" (as they were
d Foxes,—Sauks and Outagamies,—was a chief of the
ι-tai-me-she-kia-kiah¹ (Black Sparrow-Hawk), commonly
k. How he felt toward the Americans is clearly shown
by him, at Prairie du Chien, 1815, April 8th, before it
; peace had been made between Great Britain and the
ιve been sent by our chiefs," he said, "to ask for a large
e in our village. The Big Knives are so treacherous, we
ιay come up to deceive us. By having one of your large
·e will live in safety; our women will then be able to
ιe ground unmolested, and our young men will then be
families without dread of the Big Knives."² As late as
net in council on Drummond Island, Lake Huron, Lieu-
ιy, the captor of Fort Shelby. "The Americans, my
said Black Hawk, "but we are ever ready to meet them."
:onfluence of the Rock river with the Mississippi.
/hites were beginning to occupy the lead region. They
ζoes and apparently some of the Sacs and Foxes, though
l been removed. The days when the Indian held the land
ried on the commerce were almost at an end.
ιcky of whom James Johnson seems to have been leader
brought negro slaves with them. It is not known, how-
e were brought over the line into what is now Wisconsin.
ƴ and Missouri, who were the first to come, thought that
ιr north for successful farming. None the less, hundreds
ιsands rushed into the region though the whites had but
sputed possession. The Winnebagoes were the first to
In the spring of 1827 some murders, to which reference
committed by them in the neighborhood of Prairie du
ere also killed in a boat on the Mississippi near the mouth
ne 26th).
ιed a company of mounted volunteers who chose Henry
ιvernor, as their commander. It has been already stated,
aised at Green Bay also. In this were Oneida and Stock-
tunately Governor Cass was at Green Bay when the dis-
hastened to St. Louis to confer with Brigadier-General
soon started up the Mississippi with a force of regulars.
n's men and Dodge's company, the Winnebagoes fled up

ι Henry Smith, Muck-ut-tay-mick-e-kaw-kiah (*Wisconsin Historical*
ιck Hawk is sometimes called L'Epervier.
t Hawk's speech was made by Captain T. G. Anderson, of the British

owed are known in our local history as the "Winnebago war."
ows into the Mississippi from the east almost opposite the boundary
innesota.

the Wisconsin as far as the famous portage between that river and the Fox. There, by giving up three of their number who confessed responsibility for the murders that had been committed, they made end both of their flight and their struggle. The surrender of the prisoners was made to Major William Whistler of Fort Howard who had come thence with all the force of his command including the friendly Indians.[1] Among these may have been some Menomonees.

The scene was highly dramatic. On the left of the United States troops were their Indian allies. On the right hand was the band of musicians who rendered the solemn strains of "Pleyel's Hymn." The Winnebagoes approached, bearing three flags one white, the others the familiar stars and stripes. As they came into the presence of the United States commanding officer, their spokesman, the chief Car-i-mau-nee, said: "They are here. Like braves they have come in. Treat them as braves. Do not put them in irons." Then all sat down and a "talk" followed." It was of such kind as might be expected. The Indians were duly admonished in regard to their offenses and their duty.

The chief Red Bird, first of the offenders in tribal rank, then stood up. It was the great day of his life and the resources of his toilet had doubtless been exhausted in making as brave a display as possible.[2] Facing Major Whistler, he said: 'I am ready;' Then advancing a step or two, he paused and said: 'I do not wish to be put in irons. Let me be free. I have given away my life'— stooping and taking dust between his finger and thumb and blowing it away— 'like that,' eyeing the dust as it fell and vanished, then adding: "I will not take it back. It is gone." Having thus spoken, he threw his hands behind him, and marched up to Major Whistler, breast to breast."

Red Bird's request was granted. He was not put in irons. While the guard-tent was made ready the sound of Atkinson's cannon was heard. Soon came also Dodge's company.

Before the time for his trial Red Bird died a prisoner at Fort Crawford. His accomplices, We-kau and Chic-hon-sic were convicted of murder, but received from President John Quincy Adams a pardon bearing date 1828, November 3rd.

With the Winnebagoes thus humbled and the Sacs and Foxes under treaty

---

[1] He arrived at the portage September 1st. Having been commanded by Atkinson to await his arrival there, Major Whistler encamped on the hight where in the following year the erection of Fort Winnebago was begun.

[2] His face was painted, on one side red, the other intermixed with green and white. He was clothed in a Yankton suit of dressed elk-skin, perfectly white, and as soft as a kid glove, new and beautiful. On his feet he wore moccasins. On each shoulder, in place of an epaulette, was fastened a preserved red bird. Around his neck he wore a collar of blue wampum, beautifully mixed with white, whilst the claws of a panther or wild cat, with their points inward, formed the rim of the collar. Around his neck were hanging strands of wampum of various lengths, the circles enlarging as they descended. There was no attempt at ornamenting the hair, after the Indian style; but it was cut after the fashion of the most civilized. Across his breast, in a diagonal position, and bound tightly to it, was his war pipe, at least three feet long, brightly ornamented with dyed horse hair, and the feathers and bills of birds. In one of his hands he held the white flag, and in the other the calumet or pipe of peace.— Strong's "History of the Territory of Wisconsin."

obligation to remove west of the Mississippi, the white immigrants felt safe in their new homes.

At first all settlers in the lead region were practically tenants at will of the United States. No one might settle there, or mine, or smelt without a permit from the government agent who was usually an army officer. These settled disputes without the help, -or hindrance,--of lawyers, and officiated at the first marriages. It was not until early in the session of 1846-47 that Congress authorized the sale of ore-bearing lands.[1] But after 1836 little attention was paid to the regulations first established. What these were is shown in a letter written by Dr. Horatio Newhall, of whom we shall hear as being some years later at Fort Winnebago. Under date of 1827, November 20th, he wrote to his brother Isaac Newhall, of Salem, Massachusetts. The letter bears the superscription: "Galena, Fevre River Lead Mines, supposed to be in Illinois." He gives us a lively and interesting picture of the country as it was then.

"I received, by the last mail brought here by steamboat "Josephine," a newspaper from you on the margin of which were endorsed the following words: 'Write a full account.' I was rejoiced to see once more a Massachusetts paper, and presume you meant by the endorsement a full account of Fevre River. This would puzzle me or any other person on the river. It is a nondescript. It is such a place as no one could conceive of without seeing it. Strangers hate it, and residents like it. The appearance of the country would convince any one it must be healthy; yet last season, it was more sickly than Havana or New Orleans. There is no civil law here, nor has the Gospel been yet introduced; or, to make use of a common phrase here, "neither law nor Gospel can pass the rapids of the Mississippi." The country is one immense prairie from the Rock river on the south to the Ouisconsin on the north and from the Mississippi on the west to Lake Michigan on the east. It is a hilly country, and abounding with lead ore of that species called by mineralogists 'galena' whence is derived the name of our town. The lead mines of the Upper Mississippi, as well as those of Missouri, are under the control of the Secretary of War. Lieutenant [Martin] Thomas is Superintendent. He resides at St. Louis; a sub-agent resides at this place. Any person wishing to dig gets a permit of the agent to do so, by signing certain regulations, the principal of which is that he will sell his mineral to no one but a regularly licensed smelter. He has all the mineral he can raise, and sells it at $17.50 per thousand (pounds), delivered at the furnaces. Any person who gets a permit stakes off two hundred yards square. This is his lot so long as he works it, and no one can interfere with his discoveries. Any person who will give bond to the Gov-

---

[1] Of this sale and proceedings preliminary thereto Mr. Consul Willshire Butterfield thus writes: "Meetings of miners and settlers were held throughout the mineral country, and the rights of miners were adjusted by arbitrators appointed at such meetings. Public bidders were appointed also, who were empowered to bid off the mineral lands at the sale June 1, 1847, and who afterwards deeded the tracts to each party who had been designated by the arbitrators as the rightful claimant. No opposition was permitted to the bidders, who offered only regular government prices,"— $2.50 and $1.25 per acre for farming and mineral lands

ernment for $5,000 can have half a mile square, on condition that he employs twenty laborers and pays the Government 10 per cent. of lead made from mineral raised on his survey, or sells his mineral to a public smelter. The public smelters, of whom I am one, give bond for $20,000 to pay the Government one-tenth of all lead manufactured. They buy mineral of any one who has a permit to dig, manufacture it into lead, pay the Government one-tenth monthly, and are the *great men of the country*. The mineral, lead, and cash all go into their hands. * * The privilege of working these mines, you know, was first given by the Government to Col. Johnson, of Kentucky, five years ago (in 1822). He did but little and sunk money. No lead was made here till last year. There were then four log buildings in Galena. Now there are 115 houses and stores in the place. It is the place of deposit for lead and provisions, etc., for all the mining country. There is no spot in America, of the same size, where there is one-fourth of the capital, or where so much business is done. There was manufactured here in the year ending September last, 5,000,740 pounds of lead.[1] The population consists mainly of Americans, Irish and French (that is in the diggings). There are but comparatively few females. Hence every female unmarried, who lands on these shores, is immediately married. Little girls fourteen and fifteen years old are often married here. Three young ladies who came, fellow-passengers with me, in June, and the only ones on board, are all married months since. Du'Buque's Mines, on opposite side of the Mississippi, are worked by the Fox Indians. They, however, merely skim the surface. The windlass and bucket are not known among them. Du'Buque's Mines is a delightful spot, particularly the Fox Village, on the bank of the Mississippi. But all of the places in the United States which I have seen, Rock Island, at the lower rapids of the Mississippi, called the rapids of the Des Moines, is by far the most beautiful.[2] Fort Armstrong is on this island. At the mouth of Fevre River is a trading-house of the American Fur Company. Their trading-houses are scattered up and down the Mississippi, on the river Des Moines, St. Peter, etc. Their capital is so large, and they give such extensive credit to the Indians that no private establishment can compete with them. An Indian debt is outlawed, by their own custom in one year. The fur company credits each Indian hunter a certain amount, from $100 to $500, according to his industry and skill in hunting and trapping. If, when they return in the spring, they have not furs and peltry enough to pay the debt, the trader loses it. But on the goods sold to the Indians, there is a profit of 200 or 300 per cent. made, and a profit on the furs received in payment."

In a postscript written 1827, December 7th, he adds: "Fevre River was closed with ice on the 21st of November, and of course navigation is ended, and I have not sent my letter. I now have an opportunity to forward it by pri-

---

[1] Including, of course, the region round about.

[2] Dr. Newhall makes an error here. Rock Island is at the upper rapids of the Mississippi; the lower beside which is now the city of Keokuk, Iowa, are near the mouth of the Des Moines.

vate conveyance to Vandalia.[1] We are now shut out from intercourse with the world until the river opens again in the spring. We have no mail as yet, but shall have a mail once in two weeks, to commence the first of January next. I have not received a letter from one of my friends since I have been in Fevre River. I hope you will write me before 1st of January, or as soon as you receive this letter."

Law and gospel soon came, law first, apparently, and with some provisos that we do not now take pride in recalling. What these were is suggested by an order passed 1829, March 10th, by the commissioners of Jo Daviess county, — of which Galena is the county seat,— taxing, with other property, "slaves;" also "indentured or registered servants." The latter expression is of course a mere subterfuge, taken from certain statutes of Illinois popularly known as the "black laws." By these it was sought to evade the anti-slavery clause of the state constitution adopted in conformity to the requirement of the Ordinance of 1787.

When the gospel came, it was of the genuine kind that proclaims liberty to the captives. It is to be hoped that Dr. Newhall with his New England training brought a measure of it himself. But though he afterward became a most helpful member of the First Presbyterian church of Galena, the oldest in the city, he did not enter into it at its organization.

The founder and first pastor of this church and the bishop of all the region of which Galena was then the metropolitan city,— or rather the true archbishop thereof needing no pallium from Rome as the symbol of his great office, — was Rev. Aratus Kent. This son of Connecticut and graduate of Yale in the last class taught by the senior President Dwight, was of the same Puritan family that gave to the profession of law the renowned Chancellor Kent.[2]

In the autumn of 1828, Galena was visited by Captain John Shackford, an earnest layman of one of the St. Louis churches. Moved by the spiritual destitution of the place, without church or minister or active Christian layman of any denomination, he stirred up the people so that forty-four of the citizens, not one of them a professor of religion, joined in an application to the Home Missionary society for a minister, and pledged five hundred thirty dollars toward his support.

Thus the way was prepared for Mr. Kent's coming. Is it superstitious to note that his mind was not at rest in his (Bradford) New Hampshire field of labor though his people wished him to stay? Nor did the invitation to return to a former parish at Lockport, New York, move him to say yes. "I must needs call," he says, "on Dr. Absalom Peters, secretary of the American Home Missionary society, and inquire after a field of missionary labor. He proposed the lead mines of the upper Mississippi, of which I knew nothing before, but where there were several thousand souls with no preaching. 'I go, sir,' was my prompt reply." Leaving his horse as a parting gift to the American Tract

---

[1] Then, and until 1836, the capital of Illinois.
[2] President A. L. Chapin, "Beloit College Monthly" (now "Round Table"), March, 1870. To this article I am indebted for most of what is here stated in regard to Father Kent.

society, he went without waiting even for his written commission.[1]

"I am as one that dreams," he wrote under date of 1829, April 3rd, "with my paper on a trunk and my pen trembling with the jarring of a steamboat contending with the strong current of the Mississippi. I am urging my way up the great valley, to the lead mines, not knowing the things that shall befall me there."

He landed at Galena 1829, April 18th, twenty-seven days after leaving New York. Eight of these were spent in St. Louis "where he stopped for consultation with a few ministers, the nearest to the mines."

On the day after his arrival he preached in Galena the first sermon heard there. "Here is opened," he wrote, "a great and effectual door to preach the gospel." It was a vast field to which he had come, but "his faith and courage were equal to the responsibility. On one of his early tours of exploration," says President Chapin, "he alighted from his horse and on one of the majestic bluffs in that region proclaimed aloud, 'I take possession of this land for Christ,' and events proved it not an empty boast."

He preached in the hotel dining-room,— though his first service was held in the bar-room,— and in the court-house. Not satisfied with any of these places he bought, with his own means, the old log court-house, and thus in the autumn his congregation had a stated place of worship. In the following winter, having a helper in the work of teaching, he had charge of a day-school which numbered sixty pupils.

Not until 1831, October 23rd, was Mr. Kent able to organize a church, and then with only six members.[2] Of these Galena, with a population of one thousand, furnished but two, and two lived forty miles away at Mineral Point, (then) Michigan.

Mr. Kent made his life a part of Wisconsin's history and that of the Northwest, as the term was used at that time. In November, 1843, he wrote:

"As Paul did, so may I, 'after fourteen years,' recount the events that have transpired [occurred] since I came first to the lead mines of the upper Mississippi. My parish from Rock river to the Wisconsin has been surveyed. I have preached at Prairie du Chien, Fort Winnebago, Madison, Potosi, Lancaster, Cassville, Mineral Point, Belmont, Platteville, Pecatonica (now Rockton), Rockford, Grand Detour, Lyndon, Rock Island, Albany and Savannah. I have been in perils of waters six times, perils in the wilderness three nights, several times lost.— but out of them all the Lord has delivered me. There was, when I came, no church of any denomination, either Protestant or [Roman] Catholic within two hundred miles, no Sabbath, no minister, no God recognized. Now we have churches, presbyteries, conventions and synods. Our village has become a city of three or four thousand. Our church has grown to one hundred seventy-five, besides those gone to four new churches. We have

---

[1] Very possibly some formal action had to be taken before this could be issued. It bears date, 1829, March 21st.

[2] Facts due, no doubt, to his high standard of church-membership.

thirteen Sabbath-schools in the country, and have raised for foreign missions $1,530. God has done great things for us."

During the period of which Mr. Kent wrote, his labors were interrupted by the Black Hawk war. The sad, and in some respects disgraceful, story of that war has been often written. On the one side it was the last great struggle of a warlike people; on the other it was part of the resistless and relentless movement by which a nation was extending its domain.

After the close of the second war with Britain, the treaty of 1804 with the Sacs and Foxes was renewed (1816, May 13th). But though Black Hawk then "touched the goose-quill" he afterward asserted stoutly that in what he signed there were requirements that he did not understand and to which he did not consent. So he continued to deny that his people were under any obligation to remove to the western side of the Mississippi. Moreover he remained under the influence and practically in the pay of the British.

Besides he was deluded in a measure by an Indian "prophet" who, like the others of his worse than worthless kind, was probably what among whites is called a "medium." Stronger minds than Black Hawk's have been led astray by spiritism, the form, it may be, which witchcraft takes in these modern days

Black Hawk was not a hereditary chief. But natural leaders, of whom he was one, rule by a right that all men recognize.

To David, afterward king of Israel, came in the time of his exile from Saul's court. "every one that was in distress, and every one that was in debt, and every one that was discontented * * and he became a captain. over them, and there were with him about four hundred men." Black Hawk's adherents were perhaps of the corresponding classes among his people, or, more strictly speaking, those who were restive under what was to the Indians legal authority. Keokuk, the tribal chief, removed in 1830 or thereabout to the western side of the Mississippi. With him were most of the tribe.

The treaty of 1804 permitted the Indians to remain in their old possessions until settlers occupied the land. Black Hawk who was deeply attached to his home, which was also the place of his nativity, remained at his village at the mouth of the Rock. The story of the injuries which he and his people received there from the whites, and probably returned in full measure whenever they had opportunity, is a sorrowful one. More than once when the Indians returned from their hunting expeditions they found that their lodges had been burned. The sentiment prevailed among some of the border settlers that an Indian "has no rights which a white man is bound to respect."

Having returned in the spring of 1831 from a winter's hunt in what is now Iowa, Black Hawk and his people found that the site of their village had been pre-empted by some white men and that the burial place of their fathers had been turned into a plowed field. Naturally the Indians were furious. They took possession of what they regarded as their own. Met with commands to recross the Mississippi they retorted by injuring or destroying property belonging to the white settlers and, it is said, threatened them with death if they did not leave. But Black Hawk claims that they did not intend to shed blood unless in defense of their homes or their people.

There has been, it must be confessed, much senseless bluster in the official papers issued by many of our state executives. At this time Governor John Reynolds of Illinois called for volunteers "to repel the invasion of the British band." Fifteen hundred or more answered the call. These with a force of United States regulars under Brigadier-General Edmund P. Gaines, came 1831, June 26th, to Black Hawk's village. But the night before the Indians had found safety on the other side of the great river, and on the 30th of June, Black Hawk and his party agreed not to return to the eastern side without permission from the President or the governor (of Illinois).

The exiles had come to the trans-Mississippi part of Michigan, now Iowa, too late to raise a crop. They got little game for the next winter. Malcontents among the Winnebagoes and Pottawatomies encouraged them to take up arms. No doubt the "prophet" used his baleful influence. Accordingly in the spring of 1832, Black Hawk made a mistake that will connect his name forever with the history of all this region. He crossed the Mississippi, April 6th, with a band of five hundred warriors, mostly Sauks like himself, their women and children. War followed as a matter of course.

The campaign on the part of the Indians may be described as a flight up the Rock to Lake Koshkonong, thence by way of the Four Lakes (of Madison) to the Wisconsin where it divides Dane county from Sauk, thence westward to where the Bad Axe flows into the Mississippi.

More in detail: The Indians first went to Prophetstown on the Rock. Atkinson bade them recross the Mississippi. "If you wish to fight us, come on," was Black Hawk's reply. Some of the Illinois volunteers under Major Stillman thought that they did wish to fight them, and went on with a great show of bravery. They thought that they were on a "big frolic" and conducted themselves accordingly.

While this choice band was in camp on the creek in Ogle county, Illinois, that now bears the name of their commander, on the afternoon of the 14th of May, they saw at a distance three Indians. These were Black Hawk's messengers to say that he wished to come to terms. But the half-drunken white wretches who had been filling themselves with whisky gave chase to the Indians and killed one of them, if not two. These were the first victims of the war and their blood the first shed therein.

Black Hawk, seeing how his messengers of peace were treated, placed his men in ambush and awaited the coming of the pursuers. A volley from the Indians put the rangers to flight. Some of them did not pull rein until they got to their own homes, but most were content to stop at Dixon, more especially as a Captain Adams, who lost his life thereby, had put himself with his command between them and their Indian pursuers. This "spy batallion" of two hundred seventy-five, disgracefully routed by a party said to number not more than a hundred of whom thirty-five joined in the pursuit, reported that Black

Hawk had under his command two thousand warriors." The Illinois militia who had so promptly enlisted, were now quite as prompt in disbanding.[1] However, out of their number a regiment was formed for further service, and their former commander, Brigadier-General[2] Samuel Whiteside enlisted as a private and showed himself a brave fighter. Better men[3] than the skulkers and more of them took their places. Illinois put two thousand volunteers in the field. As they had done in the Winnebago "war," so now the miners in Wisconsin and about Galena raised a force of mounted men,—two hundred without the Galena company,—and again Henry Dodge was made commander. Black Hawk afterward said: "If it had not been for that chief Dodge, 'the hairy face' I could easily have whipped the whites; I could have gone anywhere my people pleased in the mining country."[4]

Before new levies were ready to take the field the settlers in the lead region, the part of (the future) Wisconsin which suffered most in the Black Hawk war, were exposed to great danger. Much killing was done on both sides,— murder, if of whites by Indians; war, if of Indians by whites. One of the worst deeds was by Pottawatomies and Sauks under command of a white renegade Mike Girty. "In these border strifes," says Mr. Thwaites, "fully two hundred whites and nearly as many Indians lost their lives, and there were numerous instances of romantic heroism on the part of settlers, men and women alike."

Soon Atkinson had at his command sufficient force to take the field. After Stillman's defeat, Black Hawk put his non-combatants in safety at Lake Koshkonong where they stayed while the warriors engaged in forays about the country.

Driven from Lake Koshkonong the Indians made a stand in what is now the town of Roxbury, Dane county. There, almost opposite the site of Prairie du Sac, was fought the "battle of Wisconsin Hights." In this, though defeated, Black Hawk showed the qualities of a good commander and protected the retreat of his people.

But the end was at hand. Without the possibility of reinforcements, with-

---

[1] The first intelligence received of the runaway troops by Gen. Atkinson, was that they had proceeded across the country to the Illinois river, and disbanded themselves or had been discharged. This was said to have been brought about from some cause connected with the local politics of the state. It may be well to add the fact that Stillman's corps had never been for an instant under Gen. Atkinson's orders, they having joined Gov. Reynolds at Dixon's, by a march through the country.—Captain Henry Smith.

[2] In state service.

[3] Among these was Abraham Lincoln who, after the first set of volunteers had been disbanded, was mustered into the service 1832, May 29th, by Robert Anderson whom in 1861, he made brigadier-general for so faithfully defending Fort Sumpter.

[4] There are those to whom the mere mention of Calvinism is like shaking a red rag before some turkey gobblers: it sets them to making a noise. But as study of human thought, if nothing more, it is interesting to note the attraction this form of philosophical and theological dogma has had for many of the world's strong and determined men. Thus Dodge, once probably an irreligious man, found in his last days a favorite study in Scott's Bible, the book that furnished this Methodist party of Stockbridges with readings which took the place of sermons. And Scott, as every one knows, though like Dodge an Episcopalian, is highly Calvinistic. Andrew Jackson joined the Presbyterian church before his death. Such Calvinists as William the Silent and Cromwell remind us of Buckle's remark that every great struggle for freedom in Europe has been preceded by some form of Calvinism in the religious belief of many or most of the people.

out supplies or shelter, the wretched fugitives went on marking with the bodies of their dead a pathway for their pursuers. Their way could also be traced, in places, by trees that had been stripped of bark for food.

"At length," says Black Hawk, "we arrived at the Mississippi having lost some of our old women and little children who perished on the way with hunger. We had been here but a little while before we saw a steamboat (the Warrior) coming. I told my braves not to shoot, as I intended going on board so that we might save our women and children. I knew the captain (Throckmorton), and was determined to give myself up to him. I then sent for my white flag. While the messenger was gone, I took a small piece of white cotton and put it on a pole, and called to the captain of the boat and told him to send his little canoe on shore and let me come on board. The people on the boat asked whether we were Sacs or Winnebagoes. I told a Winnebago to tell them we were Sacs and wanted to give ourselves up. A Winnebago on the boat called to us "to run and hide, that the whites were going to shoot." About this time, one of my braves had jumped into the river, bearing a white flag to the boat, when another sprang in after him and brought him to shore. The firing then commenced from the boat, which was returned by my braves, and continued for some time. * *

"The Winnebagoes on the steamboat must have misunderstood what was told or did not tell it to the captain correctly, because I am confident he would not have fired upon us if he had known my wishes. I have always considered him a good man and too great a brave to fire upon an enemy when suing for quarter.

* * * * * * * * *

"Early in the morning, a party of whites, being in advance of the army, came upon our people who were attempting to cross the Mississippi. They tried to give themselves up. The whites paid no attention to their entreaties, but commenced slaughtering them. In a little while the whole army arrived. Our braves, but few in number, finding that the enemy paid no respect to age or sex, and seeing that they were murdering helpless women and little children, determined to fight until they were killed. As many women as could, commenced swimming the Mississippi with children on their backs. A number of them were drowned and some shot before reaching the opposite shore.

"One of my braves, who gave me this information, piled some saddles up before him, when the fight commenced, to shield him from the enemy's fire, and killed three white men; but, seeing that the whites were coming too close for him, he crawled to the bank of the river and hid himself until the enemy retired. He then came to me and told me what had been done. After hearing this sorrowful news, I started with my little party for the Winnebago village at Prairie La Crosse."

It is only just to add that Captain Henry Smith of the regular army, apparently a brave and truthful man, says that "quarter was in no instance asked or granted. The official reports give the number killed of the enemy at one hundred and fifty, though doubtless many more were killed at the river and elsewhere, whose bodies were never seen afterwards. Our loss was but twenty-seven. The Black Hawk, the Prophet, and some other chiefs escaped from the action; but were subsequently brought in by the Winnebagoes, and the friendly Sauks, and delivered to the commanding General. After the action, a body of one hundred Sioux warriors presented themselves, and asked leave to pursue on the trail of such of the enemy as had escaped. This was granted, and the Sioux, after two days' pursuit, overtook and killed fifty or sixty, mostly, it is feared, women and children."

We who dwell in Wisconsin do not boast of this "battle."

Though the affair at the mouth of the Bad Axe reflected no credit upon the whites engaged in it, their march thither did. From the Wisconsin westward they were in a region before untraversed by white men. It is probable that the Indians led them over the worst of a very rough country,—a land of forests, streams, almost perpendicular bluffs, and hills that rise nearly to the hight of mountains.

The Black Hawk war was remarkable for the number of men engaged in it who afterward acquired national renown. Two have been named, Abraham Lincoln and Robert Anderson. Colonel Taylor commanded a regiment in which Jefferson Davis served as lieutenant.[1] Major-General Winfield Scott also was ordered to the scene of disturbance and got as far north as Prairie du Chien, but arrived too late to take any part in the fighting.[2]

The war being over, the settlers felt safe in venturing out of the dozen or more log "forts" which they had built, one at every place of any importance in the mining district. The activities of business were resumed and again southwestern Wisconsin and a little later the entire region west of Lake Michigan invited immigration.[3]

The attentive reader will have noticed that the movement which first occupied the lead region had its origin in Kentucky and Missouri and preceded the New England and New York stream of immigration which found resting-places

---

[1] A characteristic story is told of Taylor. Some of the Illinois militia infected with the state rights heresy of the time, which was then leading the authorities of South Carolina to the verge of treason and twenty years before brought disgrace upon Massachusetts and Connecticut, refused to go beyond the bounds of their state in pursuit of Black Hawk. This occurred on the banks of the Rock beyond which was the route which must be taken. Taylor stationed his regulars so that between them and the river there were the volunteers. These he then addressed, telling them that orders had been received from the President to pursue the Indians. Some of their number might yet fill the office of President. If so, they would expect to be obeyed. At any rate he intended to obey orders, and if there were any among them who did not wish to cross the river,—there stood the United States troops behind them. "Forward, march!" They marched!

Perhaps Abraham Lincoln was one of the volunteers addressed. If so we may hope that he was too careful in judgment to take part in a mutiny. It is due to the re-organized Illinois militia to say that, aside from this nonsense, they made for themselves a good reputation.

[2] With Scott and his troops came to the upper Mississippi valley, for the first time, the Asiatic cholera, an enemy that took the lives of more soldiers than were slain in the war with the hostile Sauks.

[3] The land office at Mineral Point was established 1836, August 1st. The venerable George Wallace Jones, now of Dubuque, Iowa, says that his entry of the land that includes Sinsinawa Mound was the first made.

by Lake Michigan, in the valley of the Rock, and on the prairies between them. The route of the one was by the Mississippi; of the other, by the Great Lakes. Thus for a time there were, in what is now Wisconsin, two distinct areas of settlement. Of these the one in the mining district was at first much the more important. It is no wonder some thought that, with the part of the lead region on the west side of the Mississippi, it would form the political and commercial center of a state to be formed of what is now Wisconsin and Iowa. Nor was this dream dispelled when the act was passed by which Wisconsin became an organized Territory of the United States. Said act was approved 1836, April 20th, and went into effect on the 4th of the next July.

The Black Hawk war had drawn public attention to the new Territory. It had been found out that farming could be successfully carried on as far north as the lead region. Land was in great demand there and elsewhere in the future state. But of 878,014 acres of government land sold in Wisconsin by the end of 1836, Mr. Moses M. Strong estimates that 600,000 had gone to "speculators." Much harm was done the country, especially the mining part of it, by this non-resident ownership though, as has been said, an effort was made to retain the ore-bearing lands in the possession of the government.[1] However, in spite of speculation, the farmer began his work in developing the resources of the future state. The miner of the winter was often the farmer of the summer, and thus and in other ways the two classes were easily blended.

By the census taken in August, 1836, the number of inhabitants in what is now Wisconsin was found to be 11,687. Of these nearly one-half, 5,234, were in Iowa county in which were then included Grant and La Fayette. What is now the state of Iowa,—then comprised within the counties of Des Moines and Dubuque,—had a population of 10,531. This weight of population toward the southwest naturally gave the lead region a strong claim for the location of the capital therein. It was at Mineral Point[2] that Governor Dodge took the oath of office, and the first legislature of Wisconsin met at (old) Belmont, near Platteville, in 1836, October 25th.[3]

Wisconsin thus named and organized extended from Lake Michigan to the Missouri river. Its most southern point was at the confluence of the Des Moines and the Mississippi; its most northern, the point,—to which reference has already been made,[4]— called in the British-American treaty of 1783 "the most northwestern corner" of the Lake of the Woods. In other words, it included all of the present states of Wisconsin, Iowa, Minnesota, and, of the Dakotas, those portions that lie east of the Missouri and the White Earth.

---

[1] Not until August, 1842, was there passed "an act for the relief of certain settlers in Wisconsin,"—those who had been refused pre-emption privileges because they had settled on what were regarded as mineral lands.

[2] Often called in early days by the extraordinary name of Shake-Rag or Shake-Rag-under-the-Hill from the circumstance that a woman who kept a boarding-house there made known the time when meals were ready by hanging a cloth from one of her windows.

[3] The legislative session held at Green Bay, beginning 1836, January 1st, was held in the name and under the authority of the Territory of Michigan.

[4] See page 39.

CHAPTER XIV.

WISCONSIN'S OPEN DOOR.

The beginning of a permanent settlement was made on the site of the present city of Green Bay, in 1745. The ungarrisoned French post La Baye, on the opposite side of the river, was occupied by the British, as already stated, 1761, October 12th. The garrison of Fort Edward Augustus, as it was called by its new possessors, Lieutenant James Gorrel, commander, escaped the fate of most British troops in the West at the time of Pontiac's conspiracy. By the friendly intervention of the Dakotas (Sioux), Gorrel and his men departed unmolested, 1763, June 21st. Pontiac's war was soon over, but no garrison was stationed at Fort Edward Augustus, and the name dropped out of use.

In September, 1766, Jonathan Carver visited Green Bay on his famous journey, and thus wrote: "The place is only a small village containing about twenty-five houses and sixty or seventy warriors. I found there nothing worthy of further remark.' When Carver came it was as an Englishman, a colonist to be sure, but still an Englishman loyal to George III. Soon the long union between the colonists and the mother country was broken, but Green Bay remained practically a part of Canada until after the treaty of Ghent.

In 1815, May 18th, Louis Grignon wrote: "We know nothing as yet of the news except that by the Gazette we see that we are ceded to the Americans." On the 29th of the same month he announces his departure from La Baye, apparently to join as leader a party bound for Mackinaw, adding, "I go to-morrow." It was probably about the middle of June, 1815, the British finally withdrew from Green Bay.

But the American flag did not float over the old place until 1816, July 16th, three schooners with a portion of the Third United States infantry, under command of Colonel John Miller, sailed into Fox river. In two months' time, on a site near the present station of the Chicago and Northwestern railway, Fort Howard was built.[1] Here, as already noted, were held the first Protestant services in unnamed Wisconsin.[2] These, as stated, were by Dr. Morse,

---

[1] On hearing of the proposed building of this fort, McDouall continues his lamentation that the British are to lose all control of the Indians between Lake Michigan and the Mississippi and all influence over them. He speaks of Green Bay as being in a country that the Americans did not possess before the war.

[2] The notorious Samuel Peters, "LL. D. & Clerk in Holy Orders," as he subscribes himself,

in July (probably the 9th), 1820.

The name Green Bay is not always used with precision. Thus it sometimes denotes the mission of St. Francis Xavier, sometimes Fort St. Francis, sometimes the fort called first La Baye and then Edward Augustus. Even Fort Howard is sometimes hidden under the term Green Bay. The first settlement of importance, after American possession, had its beginning when Colonel Smith in 1820 removed his troops from Fort Howard to higher land on the opposite side of the river two miles and a half up stream and half a mile from it. Between camp and river grew up a village described doubtless by its suggestive name "Shantytown." What was called the "Grignon tract" is the site of the present city of Green Bay, the northern part of which was laid out in 1830 as Navarino and the southern in 1835 as Astor.

Vaguely described as opposite Shantytown was the "old agency house," erected by Colonel John Bowyer whom Dr. Morse found exercising the office of Indian agent. Of this building, made vacant by Bowyer's death, Eleazar Williams on his second arrival, 1822, September 1st, by permission of Colonel Ninian Pinkney, took possession. Here he may have held his first public services after coming west. That he delayed this duty so long does not surprise us knowing as we do the character of the man. There is reason to believe that these services in the summer of 1823 were at Shantytown or the Agency. But in the following winter at Colonel John McNeil's invitation, they were held in Fort Howard, to which the troops had been brought back in the autumn of 1822.

Williams's successor, Rev. Norman Nash, was the first minister of the Episcopal denomination or of any Protestant church to come to what is now Wisconsin apparently with the purpose of making his home here. But as he arrived late in August, 1824, and left early the next spring, it can hardly be said that he became a resident of Wisconsin. Mission work among the Indians,—though he did very little of it,—seems to have been his main object in coming. He, too, found a home at the Agency, where, after waiting till winter, he opened a school and "preached to the neighbors on Sundays," to use the words of A. G. Ellis who was nominally his assistant, virtually, it would seem, his principal. While sustaining a like relation to Williams, Mr. Ellis, the winter before, taught the post school at Fort Howard. Now, having practically separated himself from Mr. Nash, who was apparently a good but not an energetic man, he opened a school at Shantytown where, "after Mr. Nash left," he says, "I began lay reading on Sundays and organized an Episcopal Sunday-school at my school-room." Thus in the spring of 1825, two Sunday-schools were started within the present limits of our state, this and the one by Mrs. Lockwood and Dr. James at Prairie du Chien. Which preceded the other and so was the first of our Wisconsin schools has not yet been found out.

In a community with such a population as Green Bay had in its earlier years, there was no such thing, of course, as popular education. The first set-

---

was at Green Bay in June, 1818, and baptized children, "according to the rubric of the church of England," on the fifth and ninth of June. But it does not appear that he held public service or preached there.

tler at the place, Augustine de Langlade,[1] who with his Ottawa wife removed thither from Mackinaw, probably knew at least how to read and write himself, and saw to it that his children or, certainly, one of them, Charles Michel,[2] received a measure of the same kind of training. But this,— whatever it was in extent and quality,— Charles received before his father's family removed from Mackinaw. Other children of one or more favored families may have been taught by some one or more of the few men who were employed in the fur business because they knew how to use the pen.

In 1791 Jacques Porlier removed from Montreal to Green Bay. It is said that he taught a school. But Augustine Grignon who gives us the year of Porlier's arrival and was then of such an age that a school could hardly have escaped his knowledge and his memory, says: "We had no early schools — none till after the coming of the American troops."[3] Thomas S. Johnson of Onondago, New York, was the first school-master. His first contract bears date "the 10 of November, 1817." The school was to be continued nine months, and seems to have been called,— by its master at least,— "the Green Bay Seminary." In the year when Mr. Johnson began his "seminary" there was, it is said, at least a proposition to establish a French boarding and day school. If such an institution came into being there appears no trace of its existence.

As we have learned, Dr. Morse when at Green Bay in 1820 seems to have roused the people of that place to their need of a school. We may be perfectly sure, however, that Dr. Morse had nothing to do with choosing the man who was employed as its instructor,—"J. Bte S. Jacobs," as he signed his name. Under date of "17 October, 1820," Jacobs writes to Messrs. John Lawe and Louis Grignon, "I have mentioned to you boath, that I intend to keep school, being the onley means for a Liveleyhood." But under date of 20th January, 1823, this worthy school-master wrote to Mr. Lawe from "Manomenie River:" "Had [I] been incourage to keep a school at the Bay I should be there yet but one Gallon Pease 15 lbs. Pork per Month was not anueff to supp me. I got drunk to drop the school as I could not make a Livelywood on one Gallon Pease 15 lbs. Pork per Month."

Next on the list of early teachers at Green Bay we find the names of Amos Holton, then that of Daniel Curtis, a grandfather of the wife of General Sheridan. The preceding year Curtis,— once a captain in the regular army,— had taught the post school at Fort Crawford, Prairie du Chien. The next teacher at Green Bay was A. G. Ellis, to whom we are debtors for so much of information concerning the early history of that place and of Wisconsin.

It is an evidence of the foreign sentiment at Green Bay that, in the early schools there, the soldiers' children were called by the others "the little Bostonians."

---

[1] Born at Three Rivers, Canada, in September, 1703.
[2] See page 30 for some mention of this man. He it is in honor of whom Langlade county was named. He was baptized at Mackinaw 1729, May 9th, probably, according to Roman Catholic usage, very soon after his birth. He is credited by his admirers with having been the decisive factor in the defeat of Braddock. Langlade died in January, 1800.
[3] "Historical Collections," III., 253.

In July of that year, Christ church (Episcopal) of Green Bay was organized by laymen.[1] It was thus the second Protestant church on Wisconsin soil, that — of the Congregational order — among the Stockbridges being the first.

Mr. Ellis learned in the autumn of 1825 that the Episcopal authorities had "decided to suspend operations with the Green Bay mission till a suitable superintendent could be obtained." He then became teacher in the postschool at Fort Howard where there had been "a change in the army officers and soldiers," — a change that apparently was favorable to both religion and education. "In connection with some two or three of the officers, favorably disposed, a Sunday-school was organized which was kindly put under my supervision." It would seem that this was about the time when Mr. Ellis gave up his distinctive mission work. However, he continued to report, — once in six months, — to the committee of his church. We hear nothing more about the Sunday-school that he had started in "Shanty Town."

"Regular religious services," he adds, "were also had on Sundays, alternating those of the Episcopal and Congregational churches." Who conducted these we are not told, but we may infer that Mr. Ellis himself was reader when the Episcopal ritual was used. We wish we knew who led in the services alternating with his own. For, if he has made no error, they were the second of the Congregational order, — the first save those by John Metoxen, — regularly maintained within the present limits of our state.

The first Methodist services in the Wisconsin region were held in Fort Howard by one of the officers, Samuel Ryan, commonly known as "colonel" who came thither in 1826, and immediately began evangelistic labor.[2] About this time, it would seem, Eleazar Williams, who had not then given up his absurd scheme of an Indian confederacy, "returned to the Bay," — probably from New York where he had been ordained, — "and preached a few times at the post school-house."

All these efforts were in advance of the coming of any Roman Catholic priest for permanent residence. "Father Fauvel, the first of his church, I think," says the late Morgan Lewis Martin, so well known in Wisconsin history, "to land in Green Bay after the close of the early missions," came thither, 1827, May 20th.[3] In July of this year Rev. Jesse Miner must have passed

---

[1] But a second organization, and the one recognized by Bishop Brown, was effected 1829, September 10th. Whether the first had elapsed or high churchism denies that laymen alone can organize a church I do not know. But most of us are ready to claim that the action of July, 1825, was valid and formed a real church, Christian at least, if not Episcopal.

[2] I can not but suspect that those were the services referred to above by Mr. Ellis, and there called "Congregational." This supposition is favored by the fact that a real Congregational service as far west as Green Bay would probably at that time have been called Presbyterian.

On the other hand, it will be noticed that Mr. Ellis puts the first of these services before "Colonel" Ryan's coming and would have been likely to take especial notice of Methodism as a somewhat aggressive child of his own church.

[3] Judge Martin is in error. Priests had visited Green Bay, says Rev. Chrysostom Verwyst, in 1793, 1823, 1824, and 1826. Verwyst speaks severely of Fauvel whose name he spells differently: "Rev. J. Vincent Badin, appointed a Frenchman with the name of Favrell to keep school, and allowed him to assemble the people on Sundays, read to them the gospel of the

through Green Bay on his way to the Stockbridge settlement at Grand Kaukaulin. The removal from Fort Howard of the main body of the troops closed Mr. Ellis's school and caused him to engage in other pursuits. These events also occurred, Mr. Ellis thinks, in 1827. The Sunday-school receives no mention nor the alternate Episcopal and Congregational services. It is claimed, however, by W. G. Miller, D. D., that, until the arrival at Green Bay (1832, July 21st), of Missionary Clark, to whom reference has been made in the history of the Ojibway mission, Colonel Ryan continued his preaching services. If so, and if he remained at Green Bay, it is hard to understand why he did not keep them up, for Mr. Clark went twenty-five miles from the white settlement to labor among the Oneidas,— the service for which he had come.

In 1828, Rev. Richard Fish Cadle, who served later at Fort Winnebago and Prairie du Chien came' to Shantytown, to which its more dignified inhabitants sought to give up the name Menomonee or Menomoneeville. He found a home in what had been the officers' quarters at Camp Smith, and there, in November, opened a school. In the course of the winter, land was obtained for a boarding-school, designed for Indian children, and a building erected. A school-house was built the following summer (1829), probably used also as a place of worship, and a second large building soon after. Mr. Ellis, it appears, doubted the wisdom of establishing this school. From him we learn that "after nearly three years of almost insupportable labor, fatigue and anxiety," Mr. Cadle's health failed. His successor, Rev. Daniel E. Brown, "continued the school for some two years more, when, for reasons similiar to those named to me by Rev. Mr. Ferry of Mackinaw, the establishment was reduced and finally discontinued."

Dr. Richard S. Satterlee who, with his wife, both from Massachusetts, had in 1823, in a time of revival, been added to the Mackinaw church, came to Green Bay, September, 1832. Probably we may date the real work of the church at Green Bay from the time of their coming. In the summer of 1834, Rev. Jeremiah Porter at the invitation of Mrs. Satterlee who had been at Chicago to visit her sister, Mrs. Major Wilcox, came to Green Bay and preached there. While here he baptized three children of Lieutenant (afterwards Brigadier-General) Rudolph Barnes Marcy. One of these became the wife of Major-General G. B. McClellan.

---

day, sing hymns and read prayers. But Favrell soon overstepped the limits of his permit and attempted to say mass, minus the consecration, and to make processions accompanied by the soldiers of Fort Howard. He made a trip to Europe with an Indian whom he everywhere exhibited, and the presents often made to the latter found their way into the Frenchman's pocket. To crown his hypocrisy and imposition he attempted to start a church of his own, but failed egregiously. In 1832, Very Rev. Frederic Réve was sent to Green Bay to rid the country of this impostor."

This case and that of Eleazar Williams do not particularly commend the politics which by their advocates are praised as so much superior, for example, to the Congregational in this very matter of keeping and putting unworthy men out of the office of religious teacher. In these days church discipline is ultimately what it always should have been,—simply the withdrawal of fellowship or of approval. Such action has as much weight as there is reason for it, and may be taken a church or a council as well as by a so-called bishop or any other ecclesiastical authority. We do not suppose that our advocates of vigorous discipline desire power to imprison, hang or burn anybody.

In the following year Dr. Satterlee tried, but in vain, to secure Mr. Porter as pastor of the church soon to be organized. 1835, September 21st, a meeting was held at which it was resolved "that it is expedient to form a Presbyterian church in this place." At an adjourned meeting held December 30th, a resolution was passed to invite "Rev. Cutting Marsh of the Stockbridge mission to come and form a church in this place," and another "that said church shall be conducted upon the total abstinence principle, from all intoxicating drinks."

A journey of forty miles brought Mr. Marsh to this little company of believers. On the evening of Saturday, 9th January, 1836, he organized the church with twelve members, five of whom came from the church at Mackinaw. "The old church there died some years ago," says Pastor William Crawford, writing in 1876, "but in the members it sent to Green Bay and elsewhere, it enjoys a perpetual life." The creed adopted by the new church is described as being "rigid and orthodox to the extent of heterodoxy." It was strongly Calvinistic. But there is a suspicion that the creed as found upon the records has been made to differ from the one actually adopted. Though Dr. Satterlee, the leading man in the movement, preferred the Congregational polity, the church voted to call itself Presbyterian. No one, however, seems to have been strenuous on this point. The church has never been connected with any Presbytery, and the first case of discipline was the trial of one of the elders before the church.

On the Sunday afternoon following the organization, which took place in a private house in Navarino, "public services were held in the military hospital in Fort Howard." People from both villages attended. A candidate for membership who doubted her baptism at the hands of a Romish priest received the rite from Mr. Marsh. "I remember distinctly," wrote Mrs. Satterlee forty years later, "that lovely, calm Sunday; the pale-faced convalescents sitting around; the mirror-like appearance of the river in front; the earnest prayers; the service of song; the stillness all around, making the presence of God seem nevery ar."

Thus came into organized existence the first of Wisconsin's Puritan churches that has made a record of unbroken service to the present time.

CHAPTER XV.

FORT WINNEBAGO.

Among the main topographical features of the district embraced within Sauk and Columbia counties Professor R. D. Irving enumerates[1] "the east and west ranges of the Baraboo; the Wisconsin river, which traverses the area centrally from north to south, making a great bow eastward to double the eastern point of the uniting quartzite ranges; the remarkable course of the Fox river, which, after flowing southwest directly towards the Wisconsin, turns abruptly north when but one and one-half miles from it, the two rivers traversing a flat sandy plain, without dividing ridge, and passing the one into the St. Lawrence, the other to the Gulf of Mexico."

This portage in the otherwise unbroken water-course from Lake Michigan to the Mississippi is often mentioned by the early explorers. To the commerce of the days prior to the steamboat and the railway it was a serious obstruction. For though, as in 1828 when the fifth regiment of the United States infantry passed without obstruction on their way from St. Louis to Green Bay, it was sometimes overflowed so that the Wisconsin sent water to the sea through the Great Lakes as well as through the Mississippi,[2] the times when canoes could pass from one water-course to the other were very rare.

To protect trade, perhaps to prevent extortion on the part of those engaged in the transportation business and, most of all, to command effectively a position of such importance, the United States government determined to build there a military post. Accordingly, in the summer of 1828, part of the first infantry (three companies) commanded by Major, afterward brevet Major-General, David Emanuel Twiggs (who, 1861, February 18th, surrendered to the Confederates the United States forces in Texas), was ordered from Fort Howard to build Fort Winnebago at the Fox-Wisconsin portage. Almost nothing of the old fort is left though it has given name to a town. The garrison was withdrawn in 1845.

As a matter of general interest, though not pertaining to the subject of this work, we may say that Jefferson Davis first entered active army service at Fort Crawford in 1829; was at Fort Winnebago the same year and remained there until 1831, when he was transferred to Yellow river, near Prairie du

---

[1] Chamberlin's "Geology of Wisconsin," volume II., page 580.
[2] As it does now through the canal.

Chien on the opposite side of the Mississippi. In the same year he was again at Fort Crawford where he remained until about the time of his promotion which took place 1833, March 4th. Zachary Taylor disliked Davis[1] and seems to have taken pains to keep him away from Fort Crawford. Nor was he popular among the officers at Fort Winnebago where most of his life in the Wisconsin region was spent. A new broom sweeps clean and is sometimes fond of sweeping. A certain "fussiness" is alleged of Davis. This may have been nothing but attention to details, but whatever it was, it seems to have made him disliked. While at Fort Winnebago the young West Pointer constructed certain wonderful articles of furniture which were so unique that the ladies of the garrison dubbed them by the name of the inventor. The "Davis" was "unquestionably designed for clothes-press, store-room and china-closet; such at least were the uses to which Mrs. Twiggs had appropriated the one assigned to her."

We have heard of John H. Kinzie as aiding in starting the first Sunday-school at Prairie du Chien. After his marriage he lived for a time at Fort Winnebago. His wife, from whose "Wau-bun," already referred to, I have quoted above, was a faithful Christian, a member of the Episcopal church. "It was on Sunday," she writes, "that I most missed my eastern home. I thought that, perhaps, one of our number might be found who would read a portion of the church-service, and a sermon from one of our different selections. I approached the subject cautiously. 'Are there none among the officers who are religiously disposed?' 'Oh, yes,' replied the one whom I addressed, 'there is S——; when he is half tipsy, he takes his Bible and 'Newton's Works,' and goes to bed and cries over them; he thinks in this way he is excessively pious.' The hope or any united religious service was, for the present, laid aside." But efforts were made to secure a missionary. Soon Dr. Newhall of Galena, who became one of the first trustees of Beloit college, relieved for a time the post-surgeon. It is probable that on his return he called Father Kent's attention to the needs of Fort Winnebago. But a man with a field of labor larger than many a European kingdom could not easily give time to all the places that called for his services. However, "in the course of the spring" (of 1833), continues Mrs. Kinzie, "we received a visit from the Rev. Mr. Kent, and Mrs. Kent of Galena. This event is memorable, as being the first occasion on which the gospel, according to the Protestant faith, was preached at Fort Winnebago.[2] The large parlor of the hospital was fitted up for the service, and gladly did

---

[1] This the venerable George W. Jones of Dubuque, who knew both Taylor and Davis, has told me, was not the case. But as the good, old gentleman admires Davis so much that it is almost impossible for him to imagine that any rational man could dislike the Confederate ex-president, my own opinion, as expressed above, remains unchanged.

[2] There had been Roman Catholic service in or near the Fort. "Mr. Mazzuchelli, a Roman Catholic priest, made a missionary visit to the portage, during our residence there and, after some instruction to them, about forty [of the Winnebago Indians] consented to be baptized." But Mrs. Kinzie doubts that they had much understanding of the doctrines of Christianity or any desire to learn more. However, she states that an Indian woman pointed to her crucifix in declining a glass of liquor which Mrs. Kinzie, believing the woman to be exhausted, had offered her. "I received this as a lesson more powerful than twenty sermons. It was the first time in my life that I had ever seen spiritous liquors rejected upon a religious principle."

we say to each other, 'Let us go to the house of the Lord.'

"For nearly three years had we lived here without the blessing of a public service of praise and thanksgiving. We regarded this commencement as an omen of better times, and our little sewing society, worked with renewed industry, to raise a fund which might be available hereafter, in securing the permanent service of a missionary." Was not this the first of the many sewing societies of Wisconsin?

Rev. Jeremiah Porter, addressing the Home Missionary society in a letter already quoted from, begun at Sault Ste. Marie, 1833, May 4th, and ended at Chicago ten days later, says that he has learned that "at Fort Winnebago, 150 miles to the northwest, they have already subscribed $400 for the support of a minister" who, when sent, would better go, he thinks, by way of Green Bay as there is no road from Chicago. Dr. Richard S. Satterlee, post-surgeon at Fort Howard writes also to the society, and adds to what follows a plea for the post at which he is stationed: "It gave me great pleasure to receive your letter of July 27th [1833], a few days since at Fort Winnebago; and I assure you it was a source of gratification to the officers and their families, and to many of the soldiers stationed there that there seemed some prospect that a minister would be sent to them. If one should be sent he will be well received and, I have no doubt, honorably sustained."

At last the long desired missionary came. "During the last autumn," says the report of the American Board, given in 1835, "Mr. Barber,[1] who was then connected with the Stockbridge mission, spent some weeks at Fort Winnebago. While there his labors were attended with the divine blessing, and a number of persons connected with the garrison were hopefully born again. In February (1835), Mr. Marsh, by invitation, visited the place and organized a church

---

[1] Rev. Abel Lester Barber, the first resident minister in Wisconsin to labor under commission from the American Home Missionary society, was born at Otis, Massachusetts, 1803, December 28th, and graduated at Amherst college, in the class of 1831. He received his training in theology from Rev. Allen M'Loan, of Simsbury, Connecticut, who preached the sermon at his ordination. This took place at West Hartford, in the same state, Wednesday, 25th September, 1833. He and his wife,— he was married on the 11th of the month in which he received ordination,—devoted themselves to mission service. They arrived at Mackinaw 1833, November 11th. There was some thought of their starting a mission among the Ottawas, but Mr Barber's health became impaired, and, perhaps to avoid the lake climate, he and his wife, in July, 1834, removed to Stockbridge. Thence, as we have learned, Mr. Barber went to Fort Winnebago. Later we shall find him at Milwaukee, where, for a short time, he served as pastor, and then removed to a farm. Afterward he became an editor. For a time he was connected with a Prairieville (Waukesha) paper and later with the *Free Democrat* of Milwaukee. About 1849 he removed to Kenosha. In that year or the following, while the cholera was raging at Kenosha, Mr. Barber, "broken in health and somewhat discouraged, offered his services to the city to work among those stricken with the disease. In one instance he brought to his own home a little boy who had been down with the cholera but was considered convalescent, and afterward two of his own children died of the disease, and a third," —a son from whose letter I make these quotations,— "was so near to death, apparently, that a shroud was provided for him also, as I have been told."

Those who knew Mr. Barber say that he had certain infirmities of temper that made it almost impossible for others to get on with him. But these we are glad to forget when we think of his heroism, and of his service in the anti-slavery cause. He died of nervous prostration at Wallingford, Connecticut, 1876, October 7th.

At Kenosha Mr. and Mrs. Barber became members of the Baptist church and continued in that communion to the end of their lives.

there, consisting of eleven members, some of whom had been members of other churches, and others had recently entered the kingdom. During the last fall and winter there was more or less serious attention to the concerns of the soul, and a number of hopeful conversions, in not less than three or four of the military posts on the northwestern frontier."

Brief is the remaining history of this little church. Among Mr. Marsh's papers, writes his daughter, is "a letter from Fort Winnebago written by Dr. Charles McDougall," the post-surgeon, dated 1835, October 14th. "In it he speaks of 'our little church,' and with the exception of [sermons by] Mr. Brown and Mr. Stevens of their having had no preaching since my father was there."

The need at Fort Winnebago was long a burden on the mind and heart of the few brave men like Kent and Porter who were struggling with a burden too heavy for them. The answer to that need was so long delayed that the opportunity seems, humanly speaking, to have been lost. Yet it was fitting that one (Mr. Barber) who, by way of the Great Lakes, came West, sent to Indians by the American Board of Commissioners for Foreign Missions should, at this place of the dividing of the waters,[1] join his labor to that of another (Father Kent) who, sent by the Home Missionary society to minister to the whites, came hither by way of the Ohio and the Mississippi. Religious effort had found a place of blending, and made prophecy of the time, then drawing near, when the interior of the proposed commonwealth of Wisconsin should no longer separate, with its forests and empty prairies, two distinct areas of settlement but, with farms and homes, join into one, socially and commercially, the banks of the Mississippi and the shores of Lake Michigan.

---

[1] This place has been often traversed, no doubt, from the time when man first occupied the region between Lake Michigan and the Mississippi. The Mascoutins, we may be sure, knew of this route when they told Jean Nicolet of the "Great Water." Probably Radisson and Grosseilliers journeyed by this way to the Mississippi in the summer of 1659. If so, it is probable that they were the first white men to come to this famous "Carrying Place," as Carver calls it. "I always understood," says "Colonel" John Shaw (*Hist. Coll.*, VII., 221), that when the trade between Mackinaw and the Wisconsin and Upper Mississippi had become important, the early French adventurers were induced to make a sort of pole or corduroy road over a marsh, for a mile in length, between the Fox and Wisconsin, and construct a large, clumsily formed wagon on which to transport boats across the portage, of ten tons burthen. This wagon was fully fifty-eight feet in length. The lading was carried on the backs of the boatmen or Indians, or on the rude carriage."

Hither, during the Revolutionary war (1778, May 27th) came, in British service, a nephew of Langlade's, Charles Gautier, with his party of "Scioux and folles avoines [Menomonees], and did my carrying." He calls the place "the portage of the Siskoinsin."—a name that he uses not only as that of the Wisconsin river had also, apparently, as that of the country through which he was passing. However, as there was a Sauk chief Siskoinsin, Ganiter's reference may be merely to the country claimed by said chief or by his people. To "all the Villages of Siskoinsin" had been brought in a "so-called belt [of wampum] of the Bostonnians." that is, Americans.

In the war of 1812 Francis Le Roy, a brother in-law of Jacques Vican,—who himself, about 1797 or 1798, was stationed here by the Northwest Fur company,—had at the portage what Secretary Thwaites calls "a transportation plant." The use of a horse in this business was begun by Laurent Barth in 1793. The date of building the road that Shaw speaks of,—provided it was built at all,—seems to be unknown.

CHAPTER XVI.

BY THE LAKE AND ON THE PRAIRIE.

In the autumn of 1779, his majesty's sloop of war Felicity was making the circuit of Lake Michigan. She was one of a fleet of eight vessels that, in the American revolution, made sure to the British the command of that lake as well as of those then more important, Erie and Huron. On a stormy morning, Thursday, 4th November, her crew, rated the preceding January at five men, now evidently larger, cast anchor in Milwaukee bay. To use the precise words of her pilot, Samuel Robertson, whose seamanship was doubtless better than his spelling, "At 8 A. M. a verry strong gale; we came too in 4 fathoms watter; hoist out the boat; sent out M'Gautley & 4 hands on shoer with difficulty. * * At 2 this afternoon M'Gautly returned with 3 indeans and a french man who lives at Millwakey, named Morong nephew to Monsier St. Pier."

It was a bad omen that the Felicity brought rum and tobacco "to Deliver [to] the indeans at Millwakey which is a mixed tribe of different nations." Suggestive description! These presents, too, had an object, and that, as is usually the case with such gifts, a mischievous one. "M'Gautley also told them the manner governor Sinclair could wish them to Behave, at which they seemed well satisfied." A natural combination: rum, bad politics and perhaps insincerity. For otherwise the Milwaukee Indians seem at that time to have been well disposed towards the Americans or, rather, unfriendly to the British. We remember De Peyster's "renegates of Milwakie." And in the second war with Britain the indignant Dickson writes under date of 1814, February 6th: "I will give nothing more to the Indians of Millwackee; they are a sett of Impostors." Eight days later he utters a threat of fierce vengeance against a "Poutewatamie" who had come to "Winebagoe Lake," where Dickson then was, "with an intention of cutting us off. He had previously send round tobacco to the young people about Milwackee to come here with him to dance. Perhaps he may come this way again; if he does he will not return."

Before the voyage of the Felicity the site and harbor of Milwaukee had been frequently visited in the way of exploration and trade. Who was the first to come? That no one knows. It was by way of the Illinois river and the Chicago portage that Joliet and Marquette returned from their famous voyage of 1673. As they voyaged down Lake Michigan to the mission of St. Francis

Xavier,— which they reached in September, 1674,— they may have entered Milwaukee harbor. 'Hither came Marquette in the following month (1674, October 26th) on his voyage from Green Bay to the site of Chicago. Perhaps it was in the harbor of Milwaukee that La Salle, five years later, found refuge from an October storm. No priest made his home here in the early years, nor was there a permanent trading-station until Alexander La Framboise removed hither from Mackinaw. This, Alexander Grignon thinks, was about 1785.[1] "At first he went there himself and after a while he returned to Mackinaw, and sent a brother [Francis] to manage the business for him, who remained there several years, and raised a family." A daughter, Josette, was married in the summer of 1817, at Mackinaw to Lieutenant John S. Pierce, a brother of the late exPresident of the United States. "A singularly beautiful girl," it is said that she was. But the shadow of death is over our little romance of the love of the young soldier and his sweet wife, almost the first-born of Milwaukee's fair daughters. She died in 1821.

The evidence of a letter written by his own hand shows that Francis La Framboise was living at "Milwaukis, 20 Feb., 1802." Through his mismanagement, says Grignon, the brother (Alexander) for whom he was doing business, failed. However, the Northwest Fur Company had entered the field and in 1795 made Milwaukee one of its places of business.[2] That fact quite as much as any "mismanagement" may account for the failure of an individual trader. The company's trade along the western shore of Lake Michigan seems to have been under the superintendence of Jacques Vieau, who made his home at Green Bay, coming to Milwaukee, and that with interruptions, for the winter fur-trade. He gave aid to the British in the war of 1812. His successor in trade at Milwaukee was Laurent Solomon Juneau, who became his son-in-law. Of Juneau, a son of Vieau says that he came to Milwaukee in August, 1818; that his "home also became Green Bay and remained such until about 1834 or 1835, when Milwaukee began to grow and Juneau platted the village[3] and settled there permanently. Juneau was one of the last to recognize that Milwaukee was destined to be a permanent settlement, and had to be persuaded by his friends into taking advantage of the fact. Green Bay remained his home and that of my father, despite their business interests at Milwaukee."

Juneau did not become a citizen of the United States until 1831. His name is found in the Green Bay poll-list as late as 1834.

It will be remembered that the treaty with the Menomonees[4] made at Washington 1831, February 8th, ceded to the United States government a great tract of land, including all that lies between the Milwaukee river and Lake

---

[1] The "History of Milwaukee" (Andreas) says: "In 1784, Alexander La Framboise erected an ample building of logs which he occupied some time."

[2] Other posts were established in the same year at Kewaunee, Manitowoc and Sheboygan.

[3] "Juneau and I were joint owners of the original plat of Milwaukee." "His first hint of the prospective value of his location at Milwaukee came from me."— MORGAN LEWIS MARTIN, Hist. Coll. XI., 400.

[4] Often called the Stambaugh treaty. It is the one that, as amended, provided a home for the Muh-he-ka-ne-ok. See page 60.

Michigan. Between this cession and that made by the Winnebagoes at Prairie du Chien, 1829, July 29th, were lands claimed by the Pottawatomies and ceded by them according to a treaty finally ratified 1835, February 21st.[1]

On the evening of Monday, 8th December, 1834, a party of three men, Samuel Brown, Paul Burdick and Horace Chase, passed Vieau's old trading-post. They had started from Chicago on the 4th, had come overland[2] and not forgetting to honor the day of the resurrection had rested on the Christian Sabbath. All were seeking "claims." These found, the three friends started back to Chicago on the 14th.

In Chicago, though following the peaceful occupation of builder, Samuel Brown had come to be known as "Captain." Western admiration is apt to express itself in military titles. And the most cynical must acknowledge that the spirit of the soldier is needed by the pioneer.

Early in the spring of 1835 Mr. Brown came again to Milwaukee without his family, but soon went back after them. The journey to their new home was one of five days, two after leaving Racine. On this part of the trip they were first to take a wagon over what was known later as the "lake road." Thus "the emigrants had to cut much of their way before them."[3] Food for the horses gave out and their owner was obliged to feed them on bread.

We do not know the precise date of the arrival in Milwaukee of Samuel Brown and family. The honor of making "the first raised bread" in what was to become the metropolis of Wisconsin has often been claimed for Mrs. Brown. It has been said of her that "she was the second American woman to settle in Milwaukee county, and the first in the present city."[4] Her family maintain the correctness of this statement.[5] By the children of Mrs. Paul Burdick a like claim is made in behalf of their mother. These give 1835, May 10th, as the date of their parents' arrival at Milwaukee. There the Browns and the Burdicks became neighbors.

Having, as he thought, secured his "claim" by placing his family thereon, Mr. Brown returned to Chicago for his goods.[6] There he met his brother Daniel, a man of kindred spirit who had come with his wife to find a home in the

---

[1] The last of the Pottawatomies were not removed from the neighborhood of Milwaukee until June, 1838.

[2] "They found a house at Grosse Point (now Evanston), where resided a Frenchman named Quinette. From Grosse Point they saw no house until five or six miles west of where Racine now is, at which point lived Louis and Jacques Vieau, Jr., brothers-in-law of Solomon Juneau. The next house found by the homeseekers was that of Paul Vieau, which stood on a high bluff south of the river."—"Milwaukee Sentinel," 1886, September 2nd.

[3] Dr. G. T. Ladd, formerly pastor of the Spring street (now Grand avenue) Congregational church, Milwaukee.

[4] "History of Milwaukee," published by the Western Historical Company (A. T. Andreas).

[5] The recollections of Mrs. Angeline L. Hill, Samuel Brown's oldest daughter, seem to be especially vivid. She remembers distinctly that her parents and their family reached Milwaukee on Saturday. But the day of the month she can not recall. The 10th, the day of the arrival of the Burdicks was Sunday.

[6] Making ready for the season's building, Samuel Brown hired a number of workmen in Chicago. He bought a large boat with sail and oars. Some of his men came to Milwaukee in that. They camped on the shore at night. Others came overland driving some cows and perhaps a yoke of oxen. The men got to Milwaukee before their employer did.

new settlement. Having hired a vessel of thirty tons' burden with a crew consisting of captain and mate, the brothers Brown left Chicago Monday evening and arrived at Milwaukee early in the morning of Wednesday, 10th June, 1835. As they entered the mouth of the river the men got ashore to tow the boat, and the tiller was put into the hands of Mrs. Daniel Brown.[1] Though she obediently followed directions in the matter of steering, the help of a long pole was occasionally needed to keep the boat from becoming fast upon the muddy banks.[2]

Little houses could hold more in those days than they can now, and for a time the brothers made a home together, in the cabin that Samuel built[3] before he brought his own family. But a larger house was a necessity and one was built close beside the other. It was of logs covered with "shake" shingles,[4] had two rooms on the first floor and a loft overhead. "As soon as it was finished (it might have been two weeks), Mr. Samuel Brown called in a few neighbors and held service in his own house, reading a sermon and making the first public prayer in Milwaukee." Thus writes his brother's wife. The "two weeks" are to be reckoned from the 10th of June. She thinks that the sermon was one of Finney's. Mr. Ladd tells us that about twenty were present and that others took part beside the leader. This service may have been held on the 21st or the 28th of June.

"Then and there,"[5] said Dr. Ladd in the sermon already quoted from, "was formed the first Sunday school" in Milwaukee "of which some still connected with us were original members."[6]

---

[1] Mrs. Brown was the fourth white woman to make her home in Milwaukee. In 1844 she and her husband,—now fallen asleep,—r moved to Sheboygan, where she still resides. Mr. (Daniel) Brown died 1892, March 23rd. His brother Samuel, who preceded him to Milwaukee, died there 1874, December 22nd.

[2] The Milwaukee river then flowed into the lake half a mile south of the present outlet, which is the work of man, not of nature. The first steamboat that "landed" at Milwaukee came 1835, June 17th. We may be sure that it did not enter the river.

[3] Or bought.

[4] The "shake" shingles that covered the first house, or cabin, are thus described by R. w. G. T. Ladd, now of Yale university, in his memorial sermon on Deacon Samuel Brown: "Oak shingles, four feet long, bound down with poles which were withed to the logs of the house."

[5] That is, if the services spoken of by Mrs. Daniel Brown, and those referred to by Mr. Ladd are the same. It is Mrs. Hill's impression that, regularly on the Sabbaths after bringing his family to Milwaukee, and until a minister came, her father held in his own home a public religious service.

[6] The house in which the little congregation met was in what is now the block bounded by Galena, Cherry, Second and Third Streets, near the northeast corner. Near by, where is now the corner of Cherry and Second streets, was Mr. Burdick's home. When these houses were built their owners expected to buy at the approaching government sale, which was at Green Bay and did not begin until the 31st of August, the land on which they stood. But of this Byron Kilbourn, getting ahead of them, took possession by means of a "float," that is, a United States warrant good for a given number of acres of unoccupied land. Technically all government land was unoccupied until it was sold and settlers were mere trespassers. Yet their rights were so far respected that one who would take land by means of a "float" must needs take oath that there was no actual settler upon it. He who swore falsely incurred the deepest contempt and bitter hatred of a pioneer community. Mr. Burdick's daughter has told the writer that but for her mother's entreaties Mr. Kilbourn would have been "tarred and feathered and ridden out of town on a rail." Mrs. Burdick even opened her home to Mr. Kilbourn when with wife and child he could find no other place to stay. Accommodations were limited then in Milwaukee.

In order not to have an enemy, or at least an opposer, in Mr. Brown, Kilbourn transferred

If Mark Robinson, a Methodist, and the first clergyman to come to Milwaukee, was in the village when this meeting was held, none of the little gathering, so far as can now be learned, knew of it. However, Dr. Chase, who had forgotten his name, says that Mr. Robinson came in June and preached in his (Chase's) log house. This was on the lake shore, below the old mouth of the river and near what is now the end of Mitchell street. "Of the subsequent history of Mr. Robinson we know little. His name appears no more (after 1835) in the Conference minutes."[1]

The first resident minister in Milwaukee was Abel Lester Barber of Mackinaw, the Stockbridge mission and Fort Winnebago. He, also, preached in Dr. Chase's cabin according to its owner's statement. Of this our living authorities Daniel Brown and wife, have no knowledge. But they do remember that he came to the little settlement almost before place could be found for himself, wife and child. Soon, however, a cabin was built for him "on the Chestnut street hill."[2] It was beside the old Indian trail that led toward Waukesha and probably stood near where is now the First German Methodist church.

In the "Home Missionary" for September, 1835, is the caption:

"WISCONSIN TERRITORY.

"'This is the first time we believe that we have had occasion to place the name of this region as a caption to our correspondence.

"From the Rev. A. L. Barber, Milwalkee, Wisconsin Territory, west of Lake Michigan:

"'I came here about eighteen days ago[3] and found a population of between two and three hundred, mostly from the states and of New England origin.

"'The impression is extensively prevalent that this place will, in a few years, be second in importance to none on the shores of Lake Michigan except Chicago. Four physicians and nearly thirty mechanics are already here, with a view to permanent residence, though one year has not yet elapsed since an Indian trader and the men in his employ were the only white inhabitants.

"'We have twenty-four professors of religion, belonging to evangelical denominations, of which number fifteen are in connection with Presbyterian or Congregational churches.

"'A Bible class had been commenced two Sabbaths before my arrival and

---

to him the tract on which stood the houses that Brown himself had built. Mr. J. S. Buck in his "Pioneer History of Milwaukee," says that "the first lot sold upon the west side was from Byron Killbourn to the late Deacon Samuel Brown, October 16th, 1835."

[1] History of Methodism in Wisconsin, by Rev. P. S. Bennett, A. M. The Rock River Conference then extended indefinitely northward and is the one to which Mr. Bennett makes reference.

[2] Mrs. Daniel Brown.

[3] We do not know the precise date of Mr. Barber's arrival, but as he was in "Milwalkee" eighteen days before he wrote, and his letter, borne by the slow mails of those days reached New York in time for a magazine, the "copy" for which was apparently made up by the fifteenth of August or sooner, we may reasonably suppose that his coming was as soon as the early part of July.

The population of two or three hundred was of course not a settled one.

is attended by about thirty. A weekly prayer meeting to be held Wednesday evening has been established.'"

Mr. Barber records the fact that: "We have infidelity, coarse and clamorous, much profane swearing, contempt of the Sabbath, most determined irreligion. A strong sweeping current of worldly enterprise, a push and scramble after wealth prevail as a matter of course."

At this time Samuel and Daniel Brown were building for Mr. Juneau a "store" on the west side of the street that now bears the name East Water. In this building[1] Mr. Barber found a place to preach and "there," says Daniel Brown, "we continued to worship until it was finished and goods put in for trade. Then we had other buildings under way that we occupied all the fall."

The service in Mr. Juneau's store-room seems to have been the first of the kind in Milwaukee outside of a private house. What we may call Milwaukee's first choir[2] led in song. Indians stood without listening, until Mr. Juneau, thinking apparently that their presence detracted from the dignity of the occasion, drove them off with a club. It may be that the date of this service was August 23rd.

In its issue for February, 1836, the "Home Missionary" makes the following announcement: "The board have recently resolved to assume the support of as many laborers as the parent society shall be able to procure for the territories of Ouisconsin and Missouri, and two missionaries have already been stationed on these fields, the Rev. Mr. Barber at Milwalke, Ouisconsin Territory, and the Rev. Cyrus L. Watson at Dubuque's Mills, in Missouri."[3]

The report of the Home Missionary society made at the annual meeting in May, 1836, makes mention of Mr. Barber's work. He had written: "Temperance gaining ground; field extensive and needy."

Mr. Barber's commission from the Home Missionary society was for six months from the 1st of July, 1835. He may have rendered pastoral service

---

[1] From Daniel Brown and wife I received the impression that this structure occupied the northwest corner of East Water and Wisconsin streets,—the site now occupied by the only "sky scraper" of which Milwaukee can boast. But this particular building put up by the brothers Brown has been identified by William W. Wight in "The Old White Church," as the "Pioneer Store." Of the place where it stood Mr. Wight says that "the most northerly of the stores of the Bradley & Metcalf Company, at No. 393 East Water Street, rests upon the precise spot."

[2] It consisted of Mrs. Daniel Brown, soprano; Miss Susan Burdick, Samuel Brown and Nelson Olin, tenors; Daniel Brown and Thomas Olin, bassos.

[3] An error. What is now Iowa ceased to be a part of Missouri Territory (not the state) when, 1834, June 28th, Michigan was enlarged so as to include all the region north of the state of Missouri and south of the British Possessions, lying between the Mississippi and the Missouri.

Another way of stating the fact is to say that all of the Louisiana purchase, lying north of the present state of that name, was, in 1804, made the "district of Louisiana." This, in June, 1812, was organized as "Missouri Territory." From this, in 1819, were separated the regions that now form the states of Missouri and Arkansas. Then, in 1834, as aforesaid, that portion of the vast mesopotamia of the Mississippi and the Missouri, lying north of the southern boundary line of Iowa, was made, "for temporary purposes," a portion of the Territory of Michigan.

I hope that I have not taken an unpardonable liberty in venturing to use "mesopotamia" ("between the rivers") as a common noun. We need the word. There are other mesopotamias besides the one between the Euphrates and the Tigris.

after that time expired. Rev. Henry Gregory, an Episcopal minister, who, in January, 1836, spent a Sunday at Milwaukee, speaks of there being a "Presbyterian" minister in the place. Mr. Gregory was asked to officiate, "which I did," he says, "and preached in the afternoon; and that was the first service, according to the liturgy of the Protestant Episcopal church, in Milwaukee, and was held on the first Sunday after the Epiphany, January 10, 1836." With this narrative it is interesting to compare one given the writer of these pages by Mrs. Daniel Brown, and hereto subjoined:

On a Sunday, perhaps in January, 1836, the little congregation had met in a building which the brothers Brown were putting up for Talbot Dousman on the southwest corner of Huron and East Water streets. They had no minister. Dr. J. J. Kemper, so long the Protestant Episcopal bishop of Wisconsin had come to Milwaukee on his first missionary visit to the place. He came to the little congregation and was invited to lead their worship. This he did after the forms commonly used in Congregational churches, offering prayer without book and wearing no gown. He pleased his hearers greatly and in the afternoon all come out to join in worship according to the forms of his own denomination.

I have little doubt that these accounts are of one and the same incident, that the officiating minister of the day was Mr. Gregory, and not Dr. Kemper. Whoever it was, it is pleasant to remember this fraternal beginning of the work of the Episcopal church in Milwaukee.

If Mrs. Brown is right in her recollections, it would seem that Mr. Barber's service as pastor had come to an end in January, 1836.[1] But meetings were not given up because Mr. Barber moved upon a "claim" and quit preaching. There was an admirable vigor of Christian sentiment among some of those early settlers.[2]

In the number for March, 1837, the "Home Missionary" contains an appeal from Milwaukee for a minister. "An attempt has been made to form a church on the Congregational Union plan which, as I understand it, means to break down all other denominational distinctions and to establish one on their ruins. This has been proposed and advocated by a young clergyman from western New York. * * The population at present is about 1500."

The audacious young man who, according to this evident misrepresentation, had undertaken so great a task was Jared Fordham Ostrander, who came to Milwaukee in 1836, probably in the latter part of the year. "He preached Sabbaths for six months," says his wife, "from house to house, there being no church building or school-house in the then village of one thousand inhabitants,

---

[1] No doubt he continued to serve the community in various ways as a minister might. Thus he officiated at one of the early marriages in Milwaukee, that of Barzillai Douglas and Harriet M. Church, 1836, July 17th. Mr. Douglas is the only man living who was elected to office at the first election held at Milwaukee (1835, September 19th). He now lives at Brodhead, Wisconsin.

[2] It is remembered that Mrs. Samuel Brown refused utterly to cook fish caught on Sunday by her husband's workmen. Nor would she give the use of any of her kitchen utensils when they proposed to do the cooking themselves. Some may think that she was too strict. But her strictness showed conscience. Does the prevailing laxity show anything as good?

and no organized church. He endeavored with a few earnest Christians to organize a union church, as there were so few of each denomination, but failed, as other ministers came in and Christians were divided up into small, weak churches." "A Congregationalist, a very good man and a fair preacher," says Daniel Brown in speaking of Mr. Ostrander. He had come West with an educational project in mind. This he sought to carry out at Aztalan whither he removed in 1838.

There was no organization of a Congregational or Presbyterian church until the spring of 1837. "During the preceding time," says Daniel Brown, "we had all met together as Christians. Such men came in as Deacon Hinman, A. Finch, Jr., Harrison Reed, the three Clintons, Deacon Mendell, Deacon Love and many others. As loving disciples of the dear Saviour we talked of church organization, and it was agreed that when a vote was taken the church should be called as the voters wished, each one showing preference." In February, 1837, the late John Ogden wrote earnest letters to Mr. Marsh of Stockbridge and to Rev. Moses Ordway, then serving as pastor at Green Bay, "urging them to come to Milwaukee and establish a church. Down through the Wisconsin woods, feeling their way by blazed trees, stumbling along Indian trails, braving February storms, traveled these men of God toward the Macedonian cry. After four days of exposure they reached their destination."[1]

Though it is very probable that a church-home on the west side of the river was then building for the little congregation, it seems that most of them lived on the east side. There, accordingly,—in the court-house,—were held, 1837, April 13th, the services by which was constituted the First Presbyterian church of Milwaukee.[2] On the 25th of the same month Rev. Gilbert Crawford of Albion, New York, was chosen pastor. Upon this service he entered the following July.

A church building, the first in Milwaukee, had been completed before Mr. Crawford's arrival and was dedicated when he began his pastorate there. It seems that this first church in Milwaukee was also the first in Wisconsin (save those at Indian mission stations), erected by Protestants for divine worship.[3] It was built by Samuel Brown and, according to his brother's recollections, was begun the autumn or winter before its dedication.[4] It stood on Second street near Wells,[5] was painted white, and would seat one hundred fifty persons. It was used as a house of worship until August, 1840.

---

[1] "The Old White Church," by William W. Wight.

[2] The Presbyterian polity was adopted by a majority of one. Deacon Daniel Brown and wife make the statement that "the time [of organization] was changed to one day sooner, and six of our Congregational members were out of town. * * Part of our number expected some time in the course of the year to move to Waukesha." Inasmuch as the removal was actually made, it seems probable that the majority of those who remained preferred the Presbyterian polity. The first church at Waukesha was Congregational.

[3] The Methodist congregation at Platteville was using as a church a little log building put up for a justice's office.

[4] Probably he bore most of the cost, $619.01.

[5] It was on lot thirteen, block fifty six, according to Rev. S. A. Dwinnell. He adds that it was the first painted church in the Territory.

This First church of Milwaukee, having become one with the North Presbyterian, organized in 1849, January 31st, is now Immanuel. Its influence has been great, and its history has been one of prosperity and good. If we consider this church as really existing before its formal organization, we must put first in the list of its pastors, A. L. Barber, then J. F. Ostrander. Nor should we forget Moses Ordway's temporary service. Then, July, 1837, came Rev. Gilbert Crawford. He seems to have been a leader in the organization at Milwaukee, 1839, January 17th, of the first "Presbytery of Wisconsin," a body which the ecclesiastical events of more than half a century have metamorphosed into the "Congregational Convention of Wisconsin." The old church suffered division that, in the providence of God, its aggressive sister, Plymouth, might come into life, burning with the revival spirit and the heat of the anti-slavery conflict. And it was from the pastorate of the First church that, at the call of Father Kent and others, Aaron Lucius Chapin went to become president of Beloit college.

But these events belong to a later time than that of unnamed Wisconsin. Ours is a story of explorers, traders, missionaries and pioneers. Of the last class those who came to mine,—at least many or the most of them,—had not so much the purpose of permanent settlement as of quickly acquiring wealth. But in the southeastern part of Michigan-west-of-the-lake men came with intent from the first of making homes. For such a purpose, there is scarcely a fairer land under the sun. But nature seemed to greet the new-comers with a frown. Thus in the summer of 1835 there was in the neighborhood of Racine frost every month.[1] Many immigrants turned away. Supplies of food came mostly by the way of the lakes. Flour, which during the spring and summer cost from twenty to thirty dollars a barrel, was in the autumn still as high as fourteen. John T. Kingston who gives these facts[2] adds that he was in Chicago before the opening of navigation in 1835 and saw the last barrel of flour in the market sold for twenty-eight dollars. The following winter, Mr. Kingston says, "was unusually hard on the new comers; they were mostly without sufficient means to buy the necessary provisions to last through the cold season. Many families lived entirely upon potatoes, and some even upon oats hulled and afterwards boiled. But game was plenty."

Soon came also the want of money brought about by the financial stress of 1837. Nor was the scarcity of food so soon at an end as one might expect in a country as fertile as southeastern Wisconsin. "I believe," wrote Rev. Cyrus Nichols in the "Home Missionary" for July, 1838, "nearly one-half of the people are destitute of meat; not a few families within the circle of my acquaintance are subsisting on potatoes and milk. Many during the past winter had nothing to eat for weeks in succession but potatoes and salt, and many, I am informed, subsisted weeks on turnips alone. There is no credit and almost no current money. Labor will not procure money or provisions except to a

---

[1] "Back from the immediate lake shore and east of Fox river."—*Hist. Coll. VII.*, 338. This Fox river is the one that flows into the Illinois.
[2] See reference in preceding note.

very limited extent." "Hard times," surely, there were in those early days.

Yet in the "Home Missionary" for October, 1838, the immigration into to Wisconsin is reported to be at the rate of four thousand a month. In the number for April, 1839, we are told that "the inhabitants live better this year than the last, yet very few have what they used to call the necessaries of life." "Our missionary at Racine," says the editor, "received but $60 in two years from the people." No doubt the good man remembered the apostolic injunction, "trust not in uncertain riches." But we wonder if he would have written, as Rev. Stephen Peet did in the report of a famous tour of exploration published, in the "Home Missionary" for September, 1838, "The financial struggle is over in Wisconsin."

It would seem that Mr. Nichols was the first resident minister at Racine.[1] "We greatly need help here," he wrote in the "Home Missionary" for January, 1838. "I have seen no Presbyterian or Congregational minister since we arrived here in August, 1836. There is no such minister between here and Chicago, a distance of sixty-five miles, but one between this place and Green Bay, about one hundred and fifty miles, and none between this place and the Mississippi river which is more than two hundred miles distant. Indeed I believe there are but three or four Presbyterian or Congregational ministers in this Territory on this side of the Mississippi river. * * The number of ministers of other denominations is less than is usual in a new country. The Methodist and Baptist preachers are comparatively few."

But an earlier story than that told by Mr. Nichols deserves at least a few words. It was on the 10th of October, 1699, that white men first came to the Che-pe-ka-taw sibi,[2] or Root river, which they or other early French explorers called by the corresponding name in their own language, Racine. These men were of two parties, one under command of Francis Morgan de Vincennes who in 1702 founded the first settlement in Indiana. The other party was one of Jesuit missionaries who remained in the vicinity seven days trying to find a portage to the Fox (tributary to the Illinois). It is to these, perhaps, that we owe the name Racine.

In November, 1834, Captain Gilbert Knapp brought to the mouth of Racine river the first settlers there, William and Andrew J. Luce, brothers from Indiana. In honor of Captain Knapp the new settlement was called for a time Fort Gilbert.

Though among the early settlers was William Sell, a local preacher who had been government blacksmith at Fort Dearborn, it is thought that the first religious service at or near[3] the mouth of "Root river" was in June or July, 1835 by Rev. Jesse Walker of whom we have heard as preaching at Chicago at an early time. Father Walker, as he was deservedly called, was a Methodist pioneer preacher of the best type,—a man who "was never turned aside by

---

[1] His home was at first in the town of Caledonia, where he was one of the earliest settlers.
[2] Otherwise written Chippecotton or Schipicoten.
[3] Mr. Bennett, the historian of Methodism in Wisconsin, thinks it is "probable that Mr. Walker visited a point on Root river, some distance from Racine."

dangers or hardships, always seeking out the frontier settlers, comforting and administering to the sick,— spending his life, in fact, for the good of his fellow-men." But he did not serve as pastor or stated preacher at Racine, and died in the autumn of that same year,— 1835.

In the spring of 1835 a certain exploring party came first to Milwaukee and then to Racine. But at neither place could they secure "claims." These they were seeking not only for themselves, but also for other members of a company that had been organized the winter before (February 20th) at Hannibal, New York. On the 6th of June, 1835, this party of explorers,— Waters Touslee, Sidney Roberts and Charles W. Turner, came to Pike Creek and took claims there. A post-office, to which was given the name Pike Creek, was established in 1836. In the following year Southport was chosen as the name of the place, which on becoming a city, in 1850, took the name of Kenosha. A prayer meeting was held and a Sunday school [1] organized at Pike Creek on the 2nd of August, but the first sermon in Pike Creek "was by Rev. Abner Barlow, at the house of Waters Touslee, on the north side of the river in 1835. The number of inhabitants here at that time, according to the record of Isaac G. Northway, was thirty-two. Twenty of these attended the meeting and quite filled the house, which had only one room. The dwellings of the early inhabitants were small, usually consisting of one room, and sometimes roofed with bark." Col. Michael Frank, from whom I have quoted, thinks that the time of Mr. Barlow's sermon was about December, 1835. Mr. Barlow was then in deacon's orders in the Methodist Episcopal church.[2] He afterward entered the Congregational body, and became a pioneer in religious work in Dane county, with a parish that extended over into Rock.

Not only were settlements formed beside the Mississippi,— throughout all the lead region,— and on the shores of Lake Michigan before Wisconsin had separate political existence, beginnings were made also in the interior,— on the prairie traversed by the Fox, and gemmed with lakes; and beside the Assenisibi, or Rock river,— a stream whose banks would invite settlement.

"It being natural to ask what sort of a man first set foot on the site of this city of Beloit, we have to answer, that we do not know.[3] Some pre-historic man perhaps. Next, and certainly the mound-making man, for here are his mounds, on which we stop long enough to note his eye for a situation, a good locality. Next, if next and not the same, the Indian, to whom this was a favorite

---

[1] By Jonathan Pierce and Austin Kellogg, good Methodists. Twenty-eight attended; twenty one took part.

[2] Mr. Barlow was not a resident of Pike Creek, but of the town of Pleasant Prairie which comprises the southeast corner of Wisconsin. He was one of the earliest settlers there, having passed Waukegan, Illinois, at a time when, to use his own humorous description "it consisted of a coffee mill nailed to a stump." He was ordained as an elder in the Methodist Episcopal church at Chicago, 1842, August 7th, by Bishop Robert Richford Roberts. On one occasion,— it could hardly have been in August, however,— Mr. Barlow, walking with others toward and into Chicago, was obliged to wade for twenty miles through water over his shoetops.

[3] Rev. Lucien Dwight Mears, historian of the First Congregational church of Beloit, and the first white child born in that city.

place of resort.[1] Next, the first white man to sojourn, though not to settle, the French Canadian, Joseph Thiebeau, with his two Indian wives and family of half-and-half children. Sojourner to be sure and not settler, but he was the first builder of anything more than an Indian wigwam — of a log house — the first house here. * * Next, the first real settler. Caleb Blodgett was his name, originally, I have reason to suppose, from Randolph, Vermont. Coming west by degrees, he was here in this region with one or two sons, as early as the month of May, 1836, exploring, looking for land and a location. With him also, at some time during this year 1836, now or later, the first of the original members of the [First Congregational] church to visit the locality, though he did not come to settle until the autumn of the following year, Chauncey Tuttle. In the month of June of this year 1836, Mr. Blodgett is ready to approve the judgment of the mound maker and the Indian and decide for this place. * * In December, year 1836, he brings his family, the first white family; hence the first white woman to come to stay, Mrs. Caleb Blodgett, with perhaps two of her daughters."

A story of early Wisconsin-ward emigrants is told in a paragraph of the Beloit college "Codex" issued by the class of '95:

"I heard the word Beloit in 1836 for the first time. I was standing in my father's yard in Vermont one June day, and up came four covered wagons filled with people, and among them four beautiful girls, just blooming into womanhood. They attracted my attention and I began to ask questions; they were bound for Beloit, Wisconsin."

A pretty story this, and told by a worthy man, Dr. Daniel Kendall Pearsons, of Chicago, the generous giver to Beloit college.[2] But there is some mistake or lapse of memory. In 1836, though Beloit had a mere beginning, it had not yet its present name,[3] and probably no distinctive name at all. However, we need make the date only a year later to think of such a group as Dr. Pearsons describes, emigrants perhaps from Colebrook, New Hampshire, where had been formed the "New England Emigrating Company," under the auspices of which the real settlement of Beloit was affected in 1837. Thither came in its early years Lewis Homeri Loss who, had it been possible, would have come west in response to Mr. Warren's call to found a mission among the Ojibways. At Beloit he founded a seminary which continued its existence until it furnished to Beloit college its first freshman class, of four. And thus was laid, in part, the foundation of the oldest institution of higher education in Wisconsin. A

---
[1] On the site of Beloit was a Winnebago village. Its name in English form is preserved in that of the town of which Beloit once was a part,— the town of Turtle.

[2] I believe that Dr. Pearsons's gifts to Beloit college exceed those received from any individual giver by any other Wisconsin institution.

[3] What follows here is merely from memory, but I seem to recall a story in which it was said that the place was first called New Albany; that a committee of settlers met to make choice of another name to be recommended for adoption; that while some were preparing letters to be drawn from a hat until some pronounceable combination should be secured, another was trying to recall an Indian name that he thought rhymed with "Detroit." He uttered something that was, or sounded like, "Beloit," a name that pleased all so well that resource to the hat and its contents was deemed needless.

fuller story belongs to a later time, and has been often told.

The peninsula, or, more precisely,—if we may use such an etymological monstrosity,—the "inter-lachen," whereon Wisconsin's capital was to stand and her great university to be built, had, in 1836, been neither marred nor beautified by the hand of man. Where now more than a thousand students come and go, then not a family had made a home. But observing eyes had seen the beauty of the site, and persistent advocacy by James Duane Doty,—who, we are sorry to have to add, did not refrain from bribery,—led to the choice thereof as the capital of the newly organized Territory. That was done at (old) Belmont, 1836, December 3rd. At the same place there was held the first session of the Territorial supreme court. But it was on soil not now belonging to Wisconsin,—at Burlington, Iowa, that an act was passed creating the university of Wisconsin. Not until 1850, however, did the institution begin the work of instruction, and then as a preparatory school.

Among the pioneers of 1836 was a young man—Rev. Solomon Ashley Dwinnell,—[1] who thirty years later told well and briefly the story of that early time.[2] "In the year 1836," he says, "Wisconsin was organized as a Territory of the United States, and its material, educational and religious history really began. Little had been done before that time.

"On the 25th of October, 1836, I entered Chicago on the Great Eastern Mail Stage, consisting of a common uncovered lumber wagon. This, with an extra for baggage and a few passengers, brought all the travelers from the East for the day, as navigation was then closed. Chicago was then a frontier village, with apparently some 1,500 inhabitants. A garrison of United States troops at Fort Dearborn, near the mouth of the river, protected the inhabitants from the attacks of the Indians. The village was mostly limited to a few squares east and south of the river. There were three small buildings on the west side. * *

"On the 15th of November * * I entered Wisconsin * * [and] at seven o'clock, evening, I reached the 'Outlet of Big Foot,'[3] now Geneva, having traveled thirty-five miles without seeing a human dwelling. The settlement consisted of five families, living in rude log cabins without floors, chimneys, or chambers, the roofs covered with 'shakes' and hardly a nail used in the construction of their dwellings. There were then twenty-seven families in what is now the county of Walworth, and all but four in the eastern half of it; all living in log cabins. All of them had come in since spring, and had put under cultivation about eighty acres. I settled on Spring Prairie, in what is now the town of La Fayette.

---

[1] Mr. Dwinnell, though once a student of theology at Andover, was compelled by the threatened failure of his health to choose an out-of-door-life, and did not enter the ministry until after he had been in Wisconsin many years.

[2] In the "Wisconsin Puritan," a religious paper that, in 1867, was absorbed into the "Advance" of Chicago.

[3] Big Foot was a Pottawattomie chief, whose name was borne for a time by the lake now called Geneva. Mr. Dwinnell seems to use "Outlet of Big Foot" as the name of the prospective village.

"In the fall of 1836, there were farming settlements near Kenosha, Racine and Milwaukee. There were probably twenty families on Fox River, from Burlington to Waukesha. There were twenty-seven in Walworth county. On Rock River, there were five[1] families at Beloit, three at Watertown, two at and near Janesville, and two at Fort Atkinson. The number of souls, at that time, from the settlements by the lake shore to Mineral Point and Dodgeville, could not have exceeded three hundred and fifty, nearly all of whom came in the same season. Travelers from place to place made their way by Indian trails, which were numerous, and about six inches in depth and eighteen in width.

"In 1836 the amount of land under cultivation was about three or four thousand acres, and the amount of grain raised could not have exceeded 40,000 bushels, mostly sod corn and buckwheat.

"Early settlers of a state must work for posterity. During the first fifteen years I opened two farms, upon the first of which I split and laid up three miles of rail fence with my own hands, raised thousands of bushels of grain, most of which was sold for less than the cost of production. Not a bushel of wheat was sold for a dollar; the average price in market was about sixty cents. The first grain we carried to market was the best quality of winter wheat, sold at Southport, September, 1840, at fifty-five cents per bushel. It was threshed by treading with oxen, and driven thirty-five miles to market. It must have cost $1 per bushel to produce it. In subsequent years, the farming interest somewhat improved.

"In 1836 there were four counties. Milwaukee county extended from the state of Illinois north to Manitowoc, and west to the four lakes, where Madison now stands, with a population of 2,893. Brown was north of Milwaukee —its population 2,706. Iowa county embraced all the region west of Milwaukee county to the Mississippi and Wisconsin rivers, with a population of 3,218. Crawford was north of the Wisconsin river and west of Brown County; its population 1,220. The entire population was 11,683. It is alleged that 3,000 Indians of the Oneida, Brothertown and Stockbridge tribes, not then citizens, were enumerated in that census. If so, the white population was about 9,000.

"In 1836 there were 303 miles of mail route established in the territory; from the state line of Illinois, near Kenosha, to Milwaukee, forty miles, by a two-horse lumber wagon, twice a week; from Milwaukee to Green Bay, one hundred miles, once a week, on the back of a man; from Galena to Mineral Point *via* Platteville, forty-three miles, in a one-horse wagon, once a week; from Platteville to Cassville, twenty miles, and from Platteville to Prairie du Chien, thirty miles, once a week, on horseback; and from Mineral Point to Fort Winnebago, seventy miles, once a week, on the back of a man.

"In 1836 the nearest railroad was at Utica, New York, [and] the magnetic telegraph was not invented."

---

[1] An error, doubtless. On this point Mr. Mears is much more likely to be right than is Mr. Dwinnell.

"In 1836 there were four weekly newspapers in Wisconsin. The *Green Bay Intelligencer* was established, December 11, 1833, by P. V. Suydam and A. G. Ellis; the *Green Bay Spectator*, August, 1835, by H. O. Sholes and C. C. P. Arndt. In 1836, the above named papers were consolidated, and assumed the name of the *Wisconsin Democrat*, published at Green Bay by H. O. and C. C. Sholes. The *Green Bay Free Press* was established, 1836. The *Milwaukee Advertiser* was established, July, 1836, by Daniel H. Richards; name changed to *Courier* in 1841, and to the *Wisconsin* in 1844. The *Belmont Gazette* was commenced, October, 1836, and was published during the session of the Territorial legislature at that place, for two or three months, and was then removed to Mineral Point, and became the *Miners' Free Press*, in 1837.

"In 1836 there were eight small private schools, and no public schools. There was one in Pike, now Kenosha, taught by Rev. Jason Lothrop, in a log school house. The school was opened in December, 1835. There was a school taught in Milwaukee, by —— West, in a building owned by Deacon Samuel Brown, on lot 12, block 39, second ward, now occupied as a store. The first school in Milwaukee, was taught by David Worthington, in the winter of 1835-6, in a room on East Water street, one block east of Wisconsin street. There was one in Sheboygan, in a private room, by T. M. Rublee; one in Green Bay by Miss Frances Sears of 35 scholars, in a frame school house 24x30, on Cherry street, built in 1834; one in Prairie du Chien, of thirty pupils, taught by —— and an infant school of twenty by Miss Kirby; one in the Methodist log meeting-house, at Mineral Point, of about fifty scholars, and one in Platteville, of 40 scholars, taught by Dr. A. T. Lacy, in a log school house 20 by 22 feet, built in 1834. Samuel Huntington had previously taught in the same house. The whole number of scholars taught was about 260.[1]

"In 1836, there were probably, as nearly as can at this time be ascertained, six Sabbath schools with about 185 scholars.

"It was in 1836 and onward that Eastern emigration poured into the West as a mighty stream. Just at that time Wisconsin was opened for settlement. Its lands were surveyed and emigration invited to its shores. The financial crash of 1837 succeeding the wild speculation of 1836, reduced many families

---

[1] Supplementary to the above may be made the following statements: Rev. Jason Lathrop was an eccentric, but very worthy, Baptist clergyman. Mr. West's work is mentioned in both the "History of Milwaukee" (Western Publishing company) and the "History of Education in Wisconsin." His Christian name is not given, but we are told that he afterward removed to Appleton. David Worthington was one of three who held in May or June, 1835, what Deacon Daniel Brown thinks was the first prayer meeting in Milwaukee. Mr. Worthington afterward entered the ministry of the Methodist Episcopal church. But neither he nor West taught what was absolutely the first school in Milwaukee. That was in 1835 by a Mr. or Dr. Heth. He had few pupils, save the children of Solomon and Peter Juneau. "F" instead of "T" should appear in Mr. Rublee's name.

It may be added that to Southport (Kenosha) belongs the honor of establishing the first public school in Wisconsin. Colonel Michael Frank, historian of the Congregational church of Kenosha, did more than any other man to secure the needed legislation. He it was, also, who "framed the school laws of this state, which, by subsequent modification, constitute the school code of to-day."

at the East to bankruptcy, many of whom in order to retrieve their fortunes and found new homes, emigrated here. Among these were many men and women of refinement and education, and of sterling moral and Christian character, some of whom were soon found in almost every village and settlement. Their cabins were opened for religious meetings, Sabbath schools and the preaching of the gospel. They became the members and officers of the churches soon after formed. Thus the moulding of the Territory in its laws, its educational, moral and religious institutions was largely given into the hands of Eastern people."

Well did these men do their work. They brought hither the town system of local government. They created our schools, our colleges and the most highly vitalized of our churches. They led the way wherein have followed men of multitudinous nations. Thus has been brought together in Wisconsin a polyglot people. Of these a majority were peasants in the lands whence they came,—that is men without social, political or religious responsibility, men whose chief duty was unthinking obedience to priest and king, and whose chief privilege was the stupefaction of the beer mug on Sundays.[1] Yet these men, received here into an equality of political and social privilege that perhaps has not a parallel in the world's history,[2] found place where they,—and more than they, their children,—could breathe of the spirit that was in the best of the men who, coming some from the South and more from the East, laid here the foundations of a great commonwealth,—foundations whereon were to build not only their own children and the sons and daughters of their neighbors, but also people of strange language and alien citizenship. Of Wisconsin's early pioneers, we may say in the words of Emerson that they builded better than they knew.

---

[1] Sundays, it may be added, which ecclesiastical and political tyranny were glad to have debased into times of frivolity or of anything rather than the hallowing thought that duty, rights and righteousness are found primarily in the personal relation of every soul to Almighty God.

[2] Under the laws of Wisconsin a man does not need to be a citizen to be a voter. It is enough that he has merely "declared his intention" to become a citizen and has lived one year in the state. Our present system is well illustrated in the case of President Eaton of Beloit college. That gentleman is a native of Wisconsin, was educated in her schools and, with absence for further study, made his home here until he entered upon professional life. Returning to his native state to assume the presidency of his *alma mater*, he must needs wait for the privilege of voting, as long as the foreign emigrant. That is, if a man from Sinope in Asiatic Turkey or from Bjelometschetskaja among the Caucasus mountains arrived in Wisconsin on the day that President Eaton returned thither, and on that same day the emigrant "declared his intention" to become a citizen of the United States, the one was legally entitled to vote as soon as the other. It is said that men have voted for twenty years in Wisconsin and yet been in a position to repudiate the duties of American citizenship. Save, perhaps, for the number of years, this statement is true of several voters in the little city where I am writing on the day following the autumn election of 1894.

APPENDIX.

IN MEMORIAM.

On August 12th, 1894, at the home of her son, Rev. E. P. Wheeler, in Ashland, Wisconsin, Mrs. Harriet Wood Wheeler breathed her last. Her death was the result of an accidental fall, which occasioned concussion of the brain and a broken hip. Her case was a hopeless one from the outset. She lingered along for eighteen days, enduring the greatest suffering, when the end came. A wide circle of friends, including those who appreciated the worth of her personal qualities, as well as those who knew of her missionary services, have united in asking some outline sketch of her life. Filial affection yields to this request, though with hesitation, knowing the inadequacy of the means at command to set forth in words the spirit of the life it would portray. The following, however, is given. in the hope that it may furnish some fresh suggestion of the grace that is all-sufficient.

MRS. HARRIET WOOD WHEELER.

The subject of this sketch was born in Dracut, now a part of Lowell, Massachusetts, on December 4th, 1816. She was of Puritan blood in both lines of descent. Her grandmother on her father's side was a Whiting, who had come down from a long line of godly ancestors, among whom were several ministers of the gospel. Among the earliest representatives of this class in England, was a dissenting clergyman in Lincolnshire, in the early days of non-conformity; another a mayor of Boston of the same shire, and a third "a man of considerable note in the time of Cromwell." The same family were well represented in the religious life of Boston, in the early days of New England. Cotton Mather speaks of some of them as belonging to a class of clergymen, who were "reverend, holy and faithful ministers of the gospel." The Wood ancestors were generally represented in mercantile pursuits. From them she inherited an energetic disposition and a strong constitution. Her mother was a Kendall and contributed a native refinement and delicacy in the make-up of her natural endowments. From all lines of descent, however, there was given her a Puritan conscience which subordinated all human interests to the divine will, with absolute consent. The year of her birth was a crisis in the religious life of her parents. Though both had been reared with all the strictness and fidelity common to the orthodoxy of the times, neither were members of the church. In fact, the father had tried to justify the anomalous attitude he was conscious of occupying, by the ostensible acceptance of the Unitarian faith. But the influence of early training, combined with growing responsibilities made an issue in their lives. Weeks of mental and religious struggle followed. Out of it all came the clear consciousness and acceptance of the verities of the evangelical faith. They united with the Congregational church in Dracut, and later on became charter members of the First church in Lowell. It is significant that the weekly prayer meetings of the latter church were held, during the first year of its history, in their home. Into this atmosphere of Christian zeal, Harriet Wood was born. That it had its effect upon the very beginnings of her moral consciousness, is evident from the fact that she could never in her after life, look back upon a time when she was not a Christian. Her earliest recollections were of faith and trust in the unseen Father of all. It was a life of trust too, out of which poured forth, as from a living spring, the ministries of Christian service. At the age of ten, her favorite occupation, Saturdays, was to visit the sick and needy and lavish upon them the sympathies of a full heart, as well as to supply, as generously as she could, the means for their physical comfort. When she had reached her fourteenth year, the home was bereft of the mother. Her dying charge to the daughter Harriet was that she must now become the mother to the six younger sisters and one brother. Most prayerfully and devotedly did she take up the new responsibility, throwing into it all that ardent and generous enthusiasm so native to her spirit. It was her habit on pleasant mornings to gather the children into the parlor of the old home, and, after reciting a verse or a hymn, marshal them all off into the woods for a romp before breakfast. These home cares accepted so heartily and borne with such loving faithfulness, developed her character in many directions of usefulness, especially on its religious side. And so it came about, that these early responsibilities matured in her heart the conviction that the consecrated life was the only true life to live; and it was this thought that ultimately became fixed in the settled purpose to give her life in missionary service.

During her sixteenth year, she entered Mary Lyon's school, at Ipswich. The newly-awakened zeal in missionary work was in full tide here, and Miss Lyon lost no opportunity of inspiring her pupils with the real missionary spirit. She found in Miss Wood a congenial spirit and a heart tremblingly alive to the missionary appeal. On one occasion Miss Lyon invited a missionary from Ohio to address the young ladies on the subject of Indian missions. The appeal went straight to hearts that were responsive, and they took upon themselves the support of an Indian pupil at the Mackinaw mission school. The year at Ipswich was full of significance for Miss Wood. She had evidently caught much of the spirit of that consecrated genius of common sense in Christian culture, Mary Lyon. In a letter to her father, written at this time she says: "For a few weeks past I have begun to look around and consider what I must become when I leave here, and the more I think of it, the more I am bewildered. I very much wish to form a character that will do some good; one that will be useful; not one that will live only for the gratification of selfish principles."

She returned to Lowell to take up her home duties again; but with the added purpose of serving her Master more unreservedly than ever before in all the relations of life. It was not without a struggle that she renounced her social ambitions from the worldly standpoint and entered with fresh consecration upon the work of the church with which she had become identified. Here her Christian aspiration found free play. Through the channels of the Sunday school, and through the varied avenues of parish work, her activities flowed in full tide. Her visitings among the poor and neglected classes and among the mill operatives of Lowell were especially fruitful; not only to those thus comforted, but reflexively fruitful in the culture of her rare spirit. Before the days of deaconesses, she fully sustained that relationship to her church and in such manner as to merit its official recognition. It was in the midst of these labors that she met her future husband, Leonard Hemenway Wheeler, who was completing his theological course with a view of entering upon mission work among the Chippewa Indians of Lake Superior. During his last term at Andover, he was delegated to attend certain anniversary exercises at Lowell, and was entertained at Mr. Wood's home. The acquaintance thus begun was continued for the few months Mr. Wheeler was pursuing medical studies in the office of a physician at Lowell, as supplementary to a course of medical lectures he had already taken at Pittsfield, Massachusetts. The acquaintance reached its destined culmination in marriage, April 26th, 1841. Mr. Wheeler was already under commission of the American Board to labor among the Indians, as stated. The ordination services were held in the Appleton street church, with which Mrs. Wheeler's religious activities had been so intimately identified. From its benediction and blessing they proceded to their far off and unfamiliar field of labor, visiting for a short time on their way with Mr. Wheeler's family in Vermont.

The stay at the old homestead, though necessarily brief, made its impress on the young bride. Revisiting the scenes of Mr. Wheeler's boyhood, recalling old associations, the greetings and farewells with old associates, and the mingling of all in the chalice of sweet Christian fellowship, made this final leave-taking of the old New England home seem like the passing of a sacramental cup of true communion with kindred spirits and with their common Lord. They proceeded at once to their field of labor. The journey proved a long and wearisome experience in those days of slow travel. The stage, the steam packet, the bateau and sailing craft were successively brought into requisition in the course of the trip. Arriving at Mackinaw, they found it essential and profitable to tarry a week, that they might investigate the work of the Indian mission at that point and also gain a little much needed rest. From this station they set out again; this time in the open bateau of the professional *voyageur*. It was the type of craft that had, for so many years, served the daring and zeal of the French discoverers and the Jesuit missionaries. After nine days of variable weather and rough sea-faring, in no wise tempered to the delicacy of Mrs. Wheeler's health, they reached Madelaine Island, Sunday, August 1st, 1841. The missionaries at La Pointe gave them hearty welcome, and in the evening of this first Sabbath, Mr. Wheeler preached in the mission church.

At the time of their arrival, Madelaine island was the headquarters of the American Fur company, and through this corporation the emporium of trade for all the region north and west of Mackinaw. Here was a population varying somewhat with the seasons, but at this time numbering about seven thousand souls, principally made up of Ojibway Indians. Here the Fur company had built a commodious fort and official residence for its officers and their families; and from this common center its factors and agents traversed all the adjacent territory, as well as the more remote regions of the interior, trading with the Indians for furs. The Indian agent, that elusive personality, who, in so many instances, has stood as the unknown quantity in his alleged mediatorial capacity between the Great Father at Washington and his much pillaged children of the forest, was also quartered at the island. "Payment time," in the fall of the year, was always an occasion of much interest to the red men, and brought large companies of them to this governmental "round-up," or rendezvous, to receive the annual disbursements of money and miscellaneous items due them under terms of treaty. It was in the midst of these varied conditions and more varied people, that Mr. and Mrs. Wheeler were to begin their missionary labor.

The young couple began housekeeping in the mission manse, which had already been provided by the American Board for the use of its missionaries.[1] The structure, comfortably and well built for those early days and, at that time, remote locality, amply accommodated the missionary force on the island. It still stands, and its upper rooms, long since untenanted, look out upon the ever varying phase of water-view and landscape that still yield to fancy their old-time spell of facination and charm. Besides Mr. and Mrs. Wheeler, the manse was occupied by Rev. Sherman Hall and family, founder of the mission,[2] together with Miss Abbie Spooner of Athol, Massachusetts, who had accompanied Mr. Wheeler to the island to teach in the mission school. The basement of this mission home was fitted up as a school room; and here Mrs. Wheeler took up the first golden threads of her missionary service, the day after her arrival. She began as teacher in this mission day-school, but the unstinted love of her heart saw an additional opportunity, and she soon organized a night school for mothers. Every evening from fifteen to twenty Indian mothers gathered in her rooms for instruction. She gave them lessons in sewing as well as practical talks on house-keeping; some also learning to read and write. Prayer, singing and reading of the Bible, gave wing and spiritual cheer to every session of the mothers' school; and souls born into the kingdom evidenced the Spirit's blessing on the work. Mrs. Wheeler also accompanied her husband in his daily visits to the wigwams of his parish and assisted him in his ministrations to the sick and needy. These Indians up to this time[3] were wholly innocent of those civilizing influences that lead to better things; were in the thick darkness of heathenism and deep in poverty. The chase and fishing furnished the staples of a more or less precarious subsistence. Wearing but little clothing, they were also destitute of the things that we deem the most common comforts of life. The appeal of such need went straight to the heart of Mrs. Wheeler, out of which were the issues of such untiring ministries.

She writes her parents at this time: "You can hardly imagine how much this poor people suffer in sickness. They have no comfortable houses, no soft pillows to recline their aching heads upon and no palatable food." It was her

---

[1] See page 156.
[2] I should prefer to call Mr. Ayer the "founder of the mission," though, after his first coming to La Pointe, he was not in the service of the American Board.—J. N. D.
[3] The time of the founding of the mission.

daily prayer that she might have strength and grace to exert a saving influence upon these people. She again writes home: "I have felt for some time that I could not rest satisfied until God should come by the influence of His Holy Spirit and convert this people. Pray, my dear parents, that we, who are sent here to be as light to this dark people, may be, indeed, bright and shining ones; that our hearts may be purified and sanctified, and made meet for this service."

But the demands on her time and strength did not begin and end in this service for the Indians only. During the summer months there were many arrivals of government officials, occasional tourists, and of those in search of health. The sunny temperament and rare social graces of the new hostess of the manse invariably attracted these new-comers to its hearth cheer. It was included in the charge of the American Board to its missionaries, that they should give entertainment and refreshment to the stranger within their gates; and, for this purpose, the necessary furnishings were provided. Mrs. Wheeler was the embodiment, to a remarkable degree, of unselfish, unstinted Christian cordiality. Hers was a heart always sympathetic and warm toward the stranger. Thus it came about that the mission home on the island, and later at Odanah, was a veritable "wayside inn" to many phases of humanity, as they drifted by in tireless search of wealth, health and rest. They came under the guise of explorers, tourists, government officials, timbermen, and the traditional settler. Its hospitality was impartial and its slender resources were made, by elastic adjustment, to fit all occasions. It was a tabernacle in the wilderness for those earlier days,—a place that always seemed pervaded with the sweet incense of two consecrated lives; a house of prayerful sunshine. Hither came Grace Greenwood in search of rest and health. Robert Stuart of Irving's "Astoria," Indian Commissioner Manypenny[1] and Agent Richard Smith, all friends of the Indians in the larger sense, were among the "official" guests. Professor Joseph Emerson also came from the classroom of a Yale tutorship to pass a vacation on the island[2] in those days of beginnings. He preached in the newly-built mission church, and thus were woven those golden threads of friendship, that twenty-five years later drew the missionary, worn out and broken in health, to Beloit for the education of his children. It was in this home, in later years, that J. Q. Adams Ward, the artist, passed some weeks, perfecting his models of the ideal Indian head, which he subsequently expanded into the bronze figure of the American Indian that now stands in Central Park, New York. But these digressions are leading us too widely from the main path of this sketch.

The November following their arrival found Mrs. Wheeler well nigh prostrated with the summer's work and the growing sense of the magnitude of her mission. The twenty-fifth of the month was a memorable day with her. It was the anniversary of the last Thanksgiving day spent in her New England home. She thus writes of it to her parents: "This has been an interesting, though somewhat trying, day to me, a day which I have looked forward to with

---
[1] G. W. Manypenny, commissioner of Indian affairs under President Pierce.
[2] About the time that he began work in Beloit college, and that was in 1848.

interest and dread. The power of association in my own mind is so strong, and past scenes, looks and tones come rushing upon me with such overwhelming force, that I dread anything that has a tendency to remind me of them. You will, I think, remember the occurences of that day. Oh, what a day of anxiety and trial it was to me. With what fearfulness and trembling did I come to the final decision. Never can I forget the anxious looks of my dear parents. The enquiring ones of my little sisters have come up before me to-day with a vividness and a freshness which has been very painful. The scenes of that evening have all been lived over again,—our parlor, the bright fire, my dear parents, that happy group of brothers and sisters.

"When I seated myself in my chamber this morning, the thoughts of home, and the scenes of last year came rushing upon me with such force as almost to overwhelm me. For a few moments I could do nothing but weep, but soon I was enabled to cast myself on the blessed Redeemer, to look to him for strength."

This 25th day of November, 1841, was one of great struggle in her soul, a day of crisis in her spiritual life. A Thanksgiving day turned into one of fasting and prayer sufficiently indicates the nature and intensity of the struggle. The picture is very vivid to her that day,—in the immediate foreground a life of privation in many ways, of isolation, of the giving up of social joys and its circle of kindred spirits, the seemingly narrower path of influence in a work among a degraded people, and practical renunciation of all former interests; and then for the remote background of this picture, that far away New England home, with its cheer, its comforts, its kindred and plenty. She deeply felt the urgency of committing her way unto the Lord afresh, and she can not leave that chamber of fasting and prayer, until she has, in solemn covenant, reconsecrated her life and all its future to God. That covenant, just as it was penned fifty-three years ago, is inserted at this point, as it seems the secret of the varied fruitage of all the years that followed.

COVENANT.

"Almighty and most merciful God, the author of my being and the preserver of my life, I desire at this time, with the deepest reverence, humility and self-abasement to present myself before thee, sensible of my utter unworthiness to appear in thy majesty's presence, especially on such an occasion as this; even that of entering into a solemn and everlasting covenant with the King of Kings and Lord of Lords. But this gracious proposal is from thee. Thine infinite mercy and condescension have opened the way, and thy grace, I trust, has inclined my heart to accept the terms of that gracious covenant according to which I would now heartily surrender and consecrate myself wholly to thee, to be thine forever. I acknowledge myself a great sinner and, with a penitent heart, beseech thee to be merciful to my unrighteousness, and forgive all my sins through the atonement and mediation of thy dear Son, in whom are all my hopes of acceptance. I beseech thee to pardon and receive thy prodigal child, who desires nothing so much as a place in thy family, and to be entirely devoted to thy glory. And yet such is the exceeding sinfulness of my heart and life that I cannot approach this solemn transaction without trembling. But convinced that it is but a reasonable service, I do this day, in the presence of witnessing angels, make an entire and hearty surrender of myself to thee. I yield to thee my mortal body with all its members, faculties and senses to be henceforth wholly employed in thy service and resigned to thy will. To thee I also surrender my rational and immortal soul with all its intellectual and moral powers, to be used, directed and disposed of, according to thy holy and sovereign pleasure. I also surrender and consecrate to thee all my time, property and influence, accounting myself thy servant bound to improve all to thy glory, and submit all my interests and desires to thy management and direction. At the same time I renounce all other Lords which have had dominion over me and choose and avouch the Lord Jehovah, Father, Son and Holy Spirit to be my God and portion forever. I take and own God, the Father, as my Father in heaven, engaging thus the aid of his grace to love and obey him as such, and humbly pray to be owned and blessed of him as a daughter of the Lord Almighty. The Lord Jesus Christ I accept as my only Redeemer and Saviour, beseeching him to wash my polluted soul in the fountain of his blood and make me a meek, exemplary follower of him till death and then receive me to his everlasting kingdom. The Holy Ghost I also avouch as my Enlightener, Guide, Sanctifier and Comforter entreating him to make my heart the temple of his residence, to shed abroad a Saviour's love there, to lead and enliven all my devotion, and bring every thought and desire into subjection to the divine will.

And now, O Lord, behold I am thine; oh make me a faithful servant, a willing and obedient child. Use me for thy glory as seemeth good in thy sight. Put me among thy children and number me among thy peculiar people. Feed and nourish my soul from thy bounteous table and clothe me with the robe of salvation prepared by the labors and sufferings of thy dear Son. While I live enable me to live wholly to thee, performing the duties and fulfilling the obligations of this solemn covenant, or if at any time, through indwelling sin, I violate my covenant vows, oh, let not thy loving kindness depart from me nor thy covenant of peace be removed; but grant me evangelical repentance and faith in Christ, and then save me from all my backslidings and by every fall make me more humbly watchful and prayerful, that my path may be as the rising light, which shineth brighter and brighter to the perfect day. And when my warfare shall be accomplished, my work on earth finished, receive me to thyself in that time and way which shall be most for thy glory, only grant, I beseech thee, that amid the struggles of dissolving nature, I may enjoy thy gracious presence, have the peace of God ruling in my heart and be enabled to employ the last breathings of mortality in thy praise. And when this clay tabernacle shall be returned to the earth from which it was taken, and this immortal soul, now engaged in covenant with its Maker, shall have entered on the retribution of eternity, should this memorial meet the eye of survivors, may it prove an instrument in the hands of the Spirit of awakening and saving such as are impenitent and of quickening to greater care, diligence and zeal such as have tasted that the Lord is gracious, that they may be prepared to join with the covenant people of God, who are before the throne, in ascribing blessing and honor and glory and power unto him that sitteth on the throne and to the Lamb forever and ever. Amen.

HARRIET WHEELER.

La Pointe, Lake Superior, Nov. 25th, 1841.

During the summer of 1842, Mrs. Wheeler accompanied her husband to the Fond du Lac mission, at the head of Lake Superior, to assist Missionary Ely in revival services. The mission was located not far from where Duluth now stands. They made the voyage in the mission sail-boat, camping two nights on the way. A place in which to hold the services was the first requisite after arrival. A lodge was accordingly built, its skeleton of cedar poles serving as studding and rafters; the top covered with cedar bark and the sides left open. Such was the somewhat primitive place of worship, meant to serve only a temporary purpose; but the Spirit was there in the richness of his power and builded for all eternity in the hearts of humble and contrite seekers. In a letter[1] home, Mrs. Wheeler thus writes of the services: "The meetings to-day have been very solemn and interesting, this evening especially so. It was a prayer and confessional meeting, and I have been very much interested in hearing these Spirit-taught children speak and pray. The first one who spoke had been a medicine man until within a few weeks. When the war party fitted out for the Sioux country this spring, he called on Mr. Ely, the missionary, shook hands with him, and told him if the Lord spared his life to return again, he would go to war no more, but would live differently. He went. Towards the close of a battle, the Chippeways were obliged to flee. The Sioux took another route and came out directly in front of them. The balls of the enemy were flying about his head on every side. Death stared him in the face. He says that he then promised the Lord in his heart, that, if he would spare his life, he would listen to his word. When he returned he told Mr. Ely his promise, came and settled down with his people, and ever since has been an attentive listener to the preaching of the gospel. This evening he has publicly renounced his heathenism and expressed his determination to become a Christian. He told the Indians that they must not invite him again to their *metawa* (religious) dances or their feasts. He appears to be sincere. This afternoon Mr. Wheeler visited him at his lodge and, after conversing with him, turned to his wife and asked her how she felt. 'She,' said he, 'will go with me. When I travel, she generally sits in the stern of the canoe, and I forward. She is not quite as far along as I, for I am the length of the boat before her, but

---

[1] Dated at Fond du Lac (of Lake Superior), July 20th, 1842. The Sabbath following was July 24th, "the interesting day," probably, that Mrs. Wheeler writes of in the next paragraph. Other letters that have been quoted from bear dates as follows: That from Ipswich to her father: 1832, July 27th. That from La Pointe, telling of the Indians' suffering in illness: 1841, November 20th.

she will follow.' A number of the Indians spoke this evening; one of them had recently united with the church at Sandy Lake. Before he commenced speaking, he went round and shook hands with the missionaries. This he did, he said, to keep up his fellowship with them. He expressed a strong desire that all the natives should become Christians. He said that he wished they would all be like little children, who, when any danger was near, would run to their mother and cling to her. So he wished all would flee to Christ and cling to Him. In his address to the Indians he told them to look about upon this world and to see the works of God. 'But,' said he, 'where are the tracks of our gods; we cannot see anything that they have made.' Some of the Christian Indians exhorted each other to live more holy; and to renew their consecration to the service of God. It was a solemn and interesting season. All without was calm and still. The bright moon cast its silvery rays into our little tabernacle, and here were a people recently sunk in all the horrors and degradation of heathenism; now singing the praises of God and calling upon his name. I remarked to L. [Mr. Wheeler] this evening, that it was enough to repay us for all the privation we were called to endure to witness such a scene.

"Sabbath evening: This has truly been an interesting day. This afternoon the sacrament was administered, and two Indians were admitted to the church. One of these was an old man. He is the head chief of the band. He is very tall and dignified in appearance. It was an affecting sight to see him come and kneel before the desk, and receive the ordinance of baptism. Mr. Wheeler baptized him and gave him the name of David. Two of his children were baptized also. The other person admitted was a young woman, wife of one of the native members. I cannot describe to you my emotions, as I celebrated the dying love of Jesus with this little band in the wilderness." Soon after this, the joint service with Mr. Ely of this Fond du Lac mission was brought to a close. The return trip to Madelaine island, of Mr. and Mrs. Wheeler, was not without incident. They were wind-bound for several days and their provisions failed them before it was safe to continue the voyage. They committed themselves afresh unto the care of the Lord, and during the night following the day, they had eaten the last of the food, the wind went down. They immediately set sail and reached the mission without further delay the next forenoon. Here the work was taken up again as already outlined and pushed forward with renewed zeal.

The rearing of a family began, in the year following, to engage the thought and love of Mrs. Wheeler. In March of 1843, a son was given her and in January of 1845, a daughter was added to the family. A letter to her parents at this time is interesting as setting forth her views with reference to the problem of "bringing up" missionary children. She writes:[1] "They call me here an over-anxious mother. Be this as it may. I cannot help it. Perhaps you would like to know what we intend to do with the children, should they be spared us. My present opinion is that we shall not send them away from us,

---
[1] From La Pointe, January 4th, 1846.

at least, not until they are able to take care of themselves. I can not yet see the consistency of missionaries' neglecting their own children or of throwing them upon the care of others, that they may be at liberty to devote themselves exclusively to the heathen. Besides, the heathen need the influence and example of a well-regulated household. They need to see the great principles of the gospel embodied; acted out. A missionary's family should be a model one, exhibiting to the heathen all that is lovely and desirable. The poor, darkminded heathen want something more than a good theory. Will you not pray, my dear parents, that your children may be enabled to emit a steady, unwavering light in this dark land. Oh, never did I know the crushing weight of responsibility, until I had the charge of a family on missionary ground."

It soon became apparent to Mr. Wheeler, that the location of the mission on Madelaine island, did not admit of reaching the Indians under settled conditions of life. He felt that the work could not be established there on permanent foundations. While the Indians resorted to the island in large numbers for their "payments" and for trading, the conditions did not seem suited to the support of a settled population. And even these attractions would soon be wanting, in the withdrawal of the American Fur company, with its stores, supplies and trading retinue. Accordingly, early in 1845, Mr. Wheeler had selected a site at the confluence of the White with the Bad river, as a point having resources in its soil and products that would invite permanent settlement. It was easily accessible from the main lake through Bad river, and from Chequamegon bay through the Caucaugon. The soil of the river bottom was very responsive to cultivation and the remoter banks of both streams heavily timbered, including a large percentage of hard maple, which Indian enterprise soon developed into thriving "sugar bushes." Extensive fields of wild rice also flanked the sluggish current of the Caucaugon on either side. Here Mr. Wheeler proceeded to make a clearing and to build the necessary structures in which to begin the work of a branch mission. The place soon came to be known as Odanah, the Indians later adding the more descriptive appellative of "The Gardens." In the summer of 1845, Mrs. Wheeler came to Odanah. The house she occupied that first season was a primitive affair of logs, with a bark roof. The space thus inclosed served as parlor, sleeping, dining and school room, and on the Sabbath as a chapel. In regard to the Odanah enterprise thus early undertaken, Mrs. Wheeler writes: "We feel that there is but little prospect of doing the Indians permanent good, while they are wandering about from place to place. Nothing can be done for their civilization under such circumstances; and we find that Christianity and civilization go hand in hand. They are inseparable." At Odanah she soon gathered for instruction about fifty pupils, the majority of whom were boys. It was indeed at first hand that she took them for training, wholly innocent hitherto of any touch of culture. She thus describes[1] their appearance: "Some of them came with their long black hair streaming over their shoulders. Other with it braided,

---

[1] Winter of 1845.

with thimbles and potato balls attached to the ends. Others with it tied up with a string of red flannel, and others again, still more exquisite in their tastes, had a bunch of wild flowers tied in. Their hands and faces looked as if they were perfect strangers to the blessings of cold water. However, I could not help loving some of them at least; and I spent many happy hours with my wild, bright-eyed Indian children in the shanty." An extract from a letter written to the Young People's Missionary society of Lowell, Massachusetts, is interesting as showing how one's estimate of the Indian character may need revision after actual contract with them. She writes: * * "This whole subject is invested with such a sacredness and encircled with such a halo of romance, that it is impossible for others to get the subject before their minds in a true light; to obtain a correct impression. They have heard so much of the poetry of Indian character, of his proud and lofty bearing, of his gratitude for favors, and of the beautiful simplicity of nature's children, that they entirely lose sight of the darker shades of the picture. Perhaps few have had more of this feeling than I had myself when I first came to this country; but I can assure you that it did not require many weeks of actual experience on the ground, to put to flight all such ideas. I found it was sober, prose business; a stern reality, but yet a most precious, a most blessed work." Mr. Wheeler, while appreciating the difficulty of the problem, felt that the work was indeed a blessed one. He writes: "I have never seen the day yet, when I regretted having come to preach the gospel to these poor people. Could you see these poor people as we do, in all their blindness and sin, you would feel more than ever before, that it was not by might nor by power, but by the spirit of the Lord, that men are to be saved." The first snow storm of this first season at Odanah, was the signal for their return to the island to continue there the work for the winter.

In the spring of 1846, Mr. Wheeler began laying the foundations for substantial and permanent work at Odanah. The needed buildings were erected, and one, which was completed in the fall, was occupied by his family; and from that time, till the end of his missionary service, continued to be their home. It came to be a home very much endeared to the heart of every member of that household; and how could it be otherwise with two such lives to hallow it? Now that both have been gathered to the home above and the "rest that remaineth;" with what love does memory cherish all the associations of that dear old mission home, the morning and evening worship with the never-failing hymn of faith, the verses of Scripture, the prayer, and the day between these two gateways filled with its appointed routine of service. And then the anniversaries in the old home. Its Thanksgiving days, Christmasses, New Year's days and its Fourths of July, all made bright and gladsome by the "singleness" of the one heart of love of that father and mother. Nor must the 26th of April be forgotten, the anniversary of their marriage. Many a tree planted on that day keeps green the memory of that first love. But the Sabbaths of that home touch the springs of tenderest recollections. How full

of sweet solicitude were these hearts, lest the day should be misspent and its blessings unappreciated. How careful were they that every thing in that home should be in order the night before and that nothing obtrude to weaken the sense of sacredness that their convictions told them belonged to the Sabbath, and all this without making the children feel that it was either an irksome or tiresome day. But the sentiment of that line of the old hymn came to be theirs:
"Thine earthly Sabbaths Lord we love,"
And again as expressed in those other lines of the hymn:
"Day of all the week the best,
Emblem of eternal rest."

Aside from the regular church services, the sweet songs of Zion from the old "Plymouth Collection" and from other sources, had a prominent place in the home observance of the day; and as the twilight deepened into night, the family never failed to gather about the mother to listen, with rapt attention, to the old Bible stories and the lessons she invariably drew from them. But the dear old mission home can live only in memory till the coming of that day of redemption, when the God of the covenant shall complete again the household circle of those old mission days, now broken but for a time.

During this first winter in the new home at Odanah, Mr. Wheeler conducted services at the mining and logging camps in the vicinity. Mrs. Wheeler frequently accompanied him and was always courteously received. The greasy packs of cards were kept in the background and rough words held in abeyance during their stay at the camps. She never went empty-handed, but always filled with good things, as was her heart with love. The home-cooked food she would take, supplemented with papers, magazines and books that might be spared from the mission always found hungry men and appreciative hearts in these camps. The books passed from one circle of readers to another, and in this way eighteen volumes of Abbott's histories were literally read to pieces and D'Aubigne's History of the Reformation was about as seriously devoured.

In her own home, Mrs. Wheeler was the most unselfish and devoted of mothers. Her tasks had no relation to the hour-glass of mere time service, but early and late was loving toil poured forth for her family as unstintedly and joyously as a lark's song. . She was always abounding in those youthful sympathies that made her so companionable to her children and so beloved of all young people. She was always in touch with young life; an appreciative sharer of its pains and pleasures. And so it was not much less than intuitive for her to kindle, each year, the enthusiasms of her always youthful spirit over the observance of recurring anniversary days. She was the inspiration, and at the same time, the happiest expression of such occasions. Thanksgiving day must be celebrated with all its delightful features of family reunion and good cheer as in the old New England home. The blessedness of giving, rather than of receiving, was the never-failing lesson of the Christmas season. She never broke the spell with which child-wonder invested all the preliminaries leading up to the Christmas tree and the mysteries of Santa Claus. It was a very happy expectant group that gathered about the magic tree, which had been set up either in the large dining-hall of the boarding-school or in the school house, as convenience might suggest. Its glories were curtained from the little throng, — in which were included the Indian girls and boys of the boarding-school, as well as the members of the mission families,— until their exuberance of spirits had found its joyous outlet in song. And while the strains of "Happy Greeting to All" resounded on every side, those behind the curtain, and in the secret of Santa Claus, were lighting up the innumerable candles of the little mother's own making. And then the veil was drawn and the perennial miracle of the evergreen tree stood revealed. The candles twinkled to the music of dancing eyes. The numberless little cakes in every variety of form, sparkled in holiday frosting. The less numerous and half-hidden surprises of candy and nuts shown with softened glow through their dainty bags of gauze. The dazzle of Indian bead-work in many forms of fanciful pattern and rich coloring hightened the charm. The many little "mokuks" of birch bark curiously carved and filled with maple sugar, the square parcels of maple gum-sugar done up in birch bark and tied with shreds or strings of basswood bark, the pairs of moccasins with their rich embroideries, the mittens of buckskin and bright colored yarns — these, and many other kinds of fruit, burdened that tree from topmost bough to base. But that base had its own peculiar attractions for the boys. About it were grouped the coveted sled or tobbogan, the pairs of snowshoes with their bright trimmings, the gayly-stained bows and arrows, the baby ox-yoke for yoking up pet yearlings, and such other things as boys prize. Then began the disenchantment of the tree in the distribution of the gifts; and, after that, a short address, appropriate to the occasion, carried home to the heart on the wings of song. A round of good, old-fashioned games concluded the festivities. Thus flowed Christmas tide at the mission; and its warm currents of glad cheer never failed to soften down the sterner realities of the work and to make its privations and hardships seem less drear.

Mrs. Wheeler's thoughtful care, though taxed in so many directions, did not overlook the children's birthdays. In the earlier days of the mission, the mother, attired in a green Irish poplin gown of rich texture and elaborate design, was inseparably associated in the minds of the older children with those celebrations. A table, spread with the linen and set with the china, reserved for state occasions only, still further dignified such days. And then the happy recipient of these honors was remembered with some delicacy to which he was specially partial and which had been fondly hoarded till the set day had come. The opportunity was not lost of supplementing all with kindly words of counsel — often in the language of Scripture. But in her care and solicitude for her family, all days were as birthdays. How many and delightful evening hours of reading before the good nights were said; how many hours of plying of the needle after all others had retired; and, after that, how many hours spent with candle or lamp in hand, making the nightly round, simply to assure her heart that all was well with the sleeping children; and finally how many hours, reaching far into the night, of fervent prayer and of personal communing with God and his Scriptures. The sum of them all is known to Him only, "who seeth in secret." Nor were these outgoings of her life for her own children alone; but under the hovering of these wings of her care and solicitude, were gathered, at various times and for periods of many years in some instances, the motherless girl, the homeless boy, the tired-out teacher and the broken-down missionary.

The days that brought the missionary box and annual supplies from "below" (a word mysteriously significant, in the minds of the children, of teeming cities and of cultured white people), came to be somewhat of the nature of anniversary days, and looked forward to with expectation that was never disappointed. The box came from the church and Lowell relatives of Mrs. Wheeler, and its opening at the mission home was always an occasion of joy, not unmingled with the tear that the heart could not keep back as the tokens of loving remembrance were brought to view. But this sketch, in its unfolding, must not linger too long within the magnetic circle of that purely household life; though a return to the chronological development of the work may seem somewhat abrupt.

The progress of the work among the Indians at Odanah is indicated in the following extract from a letter[1] of Mr. Wheeler's to his father. * "We have had a very good season here this year. The Indians have gathered quite a crop of corn this fall and their potatoes will be good. This people are making sure progress in civilization, and, during the spring and summer, more attended the meetings than at any other time since we have been here, and our school also has been better attended. But what will be the result of all our labor here yet, we can not tell. One thing to our minds is certain, that the gospel is the only thing that will ever save this people even for time. I am fully convinced that they will be civilized only in proportion as they are brought under the influences of religion. We feel that the present is a most critical time with the Indians in this vicinity. The laws of the state are such that any Indian who adopts the habits of civilized life, can become a citizen. And as the gospel is that alone which will make any fundamental change in their habits, we feel that a great weight of responsibility rests upon us, to do what we can to interpose this saving influence between them and annihilation; and what we do must be done quickly."

In the fall of 1850, Mrs. Wheeler with the children returned, for the first time since marriage, to her Lowell home. She not only needed the change and rest, but wished to give her children the advantage of a winter's schooling in a thriving city. The opportunity was well improved, and all returned to Odanah the following summer. At once Mrs. Wheeler entered upon the work that, for the few months of her absence, had been intermitted. It was gratifying to note evidences of advancement on the part of the Indians. One by one they forsook their wigwams and began to establish themselves in more permanent dwellings, to cultivate larger tracts of land, to send their children to school more freely, and in many ways to adopt the white man's methods. But the

---

[1] Dated at Bad River, September 28th, 1848.

missionaries felt more than ever that gospel motives should be the basis of this upward movement in the lives of the Indians. In a letter written at this time, Mr. Wheeler gives expression to this feeling: "We are becoming more thoroughly convinced that, if this people are ever saved for time as well as eternity, it must be through the instrumentality of a preached gospel. No radical changes can be expected, even in their mode of life, except they be made upon a gospel basis. Civilizing influences only, do not go deep enough. Not even schools or boarding-schools should be sustained at the expense of the direct preaching of the gospel; though they are both [to be] desired when both can go together." Again he writes: "Those children who are most regular at school are most constant in their attendance upon our meetings. The parents of these children, too, are among our most constant hearers on the Sabbath, and thus our school becomes a door of entrance to the sanctuary." A more extended extract from a letter[1] to his father, details some interesting phases of the work: "We have had a very pleasant winter thus far. The snow is not over two feet deep. We rarely have more than three feet of snow in this region, though back on the hills it is from five to six. Our Indians received their payment again last fall at La Pointe,[2] in goods and money. There is a prospect that they will be permitted permanently to remain here, and have their farmer, carpenter and blacksmith restored to them. The people feel quite encouraged. They are making great calculations about planting next spring, and we shall do all we can to aid them. There will be more Indians here than we have seen for years. Our people were never more quiet and orderly than now. There is no liquor among them. I have not seen an Indian drunk since last fall, and that was not here. They feel fully resolved to put away permanently the 'Ish-ko-da-wa-bo,' 'fire water.' I hope they will be as good as their word. Our meetings were never so well attended as this winter. Our school-house is full and some of them listen with serious attention. Miss Spooner also has a good school; much better than we have ever had before. We have a singing-school also once a week, attended by nearly all the children and youth of the place. The singing is mostly in Indian. They sing by rote, knowing nothing about the rules; but you would be pleased to see what fine voices some of them have. We have also a Sabbath school which embraces nearly all the young people of the place. So you see I have enough to occupy all my working hours, week days and Sabbaths. Our religious exercises are in Indian, which requires considerable labor and study to prepare for. We hope the season will not pass away without our seeing some fruit of our labor, some souls brought to a saving knowledge of the truth. There are a few cases of earnest religious enquiry. It would be our greatest source of joy, could we see some of these dark-minded ones coming to Christ for salvation. Our station needs much to be re-inforced. There is not a Christian brother to offer a prayer nearer than a hundred miles in any direction. No American family nearer than fifteen

---

[1] Dated at Bad River, January 31st, 1854.
[2] See page 169.

miles and but three of them within a hundred miles."

But "these dark-minded ones" had mortal bodies that needed redemption as well as minds to enlighten and souls to save, and so these two servants of God found that the medical side of their work was no small tax upon their sympathies and strength. A meager set of dentist's instruments, a medicine chest well filled, a pocket leather-case of surgical instruments, and a small magnetic battery, comprised the equipment for this branch of the work. The unenlightened aboriginal mind naturally invested them with magical powers. But this soon gave way before the subtler magic of sympathizing hearts, pouring the oil and wine of self-sacrificing love into lives whose very helplessness constituted the strong appeal; "For I was an hungred, and ye gave me meat: I was thirsty, and ye gave me drink: I was a stranger, and ye took me in naked and ye clothed me: I was sick, and ye visited me: I was in prison, and ye came unto me." During the early spring of 1854, the epidemic of small pox swept the reservation. Two Frenchmen from St. Paul had brought the contagion to Madelaine island, where many were exposed before the nature of the disease was known. Mr. Wheeler, however, was sent for, and promptly vaccinated every inhabitant of La Pointe. Returning to the reservation, he found the epidemic had preceded him and the Indians in a state of panic in consequence. Vigorous measures were necessary, and carefully complied with, on the part of the people. It was a trying ordeal for the two missionaries. The little daughter Julia, in a letter to her grandparents, uses this language: "Mother would write you if she had time to do so. She has to work very hard, and sits up at night to sew. The small pox is at L. P. [La Pointe] and yesterday father vaccinated the Indians till he was faint, and then mother vaccinated a while." A month later Mrs. Wheeler writes her parents, under date of March 6th, 1854: "I had intended to write you and several other Lowell friends long letters by this mail, but the past fortnight has been one of peculiar trial and anxiety to us. We have passed through all the horrors of the small pox. A fortnight ago, a company of Indians came here from across the lake in a state of the greatest excitement and alarm. Three or four of their number had been taken down with the small pox: these they had left behind. Mr. Wheeler immediately vaccinated all of them, but the next day two more were taken down. Mr. Wheeler fitted up a house and put them into it, and hired a Frenchman and his wife, who had had the disease, to take care of them. The next day there were three others brought down. One of them had the most virulent kind; the confluent small pox, and died in about a week after he was taken. The others are all recovering, and we think will be able to be out this week. We have all been much exposed, particularly Mr. Wheeler, as he visited the patients almost every day. We have used every preventive in our power. I smoked Mr. Wheeler most thoroughly, I can assure you, every time after coming from the hospital; and every time before he went in, he tied up his face and put a rag round, wet with the chloride of lime. The families that have been exposed, have been kept entirely separate from the others. Vaccination has taken well everywhere, and we hope the disease is arrested. We are all in the hands of our Heavenly Father, and here we feel we are safe. We do find it good to trust in the Lord." The usual routine of school and church work was necessarily intermitted for the time. In writing home of the matter, Mrs. Wheeler says: " We have dismissed our schools, and shall have no meetings for the present. Mr. Wheeler advised the Indians not to visit from house to house, but to remain quietly at home. It has seemed very lonely here to-day, no one moving about. The people acquiesce very cheerfully in any regulation Mr. Wheeler proposes. One man told me yesterday that the Indians had given their bodies to Mr. Wheeler. They trust in him, and anything he told them to do they should do." All the ill effects of this period of epidemic were soon overcome, and work resumed again in its normal order. The lessons of this visitation were full of significance to the Indians. It helped to reveal to them unmistakably the character of missionary effort in their behalf. It melted the cold reserve that excluded the gospel and opened their hearts more than ever to Christian influences. From the sanitary standpoint much was taught them which served its purpose in averting any repetition of such an experience.

Many incidents of interest might be cited from this medical branch of the work, as showing the versatility requisite to meet emergencies of frequent recurrence. One case will serve as illustrative of this feature of compulsory readiness on the part of the missionary to meet the unexpected in his work. The head chief, while off the reservation, had yielded to liquor and in a drunken brawl, had received, in the fleshy part of the leg, an ugly gash six inches long that laid bare the bone. In this condition he remained for two days on the sands of Chequamegon Point, under the stupor of the accursed "fire water." On the third day he was brought to his home at Odanah and the help of the Mission summoned. Mr. Wheeler was away, and there was no other alternative but for Mrs. Wheeler to respond to the call. She found the chief in much pain and discomfort, but very humble. An examination of the wound disclosed a condition of things from which she instinctively shrank, and yet taxed her sympathies to the utmost. The sand, with neglect and hot summer weather, had contributed very materially to the repulsiveness of the task of dressing such a wound. A thorough cleansing was the first process. The gaping edges were then brought together as closely as possible with long strips of adhesive plaster. It taxed to the limit all the strength and courage she could command, to push the surgeon's needle through the toughened cuticle and make secure the stitches that had to be taken. A liberal anointing of fur balsam was next applied, and the necessary bandaging to keep all in place completed the dressing. In three weeks the chief was about as usual; but just prior to the next occasion that called him from the reservation, he came to Mr. Wheeler to borrow his hat which, he said, would keep off the evil spirit. It would be more accurate to infer that, as there had never been a "brick in that hat," its efficacy to protect the wearer against bad spirits would be more apparent.

It was in these, as well as other ways, that Mrs. Wheeler exhibited remarkable powers of endurance. In a letter to friends, Mr. Wheeler writes: "Harriet is truly a wonderful woman. With an amount of care and toil which would crush an ordinary woman, she somehow makes her way through it. But she has a wonderfully elastic constitution." And yet the constant over-straining of that "elastic constitution" made serious inroads on her health and, under date of July 2nd, 1858, Mrs. Wheeler writes her parents: "My health during the last year has been very miserable. Last fall and winter I had two attacks of congestion of the lungs; and I have not yet fully recovered from the effects of them. I was very much disappointed in not being able to visit home last fall; but my health was such that it was impossible to get there. You have, doubtless, thought it very strange that I did not write you; but I am sure, could you see how I am situated, you would feel that I am excusable. I find enough to do to consume three times the amount of time and strength I have, and I am obliged to leave undone many things which seem absolutely necessary to be done. My children suffered much last fall for the want of suitable clothing; and when I was able to work, I worked day and night. Twelve, and sometimes one o'clock at night, still found me plying my needle. About the middle of February I took a severe cold which settled on my lungs, and for three weeks I could not speak a loud word and, for as many more, only with the greatest difficulty. I have now a little daughter three months old. Physicians still tell me, that if I wish to live, I must leave here. The Prudential Committee at Boston have given me leave to visit the states, and Mr. Clark, one of the district agents of the Board, who is now on a visit to us, says I must go by all means, as soon as it is safe to leave here." Acting under these instructions, Mrs. Wheeler and her children left the mission early in September, to spend the winter in Lowell. Mr. Wheeler accompanied his family as far as Detroit, where they attended the annual meeting of the American Board, and then on to Cleveland, where the two older children at school were to join the mother in the trip to the East.

From Cleveland Mr. Wheeler returned to Odanah to superintend the completion of the buildings of the manual labor training-school, which care he found it necessary to carry in addition to his usual duties. Mrs. Wheeler, in the letter just quoted from, writes of the matter as follows: "We are now in the midst of the care, labor and anxiety of erecting buildings for our boarding-school operation. Our school house is most finished, and the boarding-house will be commenced in a few days. This is a great addition to Mr. Wheeler's cares and labors, and I sometimes feel he will sink under it. Under these circumstances it is very trying for me to leave him here alone. Pray much for us, my dear parents, that we may be guided by infinite wisdom, and that as our day is, so our strength may be." Aside from his Sabbath day ministrations, which comprised two, and sometimes three services, his daily rounds through the dwellings of the settlement to read and expound the Scriptures and visit the sick, necessarily took much of his time.

Early in the year 1859, Mr. Wheeler learned that the government was planning to open for sale the Red Cliff and La Pointe portions of the Indian reservation, through a misconception of the intimate relation these localities sustained to the Odanah reserve, and so not appreciating the effect such ill-advised action would have on all the Indians of that region. It had also come to his knowledge that the Lac Court Oreilles reserve, of three townships, was to be subdivided and offered for sale, without making provision for another locality for those Indians. These, with other matters relating to the welfare of the Odanah Indians, made it necessary for him to go to Washington at once. With an Indian guide he set out in the depth of winter, through the woods as far as Chippewa Falls. The exposure and hardship incident to this initial stage of the journey were very trying. But immediate action and personal representation at Washington in behalf of the Indians, were essential. While on his way, he writes from Oberlin, Ohio, under date of March 12th, 1859, to Mrs. Wheeler at Lowell:

"I wish to leave by the middle of the week, but must come East by way of Washington. Business affecting the welfare of our Indians and that of the Lac Court Oreilles Indians, concerning their reserve, require the prompt attention of the department. The whole of the Lac Court Oreilles reserve, three townships, has been recently subdivided, and, by proclamation of the President, is to be offered for sale. I called at the land-office at Eau Claire on my way down, and found that no instructions had been left at the office to reserve any land for the Indians. Mr. Fitch [of the Michigan agency] had instructions from the department to locate this reserve, but neglected to do so. I noted down the townships, covering the land the Indians want, while at the land-office. Mr. Fitch gives me a letter recommending these townships to be withheld from sale. The object is to get an order from the Indian department to the land-office at Eau Claire, to respect the Indian reserve, and all will be right. One hundred thousand acres is too much for the Indians to lose. Other matters require attention, affecting the interests of our people and the Indians at Lac du Flambeau." A further quotation from a letter[1] to Mrs. Wheeler indicates a favorable consideration of the object of his mission to the capital: "I attended an interesting prayer-meeting this morning, where something like a dozen clergymen, of different denominations, for the most part conducted the devotions. Saw my old friend, now Dr. Sunderland, a warm-hearted Christian and earnest preacher of the gospel. He went with me to see the commissioner [of Indian affairs]. To-day has been a day of progress with me in Indian matters. I have had a very free talk with Mr. Mix, and he is disposed to look carefully into the affairs of our Indians and see that some of the promises made our people by different agents, are fulfilled. But we could not finish our business to-day. He wishes me to call again to-morrow morning. I shall think the day well spent, if we can make as much progress as we have to-day. Let us have patience then."

---

[1] Dated at Washington, D. C., March 23rd, 1859.

After bringing his business at Washington to a satisfactory conclusion, he joined his family at Lowell, very much worn with the multiplicity of his cares. A two weeks' rest was the utmost limit of time he felt he could allow himself, before undertaking the return journey with his family to the mission field. They arrived at Odanah early in May. Two weeks after, Mr. Wheeler was taken with hemorrhage of the lungs, and for weeks his life was despaired of. In a letter[1] to her parents, Mrs. Wheeler writes of his critical condition: "He told me last night that he felt he was standing on the verge of the dark valley, ready to go down into it, or to return to life just as the Great Master should see best. I feel exceedingly anxious about him. It seems as if he could not be spared from his family now; and our poor people — what will they do without him? They express a great deal of sympathy and anxiety. Some of them say they can not sleep, for they feel as if their father was to be taken away from them. Others, as they take my hand, exclaim: 'Oh, surely trouble has come to us now.' * * I have admitted a few to see him and they invariably thank the Great Spirit for permitting them to see him again." Mrs. Wheeler also writes of the many kindly services of the white friends at Ashland and Bay City. With the return of warmer weather, Mr. Wheeler's strength rallied somewhat. His physician warned him, however, that he must discontinue preaching if he hoped at all to regain any measure of health. But the missionary could not let go the work, into which his heart's life and faith had gone so deeply; and he decided to remain at his post, though under ever narrowing limitation of strength. The burden of responsibility rested each year more heavily on Mrs. Wheeler. While the work of the mission was carried on as usual, she was untiring in tender care of her husband, cheering him with the companionship of her sunny heart; but the shadow of wasting consumption was creeping on apace. In the fall of 1866, the physician told them that Mr. Wheeler could not survive the winter at Odanah. Removal was imperative, and providential indications seemed to point out Beloit as their future home. This sketch can not dwell on the sad details of the breaking up of that mission home and of the sundering of ties that had taken deep root there.

On the morning of departure, the baptism of a child of Christian Indian parents, in the dining-hall of the boarding-school, was the impressive close of a missionary service of twenty-five years. When the family reached the bank of the river, where the mission sail-boat was awaiting them, they found the entire village gathered to bid them farewell. It was the language of the heart that spoke in tears as the boat bore from their sight forever, their counselor and trusted friend of a quarter of a century. In touching incident, it was not unlike that historic leave-taking set forth in such tender simplicity in the closing verses of the twentieth chapter of the Acts.

That first winter in Beloit was memorable for the untried responsibilities it brought to the mother of that household. With limited means of subsistence,

---

[1] Dated at Odanah, June 24th, 1859.

the courage of faith was taxed daily to meet the problems involved in the care
of a stricken husband and the providing, in a large measure, for the necessities
of eight children. It was an experience requiring a rare degree of Christian
fortitude, and yet one made the more memorable by the love and helpfulness
of new-found friends. And thus were the tendrils of new friendships rooted
in the soil of apparent adversity. The faith of the true believer is ever finding its fruitage in a new hope. And so did this first winter of trial of faith at
length merge into the spring-time of fresh hopefulness. Mr. Wheeler's health
seemed to improve and, as strength returned, he devoted his time to the further
working out of a new principle as applied to windmills, which, in its cruder
form, had already been put to practical test on mission ground. His cousin,
Samuel Chipman, Esq., of Warsaw, Indiana, visited him at this time, and was
deeply interested in the new principle for regulating windmills. He encouraged Mr. Wheeler to work out the necessary drawings and model for the patent
office. This was done and, with the financial aid generously contributed by
Mr. Chipman, the patent was granted September 10th. 1867. Under date of
January 23rd, 1868, Mr. Wheeler writes his father, now well on in years, and
still at the old Vermont homestead: "I do not regret coming to this place.
We find many kind friends here, and society is all that could be desired. We
have a snug little home, which makes us quite comfortable this winter weather.
I got no bees as I expected last spring; as my windmill has fully occupied
my time, and may take me away from home much for the next few months,
if health will permit me to travel. You will like to know, perhaps, how I
succeeded with the mill. I have spent a good deal of time on it, experiment-
ing and getting it into good shape. It now suits, so far as the general plan of
it is concerned. Two points have especially engaged my attention: 1: To
get the mill so as to run nicely. 2: To simplify and improve the construction of it, so that it will be strong and cheaply built. I have, as yet, put up
but two hundred-dollar mills, both of which drive pumps in wells fifty feet
deep, and give good satisfaction. Practical mechanics and machinists are much
pleased with it.—it is so simple in its construction and accomplishes such important ends. It is self-regulating and will take care of itself in any wind,
however gusty and strong it may blow. For deep wells on our prairies to raise
water for watering stock, it is a mill, we think, which will be much wanted. It
is not yet remunerative, the balance has been out of pocket thus far, but I hope
the scale will turn it my favor before long. I suffer, as many inventors do, in
not having the means to bring it rapidly into notice. But, as in every new thing,
we must be contented to move slowly and wait patiently for results. The mill
in its present form, is used only to work pumps. I hope soon to get up another
form for driving machinery. I feel quite confident I can get one up in a shape
that will give better satisfaction than anything now out, though it must be confessed there are not a few difficulties in the way. So you see I continue to
keep busy, and, having something of the versatility common to the Yankees, if
I can not do one thing I turn my hand to another. I shall never be able to

preach any more, but if I can get up a useful mill and provide for the wants of my family, one part of the end of life will be answered."

In the mind of the inventor, as well as in that of Mrs. Wheeler, the evolution of the "Eclipse" wind-mill was held to be in the direct line of their faith and as much the outcome of that same missionary spirit and effort as was the fruitage of their labors among the Indians. Five years of life were left Mr. Wheeler in which to lay the foundations for a new business. In the early winter of 1871, he was again prostrated with hemorrhage and, after a lingering illness, the gentle spirit of this most patient sufferer was called home Sunday evening, February 25th, 1872. This sketch does not attempt to portray the character of Leonard Hemenway Wheeler; a man strong in his convictions of right, but not obtrusive, one who combined Christian gentility with sanctified tact. The funeral discourse, by his pastor, Rev. George Bushnell, was sympathetic and responsive to all the traits of that character which were justly and beautifully summed up in his text: "Behold an Israelite indeed, in whom is no guile."

This stroke of bereavement pressed with almost crushing weight upon Mrs. Wheeler. In a letter to her father two days before his death, she writes: "My dear father, I fear my precious husband is going rapidly down to the grave. Pray for us. Pray that he may be sustained to the last; and that he may be spared protracted suffering. It seems to me I can not bear to see him suffer. I can not tell you how dark and desolate the future looks to me without him. But I know the Lord can make it all light." She kept the letter till Monday morning, when these few lines were added:

"My dear father, brother and sisters: My precious husband has gone home to his rest. He died last night at nine o'clock. Will be buried Wednesday. Pray for us." She took this cup of affliction as from her Master.

Again, in September of 1873, was Mrs. Wheeler's heart stricken;—this time in the death of her eldest daughter, Julia. In a letter to her father under date of November 6th, 1873, she writes: "I found after all was over and sister Hannah had left me, I was completely prostrated. I was very weak and a little exertion would bring on trembling and palpitation of the heart. I have been passing through the deep waters, my dear father. You have doubtless heard before this something about Julia's death. She died very suddenly at last. We thought she would live until cold weather. She failed very rapidly after her return. She seemed to make a great effort to keep about until she could get home. She had no wish or expectation of getting well for three months before she died. She said to me that her only hope of salvation was that Jesus had died for her. She frequently asked us to read to her the 53rd chapter of Isaiah and the hymn 'Just as I am without one plea.' She said to me one day that it seemed to her that this hymn expressed the whole gospel.

"I have hope that she is now at rest with her dear father in the better land. Oh, my dear father, I can not tell you what a comfort it is to me, in my bereavements and loneliness, to feel that they are at rest. Earth seems so changed to me, and heaven *so much nearer.*"

It would seem not inappropriate to the purpose of this memorial that some further account of this daughter Julia be given at this point. She was possessed of a gifted mind, precocious in her studies and an omniverous reader. None of the books at the mission escaped her, not excepting Neander's church history and some bulky volumes in theology. At seventeen, she was teaching in the public schools of Houghton, Michigan, where she found opportunity, in a family of culture, of still further enlarging her acquaintance with books. She had marked literary instincts and recognized ability as a writer. She contributed a series of sketches on "Early Protestant Missions on Lake Superior," to the Lake Superior *Miner*, over the signature "Kitche-gume-wekwa" (Lady of the Great Lake), a name her Indian friends had given her. It was natural that she should soon come to have a deep interest in the welfare of the Indians, the sense of justice being a marked part of her strongly developed moral nature. As she became familiar with his character and acquainted with the wrongs he suffered at the hands of unscrupulous whites, she championed the cause of the red man with the intensity of infatuation. She wrote about it and addressed Christian audiences in its behalf. She took up the matter by correspondence with Senator Sumner who was interested to the degree of seeking further suggestions and of engaging the attention of Judge Doolittle, chairman of the committee on judicial affairs, with whom she subsequently corresponded. Senator Sumner's first letter is given in full, since it touches the core of the difficulty, as it then existed:

SENATE CHAMBER, JAN. 18th, 1865.

"I hasten to acknowledge your letter of January 13th. The condition of our Indian tribes has always caused me solicitude. The difficulty seems to me to be not so much in the system as in the men who are employed to carry it out. The same spirit animating its agents, no system could succeed, and the problem is to find men who, coming from the West, and familiar with Indian character and habits, are at once honest, unprejudiced and willing to work for the small compensation which the government can offer. Even if such men could be found, it is not easy for the appointing power to discriminate between honest men and well recommended rogues; and once appointed, there are great difficulties in detecting fraud, especially as the feeling of the border population upon the subject of the Indians is far from just. I shall be glad of any suggestions you may be able to give me. Accept my best wishes and believe me
Faithfully yours,
CHARLES SUMNER."

While the direct outcome of her effort may not have been apparent at the time, in any immediate and favorable bearing upon the Indians, it may have had some weight in subsequently shaping the so-called peace policy of President Grant, as carried out in the department of Indian affairs.

Mrs. Wheeler was wont to think of her life as divided into periods of twenty-five years. The first quadrant of this life-circle arched itself over the days of girlhood and young womanhood passed under the home roof at Lowell, Massachusetts. One base limb of this bow of promise rested on the date of her birth, December 4th, 1816, and the other upon the date that closed the period culminating in marriage, April 26th, 1841. The second period was spanned by the shining arc of twenty-five years of consecrated missionary service among the Ojibway Indians of Lake Superior, from 1841 to 1866. The third quarter of the circle bent its strong bow over varied experiences and successful activities that witnessed the firm establishment of a large manufacturing business at Beloit. She made no note of the fact that five years more than the alloted "three score years and ten" of life had already passed over her; but her always young and hopeful spirit looked to the future with expectancy. Over what enterprise for Christ would the last quadrant of the circle of this charmed life, arch the halo of its benediction?

Early in 1890, her son, Rev. E. P. Wheeler, was called to the pastorate of the First Congregational church of Ashland, Wisconsin.

He recognized in the call an opportunity to take up some phases of the work so reluctantly laid down by the father, and to link the history of past service with a renewed effort toward larger things for the larger community to which he might minister. At the same time, it gave opportunity to enter again the gospel ministry, from which broken health had compelled him to withdraw for a time. While he felt drawn to the field by every consideration of past associations that had become historic, and especially constrained also by the evident extremity of the church extending the call, yet he felt that the mother's counsel must determine his final decision. Without disclosing his own feelings in the matter, he sought her advice. As was her wont, she canvassed the whole question before God in most earnest prayer; and, when, on certain Sunday evening, he asked to know the conclusion she had reached, she told him she thought the call to go to Ashland was from above. On the following Monday morning, he telegraphed the committee his acceptance. The prayer of the mother preceded him as he went to take up the work, nor, while life remained, did her prayers cease for that work, which, under the brooding of the Spirit, she saw develop and expand in new and unexpected directions.

It is not within the limitations of this sketch to follow in detail the growth of these new phases of the work referred to, which seemed the direct outcome of the acceptance of that call. As the work unfolded, Mr. Wheeler felt more and more the significance of the early missionary labors in those regions, especially in their relation to the mission he was sent to fulfill. The rapid movement of events could not but deepen the impression that, under Providence, he had, in an important sense, "entered into their labors." He found a growing interest among Christians generally, and especially among Congregationalists, in all that pertained to the history of those early mission days.

This newly awakened interest centered locally in the old church and mission-house still standing on Madeleine island. These stirrings of the old faith in new hearts, crystallized in the organization of the Lake Superior Congregational club. The question of Christian education as an evangelizing agent for North Wisconsin, was also in the air of these latter days of new beginnings. This aspiration and prayer, in the hearts of a few, soon took on the significance of a movement culminating in the conference at Pratt, Wisconsin, in July, 1891. In its deliberations were represented the clergy and prominent Christian laity of North Wisconsin, and leading Christian educators from other parts of the state and Minnesota. Their counsels resulted in the incorporation of the North Wisconsin academy, and this action was subsequently endorsed by the Winnebago convention of the Congregational body.

The new academy enterprise, to stand for the higher ideals of Christian education, readily gathered to itself the support of all the Christian element as well as the encouragement of all those not professedly Christian who yet appreciated the value of having such an institution in their community. Prominent citizens of Ashland, by liberal offers of land for a site and generous pledges to the subscription list for necessary buildings, secured the location of the academy to their city. It is fitting, in connection with this movement, to mention the name of Dr. Edwin Ellis, the old-time friend and helper of missionary days. The academy from the beginning was much in the heart and prayer of Mrs. Wheeler. It seemed to take up again the scarlet thread of promise that had run through the texture of those former days of consecration to Christ's kingdom in North Wisconsin.

In June of 1892, she received an invitation from the Lake Superior Congregational club to be present at exercises to be held on Madeleine island and at Ashland commemorative in part of the work of early Protestant missions on the island, and in part to give "local habitation and a name" to the academy movement in the laying of its corner-stone at Ashland. It was a great joy to Mrs. Wheeler to be able to accept the invitation and recognize in what she subsequently saw and heard, the good hand of the Lord in it all. By courtesy of Rev. J. N. Davidson, the following extracts are from his notes made at the time. "For years the old church at La Pointe stood unused and desolate. As it was but a few feet from the lake, it was at a latter time degraded by becoming a shelter for the building of boats. From this fate it was rescued by one who had received part of his early religious training within its walls, Rev. Edward Payson Wheeler; then Congregational bishop of Ashland. Having obtained possession of the old church, he formally presented the title deed thereof to Mr. Eugene Arthur Shores, as trustee of the Lake Superior Congregational club. This was on Tuesday, July 12th, 1892. The exercises took place in a tent used by General Missionary George W. Nelson in his evangelistic work in the new villages of Northern Wisconsin. The tent was spread between the church and the lake. Among those present was the gracious woman, who, fifty-one years before had come to those shores as a bride. Beloit college and

Carleton were represented, and there was attendance also from Chicago and Milwaukee. From the old Bible presented to the mission by Mr. L. M. Warren, and bearing in his handwriting the date, 'July 10th, 1834,' Rev. T. G. Grassie, secretary of the Wisconsin Home Missionary society, read the ninetieth psalm. There followed the statement of some facts relating to the early history of the mission and the work therein of Mr. and Mrs. Wheeler. Secretary Joseph E. Roy showed how missionary service done for the Indians, had blessed in every way this whole nation. A Scripture lesson in the Ojibway language was read by Rev. John Clark. Then followed, as already mentioned, the formal transfer of the church property. The reverent voice, active mind and tender heart of our beloved Professor Blaisdell led in the memorial prayer. The day closed with an address on the 'Pilgrim Faith' by Rev. Judson Titsworth of Milwaukee.

"Fittingly July 13th was called Educational Day. Ex-President Merrell of Ripon college and Professor A. H. Pearson of Carleton, spoke of different aspects of Christian education. A party visited the old mission-house wherein Pastor Wheeler was born. Others sought the site of the old "Fort." A delegation of Ojibways from Odanah came again to the place where their fathers had been taught the lessons of the gospel. On this day also, there was organized, in the old church, the North Wisconsin Home Missionary society.

"Not formally connected with the history either of the mission or of the Ojibways, but in very truth with that of both, came, at Ashland, on Thursday, July 14th, 1892, the laying of the corner stone of the North Wisconsin academy."

The following extracts from a letter written at Ashland at this time by Mrs. Wheeler, to the home at Beloit, show her deep interest in the occasion: "We reached here after a tedious trip Saturday at ten o'clock and have been in one whirl ever since. The two days of conference closed yesterday, and such days! Edward's hopes and expectations have been more than realized. Crowds have attended and the papers that have been read have been remarkable papers. Dr. Roy's paper made a very deep impression. I can give you no idea of it till I see you. I hope it will be published. The weather has been perfect. Had it been ordered for the occasion it could not have been improved. How I wish I could give you all a picture of the day, as the boats moved out with band playing, flags floating in the breeze and loaded down to the gunwale with a happy, enthusiastic crowd. The wind was strong enough to ripple the water thoroughly but not enough to make us seasick. Professors Blaisdell and Burr enjoyed it to the full. I shall not attempt to tell you about the meetings on the island until I see you.

"July 15th. I supposed we had had our best things at the island, but the interest culminated yesterday at the laying of the corner-stone of the academy. I send you a programme. Professor Blaisdell outdid himself. He made a most profound impression. I think the citizens of Ashland will not soon forget him."

The occasion, as a whole as well as in all its details, was one of rare significance to Mrs. Wheeler. The old enthusiasms thrilled her soul as the story of those morning days of missionary consecration was rehearsed. Her lively imagination again recalled the old scenes and lived over the old experiences. The old faces and old fellowships came again to a memory that made no account of the half century that had passed away. So were her spiritual eyes lifted up unto the hills of God.

The remaining days of this memorable summer of 1892 Mrs. Wheeler spent at Ashland and vicinity, greeting again the narrowing circle of old friends that had grown more dear to her as time passed. She revisited Odanah, the Indian mission with the founding and growth of which her prayer and life were so intimately associated.

With what tender regard did the heart of those Indians flow out to her, their old-time teacher and helper. How they clung to her and drank in every word she had for them. With the pathos of genuineness did they call to mind the old days memorable with the many-sided helpfulness of her own life and effort in their behalf. "Now when we are sick," they would tell her, "there is none to help as you did, and we die." While at the mission, it was a joy to her to visit once more the man who had been the faithful interpreter and assistant pastor for Mr. Wheeler during all the years of his ministry to that people, — Rev. Henry Blatchford, subsequently ordained as pastor by the presbytery and still ministering to the Indians in spiritual things. For fifty-three years has he witnessed for Christ among his people and the evening twilight of his days finds his life molded into a character that will endure.

In the early autumn Mrs. Wheeler returned to the home at Beloit with much improved health and buoyancy of spirit. For a number of years previous she had not known what it was to go through a winter entirely free from any illness that required a physician's care. During the winter of 1892 and 1893, following her return, she, however, enjoyed exceptionally good health. With renewed interest and love, she took up again the thread of household affairs and felt again the enriching influences of all those fellowships with neighbors and friends and of that which came through the activities of the church, all of which, in their combined effect, made her so appreciative of such privileges. Her affection for the old church had deepened under the pulpit and parish ministrations of her beloved pastor, Rev. Cyrus Hamlin, for whom she had the highest esteem. Thus environed she felt herself still a child of the covenant, one to whom the promises of a loving Father had been fulfilled. "At evening time there shall be light." She had already lived a long and serviceable life, whether the time be measured by the flight of years, or by the deeds that were the fruitage of a consuming zeal for good works.

The spring and summer of 1893 found her health very variable, culminating in the winter of the same year in a severe attack of *la grippe*. So prostrating and prolonged was this illness that she at times felt she could never rally from it. The spring of 1894 brought her the courage to undertake a visit to her son and family in Chicago in the hope that the change might prove beneficial. Though every effort was made to relieve her of all burden and to surround her with all that ministering love might suggest, her stay, thoroughly enjoyed as far as strength permitted, served to reveal how broken was her strength. On her return it was a source of regret to her, to which she gave expression at different times, that extreme prostration made it impossible to call on dear friends, in Chicago, whom she felt she would not see again in the earthly life. Her constitution was of that responsive type that quickly regains its balance when recovery has once set in. But, in this instance, vitality was so slow in asserting itself that her physician felt she must have the tonic of a more invigorating air than prevailed at Beloit during the summer months, in order, if possible, to regain lost ground before entering another winter. She knew what the oxygen of Lake Superior air had done for her depleted strength in other days, and it was thought best that she spend three months or more at Ashland, Madeleine island and vicinity. It was originally planned that she should leave for the north July 1st, but she could not bear the thought of thus missing the intended visit of the two grandchildren, who with their father and his recent bride were to spend the 4th of July at the old home. The departure was accordingly postponed till the 10th. As the date approached, it occurred to the elder daughter, Mrs. Leonard, that a gathering of old neighbors and friends with a family reunion would be a very pleasant association for the mother to carry with her. The plan was no sooner conceived than put into effect. The thought was a happy one delightfully carried out. That evening of greetings, good fellowship overflowing in songs, the genial and happy mood of every one present, and then the farewells,— it surely was, not then revealed to any one of that dear circle that "Mother" Wheeler would never be greeted again save in the home on high.

On the afternoon of the 10th, in company with her daughter Hattie, the journey to Ashland was undertaken. Her son's home at Ashland was reached the day following. Though forest fires had been prevailing in the vicinity for some days and the smoke continued to shroud the city, intensifying the heated term through which it was passing, yet the nights were cool and the air of the tonic nature that induces sleep. Mrs. Wheeler gained strength from the first, and for two weeks enjoyed the sense of slowly returning health. The two weeks were also a time of rare blessing to her in that she was privileged again to meet with old friends and to receive the greetings and kindly attentions of many who loved her. Above all, was she glad to revisit once more the scenes and recall the memories of earlier days. In a letter home dated July 21st, 1894, she writes: "I have not been able to go on the lake yet, but hope to go this evening. Mr. Shores has a new steamboat, to be christened to-night. He has invited us all to be present and to go over to Bayfield on an excursion trip. Mrs. Shores very kindly offered to send her carriage if I would go." And then with the buoyancy of her always youthful spirit she speaks in the letter of the calls she had received, the invitations to pass the summer on Madeleine island, and the kindness of all. And so it seemed, from every human consideration, that Mrs. Wheeler was to pass a season under most favorable conditions for the regaining of lost strength. But the Father, in whose hands are the times and the seasons, had appointed otherwise.

The letter just referred to was received at Beloit on the 24th of July and on the evening of the 25th, occured the accident, as we say in our human way, through which the Lord who had given took again his own to himself. It was a very happy group of three that sat in a happy home, chatting of plans for the morrow. They were the mother, the daughter and the granddaughter, all of the same age in the lively interest manifested. The son, Rev. E. P. Wheeler, was not at home that evening. About nine o'clock, the youngest of the three counted the strokes of a fire-alarm and ran to the door with the remark that it meant their district. The other two followed and saw the burning building in a neighboring block in the direction of the woods. A short walk leads from the front steps, terminating in two steps down to the broad street-walk. After going down the front steps, the mother had apparently gone for a better view diagonally across the lawn and, at the edge of it, not appreciating at night the difference in level, fell forward upon the walk below. Loving helpers were at her side instantly only to hear her exclaim, "Oh, Hattie, I have broken my hip; send for Dr. Ellis at once." And then the prayer that she might be spared to her family. Next door neighbors, the family of Superintendent Grassie, rendered prompt assistance and the poor bruised body was tenderly borne into the house. Two physicians with a trained nurse soon arrived and a few moments later came Dr. Edwin Ellis, "the beloved physician" of mission days. As he took the hand of his old-time patient and life-long friend he managed to speak, as a physician, in a tone of confidence, warmly sympathetic and reassuring; but as he felt every nerve of that sensitive body quivering under the shock, the heart of the friend was wrung with agony. After all had been done that professional skill could suggest and the sufferer made as comfortable as possible, Dr. Ellis inquired of the family in a low tone, "How did this happen?" Before other reply could be made, Mrs. Wheeler spoke up quickly, "Oh, Doctor, this is all for the best. It is sent to teach some lesson. Some good will come of this."

Mrs. Wheeler lingered for three weeks, and much more than has already been written would fail in the attempt to set forth all the revealings of that heart in its expressions of love and thoughtfulness toward all who were privileged to be with her in those last days. To the attending physician and nurse the scene was an unusual exhibition of character. In the wanderings of fevered delirium her thought was always for others. How it would run out to the children and grandchildren, recalling their names and uttering some prayer for their welfare; and then she would fancy herself back in her own home imagining her family physician was attending her, and speaking of neighbors and friends. Her love for little children was expressed in a touching way at this time. Three little German children were indulging in childish prattle in the yard not far from the window of the sick chamber. The attendant at the bedside did not suppose she noticed the young voices; but presently she asked who they were. The attendant told her, and said that he would go and tell them to go home. She quickly replied "Oh no, I love to hear them."

As the days wore on the inherited vitality of an elastic constitution would, at intervals, assert itself in a way to inspire hope, and yet only for a brief time. Under date of August 11th, one of the sons writes home: "Our hopes of mother's getting better are again under a cloud. She has passed through a night of much agony; not continuous or she could not have survived. [Once], when pain was extreme, she repeated the two familiar lines:

'Jesus, lover of my soul,
Let me to thy bosom fly,'

putting the emphasis on the word 'let.' God's mercies, the kindnesses of friends, etc., are the ever recurring themes of her wandering talk; that is, outside her own family. * But I must tell you of what occurred yesterday in the early evening. It seems that in the afternoon, when mother seemed quiet and a little rested, Emily told her of the letter she had received from Mrs. Dustin and how the neighbors were all anxious to hear how she was getting along. Well, it made its impression on her mind, and as it began to wander again in the early evening, she was back home again with all the old friends and neighbors, and it seems thought she was entertaining them at supper in the old home. Edward came into the room,—I was already there,—and remarked, 'Mother, you look as bright as a dollar.' She replied 'Now, Edward, I know I must prink up a little,' and began to try to fix her hair. Her smile and look were so natural that Edward stooped down and kissed her. She looked up with a coy smile and said, 'O, I know what you mean; you are trying to make me think I do look well.' And then as Edward sat down in a chair beside me at the bedside, she thought we were all at the table, and said in her old sweet voice so full of sympathy, "Edward, will you ask the blessing?" This he did, and the blessing was expanded into a fervent petition for the suffering mother. When he had finished, she said, "Now turn the coffee, please," and then for half an hour or more, how radiant was her face with that 'light that never was on sea or land,' as she thought herself entertaining all her old neighbors. She began to greet this one and that one with her old-time warmth. Just then the nurse stepped into the room and mother thought it was another old neighbor and stretched out her hand with 'I'm so glad to see all my dear old friends again. I don't, just for the moment, recall your face, but all my good neighbors are welcome to my hearth and home.' Then she made an address to her neighbors recounting, 'how many good feasts of the heart we have had together and this last seems the best of all,' thanking them again and again for their many kindnesses to her and telling them how they had helped her along the different steps of the pathway of life, and closing with 'but Christ will help us all to take the last step into the glad morning land of the new life.' And then her heart's love overflowed in prayer for her 'dear neighbors.' She commended them all to her Saviour in most touching simplicity and heart-felt fervor. * It was such a spectacle of the soul conquering the pain-racked body. She was supremely happy and showed it in every line and feature of her dear face. Emily and Hattie stepped into the room just before mother finished and not hearing did not quite comprehend. But the nurse told them. 'O,' she said, 'I wish you could have heard the sweet prayer your mother made for her old neighbors.'

The day following the writing of this letter was the Sabbath, August 12th. The symptoms of final dissolution were marked; a morning and forenoon of much evident distress and restlessness of which the physician assured the family the sufferer was not conscious to any great degree. The final struggle of mortality had set in, reaching its climax in one triumphantly spoken "amen." It was the last word of one who had always unhesitatingly accepted the dealings of a heavenly Father as "yea and amen." As the morning wore toward noon, the daughters felt something might be given their mother to ally in some measure the expression of distress. The younger got the mother's attention and suggested an anodyne. She indicated assent and as soon as it was administered smiled back her gratitude, reached out her arms and drew to her lips the face of her child for the parting and final expression of a mother's love. And then every outward evidence of distress faded,—every muscle at rest, no further recognition or consciousness of things mortal, only the soft passing of that breath God had given. Thus all the hours of that Sabbath afternoon ebbed away and, as twilight came on, the peace and stillness of the scene in that chamber seemed only emphasized as the tones of the church bell called to evening service:

> "And in these ears till hearing dies,
>   One set slow bell will soon to toll
> The passing of the sweetest soul,
>   That ever looked with human eyes."

While the bell still tolled and the twilight deepened, that soul passed through the "valley of the shadow." And then the quiet dawn of eternal day broke over the pain-worn features, transfiguring every line of suffering and leaving on the whole face an expression of ineffable sweetness as of one who had conquered.

> "Life, we've been long together,
>   Through pleasant and through cloudy weather.
> 'Tis hard to part when friends are dear:
>   Perhaps 'twill cost a sigh, a tear:
> Then steal away, give little warning;
>   Choose thine own time:
> Say not good-night, but in some brighter clime
>   Bid me good-morning.

TRIBUTES.

MEMORIES OF THE HOME LIFE.

The early memories of my sister are very sweet to me. From earliest childhood, I remember two faces bending over me, filled with love, and tender solicitude; one was that of my mother, the other of sister Harriet. She was the eldest of a family of seven children,—I, the youngest; and mother used to say her *little* children had two mothers, for Harriet was always so loving and helpful to us all. And how devotedly we loved her in return!

I remember Sabbath days, when a sister, three years older than myself, and I were kept home from church and Sabbath-school by storm or illness. Harriet was always ready to stay with us, when it was possible for her to do so, and she would tell us stories from the Bible, or read to us; and then she would tell us how to be like Him, whom not having seen, she loved. In memory it is sacred still—the closet where she knelt—and prayed that our hearts might be filled with the blessed Spirit, and our young lives guided and controlled by Him.

Although I was young when she left us to enter upon her missionary life, I remember her work among the poor and needy in our city. She was frail in those early days, and was often laid aside for weeks, but as soon as she was able to take up her work again, it was done with the same earnestness as before. She taught for three or four years, and, after spending all the week in the school-room, Saturday found her going from house to house, among the needy, and her missionary life really began before she left her girlhood home. In the city, there was one street that was her greatest care. It was filled with the poor from other lands, and many would have been deterred from going there by fear; but, for a time, every week found her among those people, caring for the children, crooning over the babies, hushing them to sleep, or giving help to weary and sick mothers. When we had servants in the house, she was always interested in their welfare, and sought to lead them into a spiritual life.

After she had been from home seven or eight years, one Sabbath just as we were going out to church, to the afternoon service (which was always held in those days), we met a woman and two children at the door. She had been a washerwoman in the family years before. She asked, "Will you tell me where

I can find Miss Harriet's church? I promised her before she went away I would sometime go to her church and I have never been." We directed her to Appleton-street church, with which sister was so closely identified. She became interested in the service, and some one became interested in her. She took her children to the Sabbath school and after a few months united with the church herself in spite of opposition and persecution, for her life was imperiled, her Bible was stolen from her room, and she was publicly cursed, and excommunicated from the Catholic church. How many seeds of goodness sown in human hearts by our sister's loving thought, have ripened and born fruit to the honor of the Master will never be known, until the harvest time, when the secrets of all hearts shall be revealed.

But the time came when she was to go from us. The subject of missions lay very near her heart, and the great desire of her life was to go into the wider field of the world. We all knew her wishes, but their fulfilment seemed a long way off until Mr. Wheeler came so often from the seminary at Andover only ten miles distant. Then we realized that her desires were soon to be gratified. It was almost hard for my sister Hannah and me to love him, for his gain would be such a loss to us.

I remember so well that wedding day. A few intimate friends and the members of our own family were all that were present, and every one was keeping up a semblance of cheerfulness, but the shadow of departure would not be dispelled. She looked so sweet and lovely in her simple wedding attire, as she stood beside the tall handsome student, just from his studies, who was to lead her away from us. I watched every expression of her face with my poor little heart almost breaking, but when the minister bade them "join hands" it was too much for me, and a great sob broke the stillness of the room, but the dear sister struggled hard to keep her voice from faltering and to repress the tears that lay so near the surface.

Well, the wedding was over, and they left us for a few weeks of visiting with friends, after which they returned and made ready for their final departure. In these days of rapid and easy transit it would seem a light thing to travel from Massachusetts to Wisconsin, but it was not so then. One could go to India now with far less discomfort, than to travel the thousand miles they were undertaking.

But the day of parting came; breakfast was almost untasted, but it was over. Trunks and boxes were packed, waiting to be taken away, and we had all gathered in the parlor for the morning prayer. I can not recall the Scripture my father read, but I shall never forget the hymn we sang or tried to sing, "Ye Christian heroes go, proclaim." I seldom hear it now that it does not take me back to that morning with its tearful gathering, so long ago. It was a sad parting, and as the sound of the wheels that were bearing them away was lost in the distance, we returned to the house, each heart burdened with grief. How anxiously we watched for letters from her, and they came as often as the slow mails could bring them. She was happy in her new life, hopeful for the future and eager to commence her chosen work, only saddened by the thought of those she had left. There were always sweet words for the little ones, and loving counsel for us. We know something of the hardships and privations she endured, but we must add to them, home-sickness, more easily experienced than described. She said little about it, but in one of her letters to mother, she writes: "Send the children away from home, that they may become accustomed to being absent from the family circle before they leave it and suffer as I have done." But all was cheerfully borne for the love of Him whose life she sought to represent. She had her faults as we all have, but in my memory of her sweet home life there were none.

When I was asked to give some incidents in her early life, I was glad to pay a loving tribute to one so dear to me. The history of these later years is known to you all. With tears we have laid her down to rest and covered her grave with flowers. They will fade, but the memory in our hearts can never die. With her, "it is well."

GONE HOME.

Dear form so still, laid away from our sight,
    Dear lips to us closed evermore,
Dear hands,—they have ceased their service of love,
    Weary feet, they have entered heaven's door.
They shall go no more out to tread the worn path
    Of the world with its labor and strife;
They shall walk all unwearied the pavement of gold,
    And the strand of the "river of life."

I can see her now as at eventide.
    She sat with God's book in her hand,
Reading of Him she had chosen her Guide,
    And the home in the better land.
The far away look in her eyes I can see,
    As she pondered the old lessons o'er,
And silently offered the prayer of her heart
    That she might love her Saviour yet more.

But our hearts, how they ache with the thought that no more
    We shall hear the loved voice; and we weep,
Not for her who has gone, but for those who remain
    In tears the life vigil to keep.

But we pause mid our tears, would we call her back,
    Though her lips are silent and cold;
And we miss the kind word and loving caress
    And remember life's story is told?
Would we call back from her Father's side
    To battle with sorrow and sin?
To tread the life path with its light and shade!
    To be tempted without and within!

"Not my will," dear Jesus, "but thine," we ask,
    Yet we can not from heart depths say this,
Except on the cloud by our faith we can read:
    "The dear Lord doeth nothing amiss."

O teach us, dear Father, this lesson of trust,
    And may we forever abide
In the "secret place" overshadowed by Thee
    Who hast promised Thy children to hide,
There where folded hands tell of work that's all done,
    (The word of the Lord standeth sure).
"If I go, I will come and receive you myself,"
    No more cross, but the crown, evermore.

Mrs. C. F. Hardy,

Beloit, Wisconsin, September 13th 1894.

TRIBUTE OF MRS. AUGUSTA S. KENNEDY.

When we who know her so well looked at her frail physique, it seemed as if she must have been crushed beneath her load, but love and faith buoyed up her flagging health and carried her on. For the last few months, however, she has been very feeble and her one thought has been that she must have Lake Superior air or die.

How hard and mysterious it seems to us that she should have left her home and come here to meet her fate. Only two days before she had gone with a party to the christening of a steamer, and seemed as happy and delighted as any of the throng. Little did we think that it was to be her last time with us. Mercifully are the times and seasons hidden from our eyes. An alarm of fire being sounded, she rushed out in the quick way so natural to her but missed her footing and fell, to be picked up bruised and broken. For three long weeks she suffered physical torture, but whenever a gleam of consciousness shone upon her she lamented that she must be a trouble to others, entirely forgetting herself.

Attended by her devoted children she lay till Sunday night, August 12th, when, just as the gates of sunset shut out the dying day, the golden portals beyond swung open and our beloved friend passed through. Life's long, weary day ended. She bade good-night to the world, to wake in the arms of Him whose loving mercies she had so long trusted, and whom she had so faithfully served.

Truly a mother in Israel has fallen. Never till the books are made up at the end of time will she know of all good she has done.

The years of utter self-abnegation which have been hers are something wonderful when viewed in the light of these days when so much worldliness infuses itself into the best efforts.

From the east and the west, from the north and the south, will they rise up and call her blessed.

None were too lowly or too poor for her kind ministration. She did not give money alone but the pressure of the hand, the comforting word and the sympathetic tear which told so eloquently the burden was shared by her. After all, perhaps she would have chosen to die here, so near the place where her heart has always been. And in a conversation with her before the delirium came upon her she said to me, "It has always been my prayer that Dr. Ellis might be with me in my last sickness," and thus it came about.

When asked to write this notice I accepted the trust gladly as the last tribute I could pay to a loving friend, but my heart fails me when I think how feeble is my best effort to do justice to her memory.

Her words and deeds are her best monument. Her life was a constant praise-service and her death comes like the benediction that follows after prayer.

In our sorrow for our bereavement let us remember

"The strife is o'er, the battle done,
The victory of life is won.
The song of triumph is begun."

MRS. AUGUSTA S. KENNEDY.

LETTER AND POEM OF REV. H. G. McARTHUR.

FORT ATKINSON, WISCONSIN.
AUGUST 21ST, 1894.

MISS HATTIE WHEELER:

DEAR AND BEREAVED FRIEND: We learned with sorrow of the sore accident which befell your mother; and now, later, with deeper sorrow, of her death. It is difficult for us to realize that such is the fact,—that your mother and our much esteemed friend has passed into the shadow so impenetrable to human vision.

But more and more as we come to realize that she is gone, may we rise into that sweet, living faith which will enable us to feel that she has only passed from the lower to the higher; and that the same true and loving spirit is still moving on with a growing sanctified purpose and impulse toward that which is diviner and more blessed.

Mrs. McArthur joins me in expressions of heart sympathy to all the family in this, your great bereavement. And our thought and our prayer is that you all may be supported and comforted by Him who deems it best to chasten his children.

Very cordially yours,

H. G. McARTHUR.

IN MEMORIAM.

A mother in Israel, esteemed and beloved,
 Ever gracing the faith in which she moved;
So kind and so true, so pure and so good;
 So thoughtful and loving in motherhood;
So genuine her devotion to truth,
 So loyal to God from earliest youth;

With a Christly spirit within her breast
  So eager to serve to the very last,
Ready to sacrifice comfort and ease
  The needy to help, the Master to please;—
The mother, the saint and the trusted friend,—
  Alas! has reached earth's pilgrimage end.
But 'mid flowing tears we may well rejoice,
  Though gone from our sight, though hushed be her voice,
For in the Beyond what an infinite gain,
  What a deep soul-peace, what spiritual reign
. To the faithful one whose whole life below
  Seemed bathed with the light of a heavenly glow! [1]

[1] In a double sense this is a memorial of the dead. Mr. McArthur passed to the world above on the 20th of February, 1895.

LETTER OF MARY WARREN ENGLISH.

RED LAKE RESERVE, [MINNESOTA,]
NOVEMBER 4TH, 1894.

MY DEAR HATTIE: Your dear letter so full of the sad tidings of your sainted mother's death, reached me a few days since, and also the photographs;—and many thanks for the same. I said sad tidings, so it was to me, as I realized there will be no more meetings on earth between us, but oh what gain to her,— blessed rest now. The burden and worries of this life all left behind, which she has borne so long and alone, yet not alone—her God "was her very strength and refuge."

That is an excellent likeness of your mother, my eyes filled with tears as I gazed on that dear, sweet old face, for it brought to mind so many, many scenes of my earliest days, and of my girlhood when under her kind and motherly ca·e.

My first recollection of your father and mother dates from the very first hour they landed on La Pointe island. I was a little girl not five years old, and the first meeting happened in this way, (it seems like a dream to me now as I think of it but it is very vivid).

My brother William had been away to school and he was expected to return home on that same vessel which brought your parents to the island. My own parents were both away from home at the time and I was staying with my aunt Julia Defoe. As soon as the vessel landed, my aunt and myself started to find my brother, and we met him and your father and mother and Miss Abby Spooner walking up the sandy beach on their way from the "Old Company's Wharf" to the mission-house at "Middle Fort," as it was then called.

My brother knew us and after giving us a hearty greeting he turned around and introduced us to his companions, who also greeted us in a most friendly and kindly manner. I remember your mother more particularly and I thought "What a lovely lady! Such bright eyes, rosy cheeks, and curling hair each side of her face." And your father—I can well recall just how he appeared. His kindly voice as he said, "And this is little Mary," I shall never forget.

I have often thought that it was their pleasant and friendly ways and manners that made such a lasting impression even on the mind of a child and which has never faded away during the many long years that intervened since that hour, and it is just this very same cordial and friendly feeling they both possessed and exercised toward all with whom they came in contact in after years that made everybody their friend, and it is this which drew the Indians around them from the very first hour they came amongst them bearing the "glad tidings of peace" and kept them in friendship firm, steadfast to the very last hour that they parted from them twenty-five years afterward.

This was the true missionary spirit, full of good feeling and sympathy toward all with whom they had to do. I have never met their equal since, though I have lived in the Indian country all my life and have met many teachers in this midst but no one like them, not one.

That was a wonderful covenant of November 25th, 1841, and how well it has been kept even to the close of life. I have read it over several times and have been impressed by its purity and perfect faith. It has been a real lesson to me and it is my most earnest prayer that I may remain true and faithful to my profession, even like these dear departed friends whom God raised up for me, in years after, when I was left homeless, fatherless and motherless, and through their faithful teachings of Christian principles and with God's help I have been enabled to keep the faith, even in the most trying scenes and trials of later years.

MARY WARREN ENGLISH.

LETTER OF MRS. M. E. VAUGHN.

ASHLAND, WISCONSIN,
SEPTEMBER 28th, 1894.

MY DEAR MISS WHEELER: Nothing could have made me happier than your kind letter with the accompanying pictures and the covenant. How many pleasant associations these dear faces recall,—the happiest of my life. You can never, unless placed in similar circumstances, realize what your dear mother was to us strangers, who came to Lake Superior in those early years. I have often wondered how she, coming without any such greeting, ever endured the loneliness of the first few years. The dear Lord was very good to her to give her not only strength and patience for her own cares, but enough to spare for others. She was, to my mind, the best example of a perfect woman I ever saw,—and I am so thankful to you for sending me the photographs.

(Mrs.) M. E. VAUGHN.

LETTER OF PROFESSOR H. M. WHITNEY.

SALISBURY, WILTSHIRE, ENGLAND,
AUGUST 27TH, 1894.

MY DEAR EUGENE: I have just heard from my home of the death and burial of your honored and beloved mother, and, though far away, I will not wait to get home in order to bear my testimony to her worth. The testimony is all one way, as you had ample occasion to find out even before she was taken away.

You were all comparatively new in Beloit when we came there to live (in 1871), and it took me a good while to find you all out and to begin upon that substantial friendship that my wife and I so much rejoice in now. But your mother was alert with the kind word and deed toward us as well as toward others. And she always wanted the best things. Her memory is blessed. I never knew your father, but I shall always cherish my recollections of your mother. Give my warm sympathy, and indeed I may well say congratulations, to all your family circle. When the saints are gathered in fulness of years, it is a matter for joy that triumphs over grief.

Sincerely your friend,

H. M. WHITNEY.

LETTER OF MRS. ANNA S. ROGERS.

MY DEAR MISS HATTIE: Ever since the sad news of your dear mother's death reached me, I have been wanting to tell you, how much I sympathize with you and your family in your great sorrow. I can indeed sympathize with you, for I know the terrible sense of loneliness that comes from losing a dear parent. But what a comfort it is that these separations are only for a season, and what a help in our grief the assurance of the unspeakable gain to our dear ones. Though so far away from Beloit, I shall always cherish the deepest affection for my friends there; and your mother, the mother of "our neighborhood," always had a very warm place in my heart. Her loss comes to me very deeply. She was one of those women who are a help and inspiration to all about them,—always doing good, always a kind word for every one. And her noble Christian character,—beautiful example for us all.

ANNA S. ROGERS.

LETTER OF DR. J. E. ROY.

AMERICAN MISSIONARY ASSOCIATION,
BIBLE HOUSE, NEW YORK CITY.
WESTERN DISTRICT.
DISTRICT SECRETARY:
REV. J. E. ROY,
OFFICE, 151 WASHINGTON STREET.
CHICAGO, ILLINOIS,
AUGUST 22ND, 1894.

REV. E. P. WHEELER,
ASHLAND, WISCONSIN:

DEAR BROTHER: On the same day I received "The Evangel" with the account of your mother's accident, and the Beloit "Free Press" with a copy of the long article from the Ashland daily press, reporting the death and the useful life. The sad demise reminds me of the first time I saw your mother when I went to Beloit to secure yourself for Colorado. At that time she impressed me with the geniality and the breadth of her character, all of which was confirmed when I saw her, the one only other time, at the old mission. It seems sad that one who had come up to the years of three score and eighteen, should then be taken away by what we call an accident. What an inspiration has that name, Harriet Newell, been to the missionary cause these eighty years! Your family have been wonderfully blessed in that she has been preserved to you so long after the taking away of your father. Such a life written out would be a romance of unusual thrill, and all of it is in the mind of your boys more indelibly imprinted than if it were in a book. It will always be a comfort to me that my first paper,—read at the old mission,—upon "The Outside Influence of the Indian Missionaries" was a comfort to her.

I see by "The Evangel" that you are now to be the principal of the academy. I hope that you may yet realize your largest aspiration in that institution.

Sincerely yours,
J. E. Roy.

LETTER OF MRS. MARY H. HULL.

ARMOUR MISSION,
CORNER OF 33RD STREET AND ARMOUR AVENUE,
CHICAGO, ILLINOIS.

AUGUST 30TH, 1894.

How much it brings up to me to read of your dear mother's life and death, which is only life anew! Please let me share with others the sorrow at her loss. * * It is gain to her How sad, though, must have been her pain and yours at the last. But her life was so full of heroism with an element of tragedy in it, it seems but a part of the heroic to have it go out in such a way. God knows whom to trust.

MARY H. HULL.

A NEIGHBOR'S MESSAGE.

A letter, highly appreciated by the family, is one received, during Mrs. Wheeler's illness, from Miss H. S. Martindale of Beloit:

649 CHURCH STREET, BELOIT.

MY DEAR HATTIE: You don't know how many thoughts are going out to Ashland, and how many prayers are rising to Heaven from our dear church, as we remember your afflicted family. We do not love to have you so far away; we do not love to be told that we can not see the dear mother again, whose face always reflected so much of the radiance of heaven. We ought to rejoice that the earthly labor and discipline are so nearly over, but it seems as if we could spare no more of our *Saints*. Our pastor was with us again yesterday and he did not forget those who are so painfully missing. Your family pew is too suggestive of life's sad changes. By and by we will try to look upward along the radiant pathway, and rejoice in the clear vision of blessedness wrought out of so many years of patient and cheerful endurance of the Father's good pleasure; but now, while the dear one lingers, we must "hope against hope" and pray to keep her a little longer *if she can live comfortably.* We are grateful that so many of her children can minister to her comfort and be to her such a consolation in their loving fidelity. And we are grateful for the cooler weather rendering a sick bed so much more endurable. It has been hard for even the well to endure.

I shall always think of your mother as when I saw her last, in such cheery circumstances. * * * * If she still lives and can think of us, please assure her of our most loving sympathy, and our hope of meeting her again in our *one* Home.

With love to all the family from Mrs. Hill and myself.

H. S. MARTINDALE.

FROM A FRIEND OF HER LAST YEARS.

When one has been lifted up by the hallelujah chorus of the "Messiah," he is likely to feel, when he hears the remaining part of the oratorio, that it is but a rhythmic descent to the plane of ordinary emotion. From a "crowded hour of glorious life" on the Rigi-Kulm or even on the majestic tribune of one of the innumerable basilicas which the Creator's hand built in the ancient shores of the upper Mississippi, it is with hesitation and reluctance that we turn again to the world and its work. After the "amen" that fell from the lips to become so soon silent forever there seems, at first, place for nothing but tears and mournful memories. But no one could remember Mrs. Wheeler without being recalled to duty, and so, from the soft turf of the God's-acre where tender hands laid away her covering of flesh, we go to put our hands once more to plow or pen.

To me, who can not abide words that have not been weighed in the scale of truth, the tributes of Mrs. Wheeler's friends seem to set forth what she really was. My intimate acquaintance with her began when I sought information that she could give better than any other then among the living. Telling the story in her own way, she almost confused me at first with her vivid setting forth of the wrong done to the Wisconsin Ojibways in the attempt to make them give up their ancestral homes and remove to a dangerous nearness to their persistent and ferocious enemies, the Sioux. But how tender was her conscience, and how careful she was lest she should say something that was unjust!

Nor was her feeling that worse than weak sentimentality that practically ignores the difference between right and wrong. She distinguished between one who was merely misled and those who, if only a proposed measure offered to themselves a promise of gain, did not care much, if at all, whether, to the Indians, it would bring evil or good. Clearness of moral vision was a characteristic of Mrs. Wheeler. Her eye was single, the body of her activities and interest full of light. The poor, petty act of Bishop Baraga in removing children from the best school within their reach, because all the pupils were taught to pray the Lord's prayer together, did not prevent Mrs. Wheeler,—though it was her own school from which the children were withdrawn,—from recognizing the man's real worth and excellence. But I doubt that she would have agreed with the bishop's remark, as repeated by Mr. Parton, when, speaking of the Ojibways, he said "I make pretty good Christians of some of them. But *men?*—no, it is impossible." Indeed, I don't believe that Mrs. Wheeler could think of any one, whether Indian or of any other race, as being a Christian without true manliness or its corresponding quality in woman.

The hardships and trials of missionary life were not favorite themes with Mrs. Wheeler. She was never the heroine of any narrative of her own. But interested questions would recall the oppressive sense of loneliness and isolation that fell upon the mission families as they watched the last boat of the season glide down the vast curve of the world that is measured by the ocean-like expanse of Lake Superior. There was plenty of food to be sure, but how limited in variety! How children and adults as well, were,— as the Scotch say,—"scunnered" with fresh fish! The time was when, in the spring, the seed potatoes must be so cut as to yield a portion for food as well as the parts needed for planting. There were hours that seemed dark. One such was when the husband, already worn with the disease that ended his life, had broken his wrist, and the eldest son was brought home, from an attempted journey to St. Paul, injured in the knee and lame because of hurt received in the falling of a bough as he was cutting wood for the evening camp-fire. This was one of the dark hours that come before the dawn, and then it was that father and son wrought together to make the model of the "Eclipse" windmill. By his successful invention the father provided for the needs of the family that he was so soon thereafter called to leave. The success of the business which he established made Mrs. Wheeler both glad and grateful. But more glad and grateful was she that he had won the hearts of the people to whom he gave the best of his life; that he loved righteousness, hated iniquity and fought it with the persistency of a Calvinist and the courage of a soldier.

Let no one be displeased if we seem to have passed in our narrative from the story of the wife to that of the husband. She would have wished it so.

Happiest of my memories of Mrs. Wheeler,—and all are pleasant,—is that of those stirring days at La Pointe and Ashland when the dear mother rejoiced not only over what had been accomplished in the past but yet more over what she believed would be done in years to come. There and then the happy little

Puritan became our uncrowned queen!

At that time there had been taken from the quarries at Prentice, on the rock-bound western shore of the beautiful Chequamegon, a huge monolith designed for the Columbian Exhibition. This shaft of stone surpasses in size the largest of Egypt's famed obelisks. But hopes were disappointed. Where it lay when the quarrymen had moved it from its ancient bed there it lies yet. It may never point toward the sky. It was not needed as a memorial of the exhibition. No more fitting use could be made of this obelisk of iron-reddened sandstone than to place it erect engraven with the names of Ayer, Hall, Wheeler,—husbands and wives,—and of those who labored with them. But these men and women have a better memorial than one of stone. In the lives and love of those, both in heaven and on earth, whom they served, and "in God's still memory folded deep" is their record both of deed and name.

It is an easy transition from a memorial of Mrs. Wheeler to a letter by her friend and associate Mrs. E. T. Ayer, one of the few survivors of that heroic mission band of half a century ago. It is fitting that both these narratives appear in the story of "Unnamed Wisconsin." For it was not until a comparatively late time that the people dwelling there thought of the Lake Superior region as really belonging to Wisconsin. Long after the Territory was organized they dated their letters at "La Pointe, Lake Superior."

Mrs. Ayer's letter is written with the delicacy and firmness of hand of a school-girl. An answer has as yet brought no reply but, so far as I know, the good lady is still among the living:

BELLE PRAIRIE, January 26th, 1891.

REV. J. N. DAVIDSON:

Yours of the 17th inst. was duly received. I have to say that you sent to a dry source for anything like dates of a *day* concerning the early missions in Wisconsin. We always kept dates of important occurences in our journals, which were quite voluminous (particularly my husband's) but when we left Red Lake, our last station among the Ojibwas, they were accidentally burned. In some cases I am not able to tell, without some considerable thought, even the *year*, in which certain events occurred.

Now in my 89th year, I do not dwell much on the past, nor have I for years. Forgetting the things that are behind, I am pressing forward to those that are before—learning more fully how we are saved by Jesus Christ; and I find that it is not by His "paying all the debt we owe," no, no. His work was far greater, and far more necessary than this, and in it I rejoice.

I hope you may be successful in your undertaking. My best wishes attend you.

ELIZABETH TAYLOR AYER.

Frederic Ayer was born in 1803, in Stockbridge, Massachusetts, but from two years old he lived in central New York, where his father was for many years a home missionary. He, too, was set apart by his parents for the ministry, but his health was not sufficient to carry him through his necessary studies and he took a clerkship in a bookstore in Utica. In 1829 the Indian mission at Mackinaw needed a helper, and, hearing of Mr. Ayer, they were so sure that he was the man for them, that one of the missionaries went to Utica in person and persuaded him to leave his business and come to their relief. But his labors in school, with a class of small boys out of school in addition, were too much, and, as he was an independent worker in 1830, he went up Lake Superior with the fur traders, wintered with Mr. Warren at La Pointe, taught Mr. Warren's children and the children of his employers, and studied the Ojibwa language. In 1831 missionaries were sent out by the American Board to La Pointe, and Mr. Ayer wintered there the second time, studying and teaching. The next winter he went on farther, to Sandy Lake. Here he finished an Ojibwa spelling-book and started off on foot with an experienced guide for Mackinaw early in the spring. He was bound for Utica to get his book printed early enough to go up Lake Superior with the traders.

This year, 1833, Mr. Ayer put himself under the direction of the A. B. C. F. M., and was sent to Yellow Lake. During his third year there, he was invited by another band to a more promising field of labor, and was directed to go there. The mission family there consisted of Mr. Ayer and wife, John L. Seymour, and Miss Sabina Stevens. Miss Crooks, who was there in the beginning, had married Rev. W. T. Boutwell, and had gone to Leech Lake. The mission at Pokeguma, on Snake River, was very prosperous for a few years, but in 1840 the Sioux came there to avenge some real or supposed wrongs, and the Indians were scattered and dared not return. Mr. Ayer afterwards spent a few years at Red Lake, and in the winter of '48-9 settled on the borders of the newly-purchased Territory [of Minnesota] and, in due time, opened a school there for the more promising children in different parts of the Indian country. This school was kept up for several years and when Belle Prairie was sufficiently settled to have an organization they joined with us. We worked together till the commencement of the civil war.

Mr. Ayer was a "man of his word," therefore he was trusted. When living on the St. Croix, an Indian came in one evening, and after sitting a while in silence, he said, "I did not sleep much last night, I was thinking hard, and puzzled. I never saw a man, before you, but what had two tongues," and crossing his two fore-fingers held them up as an explanation. "I notice *you* have but one tongue,—that is the reason the Indians like you." Wherever Mr.

Ayer lived, this trait of character was noticeable. In 1865, after the close of the civil war, he went South to labor among the freedmen, and in building two large houses and remodeling another of still greater dimensions for a church, furnishing material and hiring laborers, he had much to do with the business men of the city, and this trait of character was greatly to his advantage. He gained many warm friends, even among the rebels.

Yours in Christian bonds,
E. T. AYER.

Mr. Ayer's biography — as yet written only in fragments.— unites closely the history of Wisconsin and of Minnesota. A school that he established was probably the first within the limits of the last named state. He binds together also the narrative of the work, among the Ojibways, both of the American Board and the American Missionary Association.

Of those who labored with him nearly all have passed away. S. G. Wright is left at Oberlin, Ohio, and Alonzo Barnard at Benzonia, Michigan. Mr. Barnard was compelled to leave St. Joseph (Walhalla), North Dakota, in 1855. He removed to the Lake Winnipeg region where he did missionary work among the Indians until 1863, when he removed to his present home.

Of Rev. Cutting Marsh, Mrs. R. M. Hutton, wife of Professor A. J. Hutton of the Whitewater normal school writes, under date of 1895, March 4th: "Dr. Marsh was our pastor when I was a child. A more thoroughly consecrated man never lived." A brief sketch of his life is furnished by his daughter, Miss Sarah E. Marsh, of Chicago:

Cutting Marsh was born July 20th, 1800, in the town of Danville, Vermont, and the early years of his boyhood were spent on his father's farm. He graduated from Dartmouth college in 1826, and from the seminary at Andover in 1829.

In the fall of that same year, he came west, expecting to go to Green Bay to labor among the Indians for a year, but on reaching Detroit, he found that the last boat up the lakes for the season had left two months before his arrival. Accordingly, he went to Maumee, where there was a missionary station among the Ottawas, and spent the winter. In the spring he went to Green Bay, and from there to the station among the Stockbridges, about twenty miles up the river.

When the Indians moved to Stockbridge, he went with them and stayed until the American Board discontinued its work among them in 1848.

In 1837, he was married at Green Bay to Miss Eunice Osmer, a lady who had been for twelve years a teacher in the mission school at Mackinaw.

After the mission at Stockbridge was broken up, Mr. Marsh moved to Green Bay, and lived there three years, and there it was that he was employed by the Home Missionary society to travel as an itinerant missionary, looking up church members, organizing them into churches, and starting Sunday-schools.

In the year 1851, he moved to Waupaca, situated on an Indian reservation, the land of which had just been opened for settlement. The country was new, and for several years he had appointments for preaching at different places every Sunday in the month, some of these being twenty miles from the home. His wife, his wise and faithful helper, went to her heavenly home in 1855. And, worn with his many labors and hardships, he fell asleep in the morning of the Fourth of July, in 1873.

Of Chauncey (not Sherman) Hall, the coadjutor of Mr. Marsh, the novelist "Ida Glenwood" (Mrs. C. M. R. Gorton of Fenton, Michigan), writing under date of 1893, March 20th, said: "I boarded with him and family in Utica, New York. * * He was a colporteur. Perhaps you do not know that I am blind, and it was while attending to my eyes at the oculist's that I became acquainted with himself and family. * * I received the foundation of "The Fatal Secret" [one of her books] from Messrs. Hall and Ferry (the founder of the Mackinac school as you probably know), while Mr. Ferry was visiting Mr. Hall and family." Mrs. Gorton does not give the date of Mr. Hall's death but intimates that it occurred not "many months" after 1876. "His wife and daughter preceded him to the other world. Jennie was a sweet girl, and father and child were tender lovers."

The unusual length of time that this book has been in press has brought somewhat of correction and more of information. Part of this material was utilized even after the manuscript was in the printer's hands. Some other things I subjoin:

To the account given of Radisson and Groseilliers it should be added that, if Dr. Neill is right, they were of Huguenot origin. If so, as I presume was the case, we have another reason for their preferring to serve the English government rather than the French king,—especially as that king was Louis XIV. Dragonades and the disposition that made them were not likely to win the loyalty of men whom the woods had made free.

But early and extended as were the "voyages" of Radisson, I should not now speak of him and Groseilliers as probably the discoverers of Lake Superior.

But they were among its earliest explorers. And so great, for many reasons, is the honor due them that, if Wisconsin should have, in one of the two niches assigned her in the old representatives' hall of our national capitol, the statue of any man of the seventeenth century,[1] the form should be that of Radisson, the self-reliant explorer, rather than that of Marquette, one of that type of ecclesiastics who think as they are told and do as they are bidden.

If any French missionary could rightly occupy the place of honor given by an ignorant legislature to Marquette,— who, moreover, belongs in much less degree to the history of the Wisconsin region than to that of a small part of what is now Michigan,— no one has a better claim than the faithful Menard.

Since the first part of this book was in type the view therein set forth of the Franco-British wars that followed the accession of William and Mary has been published to the world by one of the most eminent of American historians, Professor John Fiske. It may be permitted me to say that my conclusions were reached independently, so far as I can remember, of suggestion from any one.

It would be absurd to blame the few civilized (or half-civilized) inhabitants of the "parish of Green Bay,"[2] as this region was sometimes called, for the part that they took in the wars aforesaid. At the same time it is ignorance not to know that they fought and the Canadian clergy prayed against the movement whose issue was the founding of our nation. It was the democracy of Calvinism and not the aristocracy of Roman Catholicism and of Episcopacy that made the Americans not only a free people,— that was accomplished before our Revolution,— but also a nation separate from the mother country. That other vigorous form of Puritanism that is now most numerously represented in the great and patriotic Methodist Episcopal church[3] had, in America, during the war of separation, scarcely an existence.

It may seem that disproportionate space has been given to the narrative concerning the Stockbridge Indians. Certainly one would think so if he judged merely from the present insignificance and deplorable condition of the tribe. But that, as a people, they were once entitled to greater consideration than they are now, and actually received it, has been, I think, clearly shown. And since the chapters that give account of them were in print, I have found part of the record that they made during the Revolution in volume II. of Peter Force's reprint of American archives;— a "speech delivered by Captain Solomon Unhaunauwaunmet,[4] Chief Sachem of [the] Moheakunnut Tribe of Indians residing at Stockbridge, on the 11th day of April, 1775, after sitting in Council

---

[1] Which I, for one, do not believe.
[2] "A parish" sometimes spoken of as if it extended as far northward as Lake Athabasca.
[3] As every one knows, Methodism is essentially Puritanic; and, in spite of the logomachy of theologians, really Calvinistic.
[4] See page 112.

two days, being an answer to a Message sent them by the Congress."[1]

"South Kaukauna" is a better name than "Statesburg." But the latter, for an Indian settlement, is certainly suggestive. Under date of 10th August, 1894, Dr. (and Mayor) Tanner of South Kaukauna, wrote:

"I am unable to find any one here who knows anything about the reason for the name Statesburg. They know it was called that, but the naming was too early for them."

He adds: "I took a trip out to the cemetery and I am sure I have a correct copy of the inscription, which I enclose."[2]

"The faithful memory" spoken of on page 140 is that of Sabra Howes Adams, now the wife of Rev. H. H. Benson of Wauwatosa, Wisconsin.

Of note 2, page 3, Rev. E. P. Wheeler says:

"Whatever may have been the case in 1671, the Ojibways now use the term Nadouessi as applying only to the Iroquois and the Hurons, not to the Sioux.

"On page 166 you spell the name of Moose Tail, Moo-zoo-jeele.[3] It should be Mo-zo-geede."[4]

Hennepin's statement as given in note 2, page 15 becomes somewhat less absurd when it is known that it was made in regard to the falls of Niagara, not those of St. Anthony.

To the note on page 149, it may be added that the "Presbyterian mission-school" was one established and supported by the American Board.

The note on page 151 should be corrected by the statement that Mrs. M. W. English is employed in the government school at Red Lake, and not in the Episcopal mission.

An error in note 2, page 234 is corrected in the account of Mr. Ayer's life.

Other annoying errors are these: "Country," for "county," line 3, note 1, page 37; "advice" for "avarice," page 64, line 25; "story" for "tory" in note 2, page 181; the omission of "not" before "as keen" on page 187, line 10; "elapsed" for "lapsed," note 1, page 204; "or" for "of" on page 208, line 25.

On page 222 "Kendall" instead of "Kimball" is given as Dr. Pearsons's middle name, and on page 225 the blank before Mr. West's name should be filled with "Edward."

It may be added that Mr. West still lives, has been, since 1852, a resident of Appleton and believes that he was the first man to teach in Wisconsin

---

[1] See page 95.

[2] IN MEMORY OF
REV. JESSE MINER,
BORN SEPT. 29, 1781.
COMMENCED THE MOHEAKUMUK
MISSION AT THIS PLACE,
JUNE 20, 1828.
DIED MARCH 22, 1829.
AGED 47.
"and he shall assemble the outcasts of Israel."
ISA. 11, 12.

[3] I followed the spelling of the author from whom I made the quotation.

[4] Accurate, non cauda sed anus.

under a regularly organized school-board. This was in the winter of '36-37. For this school a frame building was erected in "Kilbourntown." The boys and girls of to-day will think it strange that among his duties was the making of goose-quill pens. On this last subject ex-Judge J. T. Mills, now of Manitowoc, says of his life in the family of Colonel Zachary Taylor, while at Prairie du Chien: "I did some of his writing, and there I first saw a steel pen and wrote with it."

Principal E. P. Wheeler of Ashland thinks that Cadeau came to the Lake Superior region at a much later date than 1671 (p. 148). He is sure that of the two church buildings at La Pointe, the one that belonged to the Protestant mission is the older (p. 160). He adds: "I would not add your authority to the idea that there is any question at all as to which is the older building."

In the criticism that follows, I do not think that Mr. Wheeler establishes his point. I take it that nearly all cannibalism had its origin in the belief he describes:

"On page 170 you comment on the incident related in Brother Leonard's letter, that it was the last trace of cannibalism in Wisconsin. This is not a correct inference from the story which he relates. The practice of warriors' eating a piece of the flesh (usually the heart) of their foes when killed was in obedience to a vindictive instinct, and under the idea that the strength of the victim, thus eaten, becomes transferred by the act to the victor. It was a usage of war therefore that led the Indian in question to eat a piece of that Frenchman." None the less it was cannibalism: "The eating of human flesh by human beings."

He who would do such work as, in the foregoing pages, I have attempted, must needs learn all he can of those whose years have brought them close to the borders of the unseen world. A happy part of my long task has been to try to get and put on record things preserved in the memory of Jeremiah Porter,— in the majestic presence of death let us drop the titles given by councils and schools,— Aaron Lucius Chapin, Luther Clapp, Mrs. Harriet Wood Wheeler, Daniel Brown and Philo S. Bennett. To try to name all others of the dead and the living who by their reminiscences have given me help, would be, of necessity, a work so likely to be unsatisfactory that it is better, perhaps, to leave it wholly undone. This, perhaps, should be said that the contributions of President Chapin and Father Clapp have been chiefly of material that must be reserved for another volume. However, it was in view of meeting their judgment and, not less, that of men like them that this book was written. If it stand the test, I have succeeded in a part, at least, of what I sought to do.

INDEX.

Abbott's Histories, 242.
Abbott, Judge ——, 179.
A-boin-ug, the, 146.
Abolitionists from the South, 184.
Abraham (of Scripture), 149.
Abrams, Abram, 123.
Abstinence, total, among Indians, 83.
Academy, North Wisconsin, 255, 256.
Aceldama, a veritable, 24.
Adams, Captain (Henry?), 196.
Adams, Daniel, 66, 128.
Adams, John, 29.
Adams, President J. Q., 149, 190.
Adams, Sabra Howes, 279.
Advance, The, 223.
Advertiser, The Milwaukee, 225.
Agmegue, (Gagmegue), 94.
Agriculture among the Ojibways, 244.
Aitkin, Alfred, 160.
Aitkin county (Minnesota), 156.
Aitkin, W. A., 156, 157, 160.
Albany (Illinois), 194.
Albany (New York), 30, 47, 71, 78, 89, 94, 164, 177.
Albion (New York), 218.
Algics (Algonkins, Algonquians, Algonquins), 7, 10, 55, 56, 94, 108.
Alleghany river, 185.
Allen, Lieutenant ——, 166.
Alps, 134.
Altamaha river, 29.

Ambler, Augustus, 115, 151.
America, Protestant episcopate in, 30.
America, state papers of, 34.
Americans, 27, 28, 32, 39, 40, 42, 43, 44, 46, 100, 106, 119, 126.
American Articles of Confederation, 29.
American Bible society, 164.
American Board, 11, 47, 49, 114, 133, 129, 130, 135, 136, 138, 139, 141, 149, 162, 163, 164, 166, 168, 169, 172, 209, 210, 233, 234, 235, 248, 275, 276.
American college, origin of the, 32.
American commonwealths, majority of the newer, 34.
American flag, first in Wisconsin (?), 32.
American Fur company, 47, 49, 134, 148, 151, 158, 159, 180, 192, 233, 240.
American government, establishment of, in the Old Northwest, 35.
American Home Missionary society, 182, 183, 193, 209, 216.
American Lakes, Tour of the, 58.
American Missionary Association, 144, 162, 163, 270, 276.
American Revolution, the, 23, 29, 32, 54, 100,
American Tract society, 193.
American Union, the Old Northwest

becomes a part of the, 32.
Amherst college, 209.
Anderson, Captain T. G., 189.
Anderson, General Robert, 197, 199.
Andover seminary, 155, 223, 233, 263, 276.
Andreas, A. T., 213.
Andrews, President I. W., 34.
Anglo-Americans, 74, 75.
Angus, John Daniel, 159, 160.
Annals of Prairie du Chien, 186.
Antoinette, Marie, 65.
Anthony, John, 57.
Appenoose, an Indian chief, 134.
Appleton's Cyclopædia, 74.
Appleton-street church, Lowell, 233.
Arabian story of the camel, 95.
Arctic zone, 26.
Arkansas, 216.
Armour mission, 271.
Arnold, Benedict, 96.
Ashland, 4, 147, 165, 167, 168, 229, 250, 254, 255, 256, 257, 258, 268, 270, 271, 273, 280.
Ashley, John, Esq., 80.
Asiatic Turkey, 108.
Assembly of Massachusetts, 30.
Asseni sibi, 221.
Associate Reformed synod, 109.
Astor, John Jacob, 47.
Astoria, 47, 51, 158, 235.
Athol (Massachusetts), 234.
Atkinson, General Henry, 189, 190, 197.
Atlanta, 162.
Atlantic coast, 73, 75.
Atlantic states, emigration from, 39.
Atlantic, The, 173.
Aunauwauneekhheck Jeremy, 84.
Aupaumut, Captain Hendrick, 116, 124.
Austria, 42, 159.
Autsequitt, Neddy, 57.

Ayer, Mrs. F. T., 157, 162, 163, 274, 275, 276.
Ayer, Rev. Frederic, 13, 151, 152, 156, 157, 161, 162, 163, 234, 274, 275, 276.
Ayscough, Rev. Dr. Francis, 90.
Aztalan, 218.
Bacon, Rev. David, 46.
Bad Axe, battle of the, 198, 199.
Bad river, 168, 169, 240, 244, 245.
Bad Smell, Bay of the, 14.
Badin, Rev. J. V., 204.
Balfour (or Belfour) Captain Henry, 26, 45.
Baltimore, 27.
Bancroft, George, 11, 13.
Banks, Sir Joseph, 30.
Baptist preachers, few in number, 220.
Baptism of an Indian, 239.
Baraboo ranges, 207.
Barber, Rev. Abel L., 209, 210, 215, 216, 217.
Barber, Mrs. A. L. (Elizabeth Woodford), 209.
Barclay, Rev. Henry, 64, 78, 89.
Barlow, Rev. Abner, 221.
Barnard, Rev. Alonzo, 163.
    do   Mrs. Alonzo, 163.
Barre, Mons. de la, 6.
Barega, Rev. Frederic, 159, 170, 171, 173.
Basel, 134; treaty of, 28.
Batteaux on Lake Superior, 152.
Bay City (Wisconsin), 250.
Bay des Enock, 121.
Bayfield, 11, 147, 167.
Bayfield county, 5.
Beard, Mr., an Oneida Indian, 123.
Beauharnois, M. de, 19, 20, 21, 22, 23.
Beaulieu, Abraham, 159.
Beecher, Edward, 184.
Belcher, Governor Jonathan, 75, 77, 80, 82.

Bellamy, Joseph, D. D., 77, 93.
Belle Prairie (Minnesota), 162, 274, 275.
Belmont Gazette, 225.
Belmont (Wisconsin), 185, 194, 200, 223.
Beloit, 172, 175, 224, 235, 250, 254, 256, 257, 258, 259, 269, 270, 271.
Beloit college, 208, 219, 222, 226, 235, 255.
Beloit College Monthly, 193.
Beloit convention, 145.
Beloit, First church of, 173, 221, 222.
Beloit, first white child born at, 221.
Beloit, naming of, 222.
Beloit seminary, 222.
Bennet, Elizabeth, 128.
Bennet, John, 128.
Bennett, Lieutenant Thomas, 156.
Bennett, Rev. P. S., 66, 166, 215, 220.
Benson, Mrs. H. H. (Sabra Howes Adams), 141.
Benzonia (Michigan), 276.
Berkshire county (Massachusetts), 148.
Berlin, 159.
Bethlehem, 69.
Bethlehem (Pennsylvania), 109.
Bethlem (Connecticut), 93.
Bible, authorized version of, 175.
Bibliography of the Algonquian Languages, 167.
Big Butte des Morts, 132.
Big Foot, 223.
"Big Knives," 42, 44, 189.
Billings, 38.
Bingham, Rev. Abel, 152.
Bingham's Columbian Orator, 95.
Binghamton (New York), 93.
Bjelometschetskaja, 226.
Black Hawk, 43, 132, 133, 184, 189, 195, 196, 197, 198, 199.
Black Hawk war, 24, 184, 195, 200.
"Black laws" of Illinois, 193; of Indiana, 38.
Black Prince, Edward the, 1.
Black river, 9.
Black Sparrow-Hawk, 189.
Blaisdell, Professor J. J., 256.
Blatchford, Henry, 164, 171, 172, 257.
Blodgett, Caleb, 222.
Blodgett, Mrs. Caleb, 222.
Board of Indian Commissioners, 76, 79, 82, 92.
Board of Overseers of Harvard college, 47.
Boilvin, Nicholas, 39, 40, 43, 178, 188.
Bois Brule, 18, 156.
Bonham, Rev. B. B., 185.
Borup, C. W., 157.
Borup, Mrs. E., 157.
Boston, 5, 16, 30, 38, 76, 77, 82, 90, 92, 123, 177, 186.
Boston, Old South church of, 4, 94.
Boston, Prince society of, 4.
"Boston, tea-party," 156.
"Bostonians," 32, 203, 210.
Bourbons, the, 26,
Bourbon county (Kentucky), 184.
Boutwell, Mrs. W. T. (Hester Crooks), 158.
Boutwell, Rev. Wm. Thurston, 153, 154, 155, 156, 157, 158, 160, 275.
Bowyer, John, Indian agent, 56, 64, 202.
Boyd, George, 125, 136, 138.
Boyd, Rev. O. E., 182.
Boyle, Robert, 69.
Braddock, defeat of, 30, 203.
Bradford (New Hampshire), 193.
Bradford, William, 33.
Brainerd, David, 86, 124.
Brant, Joseph, 68, 94.
Bread, Daniel, 57.
Breck, Rev. Daniel, 38.
Bribery, 223.
Brisbois, B. W., 175.

Britain, 26, 35, 39, 42, 47.
British army, the. 30.
"British band," 189, 196.
British Columbia, 6.
British dominion, period of, 28, 44.
British government, the, 29, 32, 34.
British king, the, 32.
British North America, 28.
British Parliament, the, 29, 30.
Britons, 1.
Brothertown Indians, 57, 60, 61, 62, 67, 68, 69, 70, 71, 72, 98, 108, 117, 120, 121, 137, 224.
Brothertown (New York), 69, 70, 71, 97, 101, 105.
Brothertown, (Wisconsin), 72.
Brown county, 224.
Brown, Daniel, 213, 214, 215, 216, 217, 218, 225, 280;—Mrs. D., 214, 215, 216, 217.
Brown, J. H. H., Protestant Episcopal bishop, 204.
Brown, Rev. D. E., 205, 210.
Brown, Samuel, 213, 214, 216, 218, 225;—Mrs. Samuel, 213.
Brown's History of Missions, 100, 105, 106.
Brule-St. Croix portage, 18, 156, 187.
Brunson, Rev. Alfred, 134, 165, 166, 167, 185, 186.
Buck, J. S. 215.
Buckle, Henry Thomas, 197.
Buffalo (New York), 149.
Buffalo Creek (New York), 61.
Bulger, Capt. Andrew A., 43, 44.
Burdick, Miss Susan, 216.
Burdick, Mrs. Paul, 213, 214.
Burdick, Paul, 213, 214.
Bull, Rev, Nehemiah, 77.
Burgoyne. surrender of, 96, 106, 126.
Burns, Robert, 32.
Burlington (Iowa), 223.
Burr, Aaron, 77.
Burr, Professor A. W., 256.

Bushnell, George, D. D., 252.
Butte des Morts, the great, 25.
Butterfield, C. W., 16, 28, 184, 191.
Cadeau, Mons. 148, 280.
Cades (Wisconsin), 111.
Cadillac, La Mothe, 21, 45.
Cadle, Rev. Richard F., 65, 122, 127, 205
Cadotte, Jean Baptiste, 148.
Cadotte, Michael, 148.
Cahokia, (Illinois), 31.
Caientouton, island of, 14.
Calhoun, John Caldwell, 55.
Calhoun (Minnesota), 149.
California, 12, 148.
California, gulf of, 85.
Calumet county, 72, 137.
Calumetville, 145.
Calvert, Cecil (Lord Baltimore), 33.
Calvinism, 197; democracy of, 278.
Camp Smith, 205.
Campbell, John, 157.
Campbell, Lieutenant John, 43.
Campbell, Mrs. Elizabeth, 102, 157.
Canada, 1, 2, 6, 15, 18, 27, 28, 29, 31, 32, 40, 48, 54, 65, 75, 78, 85, 94, 95, 96, 100, 153, 165, 175, 180, 201, 203.
Canadian traders, 39.
Canajoharie, 68, 93, 94.
Cannibalism in Wisconsin, 28, 170, 280.
Canning, E. W. B., 76, 93, 97, 108.
Canterbury, (Conn.), 30.
Canton, (China). 108.
Capital fixed at Madison. 223.
Cardillac, 45.
Car-i-mau-nee, Winnebago chief, 190.
Carleton college, 256.
Carlisle, Indian school at, 87.
Carver, Captain Jonathan, 30, 176, 177, 181, 201, 210.
"Carver's grant," 30, 181.
Carver, John, Governor, 30.

INDEX.

"Carver's Travels," 30, 75.
Cass Lake, 155, 163.
Cass, Lewis, 112, 113, 148, 181, 189.
Cassville, 183, 194, 224.
Catlin, George, 133, 136.
Catlin's North American Indians, 109.
Caughnawaga (Canada), 65.
Caulking, Mr. ———, 100, 104.
Cayugas, the, 55.
Central Park, New York, 235.
Chambers, Colonel Talbot, 178.
Chamberlin's Geology, 207.
Chapin, Aaron L., 193, 194, 219, 280.
Chapin, Rev. Walter, 48.
Chardon, J. B., 19.
Charles, Cornelius S., 129.
Charles II. of England, 3, 69.
Charlestown (Rhode Island), 69.
Charlevoix, P. F. X., 2, 3, 19, 55.
Chase, Enoch, 215; Horace, 212.
Chepekataw sibi, 220.
Chequamegon bay, 4, 10, 11, 12, 13, 26, 45, 49, 146, 147, 148, 240, 274.
Chequamegon point, 147.
Chester, William, D. D., 47.
Chester, Rev. William, 47.
Childs, "Colonel" Ebenezer, 113.
Chicago, 31, 36, 42, 154, 180, 186, 205, 209, 212, 213, 214, 215, 219, 220, 223, 256, 258, 270, 271, 276.
Chicago, portage at, 18, 211.
Chicago river, 18, 110.
Chic-hon-sic, a Winnebago, 190.
Chicks, Jacob C., 57, 125.
Chicks, J. N., 139, 140, 142.
China, 168, 171, 185.
China damask, garment of, 1.
Chipman, Samuel, 251.
Chippecotton sibi, 220.
Chippewas (Chippewaus), 75, 163, 173, 175; 233, 238; their language, 154.
Chippewa Falls, 167, 249.
Chippewa river, 4, 181.
"Chippewau," 48.

Choate, Rufus, 34.
Choctaw Indians, 115.
Choir, first at Milwaukee, 216.
Cholera in upper Mississippi region, 199.
Chouart, Medart, 2.
Christinos, 3, 5.
Christmas at the Odanah mission, 242.
Church, first in Milwaukee, 218.
Church discipline, 205.
Church, Harriet M., 217.
Church of England, 29.
Cincinnati, Catholic Institute of, 15.
Citizenship given to the Muh-he-ka-ne-ok, 139.
Claims, court of, 61, 67.
Clapp, Father Luther, 280.
Clark, Colonel George Rogers, 31, 32, 36, 40.
Clark, Rev. John, 66, 123, 165, 166.
Clark, Rev. John (an Ojibway), 4, 256.
Clark, William, governor, 40, 41.
Clergyman, first in Milwaukee, 215.
"Clerk of the Closet," 90.
Cleveland (Ohio), 46, 248.
Clinton brothers, early settlers in Milwaukee, 218.
Clinton, Governor De Witt, 63.
Clinton (New York), 63, 98.
Cochran, Andrew, 184.
Codex, Beloit College, 222.
Codman, John, D. D., 123.
Coe, Alvin, 148–151, 182, 183.
Cohokia (Illinois), 32.
Colebrook (New Hampshire), 222.
Colman, Rev. Benjamin, D. D., 82, 83, 86, 90, 99, 108.
Colonial troops in Wisconsin (?), 177.
Colorado, 270.
Colton, Professor Calvin, 54, 57, 58, 116–118, 127, 135.
Columbia county, 207.
Columbian exhibition, 274.
Comet (steamer), 42.
Commentary, Scott's, 110, 197.

Commuck, Thomas, 72, 137.
Communion service among Indians, 239.
Comstock, Dr. William S., 53.
Concert of prayer, 183.
Congregational church. the first in Wisconsin, 114; the first one organized in Wisconsin, 157.
Congregational convention of Wisconsin, 219. *See* Presbyterian and Congregational convention.
Congregational club of Lake Superior, 255.
Congregational Quarterly, 46, 98.
Congress (of the Confederation), 33, 34, 35.
Connecticut, 30, 69, 85, 115, 181, 186, 209; academy of arts and sciences, 74; "board of correspondents," 63; missionary society 46, 182.
Connecticut river, 85.
Convention, Presbyterian and Congregational, 142, 145. *See* Congregational convention.
Cook, Delia, 157, 160.
Cooley, Jennie S., 171.
Copper river, 9.
Copway, George, 165, 166.
Coram, Thomas, 90, 96.
Coureurs de bois, 15.
Coutume de Paris, 179.
Covenant of Ojibway churches, 173.
Crasbury, Mr. ——, 103.
Crawford county, history of, 184.
Crawford Miss ——, 180, 181.
Crawford, Rev. Gilbert, 218, 219.
Crawford, T. H., 98.
Crawford, W. H., 178.
Crecy, battle of, 1.
Crees, the 3.
Crespel, Rev. Emanuel, 19.
Creswell, Rev. R. J., 163.
Cromwell, Oliver, 197.
Crooks, Hester, 158.
Crooks, Ramsey, 47, 158.

Crow river, 141.
Crow Wing, 167, 170.
Crown Point, 94.
Culloden, victor at, 90.
Cumberland Presbyterians, 132, 182, 183.
Cumberland University, 185.
Curtis, Daniel, 203.
Cushik, 103, 108.
Cutler, Colonel Enos, 132.
Cutler, Ephraim. 37; Rev. Manasseh, 33, 34, 35, 38, 39.
Dakota Indians, 5, 15, 57, 146. 201. *See* Sioux.
Dakotas, the (states), 127, 200.
Dane county, 196, 221.
Dane, Nathan, 34.
Danville (Vermont), 276.
Dartmouth college, 54, 68, 69, 70, 112, 144, 155, 276.
D'Aubigne's History of the Reformation, 242.
Daumont, Simon Francais, 13, 148.
Davenport (Iowa), 133.
Davenport, George, 133.
Davidson, J. N., 38, 255, 274.
Davis, Jefferson, 127, 207, 208.
Deansburg, 72.
Death penalty inflicted by the Stockbridges in Wisconsin. 137; death rate lessened among them, 138.
Deerfield (Massachusetts), 65. 86; *History and Genealogy of*, 65.
Deer Park (Illinois), 22.
Defoe, Julia, 267.
Delawares, (Leni-Lennappes), 54, 55, 73, 86, 99, 100, 105–109, 111, 132, 137; their language, 75.
Delaware river, 73, 87
Denton, Rev. Samuel. 134.
De Pere, 13, 14, 23.
De Peyster, Major A. S. 30, 31.
Des Moines county, 200; river, 22, 133, 134, 192, 200.

INDEX.

Destitution in Wisconsin, 219.
Detroit, 16–18, 28, 30, 31, 40, 45, 46, 50, 54, 64, 116, 122, 148, 181, 248, 276.
Dick, Alonzo, 72; E. M., 72; William, 57; W. H., 72.
Dickinson, Rev. C. E. 38; "General" William, 113.
Dickson, Robert, 40, 41, 178, 211.
"Diggings" population in the, 192.
Discipline of churches, 205.
Dixon (Illinois), 196, 197.
Dog Plains. See Prairie du Chien.
Dodgeville, 224.
Doolittle. Senator J. R., 253.
Doty. Ex-Governor, 31, 120, 139, 223.
Douglas, Barzillai 217.
Dracut (Massachusetts), 231.
Dragonades, 277.
Drake's North American Indians, 3.
Draper, L. C., 11, 72.
Dress, mode of among the Stockbridges, 140; of a Winnebago chief, 190.
Drexel, Miss Catherine, 172.
Drummond, George, Esq., 99.
Drummond, Lieutenant General Sir George Gordon, 40.
Drummond's Island, 44, 189.
Du Buisson, Sieur ———, 24.
Dubuque, 188, 199; county, 200.
Dubuque, Julien, 187, 188.
"Dubuque's Mines," 192.
Duche, Rev. Jacob, 32.
Duck Creek, 64, 67, 122, 129.
Duke of Cumberland, 90; of Kent, 28.
Du Lhut (Luth), Daniel Grayson, 147.
Duperon, Joseph Imbert, 4.
Du Quesne, Marquis ———, 26.
Dunand, Rev. M., 180.
Durant, Henry Fowle, 154; Pauline Adeline, 154.
Durrie Daniel S., 114.
Dustin, Mrs. Hannah, 252.
Dutch, the, 2, 4; settlements of, 85, 95.

Dwight't Travels 105, 126.
Dwinnell, Rev. S. A., 218, 223, 224.
Early History of Michigan, 45.
Eaton, President E. D., 226.
Eatonville, 149.
Eau Claire land-office, 249.
"Eclipse" wind-mill, 168, 251, 252, 273.
Edinburgh, 99.
Education in Wisconsin, History of, 115.
Edward the Black Prince, 1.
Edwards, Jonathan, 67, 91–93, 95, 99, 111, 114, 145.
Edwards, Jonathan, the younger, 74, 75, 94, 98.
Edwards, Timothy, 96.
Edwards, Rev. Tryon, D. D., 74.
Ee-tow-o-kaum, (Austin E. Quinney), 109.
Egypt, 274.
Ekaentouton, 13.
Election, first in Milwaukee, 217.
Eliot's Bible, 69, 74, 75, 124.
Eliot, John, 11, 69, 85, 86.
Ellis, A. G., 49, 57, 60, 64, 65, 110, 111, 119, 121, 202, 203, 204, 205.
Ellis, Edwin, 165, 167, 173, 255, 259, 266.
Elk Creek, 155.
Elk Lake, 155, 156.
Elskwatawa (brother to Tecumseh), 106.
Ely, Rev. Edmund F., 157, 158, 162, 168, 238, 239.
Emerson, Professor Joseph, 235.
Endecott (Endicott) John, 5.
England, 5, 17, 23, 26, 68, 69, 74, 76, 79, 80, 88, 94, 133; church of, 29.
English colonies, 29.
English, Mrs. M. W., 151, 267, 268, 279.
English, the, 2, 16, 17, 18, 27, 30, 34, 78, 84, 88, 89, 92, 94, 100.

Enmegahbowk, (missionary), 166.
Enterprise (steamer), 42.
Episcopacy, aristocracy of, 278.
Episcopal church among Oneidas, 63.
Episcopal church in America, 29.
Episcopal Missionary society, 65.
Erection of buildings for missions. 66, 114, 248.
Escanaba, 121.
Escotecke, the, 3.
Esprit, Pierre d', 2.
Esprit Pointe d', 11.
Essex Institute Historical Collections, vol. VII., 156.
Ethnology, Bureau of, Report for 1885-6, 55.
Euphrates, the, 216.
Europe, 1, 28, 42, 168, 197, 205.
Eustis, Secretary William, 178.
Evanston, 213.
Everts, Jeremiah, 149.
Exeter (New Hampshire), 155.
Fairchild, ex-President James, 163.
Falls of St. Anthony, 15, 149, 279.
Faribault, Jean Baptiste, 181.
Faribault (Minnesota), 181.
Farmington, 69, 74, 105.
Farmingtons, the, 69, 74, 105.
Fast, annual, observed in Massachusetts and Wisconsin, 128, 136.
Fatal Secret, the, 277.
Fauvel (Favrell), ——, 204, 205.
"Father of waters," the, 175.
Felicity, (sloop of war), 211.
Fenton (Michigan), 277.
Ferry Hall (Lake Forest), 50.
Ferry, Thomas White, 50.
Ferry, William Montague, 48, 49, 50, 154, 205, 277.
Festivities at the Odanah mission, 241.
Fevre river, 188, 192, 193.
Field, Rev. David Dudley, D. D., 85, 88, 95, 97.
Fifty Years in the Northwest (Folsom), 157.
Finch, Asahel, Jr., 218.
Finney, C. G., 162.
Fiske, Professor John, 27, 278.
Fitch, A. M., 249.
Five Nations, the, 55.
Flambeau, Lac du, 249.
"Float" (land warrant), 214.
Florida, 27, 29, 33, 179.
Folles Avoines, 21, 210.
Folsom, W. H., 157.
Fond du Lac (Wisconsin), 60.
Fond du Lac, (Minnesota), 153, 155, 157, 158, 160-162, 167-169, 238, 239.
Force, Peter, 278.
"Forts" on Madelaine island; middle, 267; new, 153; old, 147, 153, 256.
"Forts," in the lead region, 199.
Fort Armstrong, 133, 192.
Fort Atkinson, 224, 266.
Fort Beauharnois, 19, 20.
Fort Clark, 41.
Fort Crawford, 166, 178, 179, 190, 203, 207, 208.
Fort Dearborn, 154, 220, 223.
Fort Edward Augustus, 26, 201, 202.
Fort Gilbert, 220.
Fort Harmar, garrison of, 38.
Fort Howard, 14, 21, 52, 64, 65, 190, 201, 202, 204, 205, 206, 207, 209.
Fort Jefferson, 31.
Fort Leavenworth, 137.
Fort Mackinaw, Old, 31, 45, 177; the new, 40, 46.
Fort Madison, 42.
Fort McKay, 43, 178.
Fort Morand, 224.
Fort Ponchartrain, 45.
Fort Ramsay, 153.
Fort Sackville (Indiana), 31.
Fort St. Francis, 19, 20, 21, 26, 202.
Fort Shelby, 40, 42, 43, 178, 189.
Fort Snelling, 149, 150, 158, 166, 162.

INDEX.

Fort Sumpter, 197.
Fort William Henry, 30.
Fort Winnebago, 50, 127, 145, 149, 190, 194, 205, 207, 208, 209, 210, 224.
Four Lakes, the (of Madison), 196.
Four-Legs, 118, 119.
Fowle, Major John, 154.
Fowler, David, 67, 68, 69, 71, 97; Jacob, 68, 69; Mary, 68; William, 72.
Fox Indians, the, 12, 14, 17, 19, 20, 21, 22, 23, 24, 25, 188, 192. *See* also Outagamies.
Foxes (and Sacs), 132, 134, 189, 195.
Fox river, (tributary of the Illinois), 219, 220, 221, 224.
Fox river, the, 1, 2, 13, 16, 19, 20, 25, 30, 56, 58, 60, 64, 71, 110, 117, 120, 123, 129, 130, 142, 176, 207.
Fox-Wisconsin canal, 207.
Fox-Wisconsin route and portage, 9, 12, 18, 30, 47, 175, 176, 190, 207, 210.
France, 14, 26, 27, 29, 35, 44; "His Christian Majesty" of, 27, 175.
Franco-British Wars, 1, 278.
Frank, Colonel M., 221, 225.
Frederick, Prince of Wales, 90.
Fremont (Nebraska), 85.
French and Indian war, 25, 28, 45, 91, 147.
French colonies, loss of, 27.
French creek (Pennsylvania), 185.
French, the, 2, 3, 16, 17, 27, 28, 30, 41, 49, 78, 87, 88, 91, 93, 94, 147.
Frontenac, Marquis de, 15.
Fulton, Robert, 33.
Gagmegue (Agmegue), 94.
Gah-nu-kwash-koh-dah-ding, 11.
Gaines, General E. P., 196.
Galena (Illinois), 31, 134, 154, 187, 191-194, 197, 208, 224. *See* Fevre river.
Ga-no-a-lo-ha-le, 63.

Gardner, ——, an Indian, 129.
Garfield, President James A., 46.
Garrison, W. L., 184.
Gauthier, Charles, 210.
Gavin, Daniel, 134, 135.
Geneva (New York), 62; Wisconsin, 223.
Geology of Wisconsin, 207.
George III., 29, 44, 68, 90, 97, 147.
Georgia, 29, 162.
Germany, 35.
Ghent, treaty of, 43, 201.
Gibbon, Edward, 27.
Giddings, J. R., 46.
Gilbert, Henry, 170.
Gilman, Secretary E. W., 164.
Girty, Mike, 197.
Glacial epoch, the second, 156.
Glazier, Willard, 155.
Gleason, Rev. G L., 19.
Gorham, ——, 98.
Gorrel, Lieutenant James, 201.
Gorton, Mrs. C. M. R., 277.
Governor Clark (gunboat), 40, 42, 43.
Graham, Duncan, 186.
Grand Crossing (Chicago, Illinois), 115.
Grand Detour, 194.
Grand Haven, 50.
Grand Kau-kau-lin (South Kaukauna), 66, 110, 111, 113, 117, 120, 123, 129, 205.
Grand Portage, 147, 156.
Gratiot, Charles, 31; Henry, 31; Gratiot's Grove, 31.
Grant, President, peace policy of, 253.
Grant county, 200.
Grassie, Rev. T. G., 256, 259.
Great Barrington (Massachusetts), 77, 82, 91.
Great Britain, 27, 54, 68, 69, 86, 94, 106.
Great Lakes (and upper Lake region), 28, 30, 32, 43, 44, 46, 48, 52, 58. *See* also special names.

INDEX.

Gregorian calendar, 76, 80.
Green Bay, 3, 9, 13, 14, 18, 121.
Green Bay, region or "parish" of, 1, 3, 13, 16, 18, 21, 22, 24–27, 56, 57, 60, 64, 65, 67, 110, 111, 118, 119, 278; Indians of, 57. See also Menominees, Winnebagoes, etc.
Green Bay, post and city of, 19, 28, 30, 35, 36, 41, 42, 44, 45, 47, 49, 50, 52–54, 56, 59–61, 64–66, 110, 111, 114, 115, 116, 118, 119, 121, 122, 125, 127, 129, 130, 137, 144, 145, 147–149, 161, 177, 181, 186, 189, 200–202, 204, 205, 207, 209, 212, 218, 224, 276.
Green Bay newspapers: *Free Press, Intelligencer, Spectator,* 225.
Green, Chancellor N., 185.
Green Lake county, 2.
Greene, Secretary David, 130, 149.
Greenwood, Grace, 235,
Gregory, Rev. Henry, 217.
Grignon, Louis, 41, 201, 203; [Grignion], Augustus, 22, 24, 25, 42, 203, 212.
Grosseilliers, Sieur des, 2, 5, 6, 11, 15, 16, 210, 277.
Grosse Point, 213.
Groton (Connecticut), 69.
Guerin, Jean, 9.
Gulf of Mexico, 26, 175, 207.
Guy Park, 99.
Haldimand, Sir Frederick, Governor of Canada, 31, 32.
Hall, Chauncey, 129, 135, 136, 277; Miss Jennie, 277; Mrs. B. P., 157, 274; Rev. Sherman, 152, 153, 155, 156, 157, 160, 161, 164, 165, 167, 168, 170, 274.
Hamilton college, 49; Colonel Henry, 30, 32.
Hamlin, Rev. Cyrus, 257.
Hampton (Virginia), institution at, 87.
Hanover (New Hampshire), 68, 140, 144.
Hanson's Lost Prince, 57.
"Hard times" in Wisconsin, 220.
Hardy, Mrs. C. F., 264.
Harris, Rev. Thompson S., 62.
Harrison, Governor and President, 106, 188.
Harson's Island, 46,
Harvard college, 47, 54, 63, 82.
Hatfield (Massachusetts), 78, 86.
Hatfield's Poets of the Church, 72.
Haverhill (Massachusetts), 19.
Hawley Gideon, 93, 94.
Hayes, Sir James, 6.
Hayward (Wisconsin), 171.
Heaton, Rev. I. E., 185.
Hebberd's French Dominion in Wisconsin, 12, 21, 26.
Hefferon, Countess de, 159.
Hendrick (Aupaumut), Captain, 106, 107, 108, 112, 116, 121, 124 127; Mrs., 124; Solomon U., 56, 110; Thomas T., 129, 137.
Hennepin, Louis, 15, 279.
Henry III, 27; IV, 27; Alexander, 147, 148; Governor Patrick, 32, 36.
Hiawatha, 46.
Hill, Mrs. A. L., 213, 214.
Hinman, Deacon Samuel, 218.
Hinsdel, Rev. ——, 82.
Historical Collections. See Wisconsin, Minnesota, etc.
Historical Memoirs, 77, 108, 124.
Histories. See particular subjects.
Hoar, Senator G. F., 33, 35.
Hoard, William Dempster, 97.
Hobart, Bishop J., 64, 122.
Hocquart, ——, 22.
Holden, Samuel, Esq., 86.
Holland Land company, 60, 98, 105.
Hollis, Isaac, 82, 83, 84, 87, 91; professorship, 47; Thomas, Esq., 82.
Holton, Amos, 203.
Holy Spirit, Mission of the, 10–13.

Home Missionary, the, 185, 215–217, 219, 220.

Hooker, Thomas, 33.

Hopkins, Rev. Samuel (the elder), 76, 77, 80, 81, 91, 97. 99, 108, 124; (the younger), 91; President Mark, 90.

Houghton (Michigan), 253.

Housatonic (unnuk) Indians, 73, 75, 80; the place, 77, 82, 83, 85, 86, 99; the river, 75, 85.

Howard, General Benjamin, 41.

Hubbard, Thomas, 92.

Hudson bay, 3, 6, 18, 40; company, 6, 41; river, 75, 80, 83. 85, 95.

Huebschmann, Francis, 142.

Hughes, Rev. J. V., 144.

Huguenots, the, 5, 31, 175, 277.

Hull, Brigadier General William, 40; Mrs. Mary, 271.

Humboldt, Karl Wilhelm (?), 74.

Hundred Years' War, the first, 1; the second, 1, 17, 278.

Hunt, Wilson Price, 47.

Hunter, Lieutenant-General, 28.

Huntington, Samuel, 225.

Hurons, the, 4, 5, 7–13, 18, 22, 45, 49, 55, 61, 146, 147, 165, 279.

Hurtibis, Mr. ———, 43.

Hutton, A. J., 276; Mrs. A. J., 276.

"Ida Glenwood," 277.

Illinois, 18, 22, 24, 28, 31, 32, 36–40, 50, 54, 55, 136, 164, 166, 182, 191, 193, 224.

Illinois college, 184.

Illinois, commandant of the country of, 36.

Illinois, the (Indians), 2, 12, 24.

Illinois militia, disbandment of, 197.

Illinois river, 18, 22, 31, 41, 197, 211, 219, 220.

Illinois volunteers in Black Hawk War, 197.

Immanuel church (Milwaukee), 219.

Immigration into Wisconsin from South and East, 199, 220.

Inauguration of Wisconsin's first governor, 200.

Indian affairs, committee on, 95.

Indians' suffering in illness, 234.

Indian Puritans, 112.

Indian Territory, 61, 66.

Indian Trade, profit in, 192.

Indiana, 32 35, 37, 37, 39, 54, 100, 105, 107, 109 111, 113, 124, 166, 220.

Inquisition, 14.

"Inter-lachen," an, 223.

Intolerance, Roman Catholic, 13–15, 176.

Iowa, 35, 39, 133, 189, 195, 199, 200, 216.

Iowa county, 200, 224.

Iowas, the, 21, 188.

Ish-ko-da-wa-bo ("fire-water"), 245.

Ipswich Hamlet (Hamilton, Massachusetts), 33.

Ipswich, Mary Lyon's school at, 232.

Ireland, 37.

Iroquois (Six Nations), 2, 4, 7, 11, 12, 16, 22, 23, 55, 56, 61, 62, 93, 94, 98, 104, 108, 279.

Irving, Prof. R. D., 207.

Irving, Washington, 47, 51.

Irwin (not Erwin), Alexander J., 132.

Isaac, Dolly, 123.

Ishkado, 3.

Itasca, origin of name, 155.

Jackson, President Andrew, 197.

James, Edwin, 154, 164, 180, 181.

James, Mrs. W. L., 165.

James, Rev. W. L., 165.

Janesville, 224.

Jefferson, President Thomas, 126.

Jesuits, 4, 6, 8, 10, 15, 127, 143.

Jesuit Relations, 8, 9, 12, 13.

Jews, order for persecution of, 176.

Johnson, Colonel James, 188, 189, 192.

INDEX.

Johnson, John (Enmegahbowk), 166.
Johnson, T. S. 203.
Johnston, John, 147.
Joliet, Louis, 176, 211.
Jones, George W., 199, 208.
Jones, Miss Electa, 94, 103; her *History of Stockbridge*. 73, 81, 126, 137.
Jones, Peter, 164, 165.
Josephine, (steamboat), 191.
Jourdan, Timothy T., 129.
Journal, Carver's, 177.
Juneau, L. S., 212, 213, 216, 225.
Juneau, Peter, 225.
Julian calendar, 80.
Julius Caesar (Shakespeare), 5.
Kanadesaga, 62.
Kansas, 61; territory of 61, 137, 141.
Kaposia (Minnesota), 162, 166.
Kaskaskia (Illinois), 18, 32; death for witchcraft at, 36; court of. 36, 37.
Katakosakout, 56.
Katzer, Archbishop F. X, 36.
Kaukauna, *See* South Kaukauna and Grand Kau-kau-lin.
Kaunaumeek, 86.
Kearney, Major S. W., 178.
Keinonche, 11, 12.
Kellogg, Austin, 221; Captain Martin, 90 93.
Kemper, Bishop J. J. 217.
Kennedy, Mrs. Augusta S. 265, 266.
Kenosha, 12, 209, 221, 224, 225.
Kent, Mrs. Aratus, 208; Rev. Aratus, 154, 182, 183, 185, 193, 194, 208, 210, 219.
Kentucky, 32, 189, 199.
Keokuk (Iowa), 192; famous chief, 35, 133, 195.
Keshena, 144.
Kewaunee, 212.
Kewcenaw Point, 7; bay. 165.
Kiala, an Outagamie chief, 22.
Kickapoos, the, 14, 21; river. 22, 24, 25.

Kilbourn, Byron. 214, 215.
Killistinoes, the, 75.
Kimball, Edward Fiske, 11.
Kinderhook, 93.
Kingston, J. T., 219.
Kinzie, J. H., 180, 181, 208; Mrs. J. H., 50, 208.
Kirby, Miss ——, 225.
Kirk, Sir John, 5; daughter of, 5.
Kirkland, Rev. John Thornton, 63; Rev. Samuel, 62–64, 68, 71, 94, 98, 103, 106.
Kishkakonk nation, 12.
Knapp, Gilbert, 220.
Knox, Major-General Henry, 106.
Konkapot, B., 57; Captain John, 75–77, 79, 81, 83, 85, 94, 112; Hannah, 128; Levi, Jr., 112; Mary, 128; Robert, 128; Robert 137.
Ko-nosh-o-ni, the 55.
Lancaster Congregational church, 184.
L'Anse (Michigan), 165.
Lathrop, Rev. D. W., 183.
Latrobe, C. J., 186.
La Baye, 20, 21, 26. 177, 201, 202.
Lac Court Oreilles, 166, 170, 249.
Lac du Flambeau, 170, 249.
Lacy, Dr. A. T., 225.
Ladd, Professor G. T., 213, 214.
La Fayette, town of, 223; county of, 31, 200.
La Framboise, Alexander, 212; Fransis, 212; Josette, 212.
Lake Athabasca, 48, 278.
do. Erie, 211.
do. Forest university, 50.
do. Geneva (Wisconsin), 223; the village, 223.
do. George, 30, 94.
do. Harriet, 127, 162.
do. Huron, 2, 3, 5, 13, 14, 75, 155, 177, 189, 211.
do. Itasca, 39, 155, 156.
do. Koshkonong, 196, 197.

Lake Michigan, 1, 14, 18, 21, 26, 39, 40, 44, 45, 54, 60, 64, 66, 110, 121, 123, 146, 177, 191, 200, 201, 207, 211, 212, 215, 221.
Lake Namekagon, 4.
do. of the Woods, 39, 200.
do. Pepin, 176, 187.
do. road to Milwaukee, 213.
do. Superior region, 147, 280.
do. Superior, 148, 150-154, 156, 158, 163, 165, 168, 171, 233, 238, 253, 254, 268, 277,
do. Winnipeg (pic), 41, 156, 276.
do. Winnebago, 138, 211; builders of first steamboat on, 72.
Land speculations in Wisconsin, 200.
Langlade, Augustine, 203; Charles M. de, 30-32, 35, 203, 210; county, 203.
La Perriere, Sieur de (Boucher), 19.
La Pointe, 49-51, 147, 148, 151 153, 155-161, 163, 165, 167 170, 180, 187, 233, 234, 238, 239, 245, 249, 255, 267, 273-275; county, 167.
La Salle, 15, 176, 187. 212.
Law, John, 15; John, 175, 176.
Lawe, John, 41, 52, 203.
Laws of Canada ("Quebec act"), 29.
Lead mines, 14, 31, 187, 188, 191, 192.
Lebanon (Tennessee), 185; (Connecticut), school, 62, 67, 68.
Lee, Major-General Charles, 94.
Leech Lake, 156 158, 160, 162, 275.
Legislature, of Wisconsin, 32, 200, 278.
Leonard, Mrs. Emily, 258, 260, 261.
Le Roy, Francis, 210, 258.
Leni Lennappes, 54, 100. See also Delawares.
Le Sueur, Pierre, 14, 147, 187, 188.
L'Epervier (Black Hawk), 189.
Lewis, Captain, Meriwether, 40.
Life, loss of, in Black Hawk War, 197.
Lincoln, Abraham, 36, 172, 197, 199.
Lincolnshire, 133, 231.
Lisbon (Connecticut), 62.

"Little Chute," 56, 110, 121.
do. Crow, 162, 166.
Little Kaukauna, 60, 64 66, 71, 72, 110, 121.
do. Osage river, 61, 137.
do. Rapids, 64. See also Little Kaukauna.
Littledale, Rev. R. F., 14.
Littleman, Isaac, 137; Peter, 137.
Livingston, Hon. Philip, 78.
Lockport (New York), 193.
Lockwood, James, 78; James H., 179-183, 186; Mrs. James H. (Julianna Warren), 180, 181, 186, 202.
Longmeadow (Massachusetts), 65, 76.
Long Island, 67-69.
Long, Major, Stephen Harriman, 153.
London, 30, 86, 90.
Loss, Rev. L. H. 222.
Lothrop, Rev. Jason, 225.
Louis XIII., 15, 26, 27, 175; XIV., 13, 23, 27, 44; XV., 27, 44; XVI., 65.
Louisburg, 1.
Louisiana, 14, 15, 27, 175-177, 188, 216; purchase, 39, 216.
Louvigny, M. de, 19, 24, 45.
Love, Deacon Robert, 218; Rev. William De, 67, 70, 72, 97.
Lovejoy, Rev. Elijah Parish, 38.
Lowell (Massachusetts), 231 233, 241, 248-250, 254.
Lowrey, Rev Daniel, 183-185.
Lowrie, Rev, John C., 47.
Luce, Andrew J. 220; William, 220.
Lyndon (Illinois), 194.
Lyon, Mary, at Ipswich, 232.
McArthur, Rev. H. G., 266, 267; Mrs. H. G., 266.
McCabe, J. P. B., 137.
McCall, James, 56, 57, 59, 71, 118-121.
McCockle, James, 109.
McClellan, General G. B., wife of, 205.
McDouall, Lieut.-Col. Robert, 40, 44.

McDougall, Dr. Charles, 210.
McGaultley (British sailor), 211.
McKay, Lieutenant-Colonel William, 41, 42, 178, 189.
McKinney, Colonel Thomas L., 113.
McMaster's account of the Marietta colony, 33.
Mackinaw island, trading-post and fort, 40, 42–44, 46–52, 116, 122, 130. 148, 151, 152, 154, 156, 179, 181, 205, 212, 233.
Mackinaw (the "Old Fort"), 24, 30, 31, 32, 45, 177, 203, 210.
Mackinaw church, mission and school. 46, 48, 49, 50, 135, 165, 172, 205, 206.
Mackinaw, straits of, 45, 146, 147.
Madelaine island, 4, 11, 146 148, 151, 152, 159, 233, 239, 240, 246, 255, 258, 259.
Madison, 56, 123, 194, 224; convention (of churches), 145.
Madison county (Illinois), 182.
Madison county (New York), 96, 97.
Mail routes in 1836, 224.
Ma-ka-tau-me-she-kia-kiah, 189.
Manhattan, 4, 73.
Manitoulin islands, one of the, 3; island, 13.
Manhattas, the, 73.
Manitowoc, 184, 212, 224, 280.
Mannawahkiah river, 121.
Mann, Moody, 137.
Manuel, a Negro slave burned for witchcraft, 36.
Manypenny, Commissioner G. W., 170, 235.
Marcy, General R. B., 205.
Marest, Gabriel, 18.
Mary, Queen of England, 17.
Marietta (Ohio), 1, 33–35, 38; settlement of, 98; first Congregational church of, 34.
Marin, Perriere, 21, 24, 26, 113.

Marinette, 66.
Marksman, Peter, 166.
Marquette, Jacques, 11, 12, 13, 14, 45, 49, 127, 159, 211, 212, 278.
Marquette (Michigan), 173.
Marsh, Mrs. Eunice (Osmer), 140.
Marsh, Rev. Cutting, 99, 111, 112, 116, 120, 124–131, 134, 137–141, 206, 218, 276, 277.
Marsh, Rev. Cutting, diary of, 118, 121, 123, 125, 139.
Marsh, Sarah E., 276.
Martin, Morgan Lewis, 64, 204, 212.
Martindale, Miss H. S., 271, 272.
Martinique, 22.
Mascoutins, 2, 3, 14, 17, 21, 210.
Mason, Edward G., 36.
Mason, John T., 56, 57, 120.
Massachusetts, 1, 18, 85, 95, 98, 124, 128, 143, 148, 156, 162, 205, 208, 231, 233, 254, 275; first seal of, 69, 70; general court of, 84; historical society, 70, 75 77, 79; Indians, 11; Medical society, 33, 34, 39, 60, 65, 69; speaker of the House of, 92.
Massachusetts Bay, 33, 69.
Massawomekes, 55.
Maumee, 116, 276; river, 126, 187.
Maxwell, Thompson, 156.
Mather, Cotton, 231; Increase, 5.
May, Colonel John, 38.
Mayflower, the first, 32; the second, 1.
Mazzuchelli, Rev. Samuel, 208.
Meadville (Pennsylvania), 185.
Mears, Rev. L. D., 221, 224.
Medell, Commissioner W., 109.
Medical service of Odanah mission, 165, 246.
Memorial of Mrs. Harriet W. Wheeler, 229, *et sq.*
Menasha, 19, 177.
Menard, Rene, 7 10, 14, 61.
Mendell, Deacon Ezra, 218.
Menomonee river, 203.

Menomonees, 21, 24, 31, 42, 53, 56–61, 65, 66, 75, 88, 108, 110, 113, 119, 121, 128, 132, 143, 149, 190, 210, 212; their language, 75; their reservation, 142.
Menomoneeville, 205.
Merrell, Ex-President E. H., 256.
Messitougas, the, 75.
Messmer, Bishop S. J., 36.
Metawa, the, 238.
Meteoric shower of 1833, 128.
Methodist Episcopal church, 278; its first church building in Wisconsin, 123; missionary society, 128; preachers, few in 1838, 220.
Methodist or "Orchard" party among the Oneidas, 123.
Methodist missions among the Wyandots, 165; among the Ojibways, 153, 165, 166.
Methodism, beginning of in Minnesota, 166.
Metoxen, Catherine, 111, 112, 128; John, 26, 57, 58, 73, 109 112, 117, 122, 123, 126 129, 131, 133, 134, 139, 143, 145, 204; party of Stockbridges, 107, 109-111. 197.
Mexico, 3; Gulf of, 26, 207.
Miami land-grant, 126; river, 18.
Miamis, the, 22, 28. 107, 188.
Michigan, 7, 9, 28, 39, 40, 46, 50. 54, 148, 165, 173, 179, 187, 194, 253, 276, 277; [Indian] agency, 249; Fencibles, 41, *Historical Collections*, 43; territorial legislature of, 200; trans-Mississippi part of, 196, 216.
Michilimackinac (the region; also the Jesuit mission and post north of the strait), 12, 13, 15, 28, 45. 159.
Michilmackinac, straits of, 45, 146, 177.
Military posts in Michigan, 39.
Miller, Andrew, 129; Colonel John, 201; Ebenezer, 76; Josiah W., 129; Samuel, 124, 129, 139, 142; Weson Gage, D. D., 139, 140, 144, 205.
Mills, J. T., 184, 280.
Milwaukee, 31, 36, 47, 67, 186, 209, 212, 214, 216–218, 221, 224, 225, 256; bay of, 211; convention (of churches), 145; county, 224; first church building in, 218; harbor, 212; Indians, 211; river, 60, 121, 214; churches of: First Presbyterian, 219, Grand Avenue Congregational, 67, 213; Immanuel, 47, 145; North Presbyterian, 219; Plymouth, 219; newspapers of, *Advertiser, Courier*, 225; *Sentinel*, 213 225; *Wisconsin*, 225.
Miner, D. I., 171; Rev. Jesse, 112, 114–116, 149, 204, 278,
Miners' Free Press, 225.
Miner, Lake Superior, 253.
Mineral Point, 185, 194, 199, 200, 224, 225.
Mingoes, 55, 100.
Mining, first in Wisconsin, 188.
Mining region (Upper Mississippi), 191. See also Lead Mines, etc.
Minister, first in Wisconsin, 202.
Minneapolis, 15, 127.
Minnesota, 5, 9, 18, 29, 134, 141, 155, 156, 162, 163, 170, 171, 200, 255, 275, 276; river, 176.
Minnesota Historical Collections, Vol. VII, 134.
Miro, Governor Estavan, 14.
Missionary Gazetteer, 48; *Herald*, 50, 62, 115, 124, 131.
Mississippi valley, 17, 18; rivers of, 42.
Mississippi, rapids of the, 191, 192.
Mississippi, the, 2–5, 9, 12, 14, 18, 20, 22, 24–26, 28 35, 39 44, 47, 54, 65, 115, 127, 131, 132, 136, 139, 145, 149, 155–157, 160, 163, 166–168, 176, 177, 184 189, 191, 192, 194, 195, 198–201, 207, 210, 216, 220, 221, 224, 272; various names of, 176.

Missouri, 38, 184, 189, 216; territory of, 40, 216.
Missouri, lead mines of, 191.
Missouri river, 18, 39, 47, 127, 137, 200, 216.
Mitchell, James, John T., Samuel, 38.
Mohawk river, the, 95; the valley, 4.
Mohawks, the, 4, 55, 62, 63, 68, 78, 88, 89, 92 94; their language, 63, 64, 68, 75, 122.
Moheakumnut tribe, 278.
Mohegan language. *See* Muh-he-ka-ne-ew.
Mohegans, 69, 73-75, 137.
Moh-he-con-nuck, 143.
Mokuks of birch-bark, 243.
Monroe (Michigan), 116.
Monroe, President, 56, 57.
Monrong, ———, 211.
Montauk, 69, 105.
Montauk Indians, 68, 69; Occom's treatise on their language, 70.
Montreal, 20, 21.
Monument mountain, 83.
Moor's (or Moore's) "charity school" (Indian) 54, 67, 68, 140, 144.
Moose Tail, Moo-zoo-jeele, Mo-zo-geede (Ojibway chief), 166, 278 279.
Moraud, Captain Perriere. *See* Marin.
Moravians and Moravian missions, 97, 105, 106, 109.
More, Joshua, 68.
Moreau, a slave, 36.
Morse, Jedidiah, D. D., 47, 52-56, 60, 143, 201 203.
Morse, Richard Cary, 47; S. F. B., 47.
Mound builders, the, 221, 222.
Mount Hope (Rhode Island) 69.
Muh-he-ka-ne-ew language, 74, 125; specimens of, 90, 125; booklets in, 104, 124, 125.
Muh-he-ka-ne-ok, the, 73 77, 85, 86, 88, 91, 94 98, 105, 107-109, 113, 114, 120, 129, 131, 132, 135, 139, 140 142, 145, 212. *See* also Stockbridges.
Muh-he-ka-ne-ok (history), 73, 143.
Munsees, the, 54 56, 60, 73, 75, 100, 107, 142; their language, 75.
Mushke sibi, the, 167.
Mushkoosi (Indian word), 3.
Muskingum river, 1.
Musquakink, the, 16.
Mutiny among Illinois volunteers, 199.
Nadonoceronon, 3.
Nadouessi (sioux), 12, 14, 55, 279.
Nadowa and Nadowasie, 3.
Nanticokes (hanticks), 69, 75.
Narragansett Indians, 69, 73.
Nash, Rev. Norman, 114, 202.
Nashville, (Tennessee), 183.
Nation, The, 33.
National Board of Charities and Correction, 27.
Naunauchoowuk, 88.
Navarre, Henry of, 26.
Navarino, 206.
Neander's Church History, 253.
Nebraska, 127, 185.
Nee-koouts Hah-ta-kah, 175.
Neenah, 177.
Negro Slavery in Wisconsin, 38.
Neill, Rev. E. D., 9, 12, 147, 149, 277.
Nelson, Rev. George W., 255.
Nelson's post, 6; river, 41.
Nendrol, Cant, 100.
Netherlands (Holland), 4, 28.
New Albany, 222.
Newark (New Jersey), 16.
New Britain (Connecticut), 52.
New Brunswick, 75.
Newburyport, presbytery of, 116.
New Connecticut, 46.
Newell, Harriet, 270.
New England, 12, 19, 26, 27, 33, 35, 37, 46, 62, 67 70, 74-76, 82, 88, 136, 168, 180, 181; New England homes, 233, 235.

INDEX. 297

New England, the town and town meetings of, 32, 125.
New England emigrants and emigrating companies, 33, 98, 199, 215, 222.
New England history, 65, 97.
New England Magazine, 11.
Newspapers (Wisconsin) in 1836, 225.
New Stockbridge, 97, 99, 101, 104, 114, 124, 126, 128.
New France, 1, 2, 5, 10, 15, 16, 19, 20, 24, 26, 27, 37, 175, 176, 178.
Newhall's Sketches of Iowa, 35.
Newhall, Horatio, M. D., 191, 192, 208.
New Hampshire, 45, 68, 140, 144, 155, 193.
New Haven, 46, 47, 79, 81-83.
Newington (Connecticut), 91.
New Jersey, 76, 87; college of (Princeton), 62, 77, 95.
New London (Connecticut), 74.
New Testament (Ojibway translation), 164, 165.
Newton, Abel D., 154, 161, 208.
New Orleans, 186, 191.
New Orleans (steamboat), 42.
New York, 16, 47, 54, 55, 59-61, 63-67, 70, 71, 73, 76, 78, 80, 83, 85, 93, 94, 96, 98, 100, 101, 105, 106, 108-110, 112-114, 116, 123, 124, 128, 142, 143, 148, 157, 193, 203, 204, 217, 224, 275; emigration from, 199.
New York City, 33, 49, 194, 215, 235, 270.
"New York Indians," 52, 55 58, 60, 64, 113, 119-121.
New York, Methodist Episcopal conference of, 66.
New York Observer, the, 47, 163.
Niagara Falls, 30, 279; fort near, 34, 92, 177.
Niantic (Connecticut), 69.
Nichols, Rev. Cyrus, 220.
Nicolet, Jean, 1, 2, 3, 26, 52, 210.

Nicollet, Jean N., 160; creek called by his name, 155.
Niles, Mrs. Mary E., 108; Mary West, M. D., 108.
Ninham, Daniel (or Abraham), 96.
Nipegons, the, 75.
Non-glaciated area of Wisconsin, 187.
Nonnekagon, Lake, 4.
Norridgewock (New England), 88.
North America, 1, 6, 13, 23, 26, 27, 29, 30, 54, 90, 175; Indians of, 87, 88, 90.
North America, Travels through the Interior Part of, 30, 75, 177.
North American Indians, 109, 137.
Northampton, 76.
North Dakota, 39, 163, 276.
Northern Missionary society of New York, 47, 49, 63.
Northern Pacific railway, 155.
Northway, Isaac G., 221.
Northwest Fur company, 12.
Northwest Territory, 1, 32-34, 37 39, 55, 124; the northwest territory, 48.
North Wisconsin academy, 255, 256.
North Wisconsin Home Missionary society, 256.
Norwich (Connecticut), 68.
Not-ta-ways, the, 56.
Nova Scota, 75.
Noyelle, Sieur de, 22.
Oak Point, 4, 5.
Oberlin, 162, 163, 249, 276; college, 46; theology, 163.
Observations, President Edwards's, 74.
Occom, Rev. Samson, 62, 63, 67-72, 74, 91, 94, 97, 98, 101.
Odanah, 4, 167 173, 235, 240-242, 244, 247, 248, 250, 256, 257; reser. vation, 249.
Odgen (Holland) Land company, 55, 60, 61, 98.
Odugaumeeg, 146.
Ogden, John, 218.

Ogilvie, Rev. John, 64.
Ogle county (Illinois), 196.
Oglethorpe, General James Edward, 33.
Ohio, 1, 37, 38, 46, 109, 126, 134, 166, 171, 182, 232, 276; first constitution of, 37; Ohio, Indiana, Illinois, Michigan and Wisconsin, 29, 35.
Ohio company, the, 33, 35.
Ohio river, 33, 185, 210.
Ohnaquango (New York), 103.
Ojibway missions, distances between the, 167; mission at Sandy Lake, 129. See also La Pointe, Odanah, etc., and names of missionaries.
Ojibways, the, 4, 7, 13, 21, 42, 48, 49, 66, 146, 147, 152, 153, 161, 165-168, 170, 186, 222, 233, 254, 256, 272-276; their language, 75; Testament therein, 164, 165, 172, 175.
Ojibways, Warren's history of the, 4.
Old South church, Boston, 94.
Old White Church, The, 216, 218.
Olin, Nelson, 216; Thomas, 216.
Oliver Newbury (steamer), 130.
Oneida Castle, village of, 63; county, 96; institute, 140; lake, 63.
Oneida (New York), 98-100, 103, 107; (Wisconsin), 65; Oneida West, 66.
Oneidas, the, 55, 56, 62-64, 68, 69, 71, 92, 93, 96, 98, 100 103, 107, 108, 205, 224; certain "delegates" of, 64; Oneidas of Wisconsin, 57, 60, 61, 65-67, 94, 113, 120, 123, 128, 129, 132, 189, 205, 224; their early settlements here, 64, 122, 123, 129; capital punishment among, 137; their reservation, 60, 61.
Onion river (Wisconsin), 11.
Onohoghwage, (Oughquauga), 93, 94.
Onondagas, 4, 55, 106.
Onondaga (New York), 203.
Ontario, province of, 29, 94, 96.
Ordinance of 1787, 34, 35, 37, 38, 193.

Ordway, Rev. Moses, 218, 219.
Ore-bearing lands, sale of, 191, 200.
Oriskany Creek (New York), 67.
Oshkosh, a Menomonee chief, 57, 59.
Ostrander, Rev. J. F., 217, 219.
Oswald, Richard (British commissioner), 34.
Oswego, military post of, 34.
Ottawa river, 1, 2, 4.
Ottawas (Outaouacs), 5, 7, 11 13, 21, 52, 75, 126, 146, 276.
Otis (Massachusetts), 209.
Ouinipigou (Winnebagoes), 2.
Ouisconsin river, the, 41, 42, 177, 191; Territory, 216. See also Wisconsin.
Outagamies, the. 16-23, 42, 110, 113, 176, 188, 189; their language, 75. See also Foxes.
"Outlet of Big Foot," 223.
Pacific ocean, 14, 47, 66, 95, 123.
Paris [France], 6, 27; treaty of [in 1763, 26, 27, 176; (Kentucky), 184.
Parker, ——, ordination of, 82.
Parkman, Francis, 11, 30.
Parsons, William, Indian agent, 144.
Parton, James, 173, 273.
Paul, Moses, 70, 74.
Pearsons, Daniel Kimball, 222, 279.
Pearson, A. H., 256.
Pecatonica (Illinois), 194.
Peet, Rev. Stephen, 185, 220.
Pekitanoui (the Missouri), 18.
Pembina, 163, 186.
Penn, William, 7, 33.
Pennsylvania, 32, 37, 75, 86, 97, 105, 109, 185
Penobscot river, 73; Indians, 73, 75.
Pepin, 176; lake, 4, 19, 176, 187.
Pequods, the, 69, 73.
Perkins, Lieutenant Joseph, 40, 42.
Permoussa, an Outagamie chief, 17.
Perrot, Nicholas, 9, 13, 14, 19, 134, 176, 187.
Perry, Arthur Latham, D. D., 84, 108.

INDEX.

Peters, Samuel Andrews, LL. D., (tory clergyman), 30, 181, 201; Secretary Absolom, 193; Ziba T., 142.
Petit Marais, 153.
Phelps, Oliver, 98; William, 134.
Philadelphia, 7, 33, 56, 178, 186.
Pierce, President Franklin, 212, 255; J. S., 212; Jonathan, 226.
Pigeon river (Minnesota), 147, 156.
Pillagers, the (an Ojibway tribe), 160.
Pilling, J. C., 124, 126, 167.
Pike, General Z. M., 178.
Pine Bend, 133.
Pinkney, Colonel Ninian, 202.
Pioneer History of Milwaukee, 215.
Pioria's Fort, 41.
Pittsfield (Massachusetts), 95, 233.
Pittsburg, 33, 38, 185; synod of, 182.
Platteville, 194, 218, 224, 225.
Pleyel's Hymn, 190.
Plymouth, 1, 18, 35, 38; colony, 33, 38; rock, 38.
Poets of the Church, 72.
Pokeguma lake and mission, 160 162, 167, 275.
Ponchartrain, 18; (Fort) 45.
Porlier, Jacques, 203.
Portage, Fox-Wisconsin, 41, 42, 117, 190, 207; road at, 210; the place, 133.
Porter, George B., 60; Rev. Jeremiah, 152-154, 185, 205, 206, 209, 210, 280; Miss Mary, 185.
Potosi, 188 194.
Pottawatomies, 118, 146, 196, 197, 213.
Powles, Henry, 57.
Prairie du Chien, 28, 30, 31, 41, 42, 44, 113, 133-135, 149, 166, 176-186, 188, 189, 194, 199, 203, 205, 207, 213, 224, 280; Indian agent at, 39, 40, 43; du Sac, 197.
Pratt (Wisconsin), 255.
Prentice, 274.
Presbyterians (in time of the Revolution), 32; board of foreign missions, 47, 148, 149, 157, 172; of home missions, 157, 182; church, reunion of, 172; directory for worship, 135.
Proces-verbal, by Daumont, 13; by La Salle, 176; by Perrot, 14, 176.
Prophetstown (Illinois), 196.
Putnam, Rufus, 35, 37.
Quakers, the, 26, 97.
Quan-au-kaunt, Joseph, 112.
Quebec, 1, 2, 11, 19, 27, 29, 186.
"Quebec act," 29, 37.
Quebec, province of, 29, 37.
Queen Anne's war, 75; Indian chief's visit to England during her reign, 79.
"Quelles hures!" origin of "Huron," 2.
Quinette, a Frenchman, 213.
Quinney, Austin E., 109, 122, 137, 139, 142, 143, 145.
Quinney, Flecta W., 66, 115, 128.
Quinney, John, 104, 125.
Quinney, John W., 57, 73, 75, 112, 113, 116, 119, 121, 122, 137, 139, 143.
Quinney, Joseph, 128.
Quinney, Margaret, 128.
Racine, 213, 220, 224.
Radisson, Sieur, 2-8, 11, 12, 15, 16, 61, 176, 210, 277, 278.
Ragueneau, Paul, 4.
Railway first to cross Wisconsin, 186; nearest in 1836, 224.
Ramsey, Governor Alexander, 163.
Randolph (Vermont), 222.
Recollects (Recollets), 15, 19.
Red Bird, Winnebago chief, 190.
Red Cliff reservation, 249.
Red Dog, Sioux chief, 150.
Red Lake (Minnesota), 151, 162, 163, 274, 275, 279; reserve, 267.
Red river of the North, 186; of Wisconsin, 142, 143.
Red Springs, 143; Sea, 185.
Reed, Harrison, 218.
Reidsville (New York), 73.

300   INDEX.

Representatives, House of, 48.
Reve, Rev. Frederic, 205.
Revival at the Fond du Lac mission, 238.
Revolution and revolutionary army and war, 23, 30, 32, 34, 35, 37, 42, 46, 47, 50, 62, 63, 68, 94 97, 99, 106, 147; events of in the Wisconsin region, 177, 210, 211.
Reynolds, Governor John, 196, 197.
Rhine, the river, 134.
Rhode Island, 69.
Richards, Charles H., wife of, 56.
Richmond (Virginia), 7.
Riggs, A. L., D. D., 150; Stephen Return, Rev., 162, 166 168.
Rigi Kulm, 272.
River Indians, 75, 76, 79; Nation, 136. See also Muh-he-ka-ne-ok.
Roberts, Bishop, 221; Sidney, 221.
Robertson, Samuel, 211.
Robinson, Mark, 215.
Rockford, 194.
Rock Island (Illinois), 43, 192, 194; the island, 133.
Rock river, 24, 189, 195, 196, 224; valley of, 200; conference, 215.
Rock St. Louis, 22.
Rockton (Illinois), 194.
Rocky Mountains, the, 40, 47, 162.
Rogers, Major Robert, 45; Mrs. Anna S., 269, 270.
Rolette, Joseph, 41.
Rolfe, Benjamin, 19.
Roman Catholicism, 29.
Rome (Italy), 159; church of, 26, 65,
Roosevelt, Theodore, 32.
Root, Erastus, 56, 57, 120, 121.
Roulette, Mr. ——, 181.
Round Table, (Beloit college). 193.
Roxbury (Wisconsin), 197.
Roy, Secretary J. E., 256, 270, 271.
Rublee, F. M., 225.
Russell, Miss Caroline, 115.

Russia, 70; Russians and Cossacks, 42.
Ryan, Colonel Samuel, 204.
Sabbath begun on Saturday evening, 141; dishonored by tyranny, 226; how honored at Odanah, 241; at Stockbridge, 136; instances of Sabbath-keeping, 1, 217; early Sabbath-schools in Wisconsin, 181, 202, 204; in 1836, 225.
Sacs (Sauks), 16, 17, 19 24, 30, 75, 110, 133, 134, 175, 188, 196 199
Sacs and Foxes, 132, 134, 188 190, 195; Sauk village, 22.
Saginaw, 16.
St. Anthony, falls of, 15, 149, 279.
St. Antoine, Post of, 176.
St. Augustine, quotation from, 111.
St. Augustine [Florida], 35.
St. Clair, Governor Arthur, 38, 106.
St. Clair river, 46.
St. Croix, portage, river and valley, 18, 156, 157, 160, 187.
St. Francis [Canada], Indians of, 75.
St. Francis, Xavier, mission of, 211, 212.
St. Ignatius, mission of, 12, 45.
St. Jacobs, J. B., 203.
St. Joseph (Walhalla, North Dakota), 276; St. Joseph's river, 187.
St. Louis, 40 43; called Pencour, 31; design of capturing, 31.
St. Mary's, treaty of, 109.
St. Mary's river (of Georgia), 29; (of Michigan), 51.
St. Peter, portal of [Arched Rock], 7.
St. Peter's river, 41, 176, 192.
St. Pier, ——, 211.
St. Pierre, Rev. Paul de, 180.
St. Sebastian, fortress of, 42.
Salem, 81.
Salisbury (England), 269.
Sandusky river, 165.
Sandy Lake [Minnesota], 129, 156, 158, 167, 168, 239, 275.

INDEX. 301

San Francisco, 180.
Santa Fe, 35.
Santee Normal school, 150.
Saratoga, 126.
Sasquahannah (Susquehanna river), 87.
Satterlee, R. S., M. D., 205, 206, 209; Mrs. R. S., 205, 206.
Sauk county, 196, 207.
Saulteaux (Sauteurs), 146.
Sault St. Marie, 146-148, 152-154, 166, 209.
Sault St. Louis (Canada), 65.
Savannah (Illinois), 194.
Scattekooks, the, 88.
Schenck, Rev. Dr. A. V., 123.
Schipicoten, 220.
Schoolcraft, H. R., 3, 7, 55,-125, 146, 148, 153 155, 166, 186; island, 155.
Schools, early, in Wisconsin, 115, 138, 181, 202, 203, 225; school code of Wisconsin, 225.
Scotland, 11, 63, 68, 80, 123, 124, 128.
Scott, General Winfield, 199.
Scott's Commentary, 110, 197.
Scuranis, ——, 103.
Secombe, ——, ordination of, 82.
Selkirk colony, 186.
Sell, William, 220.
Seminole war, 179.
Senecas, the, 55, 62, 66.
Sergeant, John, 76-97, 99, 104, 105, 108, 109, 111, 117, 124, 125, 135, 145; the younger, 54, 60, 90,95, 98, 99 101,104,106-108,111,112,114, 124, 141; the third, 56, 90, 110, 121.
Seymour, J. L., 158, 161, 275.
Shackford, Captain John, 193.
Shagawaumekong Point, 146.
Shake-Rag (Mineral Point), 200.
Shake shingles, 214, 223.
Shantytown, 115, 202, 204; 205.
Shaw, Colonel John, 40, 210.
Shawanese Indians (Showanoos), 75, 84, 87, 99.
Shawano, 144; Lake, 142.
Shawano witchfinder, a, 105, 110.
Shea, John G., 7, 180.
Sheboygan, 212, 214, 225.
Sheldon, George, 65.
Sheldon's History of Michigan, 45.
Sheridan, Mrs. General P. H., 203.
Sherman, General, son of, 14.
Shonandon (an Oneida chief), 103.
Shores, E. A., 255, 258; Mrs. E. A., 258.
Shunkasha (Sioux chief), 150.
Significance of the Frontier in American History, 95.
Simcoe, Lieutenant Colonel J. G., 96.
Simsbury (Connecticut), 209.
Sinclair, Patrick, 31, 46, 177, 211.
Sinope (Asia Minor), 226.
Sinsinawa Mound (Grant county), 199.
Sioux, the, 3-5, 11, 12, 14, 17, 19 21, 41, 42, 53, 127, 132, 135, 141, 146, 149, 161, 163, 166, 168, 172, 175, 185, 199, 238, 272, 275, 279; outbreak in Minnesota, 171.
Siskoinsin, 210.
Six Nations, 55, 64, 74, 92, 93, 98, 103, 104; their language, 75. *See also* Five Nations (2, 55), and Iroquois.
Skah-kah-wah-mee-kunk, 4.
Skatekook (now Sheffield), 76, 77, 82, 83, 85, 88.
Skenectetee (Schenectady), 94.
Skinner, Miss Persis, 135.
Slavery, decree permitting, 175.
Slavery in Jo Daviess county, 193.
Slingerland, Jeremiah, 140-142; Mrs. Sarah Irene, 142.
Small-pox, epidemic of, 170, 246.
Smelters, early, in lead region, 192.
Smith, Brigadier-General E. K., 52.
Smith, Colonel Joseph Lee, 52, 202.
Smith, Henry, 189, 198.
Smith, John, 114.
Smith, Richard, 235.
Smith, Colonel T. A., 178.

Smithfield, 122, 123.
"Snake Hollow." 188.
Snake river, 275.
Snow, depth of, in Northern Wisconsin, 245.
Socialism, experiment in, 144.
Society for Promoting Christian Knowledge, 63, 99; for propagating the Gospel among the Indians in North America, 69, 78; for propagating the Gospel in Foreign Parts, 69, 78; for propagating the Gospel among the Indians (Boston), 104.
South Carolina, 67; South Dakota, 39; South Kaukauna, 60, 66, 110, 114, 116, 279; South Sea, 14.
Southport, 224.
Spain, 14, 27, 31; His Catholic Majesty of, 27; the Spaniards, 34.
Spanish and Illinois country, 31.
Spencer, D. B., 162-164, 171; Mrs. D. B., 163, 164.
Spencer, Secretary John C., 98.
Spicer, Rhoda, 171.
Spirit mediums, Indian, 146.
Spooner, Miss Abbie, 234, 245, 267.
Sprague, Henry, 73.
Springfield, 75, 77, 80, 126.
Spring Prairie, 223.
"Stabber," the, Sac chief, 133.
Stambaugh, Samuel C., 120, 121.
Standard, the, (of Chicago), 72.
Starved Rock, 22.
State church, evil done by, 30.
Statesburg, 60, 113 116, 122, 127-129, 135, 138, 144, 279.
Stevens, Comly, 57.
Stevens, Rev. Jedidiah Dwight, 49, 50, 117, 118, 123, 127, 130, 135, 148-151, 156, 182, 185, 210; Mrs. J. D., 129, 130; Miss Lucy C., 135; Miss Sabina, 158, 275.
Stillman, Major Isaiah, 196, 197.
Stillwater, 155.

Stockbridge (England), 85.
Stockbridge Indians, 54-57, 60, 61, 66, 67, 70, 71, 73-75, 84, 94-101, 104-111, 113, 117, 120, 121, 123, 129-133, 136 142, 145, 148, 149, 189, 197, 276, 278; Congregational churches among them, 70, 97, 98, 107, 108, 111, 114, 115, 128, 130, 138, 139, 144, 145, 157; tithing-men in, 117, 141; Methodist Episcopal church, 140, 144; Presbyterian, 144. See also Muh-he-ka-ne-ok. Prohibitory laws by and for, 84, 195. Interesting characters, see Aupaumut, Konkapot, Metoxen, Quinney. Also Pau-quau-nau-peet, 90; Pohquon-nop-peet, 112; Pooh-poo-nuc, 77, 81; their language, see Muh-he-ka-ne-ew; an interpretation by Mrs. Pendleton, 109.
Stockbridge Indians, White river band of, 107, 109-112, 197; at Piqua (Ohio), 109; their church, 107, 109, 128; they come to Wisconsin, 111.
Stockbridge (Massachusetts), 74, 85-87, 89, 91 97, 104, 124, 162, 278; church of, 77, 88; *History of*, see Jones, Electa.
Stockbridge reservations: in Massachusetts, 76, 85; in New York, 96; in Indiana, 107, 109; in Wisconsin (on Fox river), 56; in Calumet county, 60, 137, 138; in Shawano county, 142, 144, 145.
Stockbridge (Wisconsin, Calumet county), 73, 110, 132, 135, 139-141, 143, 209, 218; church of, 145; mission-house at, 135; (Shawano county), 143; church of, 144.
Stockbridge and West Stockbridge, 85.
Stoddard, Colonel John, 76.
Stonington, 69.
Storm, Miss Helen C., 110.
Straum, Louis, 134.

INDEX.

Street, General J. M., 182, 184.
Strong, Hon. Moses M., 24, 190, 200.
Stuart, Robert, 50, 122; Mrs. R, 51.
Sturgeon bay, 13.
Suffrage in Wisconsin, 226.
Sullivan, Captain John, 40.
Sumner, Senator Charles, letter of, 253.
Sunday, John, 165.
Sunday-school, first at Milwaukee, 214; first at Prairie du Chien, 181; first in Wisconsin, 202.
Sunderland, Rev. Byron, D. D., 219.
Sunrise river, 150, 151.
Superior, Lake, 258, 265, 273, 274, 275.
Surrender of Red Bird, 190.
Susquehanna, 93.
Tanner, Dr. H. B., 52, 116, 279.
Tanner, John, 164.
Talon, Jean Baptiste, 13.
Tatepahqsect, 105, 106, 110.
Taylor county, 9.
Taylor, General Zachary, 43, 134, 178, 179, 184, 199, 208, 280.
Teachers, early, at Green Bay, 203.
Tecumseh, 106; war, 107.
Temperance: first convention in Wisconsin, 128; first society here, 128; early work, at Prairie du Chien, 184.
Tennessee, 49, 183, 185.
Test river, 85.
Texas, 166, 185, 207.
Thames (Connecticut) river, 67.
Thanksgiving, early observance of in Wisconsin, 128, 136.
Thayendanegea. See Brant, Joseph.
Thiebeau, Joseph, 222.
Thomas, Lieutenant Martin, 191.
Thowhusquh, Esther, 128.
Three Rivers (Canada), 2, 4, 5, 10, 203.
Throckmorton, Captain John, 198.
Thwaites, R. G., 4, 103, 180, 197, 210.
Tigris river, the, 216.
"Tikenderoga," 94.
Tithing-men in Wisconsin, 135, 141.
Titsworth, Rev. Judson, 256.
Tobbogans, a Christmas gift, 243.
Todd, John, 36.
Todd, Mary (Mrs. Lincoln), 36.
Tories, clerical, in the Revolution, 32.
Toronto (Canada), 164.
Total abstinence among Indians, 83, 130, 208; total abstinence churches, 130, 206.
Tounchy, John, 166.
Touslee, Waters, 221.
Towles, N., 57.
Town, Joseph, 157.
Town system of local government, 226.
Tracy, Jean Baptiste, 10.
Travels throughout North America, 30, 75, 176.
Travels, by President Dwight, 126.
Treat, S. B., 168.
Treaty, of 1725, 75; of Paris (1763), 26, 176; (1783), 28, 200; with the Six Nations, 104; with the Sacs and Foxes (1804), 188; Ghent, 43, 201; of St. Mary's, 109; with the Menomonees (Little Butte des Morts), 57, 113; (Stambaugh), 60, 212; with the Winnebagoes, 149, 213; with the Pottawatomies, 213; of Buffalo Creek, 61.
Trempealeau, 134, 176; county, first settlement of whites therein, 134.
Trumansburg (New York), 108.
Trumbull, J. H., 7.
Triumphant Democracy, 29, 33.
Turkey, Asiatic, 226.
Turkey, Rufus, 56.
Turner, Professor F. J., 13, 95.
Turtle, town of, 222.
Tuscaroras, the, 55, 56, 62, 67, 92, 93, 101–103.
Tuttle, Chauncey, 222.
Twiggs, General D. E., 207; Mrs. D. E., 208.
Uhhaunnowwaunmut, 56.

Umpachene, Stockbridge chief, 75-77, 81, 85.
Umpachene, Johtohkuhkoonart, 81.
Unhaunauwaunmet, Solomon, 278.
Union college, 74.
Union, the, 32, 33, 40, 54, 55, army of, 67, 72; the united colonies, 69.
United Foreign Missionary society, 48, 49.
United States, the, 16, 23, 27, 32, 33, 35, 39, 43, 50, 61, 96, 106, 113, 121, 132, 226; government, 34, 40, 42, 47, 55-57, 60, 104, 108, 109, 129, 135, 165; court of claims, 61, 67; army, 46.
Un-paun-nau-waun-nutt, Solomon, 112.
Upper Canada, province of, 28, 41, 153; first governor of, 96.
Upper Lakes region, 17, 25, 27, 43.
Upper Mississippi, the, 28, 44, 110; region, 25, 40.
Upper Pennisula, Michigan, 40, 45, 48.
Utica, 67, 114, 156, 224, 275, 277.
Vaccination, by missionaries, 246.
Vandalia (Illinois), 193.
Van der Sauven, Rev. H., 180.
Vaudreuil, Governor-General Philippe de Rigaud, 18, 45.
Vaughn, Mrs. M. E., 268, 269.
Verwyst, Rev. Chrysostom, 8, 9, 159.
Vermont, 48, 222, 233, 251, 276.
Vesuvius (steamboat), 42.
Vieau, Andrew J., 212; Jacques, 210, 212, 213; Louis, 213.
Vieux Desert, Lac, 9.
Villiers, Sieur de, 22.
Vincennes (Indiana), 32.
Virginia, 7, 32, 34, 37, 38, 56; governor of, 32, 36.
Virginia (steamboat), 185.
Viroqua (Wisconsin), 26.
Voltaire, 27.
Voyaging on Lake Superior, 152; first thereon by British and colonists, 156.

Wabash river, 18, 28, 31, 187.
Wah-pa-sha (Sioux chief), 135.
Wales, 69; Prince of, 90.
Walhalla (North Dakota), 163.
Walker, Rev. Jesse, 154, 220.
Wallingford (Connecticut), 209.
Walworth county, 223, 224.
Wappecommekkoke, 105.
Wappinackies, the, 59, 120.
Wapsipunicon river, 22.
War of a Hundred Years, the first, 1; the second, 1, 17; of the French with the Iroquois, 2; King William's, 17; incident of, 65; Queen Anne's, 75; Inter-colonial, 75; following Pontiac's conspiracy, 45; in Northwest Territory, 29, 106; in Europe, 28, (Napoleonic), 42; against Tecumseh, 106, 107; of 1812, 39-43, 46; of secession, 171. *See* also French and Indian, Revolution, and the names of various Indian tribes, Outagamies, Sioux, Winnebagoes, etc. Also names of chiefs, as Black Hawk, etc.
Ward, J. Q. A., 235.
Ware, Jr., Henry, 47.
Warren, J. H., 148, 180.
Warren, Lyman Marcus, 49, 151, 157, 180, 222, 256, 275.
Warren, T. A., 148.
Warren, William Whipple, 4, 7, 48, 146, 148, 151, 152, 159, 167.
Warrior (steamboat), 198.
Warsaw (Indiana), 251.
Washburn (Wisconsin), 4, 11.
Washburne, Hon. E. B., 31; Mrs. E. B., 31; Hempstead, ex-Mayor of Chicago, 31.
Washington, General, 32, 34, 39, 96, 98, 106, 125, 126, 149, 169; his army, 96.
Washington, city of, 58, 60, 116, 120, 121, 148, 171, 212, 249, 250.

Watts, Dr. Isaac, 124.
Wau-bun, 50.
Wauhakeeshik (Black Hawk's "prophet"), 195, 196, 199.
Waukesha, 209, 215, 218, 224; called Prairieville, 209.
Waukegan, 221.
Wau-nau-con (J. W. Quinney), 73.
Waupaca, 277.
Wauwatosa, 279.
Wawauquekon, 56.
Wayne, "Mad" Anthony, 28, 106.
Webster's Dictionary, 36.
We-kau (an Indian murderer), 190.
Wellington, Lord, 42.
Wendell, Colonel ——, 83;
Wesley, John, 32.
West, Stephen, D. D., 95, 99; Edward, 225, 279; H. S., M. D., 108.
West, Winning of the, 32.
Western Evangelical Missionary society, 163.
Western Historical company, 213.
Western posts, 34; states, 33, 34.
Western Reserve association, 163.
Westfall, ——, 137.
Westfield (Massachusetts), 77, 80.
West Hartford (Connecticut), 209.
West Hills (New York), 98.
West Indies, 22, 29; markets of, 33.
Westminster abbey, 1; assembly, 104; catechism, 92.
West Point academy, 154.
West Springfield (Massachusetts), 76.
Wheeler, C. E., 269; Miss Hattie, 258, 259, 261, 271; Miss Julia, 170, 246, 252, 253; Mrs. Harriet Wood, 165, 229, 231, 233 235, 238-240, 242-244, 246-250, 252, 253-274, 280; her covenant, 236; Rev. E. P., 4, 11, 147, 229, 254, 256, 259, 260, 270, 279, 280; Rev. L. H., 165, 167-173, 233, 234, 238 242, 244-252; Leonard, 170, 280; W. H., 175.

Wheelock, D. D., Rev. Eleazar, 67.
Whipple, Bishop, H. B., 162, 166.
Whistler, Major William, 190.
Whitaker, Rev. Nathaniel, 68.
White Earth river, 39, 200.
White mountains (New Hampshire), 33.
White Plains (New York), 96.
White river and region (Indiana), 55, 105, 107, 111; (Wisconsin), 240.
Whiteside, General Samuel, 197.
Whitewater, 276.
Whitford, Superintendent W. C., 14.
Whitney, A. W., 156; Mr. and Mrs. ——, 122; Prof. H. M., 269; Mrs. M. A., 115, 116.
Whittlesey creek, 4.
Wilcox, Major D. L., 154; Mrs., 205.
William III., 1; and Mary, 17, 278.
William, the Silent, 1, 197.
Williamsburg, 36.
Williams college, 84, 90, 108.
Williamson, T. S., 132–134.
Williams, Eleazar, 55, 57, 60, 63–66, 68, 75, 107, 108, 114, 119, 122, 127, 202, 205; Ephraim, 92, 93; Eunice, 65; Rev. Dr. Stephen, 76, 77, 80; Rev. John, 65, 76; Rev. William of Hatfield, 78, 86.
Wilson, Vice-President Henry, 50.
Windham association, the, 68.
Winnebago convention, 145, 255; county, 25; Rapids, 24, 25; war, the, 113, 186, 189, 197.
Winnebago lake and region, 19, 24, 41, 60, 72, 121, 142, 144, 145.
Winnebagoes, 2, 14, 19, 21, 41, 42, 53, 56–60, 75, 113, 118, 119, 121, 132, 149, 175, 177, 183, 188, 190, 196, 198, 199, 208, 213; their language, 56, 75, 177.
Winnepeg, 156, 276.
Winona, 135.
Winsdor (New York), 93.
Winston, Richard, Esq., 36.

Winthrope, Adam, Esq., 79; John, 33.
Wisconsin, 1, 2, 4, 5, 7, 9, 10, 14, 19, 21, 24, 26-28, 30, 31, 33, 35, 37 40, 42, 44, 48, 49, 52, 54, 55, 57, 58, 60, 61, 67, 72, 88, 90, 94, 97, 98, 100, 108, 110-114, 123-125, 128, 134, 136, 139, 141, 142, 144, 145, 157, 170, 171, 176, 189, 199, 209, 215, 221, 222, 225, 226, 263, 276, 278, 279; organized as a Territory, 89, 200; non-glaciated area in 189; pioneers of, 65, 225, 226; presbytery of, 219; legislatures of, 32, 200, 278; first mining in, 188; miners raise company in Black Hawk war, 197; early schools in, 66, 115, 151, 181, 203, 225, 279, 280; university of 223; first Roman Catholic missionary in, see Menard; first Protestant missionary, see Nash; Indians of, see, Menomonees, Winnebagoes, Ojibways, Pottawattomies, etc.; wars in, see Black Hawk, Outagamies, etc.; State historical society, portrait gallery of, 96; library of, 99.
Wisconsin Blue Book, 245.
Wisconsin Democrat, the 225.
Wisconsin Hights, battle of, 197.
Wisconsin Historical Collections, Vol. VIII., 24, 57, 64, 75; Vol. III., 25, 203; Vol., II., 60, 64, 121, 180; Vol., IV., 69, 72, 143; Vol XI., 156; Vol., IX., 186; Vol., X., 189; Vol.. VII., 210, 219.
Wisconsin, Columbian History of Education in, 115.

Wisconsin river, the, 1, 9, 16, 22, 24, 25, 30, 133, 149, 176, 186, 187, 190, 207, 210, 224.
Wisconsin Puritrn, the, 223.
Wisconsin State Historical Society, Proceedings for 1892, 38, 45.
Wisconsin Territory, History of, 190.
Wisconsin, the, 225.
Witchcraft, in Britain, France, Germany, New England, Indiana, Iowa, 36; deaths for, in Illinois, 36; Major Powell's statement, 36.
Wnahtukook, 76, 82, 83, 85.
Wolf river, 142.
Wood, ——, 233.
Woodbridge, Timothy, 77-79, 81-83, 87, 93, 94, 108.
Woodstock (Vermont), 48.
Woopikamikunk (Wapikamikunk) 105.
Wright, A. O., 27; S. G., 163, 276.
Wtanshekaunhtukko, 88.
Wyandots, 2, 165.
Wyoming, massacre at, 68.
Xavier, St. Francis, Mission of, 202, 211, 212.
Yale college and university, 46, 76-78, 93, 105, 193, 214.
Yankees, the, 39; versatility of, 251.
Y-en-dats, 2.
Yellow Lake, 157, 158, 160, 275.
Yellow river (Iowa), 183, 207.
Yoghum, Captain ——, 75.
York (Toronto), 164.
York Fort (Hudson's Bay), 41.
Zeizer (Yeizer), Captain ——, 40.
Zizania aquatica (wild rice), 41.

ADVERTISEMENT.

More than one whose childhood was spent in Wisconsin has had the experience described by Hamlin Garland. He found the homes once in the possession of friends now the property of strangers,—men of foreign nativity and language. A part of the social history of our state has been, on the whole, a sad one. Much of it is the story of the displacement of a population. With this change there was brought about the extinction of many institutions,—especially of churches. One such was the spiritual home of the writer's boyhood. The names of kindred of three generations are on the short roll of its membership. The community wherein it was established, the town of Jamestown, Grant county, had but a meager intellectual and spiritual life but the best there was of it found stimulus and expression in the old church. From its pulpit there was no uncertain sound on all the great subjects of religion, and on practical applications of it in patriotism, the struggle against slavery, temperance and the keeping of the Sabbath. Surely, I thought, some one should write of the good that has thus been done; of the fathers that had come almost with the removal of the Indians, and some even before that time; of the soldier boys whose funeral sermons were preached when, in the common course of nature, the good pastor might rather have been pronouncing for them a marriage service; and of other sons and daughters also who had lived to make a little of the world's great work their own duty. To tell this story was some one's privilege; why not mine? I knew of no other claimant for the honor, and in university life one is likely to become conscious of the impulse to make some little field of work distinctively his own.

For when I came to feel thus, days at Beloit college and at Doane were behind me and I was spending a winter in Leipzig. At Beloit it had been my delight on Wednesday and Saturday afternoons,—the only times in the old days of limited privilege when the library was open,—to fish from the bottoms of seldom opened drawers old pamphlets bearing on the history of the college. At Doane, with an eagerness that I still approve though I can smile now at some of its manifestations, I made-it my duty to get and save for the library anything I could that might have historic or, indeed, any other value,—a rule that I heartily wish had been followed in earlier days at Beloit.

Not so much from the schools that I attended,—in none of which did I ever hear prayer offered,—as through the church ran the path that led me to college. There may have been some connection, though I am not conscious of any, between my feeling of gratitude and the memories that, as I used to listen to the *motteten* in the Thomaskirche on the market place in Leipzig, brought before my mental vision the old house of God where on the Sundays of a long-past summer, often after a four miles' walk, I recited to my teacher the greater part of the gospel of John. However that may be, it was with the loyalty of a son and, perhaps, with somewhat of the interest of a student that 1885, February 12th, I began, in distant Germany, to write the history, not yet finished, of a single church,—the one to which I owe so much. But with such a topic who could withhold himself from speaking of the mingling and commingling, of the coming and the going, of the currents of humanity that finally made up the population of the lead region? Moreover, across the diminishing but always majestic Mississippi lay what had been a part of Louisiana. These topics, and others like them, led me on until this volume, different from anything originally planned, is offered to the public.

But the original design has not been forgotten. Indeed it is in fulfilment of it, on a broader scale, that "In Unnamed Wisconsin" has been written. This is a narrative of preparation and of beginnings,—of that marvelous succession of changes by which the very existence of all our civic and religious institutions became possible. Thus its genesis is natural enough. The story of one church led to that of many, and this greater work came to include a narrative showing how this region became, first in name and then in reality, a part of the United States,—a change prophetic of another yet to come to a great portion of our people.

Incidentally, in the progress of these studies, there came to be published not only many newspaper articles but also "Missions on the Chequamegon Bay," "Negro Slavery in Wisconsin" and "Muh-he-ka-ne-ok, a History of the Stockbridge Nation." The first two of these were published by the Wisconsin state historical society.

In the last-named book and in this I have sought to preserve the record of a good work done among a vanishing people. Let them speak the last words of this volume,—on the following page the first part of the shorter catechism, last edition, and here, in lines like those from which I copy, the first three beatitudes and the beginning of the third chapter of John:

 3. Wuh wekoiwuk neek kauk kauktommauk kaunthechuh wehichehuhqueweh; quaum nuh wmis num numnawwuh wuh kkewaukun wuhwekoiwaukon kunnuk uhtauk.

 4. Wuh wekoiwuk eheh neek kawtummauk taunnumme- cheek quaum,neekeheh kohetommehkowwauk.

 5. Wuh wekoiwukehelneek noochmaunthecheek; quaum neekcheh nooh wkenkeyaunauwuh.

 1. Neh unnoqueh queh neh wtiyenaup nemonnauw unne wethoow Nicodemus, kiweennoow Jews sehkoke wehoi,

www.ingramcontent.com/pod-product-compliance
Lightning Source LLC
Chambersburg PA
CBHW030746230426
43667CB00007B/863